NARRATIVE HISTORY
AND ETHNIC BOUNDARIES

THE SOCIETY OF BIBLICAL LITERATURE
SEMEIA STUDIES
Edward L. Greenstein, Editor

NARRATIVE HISTORY AND ETHNIC BOUNDARIES
The Deuteronomistic Historian and the Creation of Israelite National Identity

by

E. Theodore Mullen, Jr.

Scholars Press
Atlanta, Georgia

NARRATIVE HISTORY
AND ETHNIC BOUNDARIES

Library of Congress Cataloging in Publication Data
Mullen, E. Theodore.
Narrative history and ethnic boundaries: the deuteronomistic
historian and the creation of Israelite national identity/ by E.
Theodore Mullen, Jr.
p. cm. — (Semeia studies)
Includes bibliographical references and index.
ISBN 1–55540–846–X (cloth). — ISBN 1–55540–847–8 (pbk.)
1. D document (Biblical criticism) 2. Bible. O.T. Historical
Books—Historiography. 3. Jews—History—1200–953 B.C.—
Historiography. I. Title. II. Series.
BS1181.17.M85 1993
222'.06—dc20
93–12315
CIP

Printed in the United States of America
on acid-free paper

To my parents,
with love and gratitude.

CONTENTS

Acknowledgments

The present approach to the analysis of the deuteronomistic history and, more generally, to religious literature, grew out of a series of studies on these particular materials over recent years and in response to a number of critical questions raised within the context of the faculty colloquia conducted annually by the Department of Religious Studies at Indiana University-Purdue University at Indianapolis. I should especially like to thank my colleagues, Conrad Cherry, Tony Sherrill, Jan Shipps, and Jim Smurl, for the stimulation and support provided by these opportunities to share and discuss my research. The preparation and writing of the manuscript were greatly aided by a research grant from the University for the Fall semester of 1990. I should also like to thank Edward L. Greenstein, editor of *Semeia Studies*, and associate editors Mieke Bal and Claudia V. Camp for numerous helpful comments and suggestions concerning the preparation of the manuscript. I should like to extend my thanks, too, to my excellent research assistant, Kimberly Long, who prepared the indices. Most especially, I would like to express my indebtedness to my wife, Grace, whose assistance and support at every stage of the writing, revising, and editing of this work have been indispensable. Finally, to Richard and Scarlet, I would like to express a note of thanks for knowing when to inject a dose of frivolity into the tedium of manuscript preparation.

E. Theodore Mullen, Jr.
Indiana University-Purdue University at Indianapolis
December, 1991

1

INTRODUCTION:
THE PURPOSE AND PARAMETERS
OF THE APPROACH

Modern critical study of the Hebrew Bible and ancient Israelite traditions continues to be dominated by two major methods of analysis, the historical-critical and the literary approach. During the past decade, attention to the fields of anthropology and sociology has led to the development of new insights into these materials and the adoption of a variety of models as analytical tools. Accompanying this variety of approaches, however, has been the development of an intense debate that focuses primarily upon the appropriateness, or better, the exclusiveness of one or another of these analytical models. As is common with such territorial debates concerning the standard by which one might engage in "normal science,"[1] the positions presented tend to represent polar oppositions that allow for little possibility of mediation between them. Further, the variety and intensity of the critiques aimed at the "opposition" offer little or no evidence of the possibility of a cooperative effort at interpretation.[2] Rather than developing any common ground for

---

[1] On this phrase and its implications, see T. Kuhn, *The Structure of Scientific Revolutions*, 2nd ed. (Chicago: University of Chicago Press, 1970), pp. 10–42.

[2] The tone and nature of the critiques are indicative of the divisiveness of the debate among the competing approaches or paradigms. Representative of such

discussion, the debates seem to have created a series of caricatures of the differing positions that are, in turn, easily dismissed.

The essence of the debate seems to center around the issue of a proper focus for the interpretive enterprise, one that is either historical or literary in intent. For those who emphasize the basic historical character of the narratives composing the Hebrew Bible, the tools of the literary approach are commonly utilized to recover or reconstruct an appropriate and consistent text that may be assigned a particular purpose within a specific historical epoch. But such an approach is seen as partitive, hypothetical, and somewhat outmoded, if not simply misguided, by those concentrating on the literary models, for these aim at a critical appreciation of the various texts as a whole and their effects on the reader.[3] Finally, the application of various social-scientific models tends to emphasize the ways in which the historical development of ancient Israel might be reconstructed on the basis of parallel cultural and historical

---

assessments, though not agreeing on a single model themselves, are those offered by R. Polzin (*Moses and the Deuteronomist: A Literary Study of the Deuteronomic History* [New York: Seabury, 1980], pp. 1–24 and *Samuel and the Deuteronomist: A Literary Study of the Deuteronomic History, Part 2* [San Francisco: Harper & Row, 1989], pp. 1–17), P. Miscall (*1 Samuel: A Literary Reading* [Bloomington/Indianapolis: Indiana University Press, 1986], pp. xviii–xxv), and R. Oden (*The Bible Without Theology: The Theological Tradition and Alternatives to It* [San Francisco: Harper & Row, 1987], pp. 1–39) against the dominant historical-critical approach. In contrast, a vehement defense of this approach is developed by B. Halpern (*The First Historians: The Hebrew Bible and History* [San Francisco: Harper & Row, 1988], pp. 3–35) against literary and structural approaches developed by others.

3 The dialectic that has developed between these two approaches is illustrated by the responses elicited by D. Damrosch's attempt to combine "the comparative study of Near Eastern literature, the historical study of the sources within the biblical texts, and literary analysis of the text as it develops in its canonical form" in order to produce an historical study of the genre of the biblical narrative (*The Narrative Covenant: Transformation of Genre in the Growth of Biblical Literature* [San Francisco: Harper & Row, 1987], pp. 2–3). In a review of Damrosch's work from the historical-critical perspective (*JAOS* 110 [1990] 340–43), J. Van Seters concludes that the effort "to reconcile the methods only proves that they are quite irreconcilable" (p. 343). From a literary-critical perspective, E. Greenstein reviews the work of Damrosch and, though noting the legitimacy of the approach, questions the feasibility of the project and concludes that "historians and synchronists ask different questions," a situation that may indeed necessitate separate critical strategies ("On the Genesis of Biblical Prose Narrative," *Prooftexts* 8 [1988] 353 [Review of Damrosch]).

patterns without utilizing the Hebrew narratives as a primary source for reconstruction.[4]

As with all paradigms and methods of analysis, each of these approaches is able to yield certain results that are justified on the basis of the degree to which the analysis conforms to the general practice of the method itself. Each of the approaches and their variations is able to provide interesting insight into the variety of ways in which the Hebrew narratives might be analyzed and certain sets of questions might be resolved. The present study will attempt to develop and apply a new model for analyzing a particular set of narratives contained within the Hebrew Bible. In the process, some of the methods and presuppositions of the other models will be utilized, but generally in a slightly different context, since the present approach is the result of a different set of pre-suppositions and questions from those normally associated with the analysis of Hebrew narratives. I emphasize from the outset that this approach to the Hebrew Bible claims only to present a different perspective on the materials and to contribute toward formulating and develop-ing a different set of questions that, if answered, allow for a new under-standing of some of the roles and functions that can be attributed to the literature under consideration.[5]

The object of study by which the model will be developed is that portion of the Hebrew narrative that is commonly designated by modern interpreters as the "deuteronomistic history." According to representa-tive analyses of this literary complex, the book of Deuteronomy provides an ideological statement concerning Hebrew religion and life that consti-tutes a standard by which the history of the people Israel, from the point

---

[4] This approach is exemplified in the works of N. K. Gottwald (*The Tribes of Yahweh: A Sociology of the Religion of Liberated Israel, 1250–1000 B. C. E.* [Maryknoll, N. Y.: Orbis, 1979], N. P. Lemche (*Early Israel: Anthropological and Historical Studies on the Israelite Society before the Monarchy* [VTSup 37; Leiden: E. J. Brill, 1985]), and R. Coote and K. Whitelam (*The Emergence of Early Israel in Historical Perspective* [SWBA 5; Sheffield: Almond, 1987]), among others.

[5] As such, this approach is not offered as any type of polemic against, corrective to, or defense of any of the already existing paradigms for biblical studies. Instead, it is intended as a complement to those already in use. As pointed out by I. Barbour, competing paradigms offer differing judgments with respect to acceptable solutions. Likewise, since the standards for deciding among paradigms are themselves products of those same theories, there are really no objective criteria by which to choose among the models to be employed in analysis ("Paradigms in Science and Religion," in *Paradigms and Revolutions: Appraisals and Applications of Thomas Kuhn's Philosophy of Science* (ed. by Gary Gutting; Notre Dame: University of Notre Dame Press, 1980), p. 225.

of their entry into the land of Canaan until their exile in Babylon, is evaluated. Thus, the books of Joshua, Judges, Samuel, and Kings are all assigned to the work of a "deuteronomistic historian" who compiled this account of Israel's history, utilizing various traditions and sources. Beyond this, however, there is little agreement among scholars with respect to the precise date of the composition or the unity, purpose, or function for which this "history" was produced. The voluminous materials on the deuteronomistic history that have been published since M. Noth's original presentation of the concept and the debates that have developed as a result of ongoing research constitute a source of study in their own right and stand beyond the boundaries of the present work. Likewise, only selected works that have a direct impact on the present study will be cited in the notes.

The basic theory concerning the deuteronomistic historian was proposed by Noth, who suggested that the "history" was the product of an individual "deuteronomic" author.[6] Few scholars today agree with the proposal that a single redactor produced this entire work during the period of the Babylonian exile.[7] Rather, the general proposal has been modified so that it is now approached in one of two ways. One group of scholars, following the lead of F. M. Cross,[8] argues for a "double redaction" of the history. The original edition of the history (often referred to as Dtr[1]) was produced during the reign of King Josiah and was written to support the king's religious and political reforms. Consequently, this history was revised and completed during the exile to explain the destruction of Jerusalem and Judah. This exilic edition (Cross' Dtr[2]) corresponds to Noth's original Dtr. A second position, most commonly associated with R. Smend[9] and W. Dietrich,[10] argues that the basic

---

[6] *Überlieferungsgeschichtliche Studien* (3rd ed.; Tübingen: Max Niemeyer, 1967 [originally published in 1943]), pp. 3–12.

[7] Notable exceptions to this are H.-D. Hoffmann, *Reform und Reformen: Untersuchungen zu einen Grundthema der deuteronomistischen Geschichtsschreibung* (ATANT 66; Zürich: Theologischer Verlag, 1980), and J. Van Seters, *In Search Of History: Historiography in the Ancient World and the Origins of Biblical History* (New Haven: Yale University Press, 1983), both of whom argue for the basic compositional unity of the deuteronomistic history.

[8] *Canaanite Myth and Hebrew Epic* (Cambridge: Harvard University Press, 1973), pp. 274–89.

[9] "Das Gesetz und die Völker: Ein Beitrag zur deuteronomistischen Redaktiongeschichte," in *Probleme biblischer Theologie: Festschrift für Gerhard von Rad zum 70. Geburtstag* (ed. H. W. Wolff; Munich: Kaiser, 1971), pp. 494–509.

deuteronomistic history (DtrG) was produced during the exile and was revised by a redactor interested in the concept of the fulfillment of the law, hence DtrN. According to this view, the work was then edited by an even later redactor, DtrP, who was responsible for most of the prophetic materials that have been incorporated into the work.[11]

Each of these positions, together with the variations that have appeared, concerns itself with the reconstruction of the basic process of the production of the present text and attempts to identify each stage in that process with a series of particular ideological positions for which the text might have been produced. Hardly any of the positions, however, attempt to address the present text of the deuteronomistic history as it might have functioned with respect to the formation of the community whose identity as an ethnic group was threatened by the exile with complete assimilation and ethnic dissolution.[12] It is from this position that the present attempt to develop a new model for the interpretation of Hebrew narrative begins. Additionally, none of the major studies of the deuteronomistic history attempts to address the essential religious character[13] of the text or the mythological[14] dimensions that permeate both its contents and its design.

Furthermore, there exists one aspect of the deuteronomistic narrative that has escaped all discussion in the literature—its nature and func-

---

[10] *Prophetie und Geschichte. Eine redaktionsgeschichtliche Unversuchung zum deuteronomistischen Geschichtswerk* (FRLANT 108; Göttingen: Vandenhoeck & Ruprecht, 1972).

[11] It should occasion no surprise that each of these two major positions has spawned a number of minor variations with respect to the degree and the complexity of the editorial activity. To the two basic positions noted above should be added that of B. Halpern (*The First Historians*), which, in its attempt to bridge some of the differences between the two approaches, introduces another set of sigla to the discussion.

[12] While the works of R. Polzin (see above, n. 2) address the history in its present form, they do so from a very different perspective and with a different set of questions from those utilized in the present approach.

[13] For a discussion of what is meant by "religious character," i. e., the efforts to make sense out of experience through the ordering of sacred stories and symbols, see C. Geertz's "Ethos, World View, and the Analysis of Sacred Symbols," *The Interpretation of Cultures: Selected Essays by Clifford Geertz* (New York: Basic Books, 1973), pp. 126–41.

[14] The misunderstandings associated with a negative assessment of the concept of mythology and its functions, most importantly with respect to the historicity of peoples and events that are conveyed in texts which are termed mythological, dominate the field of biblical studies. As argued by R. Oden, biblical scholars seem intentionally to have avoided the recognition that many, if not most of the narrative texts in the Hebrew Bible qualify, at least by some broadly accepted criteria, as mythological (*The Bible Without Theology*, pp. 40–91).

tion as a *written* document. What is so crucial about the recognition of this aspect of the material is that in the form in which it would have been composed in its original setting, at least to the best of modern under-standing of the Canaanite/Phoenician writing system borrowed and utilized by the Hebrews, it would have consisted of only a consonantal text.[15] The implications of this fact have been overlooked by scholars who have worked with these materials. While one might argue that the devel-opment of an alphabetic system would tend to make literacy available to a larger general public,[16] the restriction of the alphabetic representation to consonants alone confines any immediate or "spontaneous" literacy to those with the specialized knowledge of the appropriate or proper read-ing of the text at hand. Without the vowels represented, the text of the Hebrew Bible remains highly ambiguous and can be read only by some-one who has *already learned* the appropriate vocalization of the conso-nants represented in the text.[17] In short, this means that the text was originally composed and utilized by and for a very select, specialized group of people who were able to read and teach the text on the basis of the traditional reading of the materials that they themselves had already learned. By extension, then, the context for the production of the deuter-

---

[15] This characteristic extends to the whole of the Hebrew text and is not restricted to the deuteronomistic history. For a brief description of the development of the systems of vowels that were added to the Hebrew text, see E. Würthwein, *The Text of the Old Testament* (Grand Rapids, MI: Eerdmans, 1979), pp. 16–27.

[16] Such a position is implied by the arguments of A. Demsky, who suggests that the knowledge of alphabetic writing in ancient Israel led to a "passive literacy" in that society and that during the final two hundred years of the monarchy, Israel could be termed a "literate society" ("Writing in Ancient Israel and Early Judaism: Part One: The Biblical Period," in *Mikra* [CRINT, sec. 2; Assen/Maastrict/ Philadelphia: Van Gorcum/Fortress, 1988], pp. 10–16). At the same time, Demsky notes that beyond the formal scribal schools and certain elements of the priesthood, the degree of popular literacy remains debated. On some of the possible effects of literacy on social structures, see J. Goody, *The Logic of Writing and the Organization of Society* (Studies in Literacy, Family, Culture, and the State; Cambridge: Cambridge University Press, 1986).

[17] W. Graham's work on the nature of oral and written scriptures has drawn attention to the fact that for the first two hundred years of its existence, i. e., until the vowel points were added to the consonantal text, the Quran could be read only by those who already knew what the text said (*Beyond the Written Word: Oral Aspects of Scripture in the History of Religion* [Cambridge: Cambridge University Press, 1987], pp. 97–98). While it is certainly possible for a scholar to read an unpointed text or a text in a purely consonantal state, to do so is both time consuming and conjectural. To assume that unvocalized texts enjoyed any non-specialist readership would be fanciful.

onomistic narratives must have been within the priestly or scribal schools of ancient Judah. More about the possibility of identifying the author or authors will be addressed within the body of this study.

A second consideration of the nature of the text produced by and for a specialized group is the setting in which it might have been used, i.e., its functional purpose. It is the attempt to identify the function of the deuteronomistic history that is the major focus of the present model of interpretation that is under development. Though the exact psychological aspects of authorial intentionality, especially with regard to ancient authors, lie beyond the boundaries of the present investigation, the importance of the intentional application of a narrative might help to establish the manner in which the deuteronomistic history might have been utilized by those people who preserved it as part of the second section of the *Tanak*, the *Něbî'îm*, and what role it might have served within those same communities.[18]

While there is no consensus on the precise redactional process by which the deuteronomistic history was composed, there does exist firm evidence that the work could not have been completed in its final form until c. 561 BCE, when Jehoiachin was released from prison in Babylon. This date during the period of the Babylonian exile may be taken as the *terminus a quo* at which the history in its present form could have been completed. It is with this edition of the deuteronomistic history that the present investigation is concerned.[19] The function of this final history and the ways in which it might have been utilized by the exilic and/or post-exilic communities that adopted it provide the bases for attempting to

---

[18] This is not intended to suggest that these materials were used in one way and only one way, nor that they could be understood in only one manner by one or more groups. Rather, it is to suggest that there is a general way in which these materials might have been utilized by some of the constituent groups that preserved them as part of the prophetic collection of Hebrew materials.

[19] There are those who argue that there are post-deuteronomistic additions to the text (e. g., A. G. Auld in his comments on the Gideon story ["Gideon: Hacking at the Heart of the Old Testament," *VT* 39 (1989) 257–67]). It is entirely possible that various additions and editorial changes to the text of any of the biblical materials could have occurred during much of the Persian and Hellenistic periods. The present argument maintains only that the major portions of the deuteronomistic history in substantially the form in which we possess them were written in the period immediately following 561 BCE. This is not to argue against the possibility of a Hezekian or Josianic edition of the history; rather, it is to attempt to address an existing text in an empirically ascertainable form and from there to attempt to construct some cogent arguments concerning both that text and the community or communities that might have used it.

understand and interpret the deuteronomistic narrative in its final form. There seems to be little debate that this narrative referred to as the deuteronomistic history was and is to be understood as a "history" in the literary sense of the term.[20] But what is rarely addressed is the possibility of the production of this narrative for some specific cultural situation. The most common explanation for the production of the narrative is the assertion that it formed some type of "propaganda" document for a Hezekian or Josianic "cultic reform." This explanation is invariably connected with the redactional analysis and is posited on the basis of the date assigned to the earliest form of the narrative to achieve written form. How, why, or by whom such propaganda would have been used to support certain royal efforts at religious changes in the state cultus has not been developed. Further, the analysis itself must be understood as circular, for the only direct evidence for any "cultic reforms" is derived from the deuteronomistic narrative itself and serves, at least for the books of Kings, as a literary structuring device.[21]

In short, there is little that is agreed upon concerning the date, setting, and purpose for the composition of the deuteronomistic history. Additionally, there is little to suggest that the continued study of these materials in the same manner that has dominated the past forty years will add any substantive information concerning them or their functions in the exilic and post-exilic Judahite[22] communities. It is for these reasons that I propose that another model, based on a different set of questions and presuppositions, be developed by which these narratives might be approached. Most if not all of these questions and presuppositions will be revealed in the course of the investigation itself. There is little reason

---

[20] A convenient definition of "history" as a literary genre is given by B. O. Long in *1 Kings with an Introduction to Historical Literature* (FOTL 9; Grand Rapids, MI: Eerdmans, 1984), pp. 250–51.

[21] H.-D. Hoffmann, *Reform und Reformen, passim.*

[22] The distinctions between "Israel"/"Israelite" and "Judah"/"Judahite" are important. Israel may be understood as the geographical, and possibly eponymous tribal designation for the northern national state that emerged under the reign of Saul. Judah refers to the southern geographical and eponymous tribal name for the national monarchic state that arose during the time of David, who was able to extend his rule over Israel as well. After the reign of Solomon, the two monarchic states divided and were never again unified. Hence, from c. 922–722 BCE, Judah and Israel refer to different political entities. From 722–587 BCE, only Judah remained as an existing political reality. After 587 BCE, the terms tend to be used synonymously to designate some idealized view of a reconstituted group. This symbolic reapplication of the terms will be extremely important in understanding the ways in which the narrative develops and functions in the religious and cultural life of the community.

to suspect that the individual(s) responsible for the production of this narrative history invented it from whole cloth. Rather, there is every reason to suspect that various traditions and materials, some of which might have been in written form, composed a base from which an account of the past of Israel and Judah, from its entry into Canaan until its exile in Babylon, could be created. Once the deuteronomistic history was written, and the various possible "sources" incorporated into it, any reconstruction of such "sources" becomes hypothetical at best. What can be reasonably argued as a starting point is that by c. 550 BCE, the deuteronomistic history probably *did* exist and, given the historical exigencies of that time, was probably employed within a specific context.

Though much about the historical situation of the exile and the early post-exilic period remains conjectural, it is reasonable to assume that for portions of the emergent Judahite exile and restoration communities, the period was one of crisis and adjustment. With the exile in Babylon, the leading elements of Judahite society were separated from their land. Further, both the dynastic line and the temple, the dynastic royal shrine and symbol of the divine promise of dynastic continuity, lay in ruins. The crisis of assimilation, exemplified by the loss of an identifiable "Israel" after the Assyrian repopulation of that area after 722 BCE, presented both exile and non-exile with the threat of the loss of a distinct identity connected with a discernible past.[23] It was during this period that a distinctive form of ethnic identity was developed in response to the threat of a loss of the previous identifying factors that had defined "Judahite" on the basis of land, leader, and locus.[24]

---

[23] The distinctive characters of the groups in exile and those who remained in the old area of Judah, particularly in Jerusalem, and who continued to worship at the site of the temple are often overlooked in the treatment of the cultural parameters and problems involved in understanding the ways in which these groups competed with and complemented each other in the development of the new communities. It is precisely such competitive and crisis-inducing situations as those produced by the exile in Babylon that may stimulate various mechanisms for survival, e.g., structural adaptations, new leadership roles, ritual transformations, and folklore development (D. Smith, *The Religion of the Landless: The Social Context of the Babylonian Exile* [Bloomington, IN: Meyer Stone, 1989], pp. 74–88).

[24] This is not to suggest that neither Israel nor Judah had developed a sense of ethnic identity before the exile. Rather, it is to argue that with the crisis of the exile, it became necessary to redefine and recreate what would become "Israelite" and "Judahite" ethnicity. On the somewhat amorphous nature of "Israel" prior to the Assyrian and Babylonian conquests, see M. Smith, *Palestinian Parties and Politics that Shaped the Old Testament* (London: SCM, 1971), p. 13.

This was done, I would suggest, by the conscious development of social ethnic boundary limitations that, as utilized within the community, helped to develop and maintain a new social construction of Judahite reality that was both continuous with and different from the past from which it had developed.

> By invoking a collective name, by the use of symbolic images of community, by the generation of stereotypes of the community and its foes, by the ritual performance and rehearsal of ceremonies and feasts and sacrifices, by the communal recitation of past deeds and ancient heroes' exploits, men and women have been enabled to bury their sense of loneliness and insecurity in the face of natural disasters and human violence by feeling themselves to partake of a collectivity and its historic fate which transcends their individual existences.[25]

If the accomplishment of these goals is understood as a major factor supporting the creation of the deuteronomistic history and if these concerns are understood as constituting an important aspect of the ideological developments of these materials, then a new way of approaching and understanding this "history" might be appropriate. By recreating in narrative form a series of "social dramas"[26] and by using communal expressions of ritual actions, especially in the form of confessional, covenantal expressions,[27] at critical junctures within the narrative, the deuteronomistic author created a "common myth of descent,"[28] a history that could be shared by the group facing the tragedies of the exile.

If the creation and consolidation of ethnic boundaries provided the impetus for the deuteronomistic writer's composition of this account, then several additional and sometimes complicating factors must also be considered. Given the fact that the deuteronomistic history, according to the Masoretic count, consists of some 4,314 verses (5,269 verses when

---

[25] A. D. Smith, *The Ethnic Origins of Nations* (Oxford: Blackwell, 1986), p. 46.

[26] On the concept of social drama and the ways in which it can serve to address cultural crises, see V. Turner, *Dramas, Fields, and Metaphors: Symbolic Action in Human Society* (Ithaca: Cornell University Press, 1974), pp. 23–59.

[27] As with so many aspects of Hebrew religion, the origins of the idea of covenant are highly debated. For the major arguments suggesting that the religious concept of the covenant is a late, quite possibly deuteronomic development, see L. Perlitt, *Bundestheologie im Alten Testament* (WMANT 36; Neukirchen-Vluyn: Neukirchener Verlag, 1969).

[28] This aspect of a shared social history and self-understanding is what A. D. Smith has termed the *sine qua non* for ethnic community identification and action (*The Ethnic Origins of Nations*, pp. 24–25).

Deuteronomy is included), the narrative is much too lengthy to be read or recited at any single ceremony. If the materials were to have had any active liturgical function, then, it would have been within a cultic situation that extended over some period of time, most probably one of the deuteronomic pilgrimage festivals in which the male population was required to participate on a yearly basis (Deut 16:16–17). This is not to suggest that at such festivals the entire history was recited; rather, it is more likely that only selected portions of the *tôrâ* were read, the history itself serving as interpretive midrash for the explanation and exposition of the law. This possibility is suggested by Deut 31:9–13, a text that requires that "this *tôrâ*" (*hattôrâ hazzō²t*, v. 11) be read before "all Israel" every seventh year, during the year of release (*šĕnat haššĕmiṭṭâ*, v. 10) at the festival of booths, in the place that Yahweh would choose.[29] If, as conjectured by some,[30] the beginning of the tradition of the reading of the law is to be associated with the cultic reforms attributed to Josiah (2 Kgs 23:1–3) and dated to approximately 622 BCE, then the occasion for the completion of the deuteronomistic history might be associated with the ninth of such celebrations, c. 560/59 BCE. Such a dating for the history is completely conjectural, but it coincides quite well with the dating of the last narrated event in that history.

Of importance also is the activity of the reading of the law to all Israel—men, women, children, and resident aliens—and not simply to the adult males who were required to embark on the yearly pilgrimage festivals. Most telling, however, is the typically deuteronomistic phraseology concerning the location of the reading of the *tôrâ*—"in the place which he [Yahweh] will choose" (*bammāqôm ²ăšer yibḥār*, Deut 31:11). The phrase as employed here and throughout Deuteronomy is polyvocal: whereas it is a clear deuteronomistic designation for Jerusalem, it might also be interpreted as *any* place which the deity might designate, a very

---

[29] The fact that this section of Deuteronomy is commonly considered to be deuteronomistic, and hence neither early nor original to the deuteronomic law, does not detract from the present argument. Rather, it might be taken as supporting the contention that the deuteronomistic writer was actively recreating a "history" and a set of archaizing boundaries in order to recreate and consolidate this people "Israel." By adding the requirement that the whole of the deuteronomic code be read to "all Israel" every seventh year, the author was attempting to assure that the present would be continuous with the created and imagined traditions of the past.

[30] See the work of W. Holladay pertaining to the relationship of the career of Jeremiah and the structure of that book to the public reading of the *tôrâ* during the septennial recitation of the deuteronomic code (*Jeremiah 1* [Hermeneia; Philadelphia: Fortress, 1986], pp. 1–10).

desirable "tradition" to appeal to in a context when the group was no longer in possession of Jerusalem. As has been suggested by modern literary analysis,

> The Book of Deuteronomy, in its ideological and surface composition, offers the reader a bird's-eye view of the entire history of Israel shortly to be recounted in detail in Joshua-2 Kings. This book is the history's opening frame and panoramic synopsis. The *spatial* perspective of Moses' audience and the narrator's audience is similar. The hero of Deuteronomy and his audience are in Moab, that is, outside the land, hoping to possess it with God's power and mercy; the author of Deuteronomy, and *his* audience are apparently in exile, that is, also outside the land, hoping to get in once more with God's mercy and power. The one audience is told under what conditions they will *retain* the land; the other audience under what conditions they will *regain* the land.[31]

If the above analysis is taken seriously, then the book of Deuteronomy might be interpreted as a type of social manifesto that attempts to give a form and structure to an ideally visioned ethnic group called "Israel." The model for interpreting the deuteronomistic history would be based on the premise that neither the deuteronomic code nor the deuteronomistic history was or is to be understood apart from the social world within which they were created and which they attempted to recreate and maintain by virtue of their particular ideology and visions for the people whom they addressed. If the date of c. 560 BCE can be taken as a possible time for the production of this history, then the social world of the exilic group might be described in some general ways that would help to establish and interpret the role and function of the materials.

By the time of the completion of the deuteronomistic history, the Judahite exiles would have been in Babylon for approximately 25 to 30 years. This would mean that not only the glories of the past but the memories of the past would be endangered with the passing of the generation that had grown up in the land, in Jerusalem, with knowledge of both the royal court and the temple. With these now gone and with a new generation emerging that had no first-hand knowledge of such specifically Judahite traditions, a cultural crisis would have been perceptible to those most threatened by the possibility of assimilation into the

---

[31] R. Polzin, *Moses and the Deuteronomist*, p. 72.

dominant cultural and religious surroundings.[32] The most likely candidates might be sought among the priestly and scribal guilds, for it would have been they who had access to the sources and traditions from which an account of the past and a vision of the future might be produced, and they also would have been the groups with the education and skills necessary for producing such a lengthy written work. Finally, and just as importantly, it would have been these two groups that, even in the exile, had the access and ability to foster and to enforce upon the changing community certain views and ideals.

It is to be noted, too, that the deuteronomistic writer was not the only ideologue active during this period. Indeed, it is most likely that he is to be understood as but one prophetic voice among a number of competing visionaries attempting to promote their own particular views of the nature of the community. The various and sometimes conflicting traditions that guided the growth and development of the restoration community, e.g., those emphasizing kingship, priesthood, prophecy, or wisdom,[33] illustrate that the period of the exile itself was one during which a variety of solutions were sought to preserve the diversity of the components that had once constituted the ethnic self-perception of Judah. The deuteronomistic history was created within the context of this complex web of religious and cultural influences so as to provide a history, a setting within which the traditions themselves might be understood. The creative and innovative aspects of the deuteronomistic historian are best understood when perceived as "contextualizing" and "legitimizing" the pasts out of which the differing aspects of the community had emerged. At the same time, the didactic aspects of this work present, as it were, another tradition that would compete alongside

---

[32] As P. Berger and T. Luckmann have argued, the problem of legitimating and objectifying a particular version of socially constructed reality arises when the historic "structures" are to be passed on to a new generation (*The Social Construction of Reality: A Treatise in the Sociology of Knowledge* [New York: Doubleday, 1966], p. 93). Additionally, the encounter with a people having a substantially different symbolic universe than that envisioned by an opposing group would provide a stimulus for constructing devices for the maintenance of a particular version of reality (pp. 106–10).

[33] P. D. Hanson has traced the development and importance of those differing religious traditions that were important in the development of post-exilic Judahite religion ("Israelite Religion in the Early Post-exilic Period," in *Ancient Israelite Religion* [ed. P. D. Miller, Jr., P. D. Hanson, and S. D. McBride; Philadelphia: Fortress, 1987], pp. 485–508.

the others for a position in the formation and preservation of the defining characteristics of the true Judahite community.

Through the recognition of the premise that the deuteronomistic history took its final form during the period of the exile, at the approximate point when the exilic community itself was in the process of transition to a new generation,[34] a new appreciation for the importance of that period in the development of later Israelite religion might be gained. The role and function of the narrative as a context within which and by which the various religious and cultural traditions of Judah and Israel were interpreted and preserved might allow for an understanding of the importance of various forms of narrative and discourse in the creation of discrete cultural identities. The idea that ethnic groups are built upon shared memories of a common history that binds members together and separates them from others[35] provides a basis for interpreting the deuteronomistic history as a creation whose purpose was to provide a set of boundaries for the community for which it was produced. Within the context of the crisis produced by the destruction of the Judahite state, the traditions of the past were assembled in a way that would provide for the continued survival of the people who would constitute "Israel." The possibility of using this as a starting point for interpreting the deuteronomistic history is strongly supported by one clear datum: emerging from the exile in Babylon was an ethnic community that identified itself as Judahite/Israelite and asserted its identity with those communities that had preceded it and from which its members claimed to be direct and "legitimate" descendants. The development of the deuteronomistic history provided for the preservation of the particular memory of the past that would be shared by this restoration group. As such, it provides an essential insight into the manner in which religious literature can create and sustain the construction of a social world view that provides the basis by which a people may come to identify itself.[36]

---

[34] On the basis of the materials at hand, there is little to suggest whether the deuteronomistic history was written in Babylon or in Palestine. Because the leading elements of the Judahite population were taken into captivity, it seems more likely that a setting in the exilic community would best provide the context for the production and use of this work. At the same time, it is to be noted that a new generation that had little or no direct knowledge of the now defunct monarchy and its attendant state religion would also have been arising in Jerusalem and in the cities and villages that had constituted Judah.

[35] A. D. Smith, *The Ethnic Origins of Nations*, pp. 25–28.

[36] A closely related issue is the production of the materials that presently constitute the Tetrateuch. Whether these accounts in their written form antedate the exile

The recognition of the importance of narrative in the social construction of reality, especially as it applies to such ideas as national and ethnic self-consciousness, provides the basis for the application of this new approach to various materials within the Hebrew Bible. This method of interpretation concentrates on the functional and transformative natures of selected narratives as social dramas in narrative form that functioned so as to define and bound a particular people as a separate and identifiable ethnic group. When these narrativized collections achieve an authoritative status within a particular community, they may become public symbols that provide the bases for the continued redefinition and self-understanding of that group.

As modern theories of ethnicity, world construction and maintenance, and community and group formation have demonstrated, the archaic "originals" from which communities claim descent are often reconstructed and imagined more along the lines of group needs than in accord with any known empirical or historical reality.[37] The present monograph is an attempt to present some of the major aspects of a new model for understanding the role and function of the narrative materials contained in the Hebrew Bible in what is commonly designated by modern scholars as the "deuteronomistic history." The author of this work, possibly the earliest historian known to us, produced the major interpretive literary work concerning the national life of Israel and Judah in the land of Canaan. As such, it represents an important source of knowledge concerning the origins of the community that identified itself as Hebrew, Israelite, or Judahite.

The following analysis of selected major "narrative events" within the deuteronomistic history will argue that the narrator of those stories has organized them as a series of "social dramas" of ritual creation/reenactment which produce or reinforce certain ethnic boundaries that define the people "Israel." From the fabric of traditional stories, some ancient and some invented, the author "imagined" the form and content

---

remains a matter of great debate. The majority of critics argue for a lengthy period of literary development, going back to the time of Solomon for the Yahwistic stratum of the tetrateuchal materials. The writing of the Tetrateuch lies beyond the parameters of the present study, but might be addressed by the same method of approach as that outlined here. Further, this model of interpretation can provide important insights into both the collection and editing of the prophetic works, the composition of the Chronicler's history, and the formation of the canon itself.

[37] On this phenomenon, see E. Hobsbawm, "Introduction: Inventing Traditions," in *The Invention of Tradition* (ed. by E. Hobsbawm and T. Ranger; Cambridge: Cambridge University Press, 1983), pp. 1–14.

of a community and then gave it a "history" designed to define and preserve selected aspects that might be understood as unique and meaningful to the community being addressed.

As a focus for this argument, selected portions of the deuteronomistic history will be analyzed in terms of their ritually transformative efforts to produce particular sets of cultural and moral values that became the bases for the group's self-identification. After an introductory essay addressing the model and presuppositions that guide the approach to understanding the narratives as "transformative" vehicles for ethnic identification, community formation, and world maintenance, the following chapters will provide the demonstration of the usefulness of this method in ascertaining, at least in part, an essential function of the deuteronomistic history in particular and of certain forms of religious materials in general.

The book of Deuteronomy, which in its present form represents the covenantal creation of the people Israel on the plains of Moab prior to their crossing the Jordan to "conquer" the land, exemplifies a ritual manifesto of ethnic boundary formation. By mutual proclamation, Israel is defined as a holy people, a possession of Yahweh, an entity separate from and opposed to the nations surrounding it. In terms of the temporal nature of the narrative that makes this presentation, however, the community "Israel" is constituted by those present on the plains of Moab and those who will be included in the group at a later point. Hence, the ritually transformative power of the narrated stories invites a ritual participation that transverses time and includes the present in the imagined and created "Israel" that stood on the banks of the Jordan to hear and respond to the final speech of Moses before the entry into the land promised to its ancestors. The covenantal portions of Deuteronomy associated with Shechem and paralleled in the book of Joshua provide social dramas that reconfirm, in narrative form, that the identity projected by the ethnic descriptors in Deuteronomy has been realized with the conquest of the land and reconfirmed by the ritual recreation of the covenantal ceremony led by Joshua. By way of the fulfillment of the commands in Deuteronomy, at least in part, the reality of the conquest of the land is recreated for the community to "remember." This section of the history functions to provide a "blueprint" for the conquest of the land and the fulfillment of the act of becoming a "holy people."

The book of Judges, introduced by a second rendition of the conquest of the land that illustrates the ways in which Israel failed, not only to take the land but to actualize the necessary identifying characteristics to which the covenantal prescriptions had obligated the people, provides for a new social drama that requires redress on the part of the deuteronomistic history. Here, the continued failures of the people to realize the identity required by the presentations in Deuteronomy threaten a dissolution of the unity of the group. Three special areas of emphasis in Judges illustrate this: the cyclical presentation of the need for deliverance because of failure to follow Yahweh alone, the continued threats of ethnic assimilation represented by the activities of figures like Jerubbaal and Samson, and finally the complete breakdown of the Israelite value system described in the narrative account of the "outrage" at Gibeah. Each of these narratives illustrates the breakdown of the essential characteristics by which Deuteronomy had defined "Israel." In order to preserve this group identity, the author provides yet another covenantal possibility, this one in the book of Samuel, by which the quest for kingship, evaluated in several differing ways by the deuteronomistic historian, is incorporated into the ideal of the community by way of a socially enacted narrative account.

In terms of the development of the narrative, then, the crises created by the events narrated in the book of Judges provide the need for some type of social or ritual redress and either the reintegration into an ethnic group or the realization that dissolution cannot be avoided. The adoption of monarchy as an appropriate form of Israelite self-governance and as a new social descriptor dominates the narratives of Samuel. The narrative of covenant renewal recounted in 1 Samuel 12 and the integration of kingship into the covenantal standards, reflecting the charter concerning the monarchy in Deuteronomy, reconstitute the design for "Israel." The following narratives and the conflicts between Saul and David provide the narrative accounts of the ways in which the claims of competing dynastic lines were resolved and how Israel was recreated in the land, now as a monarchic state, by way of another covenant ceremony, now centering on the figure of the legitimated monarch, David.

In the final section of the history, the accounts of the continuation of the nation, its dissolution into two competing kingdoms, each with legitimating claims to the same ancestors and traditions, the subsequent loss of the northern state, and the hoped for continuation and reformation of the whole as a people again united under "David," are recounted. In the books of Kings, the deuteronomistic historian utilizes various covenantally derived ideals to maintain the line of David in the narration of the numerous events surrounding the impact of historical circumstances on social and ideological positions. As a final product, then, the deuteronomistic history serves as a narrative realization of the special nature of this people Israel and an exposition of ethnic descriptors that should be applied to them, and serves to produce a prophetically proclaimed program of restoration of this "holy people" in the land that Yahweh had promised their fathers and which they, by failing to maintain the boundaries prescribed in their "original charter," Deuteronomy, had lost.

2

Athaliah:
History and its Legitimation
— or, Recreating a Past

An idea is able to gain and retain the aura of essential truth through telling
and retelling. This process endows a cherished notion with more veracity
than a library of facts.[1]

In modern critical reconstructions of the histories of Judah and Israel,
few episodes have received consensus like that associated with the
events concerning the reign of Queen Athaliah of Judah. The points of
agreement are several. Athaliah came to the throne as the result of a coup
that succeeded only because of the decimation of the Israelite and
Judahite royal households by the rebellion of Jehu. Though Athaliah is
credited with a reign of six to seven years, there is no reason to suspect
that her rule received popular support or that she was regarded as a
legitimate monarch. At the earliest opportunity, the ʿam hāʾāreṣ, "the
people of the land," under the leadership of the Jerusalem priest
Jehoiada, overthrew Athaliah and returned the crown to the Davidic
line.[2] Hence, with the exception of this brief period of usurpation by a

---

[1] W. Arens, *The Man-Eating Myth: Anthropology & Anthropophagy* (Oxford: Oxford
University Press, 1979), p. 89.
[2] Representative of the major works that present this view are the following: J.
Bright, *A History of Israel* (3rd ed.; Philadelphia: Westminster, 1981), pp. 252, 255; H.

non-Davidide, non-male, non-Judahite ruler,[3] the dynasty of David was unbroken from its inception until the return from the exile.

Such a scholarly consensus is the result of the way in which the texts recounting the reign of Athaliah have been approached: the accounts of the usurpation and rule of Athaliah are simple, non-critical paraphrases of the biblical story. The present analysis, designed as a methodological case study, is a response, in part, to this type of approach. In order to begin to develop an alternate analytical model, a new reconstruction of the reign of Athaliah, based upon an investigation of the pertinent Hebrew and ancient Near Eastern materials, will be proposed. With a new reconstruction propounded, the task will be to explain the reasons for the particular presentation that is encountered in the text of Kings and Chronicles.[4] Finally, on the basis of such observations, an initial formulation of some of the major purposes for the composition of this story, along with the larger history of the kingdoms of Israel and Judah, will be attempted.

Donner, *Geschichte des Volkes Israel und seiner Nachbarn in Grundzügen* (GAT 4/2; Göttingen: Vandenhoeck & Ruprecht, 1986), p. 252; H. Jagersma, *A History of Israel in the Old Testament Period* (Philadelphia: Fortress, 1983), p. 145; J. M. Miller and John H. Hayes, *A History of Israel and Judah* (Philadelphia: Westminster, 1986), pp. 302–4; S. Hermann, *A History of Israel in Old Testament Times* (Philadelphia: Fortress, 1975), p. 224; and M. Noth, *The History of Israel* (rev. ed.; New York: Harper & Row, 1960), pp. 236–37. This degree of agreement should occasion little surprise. It seems to be a common assumption of those who write histories of ancient Israel and Judah that the narratives of the books of Kings constitute accurate historical records by modern standards. See the critiques of this position that are contained in the collected responses to the publication of J. Miller and J. Hayes' *A History of Israel and Judah* edited by P. R. Davies and D. M. Gunn in *JSOT* 39 (1987) 3–63.

3   Athaliah represented for the deuteronomistic writer what could only be described as the opposite of the Davidic ideal that permeates his conception of kingship. Indeed, since she was an Israelite related to the Omride household (see below, n. 6), which had been condemned in its totality by Elijah (1 Kgs 21: 21–24), she could be viewed as being under the same curse. Her death at the command of Jehoiada could be seen, then, as a fulfillment of the deuteronomistic prophecy-fulfillment structuring device so common in the books of Samuel and Kings.

4   That the Chronicler used a *Vorlage* of the books of Kings to produce his work is generally accepted. Whereas the precise nature of this *Vorlage* remains debated, it is not important for the present work. A concise statement of the major differences regarding this issue may be found in H. G. M. Williamson's lengthy review of S. L. McKenzie's *The Chronicler's Use of the Deuteronomistic History* (HSM 33; Atlanta: Scholars Press, 1984) in *VT* 37 (1987) 107–14.

I. The Reign of Athaliah—A Reconstruction

That the account of the reign of Athaliah, queen-mother of Judah,[5] is treated in a way different from the rule of any other Judahite monarch is generally accepted in the literature. Though the exact nature of her genealogical ties to the Omride dynasty remains debated,[6] the deuteronomistic writer quite unambiguously associates her with the Israelite dynasty that had introduced and propagated the cultus of Baal and had received the unconditioned condemnation of that writer.[7] Additionally, it is clear within the narrative account that Athaliah is not accorded *by the deuteronomistic historian* the status of the kings who ruled over Judah.[8]

---

[5] Though little is recorded about the role and function of the queen-mother, or *gĕbîrâ*, in the Judahite royal court, the parallels from surrounding cultures provide evidence that she occupied a very powerful position in the royal court in Jerusalem. The status of this position is further indicated by the inclusion of the name of the king's mother in the introductory formulae for the kings of Judah contained throughout the books of Kings (such is missing only for Jehoram [2 Kgs 8:16–18] and Ahaz [16:1–2]). It seems clear that she held a position of power that was political and dynastic in function and that she was second in position only to the king. For the major parallels to the role and functions of the queen-mother in the surrounding cultures, see H. Donner, "Art und Herkunft des Amtes der Königmutter im Alten Testament," in *Festschrift Johannes Friedrich* (ed. R. von Kienle, *et alia*; Heidelberg: Karl Winter, 1959), pp. 105–45. As argued by Niels-Erik A. Andreasen, her chief function, at least in Jerusalem, seems to have been as "senior counsellor" to the king ("The Role of the Queen Mother in Israelite Society," *CBQ* 45 [1983] 191). More recently, Z. Ben-Barak has questioned the power of the *gĕbîrâ* in Israel and the ancient Near East ("The Status and Right of the *Gĕbîrâ*," *JBL* 110 [1990] 23–34).

[6] According to 2 Kgs 8:26 (// 2 Chr 22:2), she was a "daughter of Omri" (*bat-ʿōmrî*). 2 Kgs 8:18 (// 2 Chr 21:6), however, calls her the "daughter of Ahab" (*bat-ʾaḥʾāb*). It is worth noting that in the latter instances, the name Athaliah is not used. Rather, it is noted simply that Jehoram, son of Jehoshaphat, was married to a daughter of Ahab. The deuteronomistic writer apparently had little interest beyond establishing that Athaliah was related to the dynasty of Omri, to which Ahab belonged.

[7] Though Athaliah is implicitly associated with Baal worship in 2 Kgs 11:18, there is no explicit connection made in the biblical materials. The general association of Athaliah with the Tyrian Jezebel provides the major impetus to connect Athaliah with the fostering of foreign religious practices. The only corroboration available is from Josephus (*Antiquities* ix. 154).

[8] Beginning with the account of the reign of Rehoboam, the deuteronomistic writer introduced the monarchs of Israel and Judah with similar regnal formulae which included both a chronistic synchronization of dates for the two kingdoms and a judgment on the reign of the monarch. Notably, no such formula or judgment is placed on Athaliah. For a discussion of the genre and function of these formulae, see B. O. Long, *1 Kings with an Introduction to Historical Literature* (FOTL 9; Grand Rapids, MI: Eerdmans, 1984), pp. 158–65. The manner in which the reign of Athaliah is nar-

Special attention must be given to this emphasis, for the view of the deuteronomistic writer might not be historically accurate, at least in this case.

Several of the facts narrated by the deuteronomistic author suggest this possibility. If the length of the reign accorded to Athaliah is correct, then the fact that she occupied the throne of Judah for six years suggests that she enjoyed substantial support from some quarter of the Judahite population. Additionally, if the accounts of the extent of the slaughter of the Israelite usurper Jehu are accurate (2 Kgs 9:27; 10:13–14), and the Chronicler's notice concerning Jehoram's murder of his brothers is accurate (2 Chr 21:4), then there must have been little remaining of "all the seed of the kingdom" (*kol-zera^c hammamlākâ*, 2 Kgs 11:1; 2 Chr 22:10),[9] purportedly murdered by Athaliah.

One might also question the motivation for such a coup. While the most common catalysts offered by the commentaries (greed for power, coupled with the non-Judahite religious concepts of monarchy that were the results of her association with the Israelite/Tyrian queen Jezebel) should not be discounted out of hand,[10] neither should they be accepted without some critical analysis. Even if one were to assume that Athaliah engineered the murder of the remainder of the dynastic heirs and forcefully seized the throne, it should be apparent that she did not act alone. It

---

rated by the historian is also most informative. The synchronizations of reigns and rulers produce a "folding over" pattern in the chronological progression of the story. (For an outline of this structure, see below, note 18.) As R. D. Nelson has noted, the author's presentation of Athaliah without the standardized formulae associated with every other king places the reign of this queen "outside" of history ("The Anatomy of the Book of Kings," *JSOT* 40 [1988] 44).

9 Though the meaning of the phrase *kol-zera^c hammamlākâ* seems clear, especially when interpreted as parallel to *běnê-hammelek* (11:2), it should be noted that the phrase occurs only here and in the parallel in Chronicles. Given the context, the translation "royal heirs" seems most appropriate.

10 Such explanations for Athaliah's actions are grounded on the assertion, which goes back at least as far as A. Alt ("Das Königtum in den Reichen Israel und Juda," *VT* 1 [1951] 2–22), that the national states of Israel and Judah operated with different conceptions of the monarchy. It is often claimed that Israel, which experienced a number of dynastic overthrows during its brief history, preserved a prophetic, or charismatic ideal of leadership, while Judah embraced a dynastic model. It is more likely, in light of recent studies, that both nations embodied the dynastic ideals. Israel had less success in approximating the ideal than did Judah. For an analysis of some of the major contributing reasons for these differences, see T. Ishida, *The Royal Dynasties in Ancient Israel: A Study on the Formation and Development of Royal-Dynastic Ideology* (BZAW 142; New York: de Gruyter, 1977), pp. 171–82.

would not be too bold to suggest that to eliminate a dynastic line that had been unbroken through five previous rulers and to hold that position undisputedly for six years would require a larger base of support than just the royal guard and palace staff. Yet the deuteronomistic author places the responsibility for the rebellion on the shoulders of Athaliah alone. For the resulting deuteronomistic history and its parallels in the Chronicler's work, this figure stands as the only interruption in the line of David, stretching from David's son Solomon through the end of the life of Jehoiachin in exile,[11] a period encompassing nearly 400 years and including twenty male rulers descended from David. This rather remarkable dynastic feat in and of itself invites close scrutiny, if not simple skepticism.[12]

A critical reading of the pertinent texts reveals that the interests of the author have really very little to do with Athaliah other than to account for a six- or seven-year period in the historian's chronology, to explain the accession of Joash to the throne of Judah at the age of seven, and to attribute to him a financial reform of the temple.[13] About Athaliah, the wife of Jehoram and mother of Ahaziah, the Judahite queen-mother (*gĕbîrâ*), little or no information is given. All the negative references made to her are either contained within the accounts of the covenant/accession

---

[11] As one might expect, there is no way of verifying this. The continuity of the line of David on the throne of Judah stands as a basic datum of the traditions contained within the Hebrew Bible. The role of this model in the reconstruction of Judah's past and in the visions of Judah's restored future, especially with regard to the development of messianic hopes within various strands of Judaism, demonstrates how thoroughly it permeates these materials. The bonding and unifying power of a religious and political ideal should not be confused with historical realities. As I shall argue below, neither should official genealogical identifications be given the status of biological realities without adequate substantiating evidence.

[12] M. Liverani has compared the story of the enthronement of Joash to the story of Idrimi, king of Alalakh (cf. *ANET*[3], 557–58), and concludes that there is no reason to believe that Joash was really of the Davidic line; rather, given the propagandistic functions of the narrative, it is most probable that he was not ("L´histoire de Joas," *VT* 24 [1974] 453).

[13] According to E. Würthwein, the theme of this section is the continuation of the Davidic line in spite of a serious threat, and not the fall of Athaliah (*Die Bücher der Könige. 1. Kön. 17– 2 Kön. 25* [ATD 11/2; Göttingen: Vandenhoeck & Ruprecht, 1984], p. 346). In this connection it is important to note that the temple reforms attributed to Joash as his major accomplishment in his reign (2 Kgs 12:5–17) are closely related to and form the background for the account of Josiah's temple restorations (2 Kgs 22:3– 7). For a discussion of these texts, see H.-D. Hoffmann, *Reform und Reformen: Untersuchungen zu einem Grundthema der deuteronomistischen Geschichtsschriebung* (ATANT 66; Zürich: Theologischer Verlag, 1980), pp. 118–25, 192–97.

events narrated about Joash or form parts of the materials concerning his reform, all of which are framed by the repeated notice of her murder (2 Kgs 11:16, 20).[14] It is tempting to suggest that the deuteronomistic writer had little more information concerning Athaliah than the length of her reign and her relationship to Jehoram and Ahaziah.[15]

A careful reading of the deuteronomistic historian's account of the reign of Athaliah (2 Kings 11) reveals several interesting facts. From the perspective of the historian, it would be incorrect to ascribe a "reign" to her. The regnal formulae that characterize the frame created by the deuteronomistic historian and which introduce and conclude, with minor variations, the accounts of each of the rulers of both Judah and Israel, are completely lacking in the account of Athaliah's seizure of power. Instead, it is simply stated that while Joash was hidden in the temple for six years, "Athaliah was ruling over the land" (waʿătalyâ

---

[14] The doublet recounting the death of Athaliah is often cited as evidence that at least two sources, a "popular" and an "official priestly" source, have been combined to form this account (vv. 1–3; 4–12; 18b–20; and 13–18a). For a discussion of these theories and an attempt to demonstrate that chap. eleven might be better analyzed in terms of a general introduction (vv. 1–2) followed by two parallel sequences that emphasize different aspects of the revolt against Athaliah (vv. 4–16; 17–20), see T. R. Hobbs, *2 Kings* (WBC 13; Waco, TX: Word, 1985), pp. 135–38. W. Rudolph has also argued strongly in favor of the unified nature of chap. 11 ("Die Einheitlichkeit der Erzählung vom Sturz der Atalja [2 Kön 11]," in *Festschrift Alfred Bertholet* [ed. W. Baumgartner, et al.; Tübingen: L. C. B. Mohr/Paul Siebeck, 1950], pp. 473–78). L. M. Barré has argued for the basic unity of a reconstructed original of 2 Kings 9–11 that has gone through a deuteronomistic and a post-deuteronomistic redaction to give the present overlapping narrative (*The Rhetoric of Political Persuasion: The Narrative Artistry and Political Intentions of 2 Kings 9–11* [CBQMS 20; Washington, DC: Catholic Biblical Association of America, 1988], pp. 120–32), but this reconstruction of numerous redactional layers remains dubious.

[15] The degree to which the deuteronomistic writer relied upon sources, either written or oral, official or popular, remains a matter of intense debate. It would seem reasonable to suppose that the deuteronomistic writer might have had access to several types of materials. On the types of sources that may have been available to him, see the analysis presented by J. Van Seters (*In Search of History: Historiography in the Ancient World and the Origins of Biblical History* [New Haven: Yale University Press, 1983], pp. 298–302). This is not to suggest, however, that the deuteronomistic history, while clearly belonging to the genre "history writing," presents a full or accurate account of the past. Rather, when compared to the parallel materials such as the Akitu Chronicle, the Synchronistic History, or the Weidner Chronicle from Mesopotamia, the ways in which particular political, historical, or religious positions can determine the presentation of the materials become most obvious. On these texts, see A. K. Grayson, *Assyrian and Babylonian Chronicles* (Texts from Cuneiform Sources; Locust Valley, NY: J. J. Augustin, 1975).

mōleket ʿal-hāʾāreṣ, v. 3).[16] Any perceived threat to the continuation of the promise to David (cf. 8:19) is immediately removed by the interweaving of the brief account of Athaliah's coup and the narrative of the saving and nurturing of the Davidide Joash in the temple (vv. 2–3).

The deuteronomistic historian's opinion of the apostate nature of Athaliah and the illegitimacy of her claim to the throne is further evidenced in the account of her assassination. In the critical seventh year,[17] at the order of the priest Jehoiada, the prearranged overthrow of Athaliah was orchestrated (vv. 4–12). Athaliah was brought out before the temple and murdered. Significantly, the order was also given to "kill with the sword anyone who follows her" (*wĕhabbāʾ ʾaḥărêhā hāmēt bĕḥereb*, v. 15). With the conclusion of the covenant among Yahweh, the king, and the people, "all the people of the land" (*kol-ʿam-hāʾāreṣ*) went to the temple of Baal (*bêt-habbaʿal*), dismantled it, and killed Mattan, its priest (v. 18). The account concludes with the notice that "all the people of the land rejoiced and the city was at peace" (*wayyiśmaḥ kol-ʿam hāʾāreṣ wĕhāʿîr šāqāṭâ*, v. 20) as a result of the murder of this idolatrous usurper and the reinvestiture of the Davidic line.

Of this ruler, nothing more is mentioned in the deuteronomistic history. While the Chronicler uses the actions of "Athaliah, the wicked woman" (*ʿătalyāhû hammirśaʿat*, 2 Chr 24:7), as the impetus for the temple reforms of Joash, these two acts are not linked in the deuteronomistic account in Kings. For the deuteronomistic author, this six- or seven-year reign serves as an awkward narrative bridge between two Davidic rulers judged as "upright," Jehoshaphat and Joash (1 Kgs 22:43–44; 2 Kgs 12:3–4), and two Davidic kings whose deeds were comparable to those of the house of Ahab, Jehoram and Ahaziah (2 Kgs 8:18–19; 8:27). Explicitly contained in this "enveloping" narrative scheme is the only account of a queen ruling independently over Judah.[18] Though the development of

---

[16] Interestingly, the writer not only denied the application of the regnal formula to Athaliah, but also chose not to use the regular finite form of the verb, *mālak*. Instead, the Qal feminine singular participle, *mōleket*, a form which occurs only here and in the parallel in 2 Chr 22:12, is used to denote her activities.

[17] The very choice of numbers presents an analytical problem, for the number seven, as a literary device, is often used to introduce the climax in a series of events (Hobbs, *2 Kings*, pp. 138–39). It has also been argued that the choice of the period "seven years" was dictated by the type of narrative employed and may have had little to do with historical actuality (Liverani, "L'histoire de Joas," p. 453).

[18] The following structural arrangement is adapted from Long, *1 Kings*, pp. 22–23. Dates are from Bright, *A History of Israel*, pp. 469–71.

End of David (1000–961)—Solomon's Reign (961–922): 1 Kgs 1:1–11:43

ISRAEL	*JUDAH*
Reign of Jeroboam (922–901)	
1 Kgs 12:1–14:20	*in the time of Jeroboam*
	1 Kgs 14:21–15:24
	Rehoboam (922–915)
in the time of Asa	Abijam (915–913)
1 Kgs 15:25–22:40	Asa (913–873)
Nadab (901–900)	
Baasha (900–877)	
Elah (877–876)	
Zimri (876)	
Omri (876–869)	
Ahab (869–850)	*in the time of Ahab*
in the time of Jehoshaphat	1 Kgs 22:41–51
1 Kgs 22:52–2 Kgs 8:15	Jehoshaphat (873–849)
Ahaziah (850–849)	
Je(ho)ram (849–843/2)	*in the time of Je(ho)ram*
	2 Kgs 8:16–9:28
	Jehoram of Judah (849–843)
	Ahaziah of Judah (843/2)
Jehu (843/2–815)	*in the time of Jehu*
2 Kgs 9:30–10:36	2 Kgs 11:1–12:22
	Athaliah (842–837)
in the time of Joash	Joash (837–800)
2 Kgs 13:1–25	
Jehoahaz (815–802)	*in the time of Jehoash*
Jehoash (802–786)	2 Kgs 14:1–22
	Amaziah (800–783)
in the time of Amaziah	
2 Kgs 14:23–29	*in the time of Jeroboam II*
Jeroboam II (786–746)	2 Kgs 15:1–7
in the time of Azariah(/Jotham)	Azariah (783–742)
2 Kgs 15:8–31	
Zechariah (746–745)	
Shallum (745)	
Menahem (745–737)	
Pekahiah (737–736)	
Pekah (736–732)	*in the time of Pekah*
	2 Kgs 15:32–16:20
	Jotham (742–735)
in the time of Ahaz	Ahaz (735–715)
2 Kgs 17:1–41	*in and after the time of Hoshea*
Hoshea (732–724)	2 Kgs 18:1–25:30
Fall of Israel	Hezekiah (715–687/6)
	Manasseh (687/6–642)

this point must be postponed until later, it is clear that Athaliah did not fit the ideological paradigm from which the deuteronomistic writer portrayed the monarchy in Judah. With the disposal of the Omride Athaliah, the "entire house of Ahab" had been eradicated from the land in fulfillment of the prophetic pronouncements of the deuteronomistic narrative.[19]

The very nature of the treatment afforded Athaliah by the deuteronomistic historian might be the best clue to a critical reconstruction of her reign. Though it is commonly maintained that women played only a minor role in the governmental structures of the ancient Near East, recent studies indicate that this is not an accurate picture. At least four princesses, the most famous of whom was Hatshepsut (15th cent. BCE), became rulers of Egypt. In Mesopotamia, Ku-Baba founded the Third Dynasty of Kish (mid-third millennium BCE); Shiptu, wife of Zimri-Lim of Mari, was active in political matters (18th cent. BCE); Sammuramat, widow of Shamshi-Adad V, ruled Assyria alongside her son Adad-nirari III (9th/8th cent. BCE).[20] While our extant records indicate that these examples were exceptions to the standard practices of the day, they also suggest that the societies of the ancient Near East were able to recognize situations in which the rulership functions could be placed in female hands, and placed them there.

The crisis precipitated by the coup of Jehu in Israel, the murder of the Judahite king Ahaziah, and the elimination of the members of the

Amon (642–640)
Josiah (640–609)
Jehoahaz (609)
Jehoiakim (609–598)
Jehoiachin (598/7)
Zedekiah (597–587)

[19] Barré is certainly correct in his argument that 2 Kgs 9–11 constitutes an entity, i. e., that the account of Athaliah's overthrow and the enthronement of Joash is patterned on and connected with the account of the coup of Jehu (2 Kgs 9–10; *The Rhetoric of Political Persuasion*, pp. 29–35). That these chapters were an originally autonomous entity composed by a single author during the 9th century BCE to justify Jehoiada's coup (pp. 52–53) needs to be demonstrated more convincingly. Nonetheless, the accounts do indeed form a unity within the larger narrative of Kings.

[20] R. Harris, "Woman in the ANE," in *The Interpreter's Dictionary of the Bible, Supp.* (ed. K. Crim; Nashville: Abingdon, 1976), p. 963.

royal household[21] could have created such a situation in Judah and formed the background for the legitimate succession of Athaliah. It might be very significant that the deuteronomistic historian did not attribute the full regnal formulae to the queen-mother, for it is possible that her role was that of regent, not of sole ruler, for the six-year period during which she was in control of the royal court. To argue that the succession of Athaliah was legitimate implies that the deuteronomistic writer either misunderstood or manipulated whatever sources or traditions were at his disposal. The probability of such is inextricably connected to the issue of the purpose for which the work was produced, the discussion of which will constitute the second portion of this chapter. For the present, it is sufficient to propose the possibility that the deuteronomistic writer manipulated the materials to address his purposes.[22]

Accepting the accuracy of the account in 2 Kings 11 forces the reader to credit Athaliah with incredible ingenuity and unbelievable stupidity at the same time. Since Athaliah had been the queen of Jehoram and the queen-mother of Ahaziah, she would undoubtedly have had the opportunities to form the political alliances necessary to attempt a coup. Yet the author of this section of the narrative presents it as the action of the queen-mother alone. Significant is the complete *lack* of support from any quarter. For the deuteronomistic writer, Judah could and would support only the offspring of David—a political situation created and sustained to perfection within the deuteronomistic narrative propaganda.[23] Though

---

[21] 2 Kgs 10:12–14 recounts Jehu's unprovoked slaughter of 42 "kinsmen of Ahaziah" (*ʾăḥê ʾăḥazyāhû*). Whether this indicates some attempt on the part of Jehu to reunify Israel and Judah remains uncertain, though it would not seem unlikely.

[22] The power of political and religious propaganda to influence the ways in which events are interpreted might be easily demonstrated by the inscriptions and efforts of the Egyptian queen Hatshepsut to overcome the sense of illegitimacy that seems always to have plagued her reign. For a discussion of the pertinent materials relating to this ruler, see D. B. Redford, *History and Chronology of the Eighteenth Dynasty of Egypt: Seven Studies* (Toronto: University of Toronto Press, 1967), pp. 57–87. In ancient Israel, the so-called "History of the Rise of David" (1 Sam 16–2 Sam 5) serves a similar purpose. K. Whitelam's observation that the simple force of arms is seldom sufficient to maintain control of a population or an area is important, for it emphasizes the crucial role that the manipulation of the various forms of the media, i. e., epigraphic and iconographic, plays in the successful wielding of power ("The Defence of David," *JSOT* 29 [1984] 61). I would extend this use of available media to the successful formation and recapitulation of a group's "historical memory" as well.

[23] The origins of the conception of the promise of an eternal Davidic dynasty remain obscure. 2 Samuel 7, which contains the oracle of Nathan and which gives the only explicit statement of this unconditional royal grant in the deuteronomistic

Athaliah had the ability to engineer her ascent to the throne with no aid or support, she apparently failed due to her inability to count. In her attempt to rid the kingdom of Davidides, the number of whom would surely have been known to the queen-mother, she failed to account for one, Joash. Further, though the young heir to the thone was being raised in the temple in Jerusalem, the queen suspected nothing until the moment of her overthrow. If, however, Athaliah appears to have been oblivious, such was not the case for the palace guards and the people of the land, for they were able to recognize Joash as a legitimate Davidide, based solely on the testimony of Jehoiada the priest. The improbability of such a series of events suggests that the author of the account might have been influenced more by the ideology of the unbroken succession of the line of David than by an accurate rendition of the past.[24]

If the reign of Athaliah might have been legitimate, as has been suggested,[25] what evidence or parallels might be adduced to support the claim? If the decimation of the Judahite royal household during the coup of Jehu is accepted as historically reliable, then the actions of Athaliah as queen-mother would be best interpreted with respect to the issue of succession to the throne, one of the most generally documented functions of the queen-mother in the ancient Near East.[26] Ahatmilku of Ugarit was an

---

account, appears, even to those commentators who insist that it reflects an historical and ancient Judahite royal tradition, "to have been touched almost everywhere by a Deuteronomistic hand" (P. Kyle McCarter, *II Samuel* [AB 9; Garden City, NY: Doubleday, 1984], p. 221; on the history of the interpretation of this chapter, see pp. 210–31). While scholars seem intent on presupposing that the traditions concerning the Davidic line and the unbroken nature of that dynastic succession are both ancient and accurate, there exists little evidence independent of the deuteronomistic narrative to corroborate such a position. Those few references to such a promise that do occur outside the deuteronomistic corpus (e.g., Pss 89:4, 36–38; 132:11–13) cannot be shown to be earlier than or independent from the deuteronomistic redaction of 2 Samuel 7. For a discussion of these passages, see T. N. D. Mettinger, *King and Messiah: The Civil and Sacral Legitimation of the Israelite Kings* (Lund: C. W. K. Gleerup, 1976), pp. 275–82.

24   As H. Donner notes, the way in which these materials are narrated indicates that the historical circumstances must have been much more complicated than this abbreviated narrative suggests (*Geschichte des Volkes Israel und seiner Nachbarn in Grundzügen*, vol. 2, p. 252).

25   This possibility has been suggested by H. Reviv ("On the Days of Athaliah and Joash," *Beth Mikra* 47 (1970/71) 541–48 [Hebrew]) and C. Levin (*Der Struz der Königin Atalja. Ein Kapitel zur Geschichte Judas im 9. Jahrhundert v. Chr.* [Stuttgarter Bibelstudien 105; Stuttgart: Katholisches Bibelwerk, 1982], pp. 83–90), though on different grounds from those that will be developed here.

26   N.-E. A. Andreason, "The Role of the Queen Mother in Israelite Society," p. 181.

important figure in the succession to the throne after the death of her husband Niqmepa (14th cent. BCE). Similarly, in Assyria, Sammuramat actually ruled as co-regent alongside her son, Adad-nirari III (9th/8th cent. BCE) and Naq'ia-Zaqutu, queen-consort of Sennacherib, was intimately involved in the succession of Esarhaddon to the throne and in the nomination of Ashurbanipal as crown prince (8th/7th cent. BCE).[27] Adad-Gupi of Babylon was instrumental in placing Nabonidus on the throne of Babylon, though his claim to legitimacy was certainly open to question (6th cent. BCE).[28]

On the basis of the parallel materials, it might seem reasonable to suggest that Athaliah, a member of the house of David by marriage, simply took the throne as regent. Thus, the power vacuum created by Jehu's purge was filled, and any possible visions of consolidation of the throne that might have been part of Jehu's plan were thwarted.[29] The suggestion that Athaliah gave Joash to Josheba to raise and thus never usurped the throne argues just this.[30] As tempting as it might be to suggest that Athaliah actually intended to rule only until Joash reached the age at which he might ascend the throne, this reconstruction is not without problems.[31] One critical assumption that is made by this suggestion is

---

[27] Ishida, *The Royal Dynasties in Ancient Israel*, pp. 155–56.

[28] Harris, "Woman in the ANE," p. 963.

[29] If Jehu intended to usurp the Judahite throne as well as the throne of Israel, it would explain his slaughter of the kinsmen of Ahaziah (2 Kgs 10:12–14). It would also give a politically expedient reason for Athaliah's seizure of the throne of Judah, i. e., to stop any such takeover attempt. A further possibility has been suggested by Miller and Hayes (*A History of Ancient Israel and Judah*, pp. 280–82). They contend that the two kingdoms had already been united for a several-year period under the rulership of Jehoram/Joram. Though the biblical text presents the reigns of two Jehorams, one over Israel and one over Judah, for nearly the identical period of time, it is likely that the compilers of the text misunderstood the records and interpreted them as indicating two different rulers. Such an instance, though not necessary to the present arguments, would provide some interesting explanations for a number of the peculiar actions recounted and could suggest that factions from the northern kingdom were involved in supporting Athaliah's hold on the throne.

[30] Reviv, "On the Days of Athaliah and Joash," pp. 541–48.

[31] There can be little doubt that the present narrative is anti-Athaliah, anti-Omride, and anti-Israelite in its present orientation. But to suggest that Athaliah was simply securing the throne until the true heir should reach an appropriate age to rule leaves unexplained the reason for her murder. If the text is correct in its account that Athaliah was assassinated, then what events would have led to the situation wherein she decided not to relinquish power to the appropriate heir? This approach seems to create more problems than it resolves. In operation here, at least in part, is what B. Long has described as the "fundamentalist premise": the idea that holy stories, when

that Joash was a member of the Davidic line who had been saved from the slaughter of the royal household. What if, on the other hand, Joash was *not* a Davidide and Athaliah was *not* acting simply as queen-regent? What if she had taken the throne as the senior surviving member of the Davidic royal house whose male offspring had been decimated in the coup of Jehu? In this instance, she might be viewed, at least from one perspective, as the legitimate ruler. Joash, then, would become the non-Davidic usurper to the throne. This possibility must not be dismissed without serious consideration of the situation as it might be understood.

If this were the case, then Athaliah's ascent to the throne may have enjoyed the support of some of the factions of the royal court and the nation.[32] It would fall to the queen-mother to take the throne in the event that there were no male heirs to assume the position of king. Such a move might avert the appearance of several claimants to the throne and the outbreak of a general civil war. Additionally, the queen-mother might continue on the throne so long as no successor were decreed.[33] What implications this might have had for the Judahite throne would be left to speculation, especially if Joash was not actually a member of the Davidic line.[34] How a new dynastic line might be decreed was answered, after a period of time, by a well-conceived rebellion against Athaliah by the priest, Jehoiada.

If this scenario is accurate, and if it is correct that there existed a covenant between the king and the ʿam hāʾāreṣ that obligated the gentry to preserve the dynastic line,[35] then the rebellion of Jehoiada becomes quite intelligible, as does the sudden appearance of the ʿam hāʾāreṣ in the narrative as a politically viable force. Athaliah's cry, "conspiracy,

---

read critically and translated into historical language, yield history ("On Finding the Hidden Premises," *JSOT* 39 [1987] 10–14).

[32] If, as suggested above, Athaliah ascended the throne to block Jehu's efforts to consolidate Israel and Judah, then she might have been able to muster a sizable degree of support for her efforts. Such support would have been even more likely if the account of Jehu's slaughter of the Judahite princes is accurate.

[33] Levin, *Der Struz der Königin Atalja*, p. 89. Levin also points out that this might provide an explanation for Jehu's murder of Jezebel.

[34] Liverani has argued for this possibility ("L'histoire de Joas," p. 452).

[35] This obligation has been noted by M. Weinfeld, *Deuteronomy and the Deuteronomic School* (Oxford: Clarendon, 1972), pp. 88–91. Though it is indeed possible that the ʿam hāʾāreṣ represent some sort of political-social element that is involved in the maintenance of the dynastic succession, we shall argue below that this is not the only possible interpretation of the deuteronomistic use of this phrase within the context of this narrative. For the major views of the role and function of the ʿam hāʾāreṣ, see the discussion by Ishida (*The Royal Dynasties in Ancient Israel*, pp. 164–67).

conspiracy!" (*qešer qešer*, v. 14), upon seeing the covenant ceremony in process was warranted from the perspective of the rightful ruling matriarch. The covenant ceremony itself might have been one designed to recognize officially, via public affirmation, the legitimacy of Joash as the covenantally proclaimed Davidic successor to his "father," the late Ahaziah. With the covenant concluded and the "usurping" queen murdered, the land could indeed be described as "at peace."

II. The Deuteronomistic Narrative—Its Roles, Purposes, and Functions

In presenting the materials in their present form, then, the deuteronomistic writer has produced, at a minimum, a piece of propaganda supporting the concept of the unbroken dynastic line of David in Judah. Our discussion must now turn to the implications of this and enter into a broader consideration of some of the related issues involved in the creation of religious documents and communities. Though the focus of our study will remain this particular text and its role and function in the narrative produced by the deuteronomistic historian, the interpretive framework for its analysis must begin within the larger context of the study of the past, especially as it pertains to the reconstructions of ancient religious movements which are still influential on cultural realities of which the interpreter is a part. While all models developed and utilized will, in large part, be reflections of the cultural and social constructs of the world of the present,[36] a major object of any investigation of the past must be the reconstruction of the social structures of the people who created the materials under consideration.[37]

---

[36] P. Berger, *The Sacred Canopy: Elements of a Sociological Theory of Religion* (Garden City, NY: Anchor, 1969), p. 8.

[37] In a highly provocative essay, C. Geertz suggests the difficulties involved in the analysis of the cultures of "others." Critical to this process, Geertz argues, is the recognition that those common human perceptions that are generally presumed to be shared by all people, i. e., "common sense," may indeed be a highly culturally conditioned and relativistic set of presuppositions that are shared and understood only by members of that particular social world. If this is correct, then a starting point in the analysis of any culture should be with those presuppositions that serve to translate the events of life into an understandable set of data ("Common Sense as a Cultural System," in *Local Knowledge: Further Essays in Interpretive Anthropology* [New York: Basic, 1983], pp. 73–93).

While no consensus exists concerning the meaning of the term "culture," even among cultural anthropologists, I would accept the basic description offered by C. Geertz, that culture is the totality of those webs of significance which humankind has "spun" and upon which it is supported.[38] Simultaneously, I would extend J. Z. Smith's argument that religion is a "second-order abstraction"[39] to apply also to the concept of culture, i.e., that it exists only as an abstraction created by those who belong to the academy and for whom it constitutes an object of study. Given this as a starting point, one must recognize at the beginning of the investigation that the biblical interpreter, if lucky, works at what might be called a third level of descriptive discourse. Those past events which are the ideal objects of investigation are not directly accessible to the biblical critic, nor are eyewitnesses or even contemporaries to such events available for interrogation or cross-examination. Hence, the initial process of experiential interpretation, culturally conditioned in all its aspects, remains somewhat inscrutable in all its intricacies. This immediate, perceptual process would constitute the primary, or first level of discourse. Such occurrences, now experienced and interpreted through the determinant matrices of innumerable and normally unconscious cultural signifiers, if discovered meaningful or significant to an individual or a group, may be developed and retained as a tradition. A tradition, then, could become another of the various signifiers within the narratives by which groups attempt to define and identify themselves and their culture. Those traditions that endure may become important in the process of the development of the identity of the group retaining them.

It must be recognized, then, that even the first level of description that might be available to the participant in an event is not without interpretive frames; hence, this first level must be understood as one which will shape the ways in which various cultures experience similar phenomena in entirely different ways.[40] Just as problematic are the inter-

---

[38] "Thick Description: Toward an Interpretive Theory of Culture," *The Interpretation of Cultures* (New York: Basic, 1973), p. 5.

[39] "'Religion' and 'Religious Studies': No Difference at All," *Soundings* 71 (1988) 233–35.

[40] In my opinion, the failure to recognize this has led to much of the insistence on the uniqueness of Israelite religion. When placed within the context of the ancient Near East and its religious expressions, the religions of Israel and Judah appear to be quite consistent in both shape and content with the religious practices of their neighbors. Many of the common elements that have been claimed as unique to Israel have been placed in the larger context by B. Albrektson (*History and the Gods. An Essay on the Idea of Historical Events As Divine Manifestations in the Ancient Near East*

pretive processes that occur inevitably at the level of the inscription of a tradition. It is too easy, methodologically, to concentrate on the inscription *or* the process of inscribing without understanding that the two are inextricably related and culturally influenced, if not determined.[41] Underlying the process of the inscription of a tradition or set of narratives (or any text, for that matter) are the matters of authorship, implied or otherwise, audience, implied or otherwise, and purpose, knowable or not.[42] The shape that a text takes will be controlled by these factors, among others. To concentrate solely on the text and the readers' response to it is to give, either intentionally or not, a set of parameters to the processes of inscription. Only if the processes that led to the development of a text form a background for understanding the particular structures and textures of that text can the interpreter gain any insight into the signification(s) for which that text was inscribed. Needless to say, the longer the periods of transmission for various traditions that have been textualized and preserved, the more complex and hypothetical the determinations of these interrelationships will be.[43]

---

and in Israel [Lund: C. W. K. Gleerup, 1967]) and H. W. F. Saggs (*The Encounter with the Divine in Mesopotamia and Israel* [London: Athlone, 1978]).

[41] Geertz, "Blurred Genres: The Refiguration of Social Thought," *Local Knowledge,* pp. 31–32.

[42] There is little doubt of the correctness of deconstruction's assertion that authorial intentionality ceases to have any ascertainable relevance once the text has been placed in the context of an audience, since it is the audience who will read and respond to the text quite independently of any such intentions on the part of the writer. At the same time, I would argue that it is precisely this phenomenon that necessitates the effort to determine the intentions of the author of a narrative, especially one that has been adopted as a type of "blueprint" for a national or religious self-identity. While clearly the way in which a community responds to and appropriates a formative document will not, in all probability, correspond with the intentions of the writer of the document, that does not mean that these original intentions are without importance. Rather, if one is to attempt to explain the formation and conceptualization of the narrative form and contents, then an understanding of the reasons for preparing the text becomes a *sine qua non* for any responsible interpretation of the materials within an historical and cultural context.

[43] Because of the complexity of the process of transmission of traditions, oral and written, through numerous social institutions and practices, the study of the composition of the deuteronomistic historian and the purposes of that writer must focus on points of reference that can be "freeze framed" and studied as points along a larger continuum. There can be little doubt that the deuteronomistic writer, in incorporating older traditional materials into his history, has changed the meanings of those materials from those they may have had in other contexts. Yet, by virtue of the process of inscribing them in a narrative form, the author has indeed, at least for an

Clearly, then, the interpreter of ancient cultural artifacts is forced to work at a third level of descriptive discourse, bound to the present cultural matrices which form the models by which the material remains of the past, epigraphic or anepigraphic, become data to be placed within interpretive models and then projected into that historical abyss that forms the conceptual bases for the present webs of cultural signification. This involves the realization that the very concepts of scholarly interpretations of the past are, always have been, and always will be processes themselves.[44] If history is thought of as "the intellectual form in which a civilization renders an account to itself of its past,"[45] then it becomes clear that historiography itself is a process that is constantly in the process of resignification.

Religion, however, might be viewed as a cultural response to the perceived flux in which meaning is embedded. While the problems involved in defining religion lie beyond the scope of this study,[46] religion might be understood as

(1) a system of symbols which acts to (2) establish powerful, pervasive, and long-lasting moods and motivations in men by (3) formulating conceptions of a general order of existence and (4) clothing these conceptions with such

---

isolated instance, given them a particular and identifiable position and relevance to the other selected instances which he chose to record. An additional aspect of the complexity of these textual interrelationships involved in the narrating of a set of events is, as argued by H. White, that every narrative, whether historical or fictive, is constructed not only on the basis of events that are recorded, but also on the basis of materials that were omitted ("The Value of Narrativity in the Representation of Reality," in *On Narrative* [ed. by W. J. T. Mitchell; Chicago: University of Chicago Press, 1981], p. 10). This process of selectivity must be considered in reconstructions of the process of narrative preparation and utilization when possible.

44 Most pertinent in this regard are the observations of T. S. Kuhn on the role and functions of paradigms and paradigm formation in the context of scientific inquiry (*The Structure of Scientific Revolutions* [2nd ed.; Chicago: University of Chicago Press, 1970]). Though Kuhn's use of the term "paradigm" has been criticized, his position on the control of such constructs over "normal science" and the means by which knowledge is created remains valid, in my opinion.

45 J. Huizinga, "A Definition of the Concept of History," in *Philosophy and History: Essays Presented to Ernst Cassirer* (ed. by R. Klibansky and H. J. Paton; New York: 1963), p. 9; quoted by J. Van Seters, *In Search of History*, p. 1.

46 For a discussion of some of the issues involved, see M. E. Spiro, "Religion: Problems of Definition and Explanation," in *Anthropological Approaches to the Study of Religion* (ed. by Michael Banton; London: Tavistock, 1966), pp. 85–126.

an aura of factuality that (5) the moods and motivations seem uniquely realistic.[47]

Religion, then, must be understood as more than simply a web or even a section of webs within the signification system conceptualized under the rubric of culture; rather, religion must be viewed as a restructuring of selected segments of those pre-existing cultural signifiers in such a way as to create a competing web. Hence, while a product of the culture within which it develops, religion claims, at the most basic level, to be the source from which culture, or "true" culture at any rate, is derived.

Spun not in a vacuum, but among the structures of the bonds of several other cultural boundaries, the web is suspended in the open and is itself in constant flux and motion. Strands, signifiers, break and require replacement, lest tears appear to threaten the stability and continuation of the structure. From within the confusion of competing signifiers and the uncertainties of continually shifting strands within the cultural web emerge islands of calm that claim to be unaffected by, indeed impervious to the weather that beats continually upon this more fully developed idea of culture as a web. Religion grants stability to those who are persuaded by the symbolic universe created and "factualized" by this common cultural phenomenon.[48]

As one attempts to address the relationships between religious group formation and religious narratives, it is precisely this issue of "factualization" that must be confronted. One of the clearest functional aspects of this symbolic "factualization" process that characterizes religious groups is the formation of group boundaries. More specifically, I would suggest, religions delineate *ethnic group boundaries*. According to F. Barth, "ethnic group" designates a population which is largely biologically self-perpetuating, shares fundamental cultural values, constitutes a field of communication and interaction, and has a membership which identifies itself, and is identified by others, as constituting a category that can be distinguished from other categories of the same order.[49] Notably, this aspect of self-ascription and identification both insures the continuity of such groups and is dependent upon the erection and maintenance

---

[47] Geertz, "Religion as a Cultural System," *Anthropological Approaches to the Study of Religion*, p. 4.

[48] As such, established religious world views are analogous to what Kuhn calls "normal science" (*Structure of Scientific Revolutions*, pp. 10–42).

[49] "Introduction," *Ethnic Groups and Boundaries: The Social Organization of Culture Difference* (ed. F. Barth; Boston: Little, Brown, 1969), pp. 10–11.

of boundaries.[50] At the same time, such boundary formation within ethnic groups must also be understood as a process, set, established, yet always changeable. Major components of this process are categories of social interaction, community formation, and the development of organizations.[51]

If a major function of religions might be viewed as the development and maintenance of ethnic groups, then some forms of religious narratives might be understood as expressions of the boundaries which define those areas of meaningful and legitimate social interaction and communal activity. Since the implication of significant and culturally important differences in behavior marks ethnic groups as significant units,[52] the erection and maintenance of those boundaries become essential to the survival of the group. Yet the group and its cultural and historical situations change; concomitantly, so do the boundaries that maintain and define them. Despite such changes, a significant aspect of ethnicity, especially in regard to its religious function, is the denial of such changes and the insistence upon an absolute continuity with the past.

III. The Deuteronomistic Writer—Position, Place, and Function

The attempt to suggest a model, then, comes now full circle. The memory and reformulation of the past in terms of history remembered, recovered, or invented[53] provide the materials from which the narrative

---

[50] Barth, "Introduction," p. 14.

[51] S. R. Charsley, "The Formation of Ethnic Groups," in *Urban Ethnicity* (ed. Abner Cohen; London: Tavistock, 1974), pp. 359–62. In general, six characteristics of ethnic groups may be delineated: (1) a past-oriented identification that emphasizes origins; (2) a concept of cultural and social distinctiveness; (3) a relationship of the group with a broader system of social relationships; (4) a size greater than kin or local groups that goes beyond known acquaintances; (5) a differentiation of meanings for ethnic categories in different social situations and for different individuals; and (6) an assumption that these categories have symbolic functions (A. P. Royce, *Ethnic Identity: Strategies of Diversity* [Bloomington/Indianapolis: Indiana University Press, 1982], p. 24). To the extent that they display these general characteristics, the major religious traditions of the world, e.g., Judaism, Christianity, Islam, Hinduism, etc., might be analyzed as "ethnic" groups.

[52] Barth, "Introduction," p. 15.

[53] As B. Lewis has noted, "remembered history" is common to all human groups and embodies a type of poetic or symbolic truth that attempts to make the past coincide with and support the self-image that a group possesses in the present. When

traditions are erected as boundaries and foundations for ethnic communities to be formed. Though only the outlines of the model have been drawn, it might be possible to sketch in portions of the whole by returning to the specifics of the deuteronomistic historian and his purpose in constructing the narrative concerning Athaliah and Joash in the context of the books of Kings. Though the date and purposes of the deuteronomistic author remain debated,[54] one point stands beyond dispute—the year 561 BCE with the release of Jehoiachin from prison (cf. 2 Kgs 25:27–30) stands as the *terminus a quo* for the present books of Kings and the deuteronomistic history.[55] Most significantly, it is during this period of crisis that some of the most basic deuteronomistic ideological foundations, e.g., the monarchy, the temple, the nation, faced disconfirmation. In part, the deuteronomistic history must be interpreted within the context of this religious and cultural crisis.

In the context of this complex set of crises, the deuteronomistic writer produced an historical narrative.[56] Notably, the fact that the deuteronomistic author is involved in writing his own history, as well as that of his people, is guided by the impulse to rank various events within that history in accord with their significance to that writer's conception of his cultural heritage. Additionally, the narrative account of the past that is produced tends to "moralize reality" and identifies it with the social moral world inhabited by the history's writer.[57] Such historical narratives may also be grounded in what V. Turner calls "social dramas," those "dramas of living" that are parts of everyone's experience

---

it ceases to support such an image, the history may come to be regarded as false or be discarded (*History—Remembered, Recovered, Invented* [Princeton: Princeton University Press, 1975], pp. 11–13).

[54] According to M. Noth (*Überlieferungsgeschichtliche Studien* [3rd ed.; Tübingen: Max Niemeyer, 1967]), the deuteronomistic history was the product of a single editor writing during the exile. More recent analyses, however, tend to posit a pre-exilic edition of the history, dating it either to the period of Josiah or even to the time of Hezekiah. For a survey of such interpretations, see the remarks of I. Provan, *Hezekiah and the Books of Kings: A Contribution to the Debate about the Composition of the Deuteronomistic History* (BZAW 172; Berlin: de Gruyter, 1988), pp. 4–21.

[55] Several Babylonian administrative documents confirm the presence of Jehoiachin and his sons under Babylonian rule. For the texts, see *ANET*[3], p. 308.

[56] That the narrative account is a "history" is clear, if what is meant by a "history" is "an extensive, continuous, written composition made up of and based upon various materials, some originally traditional and oral, others written, and devoted to a particular subject or historical period" (Long, *1 Kings*, p. 250). On the issues of historiography in Israel and the ancient Near East, see Van Seters, *In Search of History*.

[57] White, "The Value of Narrativity," pp. 10, 13–14.

and which occur in groups with shared values, interests, and common histories, either real or alleged. Narrative, as a universal cultural activity which is part of the social drama itself, may serve as one of the processes by which the social drama converts particular values and ends into a cultural system. Such dramas have four distinct phases: breach, crisis, redress, and either reintegration or recognition of schism.[58]

Recognition of such universal cultural structures and the ways in which narrativity contributes to the generation of meaning and the objectification of the past provides one additional interpretive tool for the analysis of the deuteronomistic historian's work. The crisis of the exile, for the author of these materials, was the result of Judah's breach of the covenant with Yahweh, emphasized by appeal to the renditions of the Davidic promise as offered to Solomon in its conditionalized form (cf. 1 Kgs 2:4; 3:14; 9:4–9). Alongside this theme stands, in quite some tension, the unconditional promise of dynasty to David (2 Sam 7:12–16). Notable is the failure to resolve these thematic tensions within the story, a factor that is generally interpreted by critics as evidence of different redactional hands. Most interpreters fail to understand, however, that the presuppositions of consistently "tensionless" reconstructed "originals" say nothing about the narrative frictions existing in the final redactional entity. Further, an underlying presupposition of this approach fails to address a demonstrable element of the style of this deuteronomistic writer—*parataxis*.[59] The paratactic style of the deuteronomistic history places the reigns of kings, the conflicting accounts of events and promises, "alongside-of" each other. The author does not attempt a narrative *syntaxis*, a "together-with" arrangement that consistently explicates the causality or the interconnectedness of all the "events" narrated.[60] One result of this

---

[58] "Social Dramas and Stories about Them," in *On Narrative* (ed. W. J. T. Mitchell; Chicago: University of Chicago Press, 1981), pp. 142–63; see also *Dramas, Fields, and Metaphors: Symbolic Action in Human Society* (Ithaca: Cornell University Press, 1974), pp. 23–59.

[59] This narrative device is characteristic of the deuteronomistic historiographic style. An element of this technique is the creation of patterns which, as repeated through the narration of events, provide a sense of unity and movement (Van Seters, *In Search of History*, p. 312).

[60] T. L. Estess, "The Inennarrable Contraption," *JAAR* 42 (1974) 431. What the implications of the use of parataxis as a narrative stategy are, exactly, cannot be answered. It is possible that it was no more than the standard historiographic device of the day (compare the similar style of Herodotus, for example). On the other hand, it might indicate that the deuteronomistic writer was unable to effect a synthesis of the materials at his disposal and to construct a coherent and consistent picture. In this

style is that it leaves the end of the history open and numerous thematic tensions unresolved.

One of the clearest indicators of the open nature of the ending of this history is revealed by the debate concerning the interpretation of that ending. Jehoiachin had been released from prison. An heir of David was still alive and enthroned. Under house arrest he may have been, but the promise to the Davidic house, either conditional or unconditional, remained in effect, as did the obligation to obey the words of Yahweh. Is this "event" to be interpreted as one of punishment or as one of hope? Is it a positive or a negative sign about kingship and civil authority for Judah?[61] Rather than requiring that the tensions created by the paratactic style of the history be resolved, the interpretation of the deuteronomistic history, as well as the biblical materials as a whole, might benefit from the recognition that the degree of thematic disorder that might characterize the final canonical form of the materials is a reflection of the nature of some forms of social drama itself, if not a basic component of lived experiences.

The deuteronomistic author's major purpose, I suggest, was to produce a narrative that would reveal the order underlying the past events which would provide the necessary meaning for the present situation of the exile. It is this phase, the period of redress and reflection on the crisis, that forms a liminal stage, a time "set apart from the ongoing business of quotidian life," when an interpretation is provided to make sense of the crisis.[62] But what if the author found himself unable to derive or construct a systematic explanation and a direct and dependable causal link among all the parts of the story? The events of the exile, at a very basic level, could not help but force the deuteronomistic interpreter to

---

same vein, it might be suggested that the writer's world view differed enough from ours that the tensions we perceive to be present in the narrative, the conflicts between promise and fulfillment that plague the modern analyst, were not perceived by the ancient. Whatever the explanation used for this choice of narrative construction, the paratactic style of the deuteronomistic history, along with its repetitive and conflicting compositional elements, remains the structural frame of the recounting of Israel's past.

[61] Geertz has pointed out that there are both a governing elite and a set of symbolic forms expressing the controlling activities of that elite at the center of any complexly organized society ("Centers, Kings, and Charisma: Reflections on the Symbolics of Power," *Local Knowledge*, p. 124). For Judah, the Davidic ruler, the palace, and the temple (a dynastic shrine) and its priesthood would be the most obvious symbols of the governing body.

[62] Turner, "Social Dramas and Stories about Them," p. 152.

address some of the basic ideological presuppositions that had come to characterize Judahite religion. One of these was the idea of Judah and Israel as the chosen people, the special possession of Yahweh—a people set apart and distinct from the nations.[63] To have been conquered, exiled, and territorially absorbed by one of the nations, to have had the national shrine and central administrative capital destroyed and plundered by the "others," to find oneself forcefully resettled in the midst of those who worshipped "other gods," was, at the most basic level, to find one's sense of specialness incontrovertibly profaned. The resolution of this social drama would come only by the development of a new set of ethnic signifiers which could apply now in a land not promised and for a people no longer geographically defined or bounded.[64] For the deuter-onomistic historian, the task was complex: to construct new ethnic and religious boundaries by which the descendants of Judah could rediscover the ascription "Hebrews/Israelites/ Judahites." To do this required a rehearsal of major events of the past, an evaluation of their effectiveness in this new situation, and an attempt at some resolution of the conflicting claims laid by some of these on the present. At points, the only resolution was that of parataxis—a juxtaposition of alternatives and positions.[65]

From the standpoint of interpretive method and approach, it is important to note the limitations inherent in any proposed study of the

---

[63] This assertion that Israel was the chosen people of Yahweh, developed within the deuteronomistic history at the national level, provides the basic ethnic boundary marker upon which the refinements of the meaning of this identity are developed.

[64] G. W. Ahlström has argued that "Israel" was originally a geographic, not an ethnic designation. With the establishment of the monarchy, it slowly became a national, rather than a territorial name. Finally, after the exile and restoration, when the nation no longer existed, it was restricted to those who identified themselves with the restoration community as defined by Ezra. Hence, it developed into an ethnic descriptor (*Who Were The Israelites?* [Winona Lake, IN: Eisenbrauns, 1986]).

[65] It might not be an overstatement to say that the only resolution available was the simple juxtaposition of alternatives. R. M. Green's analysis of the deep structure of religions reveals that three elements may be discovered; most significantly, two of these elements stand in direct opposition to each other. In structuralist terms, they would be perceived as "binary opposites." Hence, in the realm of morality and religious reasoning, an unresolved tension is constant between the belief in the reality of moral retribution and the opposite insistence on the necessity of suspending that same belief (*Religion and Moral Reason: A New Method for Comparative Study* [New York: Oxford University Press, 1988], pp. 3–23). Whether it is valid to extend this structure to all religious traditions is beyond the scope and purpose of this study. I would argue, however, that Green's insights are certainly valid for Judaism and its ancestors, the Israelite and Judahite religious traditions, as well as for the major modern religious traditions of the world.

functional nature of texts that have been constructed for purposes of self-definition and cultural ascription. It stands beyond the pale of possibility to capture fully the meaning of any text, especially one that functions to bind a community into a common form. All "life texts," canonized or not, are continually in an interpretive flux, for each new experience or event or epoch forces the reinterpretation and reintegration of the past if it is to remain meaningful. The result of this is that the form and content, at least at the interpretive level, are continually changing. The task of the critic is to attempt to reconstruct, as fully and substantively as possible, those cultural contexts in which a text might be located and to address the functions of the text for that situation as a type of "frozen frame picture" that might be relevant in reconstructing and understanding the history of the interpretations of the past by certain religious and cultural groups.

Before recounting more fully the various motifs and themes that the deuteronomistic writer chose to emphasize for his account of the history of the monarchies of Israel and Judah, I shall attempt a more refined description of the historical and cultural situation of this author. While there is no dearth of treatments of the implied author, there has been little or no attempt to describe adequately the situation from which he wrote or the reasons for his compositions. While it would be foolish to attempt an identification with an individual, since the text itself gives no indication of the author, it is reasonable to attempt to describe some of the cultural parameters within which the implied writer must have functioned. Given the date noted above, it is clear that the work in its present form was produced during the exilic period. More precisely, since it looks forward to the possibilities of the recovery of the land and the renewed life at the temple in Jerusalem,[66] I would date it prior to 538 BCE

---

[66] One of the most perplexing aspects of the treatments of the deuteronomistic history stems from the inability of commentators to account for its production. Hence, it is most commonly associated with the reform efforts of Josiah, or even Hezekiah, as a type of political propaganda that was necessary to legitimize their particular reforming efforts. Parallels to the literatures of other ancient Near Eastern cultures in support of the cultic activities of various rulers are generally cited as evidence of this genre and function for political and religious documents. This may indeed be a correct assessment for portions of the materials under consideration, but it does not seem to address the deuteronomistic history in its final redactional form. In this configuration, the story presents a prophetic pronouncement of the way in which Israel not only should have entered, taken, and constituted the land, but also how it should in the future, reenter, retake, and reconstitute the inheritance granted from Yahweh.

and the beginnings of the restoration community in Jerusalem. Likewise, since there are no clues of any imminent change in the community's fortunes, I would suggest a date no later than 550 BCE and the victories of Cyrus over Astyages or Croesus.[67] If a date of 560–550 BCE might serve as an appropriate chronological frame, then several inferences might be drawn about the situation of the author.

By this time those exiles taken in the first deportation (597 BCE) had been in Babylon for nearly 40 years—not simply a biblical designation for a generation. If the author of these materials had been an adult at the time of the exile, he would be 50 to 60 years of age, a time when the death of his own generation must have been imminent. This writer himself might have been a member of the Jerusalem community that remained in Judah after the defeat by Babylon, but this cannot be demonstrated. More likely, he was a member of the exilic community.[68] Interestingly, the great peroration over the destruction of Israel and Samaria (2 Kings 17)[69] is the only text that seems to reveal any real display of emotion on the part of the deuteronomistic historian, and may reveal ties with the old Levitical or country priesthoods associated with such shrines as Shiloh.[70] Given the linguistic and conceptual connections that exist between the deuteronomistic phraseology and theology and the literary traditions of Israel, it might be correct to associate this author with those predominantly northern religious traditions. If such connections as might be made between the prose sermons of Jeremiah and the deuteronomistic narratives are indicative of some such common tradition, this prophetic figure himself might serve as some type of "model" for the description of the implied author of our materials. Indeed, the prophetic aspirations and claims of the deuteronomistic writer have been amply demonstrated,[71] and help place the role of this author within a religious movement that was very active during this period.

---

[67] Miller and Hayes, *A History of Ancient Israel and Judah*, p. 438.

[68] For a summary of the various arguments pertaining to the location of the deuteronomistic author, see P. R. Ackroyd, *Exile and Restoration: A Study of Hebrew Thought of the Sixth Century B. C.* (OTL; Philadelphia: Westminster, 1968), pp. 65–68.

[69] Cross regards this as the climax of the deuteronomistic theme of the apostasy of Jeroboam and Israel (*Canaanite Myth and Hebrew Epic*, p. 281).

[70] B. Halpern, "Levitic Participation in the Reform Cult of Jeroboam I," *JBL* 95 (1976) 31–42.

[71] R. Polzin, "Reporting Speech in the Book of Deuteronomy: Toward a Compositional Analysis of the Deuteronomic History," in *Traditions in Transformation: Turning Points in Biblical Faith* (ed. B. Halpern and J. D. Levenson; Winona Lake, IN: Eisenbrauns, 1981), pp. 193–211; *idem, Moses and the Deuteronomist: A Literary Study of*

Alongside the prophetic insistence on allegiance to the word and will of Yahweh, the deuteronomistic author relied heavily upon the theme of David and the promise to him of dynastic longevity. Though the matter remains debated, the fact that there are so few references to the promise to David outside the deuteronomistic materials or those related to them would seem to suggest that this concept found an important aspect of its development, if not its very creation, at the pen of this writer. If the royal Judahite household had been supported by the propagandistic claim, possibly dating back as early as the Solomonic court,[72] that David had received the promise of an eternal dynasty from Yahweh (2 Sam. 7:13–15; cf. Pss 89:30–31; 132:12), then the destruction of the realm and the exile of the king could have brought that promise under scrutiny. At the same time, rather than simply replace the unconditional promise with one that was conditional (1 Kgs 2:4; cf. 8:25; 9:4–9) and that could serve to explain the events that gave rise to the disaster, the deuteronomistic historian maintained the hope for the continuation of the promise alongside the more functionally useful conditionalized form of the promise. Thus he was able to create a tension that reflected a basic structural component of the religious thought of that time—a need for stability and dependability in terms of covenantally based justice (hence the conditionalized form of the promise) balanced by a desire to avoid the obvious implications of failure (hence the maintenance of the unconditional promise). When projected into the divine realm, this dialectic creates a paradox that will provide a structure for the interpretation of the past and the recreation of the people "Israel."

The author has transformed the concept of a dynastic royal grant to the king and his household into a religious formulation that was a basic part of the identity of the people being defined by these descriptive elements. Whatever description of the author of these materials emerges from our analysis, it is imperative that it be one that is able to account for the importance of the role and image of David that are developed in this

---

the Deuteronomic History (New York: Seabury, 1980), pp. 25–72. An emphasis upon the prophetic aspects of the deuteronomistic author allows attention to be focused on the ways in which that figure serves as an intermediary between the divine pronouncements of Yahweh and the human realm to which they are applied. As will be demonstrated in the remainder of this study, the histories of Israel and Judah are, for the deuteronomistic writer, directly affected by their reactions to the demands of Yahweh presented to the people through a series of prophetic voices around which the narratives of the past are structured.

[72] See the discussion by McCarter, *II Samuel*, pp. 210–15.

narrative.[73] Both permanence and stability are essential ingredients of the promise to David and the continuation of the Davidic line as it operates within the domain of the books of Kings. Indeed, the only threat to that which the deuteronomistic narrative allows, apart from the exile, is the one presented by the queen-mother, Athaliah. Otherwise, the text gives no indications of any changes in the dynastic line. This stands in marked contrast with the instability and transience of the northern monarchy, which had no fewer than nine separate dynastic lines claim the throne in a 200-year period. The abject failure of every Israelite king and the final destruction and dissolution of the state leave only the remnant of Judah as the bearer of hope for the deuteronomist's vision of the future.

Such ties to the monarchic tradition, specifically the Davidic line of Judah, provide some additional insights into the identity of the author. Whatever sources underlie the narratives of Kings, be they annals, chronicles, or lists,[74] they were available to the author. Though somewhat tautologous, this observation is important, for it suggests that the author of these materials was not a commoner, but rather a highly educated person of some status, with access to court records of one sort or another. This person also had some reasonably advanced degree of training in or acquaintance with the various traditions of the acts of the kings and the prophetic sagas associated with them. At the same time, the deuteronomistic author was not simply a royal courtier with some arcane interest in the preservation of the actions, real or imaginary, of the monarchies of Israel or Judah. Rather, he was a prophetic voice who was attempting, as an intermediary with the divine,[75] to give instructions for life. With respect to the composition of the final history, it is necessary to stress that both the oral and written traditions which the author drew upon reveal him to have been a trained specialist. As already noted, the writer was operating in the redressive phase, the period in the social drama when the transition from "old rules" to "new rules" was being attempted. This reinforces the authoritative status of both the writer and the writing—

---

73 Instructive in this regard is W. Brueggemann's treatment of the theme of David. Brueggemann argues that the Hebrew Bible depicts David in a number of different ways, each of which is socially conditioned and addresses a particular set of social situations and crises (*David's Truth in Israel's Imagination and Memory* [Philadelphia: Fortress, 1985]).

74 On the characteristics of each form, see Van Seters, *In Search of History*, pp. 292–302.

75 On the role of the prophet as intermediary, see the investigation of prophecy within the context of modern anthropological theory by R. R. Wilson (*Prophecy and Society in Ancient Israel* [Philadelphia: Fortress, 1980], esp. pp. 21–88).

two of the products of the cultural matrix produced by the breach created by the exile.

While it may be valid to assume that "the stories of a society will certainly reflect the wider life of that society,"[76] the situation is much more complex than that. Though it is clear that the author of these materials appealed to the prophetic traditions associated with Moses for part of his claim to authority, the audience for whom he produced his literature and the results for which it was intended are more difficult to ascertain. It must be remembered that in historical terms *a* deuteronomistic historian produced *a version of* the deuteronomistic history which came to win an authoritative position in the community in which it found its major support.[77] This is to suggest that, while the textual evidence for such might be meager at best, it is likely that this deuteronomistic interpretive voice found itself in competition with other such speakers. Within the context of the crisis that led to the beginnings of the collection and editing of the so-called "writing prophets," this deuteronomistic author composed a competing vision of the prophetic message for a segment of the Judahite remnant. Eventually, it would be this very "history" of prophetic pronouncements that, though presented as a guide to an unlistening Israel and Judah, would become in actuality a preface to a transformation of the cultural world envisioned by the prophet and his followers.

The deuteronomistic history as a whole, at least in its final form, then, constitutes a *vaticinium post eventum* that, like other collections of prophetic materials, stands to support and direct a community. The bases of its authority are founded in the traditions of the past that were accepted as defining the very phenomenon of "official" Yahwistic prophecy (cf. Deut 18:21–22). As will be argued in the next chapter, the book of Deuteronomy, in its deuteronomistic form,[78] provides a mani-

---

[76] T. W. Overholt, *Prophecy in Cross-Cultural Perspective: A Sourcebook for Biblical Researchers* (SBLSBS 17; Atlanta, GA: Scholars Press,1986), p. 321.

[77] It cannot be determined with precision in what particular period this occurred. Since, however, the deuteronomistic hand was involved in the redactional activity associated with the book of Jeremiah and since the Chronicler used a version of the deuteronomistic history to write his version of Israel's past, it is clear that the work came to be adopted at least by the time of the Chronicler, i. e., ca. 450–350 BCE.

[78] The scholarly consensus regarding the book of Deuteronomy is twofold. First, there is a very old core to the book that dates to the early pre-exilic period and contains a number of ancient traditions. Second, the final work has been recast, by the deuteronomistic historian, as the farewell speech of Moses, and has been given a new framework that now incorporates it as the ideological basis of the deuteronomistic

festo of sorts for the boundary formation of the "people" Israel. Included in that prescription for the formation of a community is the "Law of the King" (Deut 17:14–20), a clear ideological endorsement of the institution of monarchy in the development of Israel as a monarchic state and an ethnic unity. This "constitutional" endorsement of the monarchy, along with the encompassing ethnic descriptors that the author advocates for Israelite self-identity, provides an important dimension for the profile of the deuteronomistic writer.

Deut 17:15 notes clearly that Israel should place over itself as king "one whom Yahweh your god shall choose" (ʾăšer yibḥar yhwh ʾĕlōhêkā bô), and for the deuteronomist, this was interpreted throughout as the offspring of David. Such would be only natural. Despite possible ideological and theological origins that might be traced to the northern kingdom, the deuteronomistic historian, at least as implied by the materials ascribed to him, is concerned with legitimizing the Judahite institutions associated with and attributed to David. The dynastic presentation of David's line constitutes one of the major emphases by which the Judahite state identified itself. For the deuteronomistic writer, the folk model of this single ruler dominates the story of the kingdoms and, by projection, the messianic hopes for a restoration which grew from this prophetic movement. The maintenance of this line, and hence a foundational element of the narrative and the community's identity, provides one of the values that define the social world created by this author.

IV. What to do with Athaliah?

When Athaliah, mother of Ahaziah, saw that her son was dead, she arose and destroyed all the "seed of the kingdom" (2 Kgs 11:1; reading rāʾătâ with the Qěrê).

In narrating these events, the deuteronomistic writer placed in jeopardy an essential identifying characteristic of the community: the throne and line of David. The ways in which the narrative is to be interpreted, in terms of the deuteronomistic use of the Davidic lineage as a descriptor of Judahite identity, remain to be addressed. In terms of narrated events, the deuteronomistic writer creates the breach and crisis phases of the "social drama" and provides the possibility for redress and

history. For an overview of modern analyses of Deuteronomy, see the discussion of A. D. H. Mayes (*Deuteronomy* [NCB; Grand Rapids, MI: Eerdmans, 1979], pp. 29–55).

resolution in the space of three verses. The compression of a full six years of Athaliah's reign into the space of a half-verse (2 Kgs 11:3b) telescopes the narrative through the breach and the crisis and immediately begins the redressive phase (2 Kgs 11:4–20). The narrative style makes it clear that the effort of the writer is directed toward the reestablishment and relegitimization of the lineage of David that has been threatened by the Omride pretender, no matter what her claims to the throne might have been in historical terms.

Yet such a resolution is not without problems, for the narrative states clearly that only Joash had been saved of all the royal offspring. Appropriately enough, the deuteronomist hides Joash in the temple, the house of Yahweh. The resolution of the crisis recognizes, in culturally meaningful terms, the symbolic forms of the governing elite and those who possess them. Additionally, the social drama that is played out in the narrative does not rely solely on the symbols of legitimized power, e.g., the temple, the high priest, the royal bodyguard, the "people of the land," and the "Davidic" heir, for its authoritative claims; the proper social and political order is restored by way of the performance of a ritual procedure involving those principals just noted. This use of ritual as the mode of reestablishing and repairing the perceived breach reflects a dual use of the concept: as a "model for," ritual is able to generate change; as a "model of," ritual instills the concept of order and stability.[79]

The initial phase of the resolution of the crisis begins in the critical seventh year when the priest, Jehoiada, makes a secret covenant with the palace and temple guards and shows them "the son of the king" (11:4). He then proceeds to instruct them as to what they have bound themselves to do, and the guards agree.[80] The priest gave the guard the spears and shields "that had belonged to King David" (*ʾăšer lammelek dāwīd*, v. 10), and they took their prescribed places. The entire series of events unfolds as though it had been a standard part of Judahite practice for some time, though there is no reflection of any such practice elsewhere in the narratives of Kings. The "son of the king" was then brought out, and the priest placed the *nēzer* and the *ʿēdût* on him, emblems that are clearly

---

[79] Turner, "Social Dramas and Stories about Them," p. 159.

[80] This section of the narrative (11:4–20) is fraught with textual difficulties, most of which deal with the divisions of the troops and their positioning around the temple. For a discussion of the textual problems and some proposed solutions, see Hobbs, 2 *Kings*, pp. 134–35, 138–44.

intended to be associated with kingship.[81] He is then formally acclaimed king with the clapping of hands and the cry, "May the king live!" (*yĕḥî hammelek*; 11:12 par. 2 Chr 23:11; cf. 1 Sam 10:24; 2 Sam 16:16; 1 Kgs 1:25, 31, 34, 39).

Significantly, this narrative recounting the formal declaration of the accession of the new king provides some significant parallels with the account of the succession of Solomon to the throne of David (1 Kgs 1:32–40). With Adonijah having already laid claim to the succession (1:5–10), the aging David, as a result of the manipulations of Bathsheba and the prophet Nathan (1:11–31), gave orders to the priest Zadok to anoint Solomon (1:32–37). Thus the priest, accompanied by the prophet Nathan and Benaiah, son of Jehoiada [!], commander of the royal bodyguard, led Solomon to the spring of Gihon and there anointed him king of Israel to the acclamation "May King Solomon live!" (*yĕḥî hammelek šĕlōmōh*, v. 34b). Thus David made Solomon king (1:43), a coronation that would lead eventually to the death of Adonijah (2:13–25). In the case of Solomon, it is this ritual, performed by the priest, that designates the legitimate Davidide who should sit on the throne of Israel and Judah. Though Adonijah was the elder brother and, if the concept of primogeniture was effective,[82] had a legitimate claim to the throne, and though he had the support of the Levitical priest Abiathar, he was not installed, according to the narrative account, in accord with the necessary ritual performance. Without such a legitimizing rite, Adonijah had to forfeit his claim to the throne (1 Kgs 1:50–53).

The parallelism between the two accounts is most notable because in each occurs a specially performed ritual which functions to establish or confirm the unbroken unilineal descent from David. It might be possible to suggest in this connection that the "coronation ritual" provides a parallel to certain forms of sacrificial rites in societies concerned with maintaining a specific lineage pattern. Participation in sacrificial rituals may serve to define patrilineal boundaries, distinguishing between those

---

[81] Though the precise meanings of both terms, *nēzer* and *ʿēdût*, are uncertain, it seems clear from the narrative that they denote some types of objects that are intended to convey the insignia of royal power. Whether the *ʿēdût*, "the testimonies," are intended to imply some confirmation of covenant is open to question. See the discussion of the significance of this ceremony in Gerbrandt, *Kingship According to the Deuteronomistic History*, pp. 182–87, and the literature cited therein.

[82] It appears, as Ishida has noted, that though the principle of primogeniture was fundamental to the concept of dynasty, it was not decisive. The reigning king had the power to designate an heir (*The Royal Dynasties in Ancient Israel*, p. 155).

who have a right to participate and those who do not.[83] If the ritual investitures of Solomon and Joash serve a similar redressive and integrative function, then such rites must be understood as powerful enough to "transform biological descent" for the sake of social stability.[84] Despite the fact that the Judahite formulae introducing the kings normally refer to the mother of the king by name,[85] no emphasis is placed on the importance of this role in maintaining the succession. Rather, for the deuteronomistic historian, where there might be a problem of succession, as in the cases of the king's favorite son Solomon or the proclaimed Davidide Joash, the ritual ceremony of royal investiture resolves any problems of succession, real or imagined.

The characteristics of such a ritual are developed further in the account of Joash. As vv. 14–16 indicate, the assemblage was not composed of only the priest and the royal guard, but rather "all the people of the land" (kol-ᶜam hāʾāreṣ, v. 14) were there. This first appearance of ᶜam hāʾāreṣ is interesting, for it seems clear that the phrase is to be understood in the present case in its broadest sense—"all the people of the land." The rebellion faced by Athaliah was much larger than a simple palace coup; rather, the rebels included the whole of the kingdom. It is not surprising that the queen cries out, "Treason, treason!" She is then seized and summarily executed at the order of the priest. The legitimate ruler is acclaimed; societal rules are reinstituted; "proper" order is restored to the land.

Yet the description of the ritual is not yet complete. In a repetitive style that redescribes the events just narrated,[86] the deuteronomistic author reiterates the power and significance of the ritual for the reconstitution of the proper social order. Verse 17 states clearly that the ceremony involved the concluding of "the covenant (habbĕrît) among Yahweh, the king, and the people, that they should be Yahweh's people,

---

[83] N. Jay, "Sacrifice, Descent and the Patriarchs," *VT* 38 (1988) 53.

[84] *Loc. cit.* Though Jay's analysis is directed only at the patriarchal narratives of Genesis and concentrates only on the use of sacrifice to confirm patriarchal unilineal descent when such is in doubt, it seems that the concept of a transforming and confirming ritual performance, specifically one performed publicly like those described here, could effect the same communal bonding.

[85] The name of the queen-mother is missing only in the cases of Jehoram (2 Kgs 8:16–17) and Ahaz (2 Kgs 16:1–4). Each of these kings, interestingly enough, is compared by the historian to the kings of Israel.

[86] The carefully arranged parallel structure of vv. 17–20 and vv. 4–16, which reinforce and supplement the contents of each other, is analyzed by Hobbs (2 *Kings*, pp. 137–38).

and between the king and the people." Most commentators delete the final phrase, "between the king and the people" (*ûbên hammelek ûbên hāʿām*), on the basis of the parallel in 2 Chr 23:16.[87] Yet it is precisely this phrase that serves to indicate the nature of the ritual being conducted. Whatever the form of the ceremony in actuality, as narrated the covenant contained two differing emphases: the agreement among God, king, and people, and the compact between king and people. This twofold nature of the covenant strikes at the heart of the national ethnic identification process: the reconfirmation of the fact that the people would be "Yahweh's people" reestablishes the special nature of the group. Additionally, the explicit inclusion of the new king as a partner in this pact allows this individual to receive a divine consent to his accession. The second aspect of the contract, that between king and people, aligns this ritual with a number of royal treaty forms well known from the ancient Near East. Indeed, it is by this ritual agreement that the people accept Joash as legitimate successor to the throne, and hence, as a legitimate Davidide.[88]

The performance of this ritual investiture as a public ceremony involving all the ruling elite and the populace of the land serves to reestablish the proper dynastic succession and secures it once again in the line of David. The ritualized covenantal agreement signifies that the community was willing to accept the priest's identification and declaration of Joash as the rightful heir to the throne. The conclusion of the account with the notices of the destruction of non-Yahwistic worship (v. 18) and the accession of the king to the throne (v. 19) climaxes with the rejoicing of "all the people of the land" and the city at peace, indicators that the ritual had indeed functioned to bridge the gap that had been created with the establishment of a non-Davidic ruler on the throne. The reiteration of the notice of the death of Athaliah confirmed the elimination of the "illegitimate" order and restored the social world that had been disrupted with the actions of this queen. The narrator successfully reintegrated the pre-crisis world description by means of a public ritual activity that had the effect of rewriting history. In this way, the ethnic and national signifiers so critical to the cultural crisis in which the

---

[87] The phrase is also omitted in LXX[L]. It is precisely this covenant that forms the social basis for the acceptance of Joash as a Davidide by those over whom he will rule and, for that reason, is essential to the understanding of the narrative. There is insufficient textual reason to read this phrase as a later addition or as a scribal gloss.

[88] See the parallels provided by Weinfeld, *Deuteronomy and the Deuteronomic School*, pp. 81–91.

deuteronomistic writer was entangled could be maintained despite the possibilities of historical breaches. Historical genealogical realities are created in the dramatic narration of the actions of the people in correcting and reintegrating the proper dynastic successor to the throne and, thus, the reestablishment and maintenance of the ideological presuppositions which were a part of the narrative structure itself. As the deuteronomistic author had been able to provide a social model for the maintenance and reestablishment of the line of David when it was broken by Athaliah's reign, and to incorporate a probable non-Davidide into that same lineage, so too was he able to secure a unilineal succession despite several clear crises presented by palace coups against the reigning line.

V. Summary Observations—Directions
for Further Investigation

No matter how one attempts to reconstruct the reign of Athaliah on the throne of Judah, one is faced with an incontrovertible fact: her ascent to the throne represents a break in the Davidic line. Likewise, it seems most likely that her successor to the throne, Joash, was *not* of the line of David. Despite the obvious nature and implications of these two data, commentators are, as a whole, content to insist that the line of David remained intact and unbroken on the throne of Judah for its entire national life. This acceptance is based on the narrative account produced by the deuteronomistic historian and received as historical fact by later generations.[89] Within the context of the exile and the threats to Judahite national, religious, and ethnic identity, this writer attempted to produce a narrative reformulation of what that identity should become. In doing so, he cast it in prophetic terms and projected it into the historical past. Thus, this narrated account of what was one particular vision of Judahite identity came to be accepted as an historical account of Judah's past.

---

[89] The recent work by J. W. Flanagan illustrates how the differing genealogies of David and Saul function within the context of the narratives recounting the establishment of the Davidic monarchy. As he notes, even though the genealogies were not intended as historiographic sources, once they had come to be accepted by the community, they were presumed to be accurate because they maintained the social structures and statuses of that period ("Succession and Genealogy in the Davidic Dynasty," in *The Quest for the Kingdom of God: Studies in Honor of George E. Mendenhall* [ed. by H. G. Huffmon, F. A. Spina, and A. R. Green; Winona Lake, IN: Eisenbrauns, 1983], pp. 35–55).

A prime example of the dangers of assimilation by the conquering nation and surrounding peoples is found in the history of the northern kingdom of Israel. After its conquest and resettlement by Assyrian subjects, its religion and culture survived only in those ways in which it was preserved in the social and religious worlds of its Judahite neighbor. The Samaritan sect, the one possible survivor of this tradition, came to be rejected altogether as a part of the Judahite tradition.[90] The pressures to form ethnic boundaries are most strong, I would suggest, *not* in those instances where obvious distinctions among groups, traditions, and practices might be most apparent; rather, the compulsion to define and reinforce those identity ascriptors arises most strongly when the similarities among various groups are greatest, and concomitantly, so are the possibilities of absorption. This would have been precisely the situation in which Judah found itself during the exile.

For the deuteronomistic writer, a continuing sense of self-identification for those constituting his support group could be found in the associations with the Davidic monarchy which could be traced, in an unbroken line, back to David. By way of narrative reenactments of ritual performances, the deuteronomistic author could reintegrate the genealogical ascription of a kingship unilineally descended from David into the social world view of his group. With Jehoiachin and his sons still alive, the reliance on the promises to David could be maintained and the disaster blamed on the failure of the offspring of David to fulfill their covenantal obligations. Hence, divine reality of a "moral retribution," a basic structural part of the religious world, was offset by their "transmoral" beliefs that could suspend it in order to overcome such a situation of dissonance and despair. Despite the possible internal thematic tensions that might accompany a narrative that is attempting to express such basic structural modes, the narrative past was constructed so as to leave open the historical future to the reformation of a monarchic community that would be formed within the crisscross of the various religious, cultic, national, and cultural webs that might come to constitute the future community.

This represents, however, only the beginning of an investigation of the ways in which the deuteronomistic composition of this history exemplifies an attempt to define and identify the meanings of Judah's

---

[90] On the origins and history of the Samaritans, see J. D. Purvis, *The Samaritan Pentateuch and the Origin of the Samaritan Sect* (HSM 2; Cambridge: Harvard University Press, 1968).

past in terms that would allow it to rebuild its future and to retain a sense of self-identification. In the next chapter, some of the ways in which the deuteronomistic writer attempted to define Judahite national religion will be addressed. Since the formation, bounding, and maintenance of a special community constituted a major reason for the compilation of the narrative materials, the ways in which the deuteronomistic writer chose to formulate the differences between acceptable Judahite or Israelite behavior and the unacceptable "abominations of the nations" (tôʿăbōt haggôyīm, Deut 18:9) might be understood in terms of attempts by the author to describe his community in contrast to the purported practices of its neighbors and competitors. In this way, perhaps it will be possible to understand more clearly the implications of the deuteronomistic assertion that Yahweh had chosen Israel "to be his people, a private possession (sĕgullâ), from all the peoples upon the face of the earth" (Deut 14:2).

3

DEUTERONOMY AND
THE DEFINITION OF ISRAEL

I. The Formulation of Israelite Identity

Cast in the form of a series of speeches delivered by Moses to "all Israel" gathered on the plains of Moab prior to crossing the Jordan and entering the land promised to their ancestors, the book of Deuteronomy provides a kind of social manifesto of "Israelite" ethnic identity. Originally this work formed the ideological base that introduced the following "historical works" contained in Joshua through Kings and provided the basis for the later deuteronomistic interpretation of the actions of Israel and Judah with respect to the requirements of this extended exhortation to remain loyal to Yahweh. Based upon the ideal of complete and absolute obedience to Yahweh alone, the deuteronomic[1]

---

[1] Following the distinctions made by M. Noth, the term "deuteronomic" will be used to refer to the book of Deuteronomy and to designate those ideas and ideals that are expressed therein. The adjective "deuteronomistic" will be reserved for the "history" that follows, i. e., the works of Joshua through Kings, which are clearly dependent upon the deuteronomic materials as a base (*Überlieferungsgeschichtliche Studien* [3rd ed.; Tübingen: Max Niemeyer, 1967], pp. 3–18). Unlike Noth's position, the distinction between the terms should not be understood in the present materials as implying a difference in authorship, though such might have been the case. In its present form, Deuteronomy shows clear evidence of deuteronomistic editing. While the process of the growth of the deuteronomistic history remains debated, the recent

materials define "Israel" in terms of the various ways in which particular devotion to this single deity distinguishes "Israel" from all other nations. The manner in which Deuteronomy constructs this symbolic universe and then presents acceptable and unacceptable behaviors for those who would belong to this "Israel" constitutes the general outline of the present chapter.[2]

Scholars generally agree that the present book of Deuteronomy is structured around four editorial superscriptions that introduce the materials that follow (1:1; 4:44; 28:69; 33:1). Associated with these headings is the repeated claim, found especially with respect to those materials contained in 4:44–28:69, that this *tôrâ* was a *written* account of the divine commands that were mediated by Moses to "Israel."[3] If this final form of the book comes from the hand of the deuteronomistic writer, then this form of the work itself must be placed during the period of the exile, at a time when once again "Israel" found itself without a land and in need of a self-definition that would offset the threat of cultural and religious assimilation. For the deuteronomistic author, the distinctive nature of this written account and of the identity of "Israel" could be understood only within the context of the ideal of the covenant by which Yahweh had bound his people "Israel" to him and through which this people was to be defined. At the base of this deuteronomistic presentation of the ideal "Israel" lies a fundamental paradox: Yahweh

---

theory advanced by N. Lohfink, which allows for extensive pre-exilic literary activity producing the completed narrative only in the exile, accounts for a number of the various thematic shifts that are encountered in the whole of the work ("Kerygmata des Deuteronomistischen Geschichtswerks," in *Die Botschaft und die Boten. Festschrift Für H. W. Wolff zum 70. Geburtstag* [ed. by J. Jeremias and L. Perlitt; Neukirchen-Vluyn: Neukirchener Verlag, 1981], pp. 87–100).

[2] The theoretical background for the construction of symbolic universes and their externalization and institutionalization is provided by P. Berger and T. Luckmann, *The Social Construction of Reality: A Treatise in the Sociology of Knowledge* (New York: Doubleday, 1966), pp. 47–128. In the present work, the symbolic universe that is under investigation is one that attempts to provide boundaries that separate "Israel" from the nations and by which "Israel" might identify itself as a "people."

[3] S. Dean McBride, Jr., "Polity of the Covenant People: The Book of Deuteronomy," *Int* 41 (1987) 231, esp. n. 6. As with other books in the Hebrew canon, the redactional reconstruction of the composition of Deuteronomy remains debated. For a balanced presentation of the major positions, see. A. D. H. Mayes, *Deuteronomy* (NCB; Grand Rapids; MI: Eerdmans, 1979), pp. 29–55. The reconstructions of the stages of growth and the variety of possible usages of these materials stand outside the parameters of this investigation. Rather, this final deuteronomistic form of the book of Deuteronomy will be the focus of this chapter.

had chosen "Israel" as his special possession and, at the same time, "Israel" was obligated to fulfill the requirements of the *tôrâ* as contained in covenantal form in this book.[4] The ways in which this paradox is resolved in differing situations throughout the deuteronomistic history provide an essential element in the concept of the identity of "Israel" produced by this work.

"Israel" has been placed in quotation marks to this point because of the basic ambiguity associated with the use of that term throughout the Hebrew texts. In the Hebrew scriptures, "Israel" is applied to the patriarch Jacob, to a geographical territory, to a monarchic state, and to an idealized community. Thus, it has the power of a highly flexible and transformative symbol that may be applied and reapplied in a variety of ways to a wide range of differing situations, thus making the survival of group identity a stronger possibility.[5] The "Israel" that is both addressed and envisioned, i.e., created, in the narrated and narrating speeches of Moses[6] is one that, in historical terms, did not yet exist. The "Israel" addressed by Moses is ideal, one that will exist in real terms only at a later time. This "Israel," too, will find itself outside the land as a result of exile. It has only the hope of Yahweh's forgiveness and acceptance of its repentance to cling to in the attempt to regain this ideal time that had now been lost.[7] All of this has the effect of recreating "Israel" in the days *prior* to its entry into the land,[8] i. e., prior to its failure to fulfill the obliga-

---

[4] On the covenantal form of the present book of Deuteronomy, see D. J. McCarthy, *Treaty and Covenant: A Study in Form in the Ancient Oriental Documents and in the Old Testament* (AnBib 21A, rev. ed.; Rome: Biblical Institute Press, 1978), pp. 157–205.

[5] A. P. Royce has argued for the necessity of flexible symbols in the continued maintenance and recreation of ethnic identity (*Ethnic Identity: Strategies of Diversity* [Bloomington/Indianapolis: Indiana University Press, 1982], p. 150).

[6] On the literary significance of this distinction, see the work of R. Polzin, "Reporting Speech in the Book of Deuteronomy: Toward A Compositional Analysis of the Deuteronomic History," in *Traditions in Transformation: Turning Points in Biblical Faith* (ed. B. Halpern and J. D. Levenson; Winona Lake, IN: Eisenbrauns, 1981), pp. 193–211.

[7] On the importance of the concept of an "ideal" and its loss, especially with respect to the connection of identity and land, in the formation of ethnic and national groups, see A. D. Smith, *The Ethnic Origins of Nations* (Oxford: Blackwell, 1986), pp. 191–200.

[8] G. von Rad, *Studies in Deuteronomy* (SBT; London: SCM, 1953), pp. 70–73. D. J. A. Clines notes that the Pentateuch as a whole "functions as an address to exiles, or, perhaps it would be better to say, the self-expression of exiles, who find themselves at the same point as that reached by the Israelite tribes at the end of Deuteronomy:

tions of the covenant and the consequent crisis presented by the exile and the potential loss of identity.

The symbolic nature of the designation "Israel," applied now to a nonexistent entity with the intention of *recreating* that very object, reflects a particular religious system that imparts a metaphorical description to the social unit that is addressed.[9] As a symbolic recreation of Israel at the point of its very origins, Deuteronomy is able to supply the defining characteristics to that people that will then be applied to the latter groups who accept this as a part of their ethnic history and an authoritative account of their temporal and spatial origins. The general theme of Deuteronomy, which itself implies a definition of Israel, is the exhortation to the service of one god by a divinely chosen people centered about one sanctuary, by way of obedience to the law in the land that Yahweh had given them.[10] As I shall attempt to demonstrate in the remainder of this chapter, this theme constitutes, in ethnic and religious terms, the very concept and identity of the recreated communities that designate themselves as Israel.

The deuteronomistic depiction, and hence ethnic definition, of Israel itself is presented within the context of the sermonic exhortations of the book of Deuteronomy that define the parameters of Israelite cultic religious practice. In the book of Deuteronomy, the entity "Israel" is created on the plains of Moab prior to the crossing of the Jordan. According to the covenantal schema of Deuteronomy, this occurs when people accept the obligations of the book:

> This day, Yahweh your god commands you to do these statutes and ordinances, and you will observe and do them with all your heart and soul. Today you have proclaimed[11] concerning Yahweh that he will be your god and that you will walk in his ways and observe his statutes and commandments and ordinances and will obey him. And Yahweh has proclaimed

---

the promise of God stands behind them, the promised land before them" (*The Theme of the Pentateuch* [JSOTSup 10; Sheffield: JSOT, 1978], p. 98).

[9] The power of such imaginative ideation on the understanding of social entities has been demonstrated by J. Neusner in his study of the application of "Israel" in various Jewish works produced during the first six centuries CE ("'Israel': Judaism and Its Social Metaphors," *JAAR* 55 [1987] 331–61). According to Neusner, a religious system is composed of three things: a world view, a way of life, and an address to a specific entity (p. 331).

[10] Mayes, *Deuteronomy*, pp. 57–58.

[11] For this translation of *heʾĕmartā*, see *Hebräisches und Aramäisches Lexikon zum Alten Testament* (ed. L. Koehler and W. Baumgartner; 3rd ed.; Leiden: E. J. Brill, 1967), I. 62b.

today concerning you that you will be a people for his own possession, according as he declared to you, and you will keep all his commandments and that he will set you high above all the nations which he has made, in praise and in fame and in honor, and that you shall be a people holy to Yahweh your god, as he has declared (Deut 26:16–19).[12]

This mutual proclamation defines Israel, in the first instance, through its special relationship with Yahweh, its national god. Additionally, it accords this people a special position "high above all the nations which he made,"[13] a people separated, i. e., holy (*qādôš*), a people to be Yahweh's personal possession (*sĕgullâ*). Equally important is the way in which this formal expression of the uniqueness of Israel is framed by an explicit ceremony of covenant-making to be performed immediately upon crossing into the land (Deut 11:26–30; 27:1–8) that ties the identity of the people to that land.[14] The fact that the author of the history is careful to narrate these activities as prescribed in the following section of the work (Josh 8:30–35; 24:1–28) serves to reconfirm the identity of the people as it was developed in Deuteronomy.[15] It is the description of this very relationship between Israel and its god that provides an essential component of Israelite group identity in the deuteronomistic history.

This metaphorization of Israel as a group covenantally bound in a special relationship to its deity, separated from the other nations, finds further development in terms of its relationship in distinction from, rather than by comparison to, the surrounding peoples. For Deuteron-

---

[12]   See the treatment of this position by M. Weinfeld, "The Emergence of the Deuteronomic Movement: The Historical Antecedents," in *Das Deuteronomium: Entstehung, Gestalt und Botschaft* (ed. N. Lohfink; BETL 68; Lueven: University Press, 1985), pp. 76–98.

[13]   *ʿelyôn ʿal kol-haggôyīm ʾăšer ʿāśâ.*

[14]   Important in the context is the argument of G. W. Ahlström that "Israel" was originally a geographic, not an ethnic designation (*Who Were the Israelites?* [Winona Lake, IN: Eisenbrauns, 1986]). Though this may be historically correct, it remains clear that by the time of the deuteronomistic historian, it could be used as a territorial and an ethnic descriptor.

[15]   These sections of Joshua continue to present problems to commentators. The covenant ceremony mentioned in 8:30–35 is seen, most commonly, as an *incipit* for the account in Joshua 24 that has been placed in its present context by a secondary redactor (see R. Boling and G. E. Wright, *Joshua* [AB 6; Garden City, NY: Doubleday, 1982], pp. 246–54). A consideration of this ritual reenactment of the covenant will be postponed until the next chapter. It is important to note, however, that the structural arrangement of the fulfillment passages in Joshua parallels that of the command-ments in Deuteronomy and is, I would argue, a distinctive element of the style of the author of the deuteronomistic history.

omy, Israel is to be defined in terms of both the uniqueness of Yahweh and the uniqueness of Israel. Modern scholarship has failed to recognize the possibility that these descriptions of Israel and Israelite religion might be symbolic expressions of the ethnic, social boundary formation rather than accurate ethnographic descriptions of ancient Israelite practices. This has led to the general acceptance of the descriptions of Israel and the Hebrew materials *against*, rather than *within* their ancient Near Eastern environment.[16] The failure of scholars to recognize the functional aspects of the descriptors chosen and applied within the context of the social worlds that produced the narrative descriptions and which were projected by those narrations can lead to an interesting contrast of analytical results.[17] While the necessity of cross-cultural comparison of

---

[16] This movement took much of its impetus from the biblical theology and biblical archaeology movements of the day, influenced most strongly in America by the work of W. F. Albright and his students, particularly G. Ernest Wright. Indeed, few works could better express this viewpoint than Wright's own *The Old Testament against Its Environment* (SBT 2; London: SCM, 1950) and *Biblical Archaeology* (Philadelphia: Westminster, 1957). Despite the growing recognition that the distinctive character of Israel cannot be maintained on the basis of the evidence normally cited, as represented by the work of B. Albrektson (*History and the Gods. An Essay on the Idea of Historical Events As Divine Manifestations in the Ancient Near East and in Israel* [Lund: C. W. K. Gleerup, 1967]), the continuing influence of this movement remains nearly pervasive in the field, as might be illustrated by the distinctions that may be inferred from the title of F. M. Cross' *Canaanite Myth and Hebrew Epic* (Cambridge: Harvard University Press, 1973).

[17] Two recent treatments of the issue of sacred prostitution, especially the role of the *qādēš/qĕdēšâ* in the religion of ancient Israel, present an excellent example of the differing results that may be obtained in attempts to reconstruct the religion of ancient Israel or Judah. While M. Gruber has argued most persuasively that there is little or no evidence that the terms so often associated with cultic prostitution in the ancient Near East actually mean such, he strongly maintains that the Hebrew term *qĕdēšâ* does mean "cultic prostitute" and gives adequate testimony to the existence of, or at least knowledge of, that practice by the Hebrews ("Hebrew *Qĕdēšah* and Her Canaanite and Akkadian Cognates," *UF* 18 [1986] 133–48). R. Oden, pursuing another approach, reaches the same conclusions as Gruber concerning the evidence for the existence of this practice outside Israel: there does not exist any unambiguous evidence for the practice of cultic prostitution by any of Israel's neighbors. Additionally, Oden argues that despite the fact that the terms *qādēš/qĕdēšâ* may designate cultic prostitution, this does not constitute evidence that such was practiced by Israel or by any of its neighbors. Rather, it attests to the fact that the biblical writers condemned the religious practices of the surrounding peoples and accused them of such an "abominable practice" as this ("Religious Identity and the Sacred Prostitution Accusation," *The Bible Without Theology: The Theological Tradition and Alternatives to It* [San Francisco: Harper & Row, 1987], pp. 131–53).

the religions of Israel's neighbors with the religious practices attested by Israel as its own is gaining acceptance, the process of group identity formation and ethnic boundary-making as major aspects and functions of the narratives produced by the author of these materials, and of religious materials in general, has gone uninvestigated.

The deuteronomistic exhortation attributed to Moses in Deut 4:1–40 illustrates the way in which these materials draw attention to the unique status of Israel by way of its relationship with its god.[18] In this section, the entry into the land and Israel's possession of that land are dependent upon the people's allegiance to the precepts of the covenant that are presented (4:13). Indeed, it is precisely these "statutes and ordinances" (huqqîm ûmišpāṭîm) that will constitute the wisdom and understanding of Israel and will serve to differentiate Israel from all other groups:

> For what great nation exists that has a god so near to it as Yahweh our god is to us whenever we call upon him? And what great nation exists that has statutes and ordinances (huqqîm ûmišpāṭîm) as righteous as all this tôrâ (kĕkōl hattôrâ hazzōʾt) which I am placing before you today? (4:7–8)

The explicit identification of the statutes and ordinances with the tôrâ leaves little doubt about the authority which the deuteronomistic writer attributed to these pronouncements of Moses. When the other nations hear these statutes and ordinances, they will recognize that "this great nation is a wise and discerning people" (ʿam-ḥākām wĕnābôn, 4:6). It will be Israel's performance of the stipulations of the tôrâ that will distinguish it, in the first instance, from the surrounding peoples.

The continuation of the speech in 4:15–24 emphasizes another distinguishing characteristic of Israel—its aniconic cultic practices. Since Israel saw no divine form at Horeb when Yahweh addressed them (v. 15), they were allowed to make no images of any kind (vv. 16–18). Additionally, there could be no worship of the heavenly bodies in any of their forms, for "Yahweh your God has allotted them to all the peoples under all the heavens" (v. 19). This passage makes clear the conceptual separation of Israel from all of the other peoples "under the heaven," for of all the possible objects of worship, Israel is allowed only Yahweh. All others have been assigned by Yahweh to the other nations. The demonstration of this special nature of Israel was found in Yahweh's deliver-

---

[18] On the unity of this chapter, see J. Levenson, "Who Inserted the Book of the Torah?" *HTR* 68 (1975) 203–33.

ance of them from Egypt so that they might be "a people, his own possession" (*lihyôt lô lĕʿam naḥălâ*, v. 20; cf. 9:26, 29).[19]

The concluding portion of this address reemphasizes this special connection among Yahweh, Israel, and the *tôrâ*. Deut 4:32–40 focuses on the unique nature of the way in which Israel had been selected by Yahweh:

> Has any god ever tried to come and take for himself a nation (*gôy*) from the midst of another nation (*gôy*) with signs and wonders and war and with a powerful hand and outstretched arm and with great spectacles as all that Yahweh your god did for you in Egypt before your eyes? (4:34)

Such unique actions were performed in order that Israel might know that Yahweh alone was god (v. 35). Because of his love for Israel's ancestors, Yahweh "chose their offspring after them" (*wayyibḥar bĕzarʿô ʾaḥărāyw*, 4:37) and brought them out from Egypt in order to give them the land (4:38). This idea of Israel as a people "chosen" (*bāḥar bĕ-*) by Yahweh is first defined in Deuteronomy (4:37; 7:6, 7; 10:15; 14:2) and is explained by way of Yahweh's deliverance of Israel from bondage in Egypt.[20] The gift of the land is presented by Deuteronomy as the fulfillment of the promise to Israel's ancestors.[21] The deliverance of Israel, its choice as Yahweh's own possession from all the nations of the earth, and the essence of its identity are interwoven with the possession of the land and the fulfillment of the obligations of the covenant.[22] Israel's possession of the land would depend upon its fulfillment of that covenant (4:40). If Israel should fail to follow these commands and should act in such a way as to anger Yahweh, then it would be destroyed quickly and Yahweh would scatter its inhabitants among the peoples (4:26–27). Nonetheless, this threat of punishment as the loss of the land and the scattering of the people was balanced by the ever-present possibility of repentance and return to the proper covenantal allegiance. After all, Yahweh was per-

---

[19] The term *naḥălâ*, "inheritance," carries a special connotation in the way in which it is employed in reference to Yahweh and Israel. In Israel's religious traditions, the land that Yahweh promised to the ancestors and gave to Israel was Yahweh's own personal possession (cf. Deut 32:8–9) (P. Hanson, *The People Called: The Growth of Community in the Bible* [San Francisco: Harper & Row, 1986], pp. 63–65).

[20] E. W. Nicholson, *Deuteronomy and Tradition: Literary and Historical Problems in the Book of Deuteronomy* (Philadelphia: Westminster, 1967), pp. 56–57, 97.

[21] Deut 1:8, 35; 4:31; 6:10, 18, 23; 7:8, 12–13; 8:1, 18; 9:5; 10:11; 11:9, 21; 13:18; 19:8; 26:3, 15; 29:12; 30:20; 31:7, 20, 21, 23; 34:4.

[22] As Mayes has expressed it, "for Deuteronomy life itself means life in the land in covenant with Yahweh" (*Deuteronomy*, p. 81).

ceived as a "merciful god" (*ʾēl raḥûm*) who would not forget the covenant he had sworn to the ancestors (4:31).

II. The Creation of Ethnic Distinctiveness

Israel, then, is defined in Deuteronomy as a special people, distinct from the surrounding nations by virtue of its dual relationship with its patron deity. It is this duality that creates a type of dialectic in the ideology of the deuteronomistic corpus that provides a structure for the narrative history which will be based upon these deuteronomic ideals. The ideal "Israel" is created by the "choice" of its deity, and its continuation is determined by Yahweh's mercy and by covenantal ideals. Central to both of these defining characteristics stands Israel's distinctiveness among the nations of the earth. It is precisely this concept of distinctiveness that provides the basis for understanding "Israel" in terms of ethnicity, since ethnic groups may be defined on the basis of the opposition between self and others. By the process of categorization of such oppositions, a group is able to define itself in terms of both overt signs and basic standards of value and morality.[23] Often, the true markers of ethnic boundaries are to be found not so much in any "objective" criteria, but rather in those types of standards of conduct which a group holds firm and from which its neighbors are charged with departing.[24] For ancient Israel, and for the deuteronomistic writer, an integral part of this system of values and standards is found in the descriptions of Israel's religion, especially as contrasted with the "abominations of the nations":

> When you come into the land which Yahweh your god is giving you, you will not learn to do like the abominations of those nations (*kĕtôʿăbōt haggôyîm hāhēm*, Deut 18:9).

It will be upon these particularly deuteronomic descriptions of Israelite practice and identity that this chapter will focus to demonstrate the variety of ways in which the deuteronomistic writer has developed his presentation of ancient Israelite religion and ethnicity. Deut 7:1–6 describes Israel's obligations to *destroy* completely the nations living in the land promised by god and to avoid their worship practices, and provides an excellent starting point for understanding the construction of

---

[23] F. Barth, "Introduction," in *Ethnic Groups and Boundaries: The Social Organization of Culture Difference* (ed. F. Barth; Boston: Little, Brown, 1969), pp. 13–14.

[24] Oden, *The Bible Without Theology*, p. 133.

a group identity in contrast to the surrounding peoples. Deut 12:1–5 introduces a peculiarly deuteronomistic ideal, that of the centralization of worship in one place, an ideal that will become extremely important in the development of the descriptions of Israelite national religion during the period of the monarchy. In Deut 17:14–20, the deuteronomic "law of the king," the foundation is laid for the establishment of a monarchic state, but in a specifically restricted manner. A fourth passage, Deut 18:9–14, provides for divine-human intermediation in terms of prophecy, contrasted with the practices of the surrounding peoples. Finally, Deut 29:9–20 depicts in more detail the covenantal relationship and defining characteristics of Israel and contains stern warnings against any practices that might be considered idolatrous. The process of narrative boundary formation in this ideological introduction to the deuteronomistic history developed in these selected passages provides the foundations for an alternate explanation for the religious reforms attributed to Josiah (2 Kgs 23:4–20) in the concluding portions of the deuteronomistic narrative. In this way, the importance of understanding the presentation of Israelite national religion as a form of ethnic and group boundary formation, rather than as an historical description of events and practices, might be demonstrated. Additionally, these ideal boundaries might be understood as symbolic "frames" within which the history of Israel as a "nation"[25] was presented.

The first passage, Deut 7:1–6, occurs within the deuteronomistic exhortation of Israel to remain loyal to the covenantal obligations that have been outlined. This section elaborates on the distinctive nature of this people, justifying the instructions given with the assertion that "you are a people holy to Yahweh your god" (ʿam qādôš ʾattâ, 7:6a).[26] Within

---

[25] While some might argue that the concept "nation" is a purely modern develop-ment, I would agree with the observations of Smith that while "nationalism" is clearly a modern phenomenon, there exist a number of continuities between the formation and development of ethnic and national groups, and the application of the term to earlier historical periods is not inaccurate (*The Ethnic Origins of Nations*, pp. 6–18). In the present case, the standard use of "nation" by biblical scholars to designate the numerous monarchic states that populated the ancient world will be retained, not as a description of any political or cultural actuality, but rather as a designation of potential ethnic differentiations.

[26] The phrase ʿam qādôš also occurs in Deut 14:2, 21, 26:19, and 28:9. As M. Weinfeld has pointed out, the concept of a holy people predominates in Deuterono-my's ideological view, but is completely absent from any of the earlier biblical sources (*Deuteronomy and the Deuteronomic School* [Oxford: Clarendon, 1972], pp. 227–28).

the context of Deuteronomy, the ascription of "holiness" to Israel obligates that people to participate in the prescriptions of the covenantal demands. In the first instance, this requires the recognition and acceptance that Israel must worship Yahweh alone. In a somewhat artificially constructed juxtaposition, this section presents two obligations on Israel when it enters the land: Israel is to destroy completely the nations dwelling there (vv. 2–3) and is to avoid any relationship with those people or their gods (vv. 4–5).[27] These two actions clearly develop a contrast between Israel and "the other nations."

The intensely nationalistic attitudes represented in Deuteronomy are clear in this description of the way in which Israel is to interrelate with the inhabitants of the land that Yahweh has promised to give it: the totality of the population is to be annihilated. The application of the language and ideals of "holy war" (*haḥărēm taḥărîm*, v. 2) to the collected inhabitants of the land, here represented symbolically as seven nations,[28] represents in a totally unambiguous fashion the threatening visage presented by the competing cultures with which Israel was to come into contact in the course of the narrative. The extreme which this ideal of separation from those who constitute "outsiders" represents is furthered by the command that Israel should neither make any kind of treaty with them (*běrît*)[29] nor show them any pity.

The abstract nature of this conception of complete annihilation of the nations of Canaan is confirmed by the very next verse, which disallows the possibility of any mixing of Israel with those people by forbidding intermarriage. Clearly, the realization of the first command eliminates the need for the second. Such juxtapositions of ideals, however, are common to the paratactic arrangements that characterize the deutero-

---

[27] This prefacing of the covenantal ideals and obligations by reference to the entry into the land to possess it is common to the deuteronomic tradition (cf. Deut 4:1, 5; 6:18; 7:1; 8:1; 9:1, 5; 11:8, 10, 29, 31; 12:29, 28:21, 63, 30:16, etc.).

[28] This list and variations on it are common in the Hebrew Bible as a designation of the indigenous population of the land of Canaan (cf. Gen 15:20; Exod 3:8, 17; 23:23; 33:2; 34:11; Deut 20:17; Josh 3:10; 9:1; 11:3; 12:8; 24:11; Judg 3:5; 1 Kgs 9:20; Ezra 9:1; Neh 9:8; 2 Chr 8:7). On the conduct of "holy war," see also Deut 20:1–20.

[29] For Deuteronomy and the subsequent deuteronomistic history, the formation of a *běrît* is proper only in association with Yahweh. The injunction in Exod 23:32 that no treaty should be made with the inhabitants of the land or with their gods (*lōʾ tikrōt lāhem wělēʾlōhêhem běrît*) illustrates the well documented notion that in the ancient Near East, treaties between peoples involved the recognition of the national deities of the groups involved. For Israel, this would be a violation of the ideal of exclusive recognition and worship of Yahweh.

nomic and deuteronomistic narratives. While on a tribal level Israel might be exogamous, on a nationally conceived ethnic level, the group Israel was to be thoroughly endogamous. This assertion that marriages to people outside the boundaries by which Israel is defined are forbidden is countered by the notices that such unions were common throughout the whole of the traditions incorporated into the biblical texts[30] and reinforces the previous notice of the importance of the process of metaphorization and ideational projection in the process of ethnic boundary creation.

This total separation from the indigenous peoples of Canaan,[31] the avoidance of any form of treaty or marriage, as well as the directive for their complete destruction, are incorporated into the cultic and covenantal ideals of Deuteronomy by the explanation contained in the next verse. Contact with the other nations would lead only to turning away from Yahweh and the service of "other gods" (*ʾĕlōhîm ʾăḥērîm*),[32] explicit violations of the major covenantal obligations (Deut 5:6–10) that would lead to Yahweh's anger and destruction of his own people.[33] The practi-

---

[30] In the biblical traditions, the concern with intermarriage and the enforcement of prohibitions against it does not seem to have been emphasized strongly until the post-exilic period, when the remnant of the Judahites were in danger of being assimilated into the surrounding national groups. It is only in the times of Ezra and Nehemiah that actions to dissolve and prohibit such marriages seem to have been enforced (cf. Ezra 10:1–5; Neh 10:28–30; 13:23–27). Notably, such prominent figures in Israelite traditions as Moses, Joseph, Samson, Solomon, and Ahab all married foreign wives.

[31] Modern reconstructions of the origins of Israel in the land of Canaan suggest that despite Israel's traditions that it came from outside the land, in actuality, it too might have been part of the indigenous population; cf. K. W. Whitelam, "Israel's Traditions of Origin: Reclaiming the Land," *JSOT* 44 (1989) 19–42.

[32] This concern with "going after other gods" and "serving other gods" represents a standard part of deuteronomic terminology. For references to the variations on this standard phrase, see Weinfeld, *Deuteronomy and the Deuteronomic School*, pp. 320–21. Both the style and language of this passage are closely paralleled by Exod 34:12–16, which might be interpreted as a deuteronomistic gloss on an otherwise JE narrative tradition. Such a decision is related to the manner in which the compositional history of the narratives recounting the construction of the calf images in Exodus 32 and in 1 Kings 12 is reconstructed.

[33] The internal tension produced by the ideas of a merciful deity and one who acts in strict accord with the idea of absolute justice as exemplified by the covenantal blessings and curses (cf. Deut 27:11–28:68) runs throughout the deuteronomic legislation and the deuteronomistic history in general. R. Green's analysis of the deep structure of religions suggests that such binary oppositions constitute the most

cal rationale for adhering to the principles and obligations of the covenantal agreements finds expression in the results that failure (as blessing) might produce. Israel was to be defined by its exclusive relationship to Yahweh, which entailed a complete rejection of anything associated with other gods or their worship.

The concluding command given in this section explicitly demonstrates the manner in which Israel is to act with regard to the religious practices it will encounter upon entering the land. Rather than being tempted to serve these deities (v. 4), Israel is to tear down (*nātaṣ*) their altars, smash (*šibbēr*) their *maṣṣēbōt*, break or cut down (*giddaʿ*) their *ʾăšērîm*, and burn (*śārap*) their images in the fire (v. 5).[34] The act of dismantling foreign cult places and removing the evidence of the worship of other gods would complete the process of the elimination of the indigenous peoples and their practices from the land that had been promised by Yahweh to his people. Clearly, if such ideals were realized, Israel would become a distinct nation in the land, for, by definition, there would be no other group or religious cult with whom to compete. The very sense of urgency to accomplish these goals and alienation from the surrounding cultural influences suggests the extreme threat to Israelite group-identity that the final redactor of Deuteronomy must have perceived.

This same sense of urgency and alienation is portrayed in the second example, which describes the formation of Israel in the land. In Deut 12:1–5, the instructions to the people are introduced as "the statutes and ordinances" (*hăḥuqqîm wĕhammišpāṭîm*) which the people must follow so long as they live in the land.[35] Notable in this instance is that these intro-

---

essential elements of religious traditions (*Religion and Moral Reason: A New Method for Comparative Study* [New York: Oxford University Press, 1988], pp. 3–23).

[34] Several important aspects of this command deserve notice. First, the inverted word order places emphasis on the cultic object and stresses the necessity of its obliteration. Second, the specific verbal forms chosen indicate that the destruction is to be complete. Third, as I shall demonstrate in the following pages, the choices of cultic objects that are to be destroyed and the methods of destroying them form part of the deuteronomic and deuteronomistic stylization of foreign worship practices and partially determine the ways in which the narrative is structured. Finally, the exact nature of the cultic paraphernalia that are listed, more explicitly, the *maṣṣēbōt* and the *ʾăšērîm*, remains quite obscure. What is certain is that all evidence of the worship practices of the nations is to be destroyed along with those nations.

[35] The combinations of terms used to denote the stipulations of the covenant are quite varied, but nonetheless standardized in the deuteronomic literature. The terms *mišpāṭîm, ḥuqqîm, miṣwôt,* and *ʿēdût,* in various combinations and stylized phrases, are

duce the distinctively deuteronomic ideal of cultic centralization of worship and the standardization of all ritual activities in one and only one sanctuary. The deuteronomic ideal of the election of Israel as Yahweh's special possession is detailed in the stipulations of the covenant (Deut 12:1–26:15), all of which are focused by this requirement to centralize worship.[36] The section devoted to the purity of Israel's worship practices (12:1–14:21) begins by establishing the antithetical relationship between all religious practices belonging to the nations and those that will be acceptable to the Israelites. Via a simple "framing" technique, the single religious *axis mundi* is created for Israel in opposition to the diversity of centers found in the land. The contrast is drawn between "the places (*hammĕqōmôt*) where the nations served their gods" (v. 2), which were to be destroyed (*ʾabbēd tĕʾabbĕdûn*), and "the place (*hammāqôm*) that Yahweh would choose from among all your tribes to make his name dwell."[37]

The plurality of Canaanite worship centers stands in stark contrast to the singularity and unity of Yahweh worship. As Israel was to be defined in relation to this one deity who had chosen (*bāḥar*) this people,[38] so would the worship of this deity be restricted to "the place which he would choose" (*hammāqôm ʾašer-yibḥar*).[39] It would be here that Yahweh would "make his name dwell" (*lĕšakkēn šĕmô šām*),[40] i.e., establish his

---

among the most common. For the variations and occurrences, see Weinfeld, *Deuteronomy and the Deuteronomic School*, pp. 336–38.

[36] Mayes, *Deuteronomy*, p. 61. On the theme of worship at one and only one sanctuary, see Deut 12:5, 11, 14, 18, 21, 26; 14:23–25; 15:20; 16:2, 6, 11, 15; 17:8, 10; 18:6; 26:2. Though it is often argued that these are later additions to the corpus, which elsewhere does not require such a centralized cultic arrangement, it is clear that this ideal forms a central structural element in the deuteronomic and deuteronomistic vision of what constitutes legitimate Israelite national religion.

[37] Reading *lĕšakkĕnô* for *lĕšiknô* (cf. 12:11; 14:23; 16:2, 6, 11; 26:2).

[38] Deut 4:37; 7:6, 7; 10:15; 14:2.

[39] This phrase occurs in Deut 12:5, 11, 14, 18, 21, 26; 14:23, 24, 25: 15:20; 16:2, 6, 7, 11, 15, 16; 17:8, 10; 18:6; 26:2; 31:11. It is clear that in the present form of the text, the reference here is to the temple cultus in Jerusalem, an identification made by virtue of the occurrence of the same phraseology within the deuteronomistic history (1 Kgs 8:16, 44, 48; 11:13, 32, 36; 14:21; 2 Kgs 21:7; 23:27). Interestingly, the deuteronomistic redactor avoids making explicit the exact identity of this place, preserving it for Yahweh's choice, which later will be connected with David and his dynastic line (2 Sam 7:4–17).

[40] Deut 12:11; 14:23; 16:2, 6, 11; 26:2. Note also the parallel expression, "to put his name there" (*lāśûm [ʾet-] šĕmô šām*, 12:5, 21; 14:24; 1 Kgs 9:3; 11:36; 14:21; 2 Kgs 21:4, 7). This deuteronomic "name theology" is consistently employed to connote the view that it is the name of the deity and not the deity himself that dwells in the temple. On the development of the "name" theology, see T. N. D. Mettinger, *The Dethronement of*

continuing presence in the midst of his people. This "dwelling of his name" (12:5) contrasts both directly and purposefully with the command in v. 3 that Israel "destroy their name (šĕmām, i.e., the peoples') from this place." Once again, the distance between the "peoples" and Israel was to be complete and unbreachable. Any place that had been associated with their worship of their gods was to be destroyed, from the cultic installations on the high mountains and the hills to those that were beneath the luxuriant trees.[41] In terminology which closely parallels that of Deut 7:5, the specifics of this process of annihilation are given: to tear down (nittaṣ) their altars, to smash (šibbēr) their maṣṣēbôt, to burn (śārap) their ʾăšērîm in the fire, and to break or cut down (giddaᶜ) the images of their gods (v. 3).

The suggestion that instructions such as these depict a time when Israel was in actual control of the land and able to perform such deeds[42] misunderstands the directive on several levels. First, it assumes that Deuteronomy presents a reasonably accurate description of Canaanite worship practices. Second, it posits that these practices were rejected by Israel as an historical, religious, and political reality. Third, it supposes that an ideological and practical gap existed that clearly and discernibly separated the religious activities of the indigenous population of Canaan from those of the Israelites. Finally, it seems to assume that Israel actually attempted to institute such actions as described in some systematic manner. It is clearly impossible to demonstrate that these assumptions are not in fact accurate; it is not unreasonable to note, however, that they have not been documented by any non-biblical materials. In terms of the process of symbolization of the concept of the people "Israel," however, the move from descriptive exhortation to historical description seems unwarranted and highly questionable. Given the fact that modern Syro-Palestinian archaeology has not yet been able to distinguish Israelite remains from Canaanite materials, except with the biases provided by the biblical materials, it might be reasonable to proceed on the assump-

---

Sabaoth: Studies in the Shem and Kabod Theologies (ConBOT 18; Lund: C. W. K. Gleerup, 1982), pp. 38–79.

[41] See also 1 Kgs 14:23; 2 Kgs 16:4; 17:10. In each instance, this phraseology is employed to designate worship practices that are forbidden in Israel and for which the kings permitting them are condemned. While such references are often associated with some type of peculiarly Canaanite form of worship, it is also significant to note that the references to worship on hills and beneath fertile trees may simply reflect the use of the imagery commonly associated with the ancient Near Eastern concepts of the cosmic mountain as the abode of the deity.

[42] See, e.g., the comments of C. M. Carmichael, The Laws of Deuteronomy (Ithaca: Cornell University Press, 1974), p. 37, n. 5.

tion that Israelite and Judahite culture and religion fell within the parameters of Canaanite culture in general.[43] If this is the case, then the need to define Israel is one based not on the reality of existing distinctions, but rather on the insistence that there are such distinctions.[44] The stylized manner in which these several cultic aspects of Canaanite worship are presented clearly demarcates between Canaanite and Israelite: the cultic apparatus and practices were to be destroyed; they were not to be associated in any way with the worship of Yahweh (v. 4).

The exhortation not to act in such a manner toward Yahweh is repeated in nearly identical form in Deut 12:31a [E 32a].[45] Here the categorical distinctions between Israel and Canaan are established on the basis of the perspective of the deity:

> You shall not do thus for Yahweh your god, because they do for their gods every abomination of Yahweh (kol-tôʿăbat yhwh), which he hates; they also burn their sons and daughters in fire to their gods.[46]

---

[43] On the numerous problems of the degree of continuity between Canaanite and "Israelite" cultural distinctiveness, see the summary statements of M. S. Smith, *The Early History of God: Yahweh and the Other Deities in Ancient Israel* (San Francisco: Harper & Row, 1990), pp. 1–40.

[44] Groups are often able to appreciate their existence more fully if they can construe each other as categorical opposites. When the cultural patterns of the groups involved are similar, this attempt may lead to the invention of such differences. For the ways in which these factors have worked to produce the widespread concept of cannibalism, see the arguments of W. Arens, *The Man-Eating Myth: Anthropology & Anthropophagy* (Oxford: Oxford University Press, 1979).

[45] The two differ only in the pronominal suffix used. Verse 4 uses the 2 masc. pl., and v. 31 places the address in the 2 masc. sing. While the purpose for such variations continues to elude scholars, it is quite clearly part of the style characteristic of the deuteronomic addresses.

[46] The meaning and significance of the phrase "to burn" or "to pass a child in/through the fire" (Deut 12:31; 18:10; 2 Kgs 16:3; 17:17, 31; 21:6; Jer 7:31; 19:5; 32:35), while still debated, is generally accepted as a reference to child sacrifice, especially reserved for the cult of Molech (cf. 2 Kgs 23:10; Jer 32:35). It is commonly assumed that this practice is explicitly forbidden in Lev 18:21 and 20:2–5, but the exact practices referred to in these passages remain obscure. It is notable that the practice of child sacrifice (cf. 2 Kgs 3:27) is viewed as one that could bring powerful results. Significantly, however, in the passages in the biblical materials, it is consistently presented as an act that constituted an "abomination" to Yahweh and was thus forbidden for Israel. It is most tempting to interpret this practice as another instance of boundary formation by characterizing the other groups as propagators of unthinkable deeds. To this must be added, however, the evidence for child sacrifice from fourth century BCE Punic Carthage. Though the frequency and significance of the act

In absolute terms, Yahweh hates the religious practices of the nations that are to be dispossessed because of their wickedness (Deut 9:4–5). Indeed, their actions constitute "an abomination" (*tôʿēbâ*) to Israel's deity. The application of this classification in such a widespread manner, i.e., to all such alleged worship practices (12:31; cf. 7:25, 26; 13:15; 20:18), indicates the approach of the deuteronomic writer to all activities considered outside the boundaries of appropriate Israelite behavior: they constitute an "abomination to Yahweh"[47] and are to be avoided in every sense. For Deuteronomy, quite clearly, Israel's constitution as a holy people required strictly defined parameters to separate and differentiate the people of Yahweh from those allotted to the other deities.[48]

The distinctiveness of the people Israel is extended to the types and categories of food that might be consumed. The laws contained in 14:3–21 designate forbidden foods as *tôʿēbâ* and prohibit their consumption by Israel. The distinctively Israelite character of the legislation is revealed in the concluding prohibition:

> You shall not eat any corpse (*nēbēlâ*); you shall give it to the resident alien who is in your gates and he may eat it or you may sell it to a foreigner, but you are a holy people (*ʿam qādôš*) to Yahweh your god (14:21a).

The apodictic form of the stipulation is of interest, for it is the type of law that is dominant in Deuteronomy. Though the origins of this form remain debated, it is clear that its application, at least as incorporated within the context of the biblical legal corpuses, is to regulate human

---

remain unclear, the burial tophet at Carthage gives ample substantiation for this practice at that location during a specific period in the late Iron Age. Whether this practice was ever standard or widespread remains unclear. The lack of scholarly agreement over this issue is vividly illustrated by the opposing positions on child sacrifice in the ancient Near East taken by M. Smith ("A Note on Burning Babies," *JAOS* 95 [1975] 477–79) and by M. Weinfeld, "The Worship of Molech and of the Queen of Heaven and its Background," *UF* 4 (1972) 133–54.

[47] *tôʿăbat yhwh*: Deut 12:31; 17:1, 25; 18:12; 22:5; 23:19; 25:16; 27:15. The activities which constitute "abominations" are extremely diverse. The phrase occurs in connection with the activities of the other nations in worshipping their gods, the worship of idols, the offering of an imperfect sacrifice, various forms of divination, wearing the clothing of the opposite sex, using the wages of a prostitute to fulfill a vow, or using false measures.

[48] Common to the ancient Near East was the idea that the different nations or city-states were under the tutelage of various deities and that such an allotment had been decided by the high god(s) or the divine council. For the biblical reflections of this idea, see Deut 29:25; 32:8–9 (esp. LXX and 4QDt); cf. also Sir 17:17; Jub 15:31–32.

behavior and to order social groups.[49] Since in Deuteronomy and in the deuteronomistic history the possession of the land is connected to obedience to these laws, the fulfillment of the obligations of the covenant becomes a social prerogative for the very creation and establishment of the national ethnic group identity. With respect to the food code, the separation between Israel and other peoples could not be clearer: what is *tôʿēbâ* for Israel is acceptable for others. The designation as a "holy people," made such by virtue of the ideology of divine election, necessitates the development of distinct boundary formations.[50]

The separation of Israel from the nations is further refined in Deut 18:9–14, where the forms of divine/human intermediation that will distinguish Israel from its neighbors are carefully delineated. Again, the connection of the covenantal obligations with the entry to the land is explicit, for upon entering the land, Israel is commanded: "You will not learn to act according to the abominations of those nations."[51] The cataloguing begins with the prohibition against passing one's child through fire (v. 10; cf. 12:31b). It is followed by a list of various types of divination, e.g., sorcery, augury, necromancy, etc., all of which are assumed to have been standard practices in the ancient Near East.[52] Despite the fact that the exact meanings of the terms employed are not certain, it is clear that what is presented here is intended as a generally comprehensive list of all those forms of determining the will of the divine that are commonly practiced among Israel's neighbors. Since this passage is embedded in a section that deals with matters of public office, it is further clear that it is meant to address a type of public intermediator. In contrast to

[49] On the apodictic form and its development, see the discussion of Mayes, *Deuteronomy*, pp. 74–77. To the observations noted there might be added the Hittite literary parallels adduced by M. Weinfeld, "The Origins of Apodictic Law: An Overlooked Source," *VT* 23 (1973) 63–75.

[50] Once again, the practice referred to here may indeed fall into the category of cultural accusation, like the charges of cannibalism, bestiality, sodomy, or human sacrifice, to name a few of the well-known boundary markers employed by groups to define the uncultured and uncivilized nature of the others with whom they often find so much in common. Indeed, one must see some ironic sense of self-importance in the act of giving an improperly prepared carcass to your neighbor, so long as he or she happened to be an alien, or in selling it to a foreigner. Though the status of the "resident alien" (*gēr*) in ancient Israel continues to be debated, the *gēr* seems to have been a foreigner who, by living in Israelite territory, accepted certain tribal and national obligations, but was still recognizable as non-Israelite by the "native."

[51] *lōʾ-tilmad laʿăśôt kĕtôʿăbōt haggôyīm hāhēm*, v. 9b.

[52] G. Tucker, "Deuteronomy 18:15–22," *Int* 41 (1987) 293; R. Wilson, *Prophecy and Society in Ancient Israel* (Philadelphia: Fortress, 1980), p. 150.

such various practices, Deuteronomy proclaims that only one medium of intermediation would be acceptable in Israel: a prophet (*nābîʾ*) like Moses. The implications of the selection of this particular mode of intermediation become more apparent with the realization that the authorial voice that dominates the narrative of Deuteronomy in its final form, i. e., the voice of the deuteronomistic writer, claims itself to be none other than the prophetic successor to Moses (18:15–22).[53]

By appeal to this portion of the stipulations to the covenant, the final redactor of Deuteronomy eliminates the possible competing claims of other visionaries and politically and religiously empowers himself as the sole and authoritative spokesperson, raised up by Yahweh, to proclaim the true word and will of the deity concerning the nature and identity of his people Israel. The performance of any of the acts prohibited in vv. 10–11 would be considered "an abomination of Yahweh" (*tôʿăbat yhwh*) and, it must be emphasized, it was precisely "because of these abominations" (*biglal hattôʿēbōt hāʾēlleh*) that the people of the land would be driven out (v. 12). Contrasted with such activities is the nation Israel, a group that must be "blameless" (*tāmîm*)[54] with Yahweh, its god (v. 13). In a concluding manner, the list of prohibited practices is repeated and Israel is reminded that Yahweh has not given such matters to his nation to do. Whether the other nations actually performed such rites, and the wealth of terms concerning divination and augury in the ancient Near East would suggest that some such list of practices was common, Israel must avoid them. Yahweh would communicate his will to his people only via the institutionally accepted medium, the *nābîʾ*.[55]

Via this prophetic voice, the structural parameters for the identity of Israel are established within the context of a people described and dis-

---

53 This position has been most clearly elaborated by R. Polzin, *Moses and the Deuteronomist* (New York: Seabury, 1980), pp. 25–72.

54 This term, which designates one without moral blemish, occurs only here in Deuteronomy. While Mayes (*Deuteronomy*, p. 282) suggests that the verse may be a late, secondary addition, it is nonetheless appropriate to the efforts of the deuteronomic writer in this context.

55 The figure of the prophet is prominent in reconstructions of the religion of Israel and Judah. Whether such figures actually played an important role in the development of the national religion of Israel or whether their prominent position is the result of the process of canon formation and selection remains a subject of debate. It should be noted, however, that the claim of the uniqueness of the figure of the *nābîʾ*, as generally portrayed, is open to severe criticism. On the attempt to place the Israelite prophetic figures within a broader context, see T. W. Overholt, *Prophecy in Cross-Cultural Perspective* (SBLSBS 17; Atlanta: Scholars Press, 1986).

cerned by virtue of their profession of adherence to a certain set of covenantally based values and descriptors that are to be realized in the religious and cultural practices prescribed by the stipulations of the divine/human treaty. Even the deuteronomic ideal of leadership for the nation, expressed in the "law of the king" (Deut 17:14–20), is defined and restricted by this covenantal ideal. The king would be of Yahweh's own choice (*bāḥar*). The position could be held by native Israelites alone (17:15). Restrictions *vis-à-vis* the accumulation of wealth and wives, two common measures of status in the ancient world, are articulated (vv. 16–17). The greatest restriction placed upon the king, however, is that defined by the "copy of this *tôrâ*" (*mišnēh hattôrâ hazzōʾt*), which he is to make and in accord with which he is to live and rule (vv. 18–20). Though a king might make Israel "like all the nations" (*kĕkol-haggôyīm*; v. 14), the nature of the kingship would distinguish Israel, in ideal terms, from those other groups.[56] In the third and final speech of Moses to Israel in Deuteronomy (29:1–30:20), the existence of this set of stipulations in written and final form is presumed,[57] and the group(s) to which it is to be extended is(are) further defined. Following immediately upon the account of the ceremony sealing the covenant (26:16–27:26) and the pronouncement of the blessings and curses guaranteed by it (28:1–69) is this series of speeches designed as charges to Israel to accept the obligations imposed by its selection by Yahweh as his personal possession.

In Deut 29:9–14 [E 10–15], the final exhortation preparing for the ritual transformation of this group, liminally poised on the plains of Moab, is presented.[58] "Every man of Israel" (*kōl ʾîš yiśrāʾēl*) is stationed before Yahweh, from the major officials to the lowliest of the populace.[59] This notice that it is the totality of the people Israel who are gathered there is most important to the creation of the communal identity, for the obligations to keep the covenant are not placed simply on some leading

---

[56] As McBride has pointed out, the king was to serve as a model of obedience to the covenant before the people ("Polity of the Covenant People," 241).

[57] The phrases "this book of law" (*sēper hattôrâ hazzeh*) and "in this book" (*bassēper hazzeh*) occur only in the latter portions of Deuteronomy, i.e., in chaps. 28–30. The phraseology is continued, most explicitly, in the accounts of the discovery of "the book of the covenant" by Josiah and its relation to the reforms of the temple practices.

[58] On the transformative power of ritual activities in narrative form, see V. Turner, "Social Dramas and Stories about Them," in *On Narrative* (ed. W. J. T. Mitchell; Chicago: University of Chicago Press, 1981), pp. 137–64.

[59] Notable is the fact that in Josh 23:2 and 24:1, the farewell speech of Joshua and the covenant ceremony at Shechem, a similar listing of officials representing the totality of Israel is included.

social element of the group but upon every person, including the resident alien. The temporal aspect of this speech is likewise important to note, for the speech takes place "today" (*hayyôm*), a point made by the fivefold repetition of the time in this section. This narrative device establishes the present reality of the demands of the covenant upon those who would constitute this entity, Israel.[60] Verses 13–14 further contribute to this sense of narrative presence in the exhortation to the people, for they note that the covenant being made is not just with those standing there, but also with "those who are not present today" (*ʾet-ʾăšer ʾênennû pōh ʿimmānû hayyôm*). The Israel created and bound to the god Yahweh would not be restricted to those present in the plains of Moab; rather it would be constituted by all those who entered into the covenant of Yahweh which he was establishing "today" (v. 11), the time in which, by way of the covenantal ceremony, Israel becomes Yahweh's people, he, their god (v. 12).[61] The ritual drama created by the narrative transforms both past and present into a liminal now—the time of the creation and recreation of the people Israel. The reminder that "we dwelled in Egypt" (*yāšabnû bĕʾereṣ miṣrāyim*)[62] stands in contrast to the assertion of the narrative in 2:14–16 that the generation that had come out of Egypt had died and confirms the efforts of the author to incorporate, by narrative reenactment and ideational symbolism, all who would be so bound into a commonly shared set of "historical" reminders. In the continuation of the section, the new community is reminded of the detestable practices (*šiqqûṣîm*) of the nations through which they had passed, especially "their idols" (*gillûlêhem*) of wood and stone, of silver and gold (vv. 15–16), so that no one "today" would turn away from Yahweh and serve "the gods of those nations" (*ʾĕlōhê haggôyīm hāhēm*). The importance and immediate relevance of such a warning are apparent in the following three verses. Despite problems of interpretation associated with v. 18, it is clear that failure to remain completely loyal to the obligations of the covenant

---

[60] Polzin has pointed out the clearly exilic setting of the author of the present portion of the exposition and the future orientation of this entire section. According to this analysis, emphasis is placed upon what Israel must do to regain the land, and the answer is found in obedience to the covenant and retributive justice (*Moses and the Deuteronomist*, pp. 69–71).

[61] See also 4:20; 7:6; 14:2; 26:18; 27:9; 28:9.

[62] On the significance of the theme of the return to Egypt, especially as it represents the concerns of the exilic redactor of Deuteronomy, see R. E. Friedman, "From Egypt to Egypt: Dtr¹ and Dtr²," in *Traditions in Transformation: Turning Points in Biblical Faith* (ed. B. Halpern and J. D. Levenson; Winona Lake, IN: Eisenbrauns, 1981), pp. 167–92.

would result in swift retribution from Yahweh. Indeed, "the curse (hā'ālâ) which is written in this book" would be applied immediately to anyone who would breach the commands of the covenant and thus identify himself or herself with matters non-Israelite.[63] By adherence to the commands of the covenant and by the periodic renewal and recon-firmation of this pact,[64] Israel is continually recreated and redefined in opposition to the religious practices of the surrounding peoples.[65]

III. The Ritual Reactualization of the Community

For the deuteronomistic historian, then, this covenantally based concept of renewal constituted a type of narrative charter by which restored blessing and the reestablishment of order might be effected at those times of crisis perceived as the result of the violation of the deuteronomic code. This ideological charter provides for the way in which the failures of the people, and hence the threat of destruction, might be redirected and reconstituted so as to avoid dissolution and chaos. The account of the reign and reform of King Josiah (2 Kgs 22:1–23:30), a thematic high point in the deuteronomistic history, and the manner in which this text illustrates the ideologic character of the descriptions of Israelite religion and identity confirm the way in which the "history-like" narrative functions to recreate this national ethnic group. For the writer, the history of the kingdoms of Israel and Judah since the division of the monarchy after the death of Solomon was char-acterized by continued cultic apostasy. The establishment of a national cultus in Israel by Jeroboam became, for the deuteronomistic historian,

---

[63] That the name (šēm) of the person would be wiped out of existence (v. 19b) connects the fate of those who fail to fulfill the covenant demands with that of the nations to be driven out of the land (cf. 12:3b).

[64] While the role of the "covenant renewal festival" in ancient Israel continues to be discussed and debated, Deut 31:9–13 clearly requires that this law written by Moses be read every seven years at the Feast of Booths in such a way as to insure continually the recreation or reconfirmation of the covenantal community. Most recently, W. Holladay has used this seven-year cycle to attempt to explain the career and messages of the prophet Jeremiah (Jeremiah, Vol. 1 [1–25] [Hermeneia; Philadelphia: Fortress, 1986]).

[65] This final address of Moses concludes with two short speeches, the first address-ing the destruction of the nation as a whole (29:21–28) that would result if the covenant were not upheld and the second (30:1–14) providing for the eventual return and restoration of the nation, again in relation to the fulfillment of the covenantal stipulations.

"the sin of Jeroboam" for which the nation of Israel was destroyed (2 Kgs 17:22; cf. 1 Kgs 12:25–33). The national religion of Judah, with only two reported exceptions, came no closer to the deuteronomic ideal of the worship of Yahweh alone at one and only one cultic locale. During the final years of Solomon's reign, the worship of other gods was "introduced" into the Judahite royal court (1 Kgs 11:1–10).[66] Despite cultic reforms attributed to selected Judahite kings,[67] it is only Josiah who acts in such a way as to reunify, and hence recreate, the ideal of Israel. Both religiously and nationally, his actions enforce the group identity formulated in the deuteronomic corpus.[68]

The relationship of Josiah's reforms to the stipulations of Deuteronomy is made explicit in the account of the discovery of the "book of the law" (*sēper hattôrâ*).[69] Utilizing this book as his guide, Josiah reformed the national religious cult in such a way as to postpone the punishment for the sins of Judah since Solomon and to rectify the deeds of Jeroboam that had led to such disaster for the people of Israel.[70] Additionally, this

---

[66] It is extremely difficult to speculate on the historical accuracy of any of the accounts of worship practices in the Judahite or Israelite cultus. Further, since the deuteronomistic history focuses on the activities of the royal households, it is even more difficult to extrapolate to what might have been the popular worship practices of the people. Despite the conclusions of J. H. Tigay, drawn from a study of the onomastic and inscriptional evidence pertaining to Israel and Judah, that the society was devotedly Yahwistic (*You Shall Have No Other Gods: Israelite Religion in the Light of Hebrew Inscriptions* [HSS 31; Atlanta: Scholars Press, 1986], pp. 37–41), the matter of the worship and tolerance of other deities by the populace and by the official cultus must remain open.

[67] Asa (1 Kgs 15:11–15); Jehoshaphat (1 Kgs 22:43–44); Jehoash (2 Kgs 12:2–4); Amaziah (2 Kgs 14:3–4); Azariah (2 Kgs 15:3–4); Jotham (2 Kgs 15:34–35); Hezekiah (2 Kgs 18:3–6). Notably, Hezekiah, unlike the other kings listed here, is praised for having completely eradicated the worship at the high places (*bāmôt*), a cultic practice contrary to the deuteronomic ideal of centralized worship and a conditioning factor to the otherwise positive assessment of the other kings.

[68] For a more detailed treatment of these materials, see below, chap. 8.

[69] 2 Kgs 22:8. This phrase is a common term in deuteronomistic writings (cf. Deut 17:18; 28:58, 61; 29:20, 26; 30:10; 31:24, 26; Josh 1:8; 8:31, 34; 23:6; 24:6) as well as those composed during the post-exilic period.

[70] N. Lohfink, "The Cult Reform of Josiah of Judah: 2 Kings 22–23 as a Source for the History of Israelite Religion," in *Ancient Israelite Religion: Essays in Honor of Frank Moore Cross* (ed. by P. D. Miller, Jr., P. D. Hanson, and S. D. McBride; Philadelphia: Fortress, 1987), p. 461. The parallel account of the reforms of Josiah contained in 2 Chronicles 34–35 provides a differing chronology for the reform, starting it during the eighth year of Josiah. The interpretation and efforts of the Chronicler stand outside the emphasis of this study.

emergence of Deuteronomy into the public realm and the consequent covenantal ceremony that ensued mark the beginning of the creation of the Pentateuch[71] and the process of canon formation, a development that cannot be divorced from the ideal of boundary formation in religious and cultural movements. As such, it represents the beginning of a new period for Judahite religion and society for the deuteronomistic writer.

Such a new beginning is not without some degree of tension, created in and of itself by the structure and narrative of the history. The reign of Manasseh, father of Josiah, made necessary the reforms of the young ruler. It was Manasseh who returned the cultus to a "non-deuteronomic" state like that achieved under Rehoboam (cf. 1 Kgs 14:23–24), thus bringing about the political distresses endured by the nation.[72] For the deuteronomistic writer, the deeds of Manasseh were "like the abominations of the nations (*kĕtôʿăbōt haggôyīm*) which Yahweh had driven out from before the Israelites" (2 Kgs 21:2; cf. 1 Kgs 14: 24). The worship of gods other than Yahweh, the practice of divination and sorcery (21:2–9), all practices forbidden by deuteronomic law,[73] resulted in the explicit condemnation of Judah and the prophetic proclamation of its destruction (21:10–15). By deuteronomic standards, by reverting to the religious practices of the surrounding nations, Judah had already ceased to exist. The nation so clearly separated from the others had, for reasons unspecified, chosen to become what the charter on which it was founded had forbidden. Now Judah was one of the nations.

If the demands for the complete and undifferentiated justice required by the strict covenantal presentation of Deuteronomy were followed, then the story told by the deuteronomistic historian would be at its end with the divine proclamation of the institution of the covenan-

---

[71] M. Cogan and H. Tadmor, *II Kings* (AB 11; Garden City, NY: Doubleday, 1988), p. 296.

[72] It is common to attempt to relate the cultic reforms of the rulers to the international political situation. Since it is generally maintained that political alliances with other nations involved the formal recognition of the gods of the suzerain, then in those instances where Israel or Judah was allied with a major power, external reasons for the introduction of foreign deities and worship practices into the cult may be found. The study of Assyrian treaty requirements on vassal states by J. McKay, however, calls the accuracy of this into question (*Religion in Judah under the Assyrians* [SBT 26; Naperville, IL: Alec R. Allenson, 1973]). It is clear that for the deuteronomistic historian, the failure to follow the cultic requirements of Deuteronomy results in oppression at the hands of foreign powers.

[73] Notable in this context is the mention of the condition of obedience to the *tôrâ* commanded by Moses for the maintenance of the land (2 Kgs 21:8b).

tal curses. Yet the narrative continues and the punishments were not immediately performed,[74] for the actions of King Josiah revived the national identity and postponed those curses.[75] This is confirmed by the prophetic pronouncement of Huldah, who proclaimed the validity of the "book of the law" and the inevitability of the actualization of the curses of the covenant (22:15–20), thus effectively sealing the fate of Judah and transforming the reign of Josiah from victory to tragedy. Nonetheless, the events ascribed to the actions of Josiah constituted in narrative form precisely those ritual enactments that were prescribed by Deuteronomy for the constitution of the people Israel and Judah. While they had been dissolved, conceptually, by the actions of Manasseh, they were recreated by Josiah.

Prior to the account of the reform, Josiah assembled "every man of Judah and all the inhabitants of Jerusalem,"[76] i. e., "all the people" (kol-hā'ām), and performed a ceremony of covenant renewal in which the whole of the people participated and accepted the obligations of the words written in the law book. The generational transformations projected in Deut 29:9–24 are actualized in this ritual built around this "law commanded by Moses." All of the people of Judah and Jerusalem are ritually identical to those who accepted the covenant on the plains of Moab and established the people Israel. The "today" of that covenant was actualized by the "today" of the covenant renewal, an "event" that originated in illo tempore, i. e., in that mythical time of the creation of the people itself. The people of Judah were ritually recreated as members of that ideal "Israel" that had not yet failed to fulfill the covenant and to take possession of the land. Rather, the possibilities of success lay before them

---

74 This avoidance of the immediate application of the demands of absolute justice might be explained by the basic deep structure that is posited for many religious traditions. See above, n. 33.

75 Despite the contentions of many modern critics that the original edition of the history was written as a propaganda document to justify the reform efforts of Josiah and the centralization of the cultus during his reign, and thus concluded with the note praising his greatness (23:25), the fact remains that the final edition of the work does not end with Josiah, nor does it interpret his actions as doing any more than postponing the destruction of the nation (23:26–27). For an analysis of the structure of the final form of the account of the reign of Josiah, see N. Lohfink, "The Cult Reform of Josiah of Judah," p. 461. Lohfink notes that the "reform report" (23:4–20), recounting the systematic destruction of all foreign cult objects, may have been based on older accounts, but has been "linguistically accommodated" to the structure of the passage by the deuteronomistic writer and cannot be used to reconstruct the sequence of events in any historical sense (pp. 465–67).

76 kol-'îš yĕhûdâ wĕkol-yōšĕbê yĕrûšālaîm, 23:2.

in their newly reconstituted identities. This reaffirmation of the obligations of the covenantal demands, then, provides the ideological
directions for the stylized reforms that follow.[77] The people could be
considered as established in any final sense only when the deuteronomic
commands on the centralization of the cultus and the eradication of all
non-Yahwistic worship practices as defined by Deuteronomy had been
carried out.

It occasions little surprise, then, to see in the report of the reforms
that follows the reinstitution of the covenant a stylized narrative realization and implementation of the major demands of the deuteronomic
corpus (2 Kgs 23:4–24). The completeness with which the reform efforts
are carried out is revealed by the fact that this section names some
thirteen different objects or groups of objects that are part of the reform
and, as such, might be viewed as a combination of various reform
notices, all of which are related to the demands of Deuteronomy and the
noted cultic failures of the preceding kings.[78] The reform report itself
may be divided into two parts: 23:4–14 concerns the reforms in
Judah/Jerusalem, and 23:15–20 addresses the events related to
Bethel/Samaria. In the initial portion of the account (vv. 4–7), Josiah
ordered the removal of all the cultic objects that had been made for
Baal (ba'al), Asherah (ʾăšērâ), and "all the host of heaven" (kōl ṣĕbāʾ haššā-
māyim), all of which represent Syro-Phoenician deities[79] (i. e., the gods of
the nations which were forbidden for Israel), and had them destroyed in
the fields outside of Jerusalem. With the eradication of the non-Yahwistic
cultic paraphernalia, he stopped the worship practices of the "idolatrous

---

[77] H.-D. Hoffmann, in a careful literary analysis of the narratives concerning the
reforms attributed by the deuteronomistic historian to the kings of Israel and Judah,
concludes that the account of the actions of Josiah fulfills an idealized program of cult
reform that is the creation of the deuteronomistic author and which, at best, represents little more than a possible memory that some type of cultic reforms were
instituted during the time of Josiah (*Reform und Reformen: Untersuchungen zu einem
Grundthema der deuteronomistischen Geschichtsschreibung* [ATANT 66; Zürich:
Theologischer Verlag, 1980], pp. 250–51).

[78] Hoffmann, *Reform und Reformen*, pp. 223–27. It is generally accepted that the
account of the reform in 2 Kgs 23:4–20 had an independent origin (cf. G. H. Jones, *1
and 2 Kings, Vol. 2* [NCB; Grand Rapids, MI: Eerdmans, 1984], p. 616). If this assertion
is correct, it adds little to the discussion beyond confirming that the author of the
history utilized various materials to construct his narrative.

[79] McKay, *Religion in Judah under the Assyrians*, p. 30. Note that Manasseh is
credited with having constructed altars for these deities (2 Kgs 21:3, 5).

priests" (kĕmārîm)[80] who had been established by the Judahite kings, and who "offered sacrifices to Baal and to the sun, the moon, the planets, and to all the host of heaven"[81] at the shrines (bāmôt) in the cities of Judah and in the vicinity of Jerusalem. In short, Josiah consolidated all worship practices at the only legitimate shrine in Jerusalem—the temple.[82] He then removed the ʾăšērâ ˙that had been placed in the temple by Manasseh (cf. 2 Kgs 21:7) and destroyed it in a manner reminiscent of Moses' destruction of the "golden calf" (Deut 9:21; cf. Exod 32:20). Additionally, he tore down the houses of the "sacred males" (qĕdēšîm) that were located in the temple precinct.[83]

In the second section dealing with the reforms in Judah and Jerusalem (vv. 8–14), the efforts of Josiah are extended beyond Jerusalem itself. As Deuteronomy had required that every place where the nations had worshipped their gods be destroyed (12:2), so Josiah proceeded in systematic fashion. Having dismantled the non-Yahwistic bāmôt, Josiah defiled (ṭimmēʾ) the bāmôt located in the cities of Judah where the priests[84] had offered sacrifices. These "country priests" were brought by Josiah into Jerusalem, but were not allowed to participate in the major worship practices at the temple (vv. 8–9).[85] Next, the cultic installation (tōpet) in

---

[80] This designation always carries a derogatory tone in the Hebrew Bible (cf. Hos 10:5; Zeph 1:4). Notably, kūmrāʾ is the common Aramaic term for "priest." In the present context, these cultic functionaries are clearly to be associated with the forbidden worship practices which are enumerated.

[81] hamqaṭṭĕrîm labbaʿal laššemeš wĕlayyārēaḥ wĕlammazzālôt ûlĕkōl ṣĕbāʾ haššāmayim, v. 5b. See also Deut 4:19; 17:3; Jer 8:2; etc.

[82] That the temple in Jerusalem, and Jerusalem itself, is the place chosen by Yahweh is a dominant theme in the deuteronomistic account of the Solomonic dedication of the temple (cf. 1 Kgs 8:16, 43 44, 48).

[83] On the common rendering of this term as "male prostitute," see the investigations of Oden and Gruber cited above in n. 17. In addition, the text notes that in these houses "women wove bāttîm for Baal." The translation of "garments/tunics" for the Hebrew bāttîm ("houses"), based on the Arabic battun (cf. BHS), clarifies the text, but does nothing to explain the otherwise unknown practice.

[84] Here, kōhănîm is used, possibly designating these priests as Yahwistic cultic functionaries in contrast to the kĕmārîm noted earlier. Despite numerous conjectures, the reference in v. 8b to the dismantling of the "shrines of the gates" remains quite opaque.

[85] Attention is generally drawn to the fact that this action by Josiah seems to stand in contrast to the regulations regarding the Levitical priesthood outlined in Deut 18:6–8, which seems to imply that the right to sacrifice at the central sanctuary belongs to the Levites. As R. E. Friedman has noted, Lev 21:22–23 prohibits physically blemished priests from full participation in the cultus. In like manner, the priests from the outlying shrines might have been considered to have been ritually

the valley of Hinnom, where children were "passed through the fire,"[86] was likewise defiled. Returning to the vicinity of the temple, he did away with the horses and chariots that had been dedicated to the worship of the sun, a practice not otherwise mentioned in the Hebrew text (v. 11). The altars which had been installed by Ahaz and Manasseh (cf. 20:11; 21:5) were ritually destroyed and their dust scattered in the wady Qidron (cf. 23:6). The next cultic installations to be defiled by Josiah were the *bāmôt* which Solomon had erected for his foreign wives to worship their national deities (v. 13).[87] Finally, Josiah broke (*šibbēr*) down the *maṣṣēbôt* and cut down (*kārat*) the *ʾăšērîm* in accord with deuteronomic legislation (cf. Deut 7:5; 12:3; 16:21–22) and desacralized their precincts by filling the area with human bones (v. 14).[88]

Several points concerning the reforms of Josiah in Jerusalem and Judah should be immediately apparent. The cultic activities and objects purged during his reform were precisely those outlawed by Deuteronomy. The efforts of Josiah involve the removal of all implements of worship of gods other than Yahweh and the ritual defilement of all places associated with such practices, as well as the cleansing of the Jerusalem temple of any non-Yahwistic items. That the deuteronomic ideal of cultic purity and centralization and the deuteronomic characterizations of foreign worship practices served as a blueprint for the narrative of Josiah's reform can hardly be questioned. Simultaneously, the specific notices of some of the acts of Josiah, especially the implication that the *bāmôt* that had been erected by Solomon were still active, bring into question the reforms attributed earlier to Hezekiah (2 Kgs 18:4). With Josiah, Judahite worship and religious national and ethnic identity had been reestablished in accord with the deuteronomic blueprint. The dissolution of that identity attributed to the rule of Manasseh had now been offset, if only for a short time, by the Josianic covenantal ritual enactment of the ideals of Deuteronomy.

---

blemished and hence under similar restrictions on their activities (*The Exile and Biblical Narrative* [HSM 22; Chico, CA: Scholars Press, 1981], pp. 65–66). It should be noted, however, that the priests referred to in the passage in Kings are not called Levites, and the actions of Josiah in denying them certain access to the cult may not have been related to Deut 18:6–8.

[86] On this practice, see above, n. 46.

[87] Compare this verse with the notice of Solomon's deeds in 1 Kgs 11:5–7.

[88] On the ritual impurity that could be imparted by contact with the dead, see Num 19:16–19.

Yet the national identity constructed by the boundaries erected in Deuteronomy included the defunct nation of Israel, the area to which Josiah's reforms were also directed. At the cultic installation of Bethel, a border shrine which had been central to the innovations of Jeroboam (1 Kgs 12:25–33), Josiah demolished the *bāmâ* with its altar and burned the *ʾăšērâ*. He defiled the sacred precincts in a manner similar to that described in v. 14; he burned the bones of those buried in the surrounding graves on the altar (v. 16), thus desacralizing the installation for any ritual purpose (vv. 15–16).[89] In a manner consistent with the deuteronomistic ideals, Josiah extended these practices to the shrines in Samaria, the capital of the old Israelite nation, and defiled the illegitimate shrines by sacrificing the priests of such shrines on the altars and burning human bones on them (vv. 19–20). In symbolic fashion, then, the entirety of Israel and Judah had been reconstituted in cultic terms. No places of worship existed apart from the place that Yahweh had chosen—the temple in Jerusalem.

As the final act of his reform, and in accord with the cultic ideals of Deut 16:5–6, Josiah led the people in the celebration of the Passover, not referred to in the deuteronomistic history since the time of Israel's entry into the land (Josh 5:10–11), i.e., prior to its failure to fulfill its obligations in the land. The symbolic implications of the celebration of this festival reach far beyond a simple fulfillment of deuteronomic legislation. The Passover ritual, commemorating the delivery from Egyptian bondage, was a ritual recreation of the formation of the "original" covenant community, now paralleled by this renewed Judahite community, established in a land wherein all the religious practices forbidden by the charter of Deuteronomy had been eradicated. The final reform action noting the removal of all those intermediaries forbidden of Israel (v. 24; cf. Deut 18:9–12) returns the narrative, quite effectively, to the prophetic voice of the deuteronomistic writer.

Perceived in this manner, the reign of Josiah, as recounted by the author of the deuteronomistic history, serves a dual function. As history,

---

[89] Additionally, this act fulfilled the prophecy of the "man of God" that was delivered against Jeroboam and the altar at Bethel in I Kings 13. For a study of the importance of the clear example of deuteronomistic *vaticinium ex eventu*, see W. E. Lemke, "The Way of Obedience: I Kings 13 and the Structure of the Deuteronomistic History," in *Magnalia Dei: The Mighty Acts of God* (ed. by F. M. Cross, W. E. Lemke, and P. D. Miller, Jr.; Garden City, NY: Doubleday, 1976), pp. 301–26. On the significance of the passage for the structure of the deuteronomistic history, see the treatment in chap. 8.

the deeds of this king illustrate how the blessings of the covenant might be regained and the welfare of the people insured, within the context of the religiously structured ideal of retributive justice associated with the covenant and its implications. A people ethnically and religiously defined in terms of the stipulations of the deuteronomic corpus could be ritually recreated by the proper enactment of the covenant ceremonies prescribed therein. At the same time, since the continuation of the narrative demonstrates the ultimate failure of the kings who followed Josiah to maintain his reform, as well as the divine unwillingness to forgive the deeds of Manasseh (2 Kgs 23:26–27), the ideal of exact retribution, an essential part of the deuteronomic tradition, is maintained, thus insuring a stable and reliable universe within which the entity Israel or Judah might be understood.

In a second manner, however, the prophetic aspects of the deuteronomic movement must not be overlooked. The importance of the figure of the *nābîʾ* to the deuteronomic tradition and to the deuteronomistic history in particular constitutes another aspect of this group identification. When it is recognized that the entire history is constructed as reflection on those events that had led to the exile and had brought about the demise of the nation and threatened the ethnic identity of Judah by dispersing its members among those nations from which it was to be separate and distinct, the narrative accounts serve as moralizing object lessons to a people searching for the ways necessary to regain, retain, and remain an ethnic, religious community and to avoid complete assimilation and dissolution among the nations. As Deuteronomy had provided the manifesto which proclaimed the boundaries of this people who were to be holy to Yahweh, its sole god, so Josiah had systematically and ritually fulfilled those demands, illustrating how Israel, in its future, might restore the ideals of land and people that were, for the deuteronomistic writer, so much in jeopardy. In this way, the deuteronomistic author created a partial frame around the history of "Israel" in the land that was constructed of the ethnic group "Israel," defined as an ideal in Deuteronomy, and the reconstitution of that ideal near the very end of that history in the account of the actions of Josiah. The stories of the actualizations of that identity and its loss are contained within this frame. The "today" of Deuteronomy could be ritually recovered at any time, in accord with the proper performance of the deuteronomic ritual activities which distinguished "Israel" from the surrounding nations. At the same time, the threat of destruction for breaking the covenant stood to endanger the continuation of this same idealized community as an identifiable entity. The history adopted by "Israel" as its own national past traces this people through a variety of situations that reveal a continuing recreation and reformulation of these ideal boundaries by which those identifying themselves as part of this group might distinguish themselves from the competing social and ethnic world constructions in whose midst they dwelled.

4

Joshua: The Reinvention and Reconfirmation of Ethnic Identity

I. A Background to the History

If the interpretation of the book of Deuteronomy as a ritual manifesto of ethnic boundary formation for ancient Israelite identity is correct,
then the remainder of the deuteronomistic history might be understood,
at least in part, as the varied attempts of the deuteronomistic author to
formulate and to reformulate, to define and to refine those boundaries
which would best express the ideological ideal that was known, and was
to be known, as "Israel."[1] As such, this formulation of ethnic identity
must be understood as a complex process, one which was subject to

---

[1] If it is correct that the deuteronomistic materials are to be dated, at least in their
final form, to the period of the exile, then it is important to note that both of the
dynastic states of Israel and Judah had ceased to exist as independent political
entities. Thus, the deuteronomistic use of the term "Israel" is anachronistic, in a
sense, at least as it is applied as a description for an identifiable people occupying a
particular geographical area or as an independent dynastic state. On the variety of
usages of the name "Israel," see the discussions of G. Ahlström in *Who Were the
Israelites?* (Winona Lake, IN: Eisenbrauns, 1986). It is clear that the idea of an "all
Israelite" conquest of the land of Canaan has its origins in the application of that
designation within the deuteronomistic narratives of Joshua, at least as far as can be
demonstrated on the basis of the evidence presently available.

change and interpretation within the context of the literary and political realities of the narrative as it was produced.[2] Since ethnic identity is defined and maintained through shared myths of origins, histories and cultures, by a sense of communal solidarity and an association with a specific territory,[3] it is not surprising that the narratives of Joshua are concerned with the matter of the possession of the land through which Israel will identify itself. Additionally, neither ethnicity nor national identity is self-contained; each is a highly dissociative phenomenon that expresses its essence by denying its similarities with other ethnic and national groups. Because of this, it should occasion no surprise that the literary expressions of self-identity, especially those concerned with establishing and confirming the boundaries of a given group, often involve polemical elements.

Such is clearly the case with the book of Joshua, for there, the ideological realities of obedience to "every word" (*kol-haddābār*, Deut 13:1) commanded by Yahweh through his servants, Moses and Joshua, are subject to interpretation and refinement in light of developing "realities" that emerge in the process of the attempts to apply the boundary descriptors presented by Moses on the eve of the entry into the land. It is in Joshua that the temporal shift from the future projections of "when you enter the land," commonly associated with the divine commands reported in Deuteronomy,[4] to the narrated realities of the crossing of the Jordan and the conquest and settlement in the land occurs. As structured by the deuteronomic narratives, the entry into the land itself is framed by the ritual recreation of the deliverance from Egypt and the covenantal ceremonies at Sinai and Shechem. Simultaneously, the social enactments of the ritual foundations of the emerging ethnic group Israel occasion selected modifications in the original boundaries created by Deuteronomy. As the ensuing investigation will demonstrate, this was due in part to the ongoing conflicts concerning membership in the community, a debate which was largely responsible for the production of the deuteronomistic history.[5] Such dissension produced vying interpretations of the

---

[2] A number of the special problems that result from the literary formulation of such traditions have been noted by J. Van Seters in "Tradition and Social Change in Ancient Israel," *Perspectives in Religious Studies* 7 (1980) 96–113.

[3] A. D. Smith, *The Ethnic Origins of Nations* (Oxford: Blackwell, 1986), p. 32.

[4] Cf. Deut 4:1, 5, 14, 22, 26; 6:1, 18; 7:1; 8:1; 9:1, 5; 11:8, 10, 11, 29, 31; 12:29; 28:21, 63; 30:16; 31:13; 32:47; etc.

[5] As N. K. Gottwald has emphasized, attention must be given to the process of religious conversion as one of the possible ways of gaining membership in the com-

past traditions[6] and competing prophetic visions of the form and shape of the national state and religion that would best fulfill the ideals of those who gave expression to them.[7]

The necessary elements for the formation of an ethnic identity[8] were all present within the context in which the deuteronomistic author composed his account. Remaining in the land of Judah was the majority of the peasantry who were, in all probability, affected in political, cultural, and religious terms by the major traditions connected with the urban centers. In those major urban centers were located the competing levels of priests, prophets, and bureaucrats, each of which had a vested interest in the structure of the social order. Associated with the Jerusalem royal household and dynastic shrine was a small number of cultic personnel (priests, scribes, prophets) who claimed a monopoly on the community's religious belief-system and who controlled the major ways of disseminating the elements of that system. Binding the members of the community to each other, to their land, and to their god(s) was a

---

munity ("Religious Conversion and the Societal Origins of Ancient Israel," *Perspectives in Religious Studies* 15 [1988] 49–65), though this has been strongly challenged by J. Milgrom, who argues that this type of "conversion" could not have occurred before the second temple period ("Religious Conversion and the Revolt Model for the Formation of Israel," *JBL* 101 [1982] 169–76). Caution must be exercised, however, in the movement from traditions concerning the formative experiences of early Israel, especially as constituting a type of "revitalization movement," to a description of actual social and historical realities supposed to underlie such customs. On the nature of "revitalization movements," see A. F. C. Wallace, "Revitalization Movements," *American Anthropologist* 58 (1956) 264–81.

6 Though modern scholars tend to assume that the antiquity associated with many biblical traditions is a reliable indicator that the customs and beliefs contained therein are both ancient and accurate, notice must be taken of recent anthropological work regarding the "creation and invention" of national and ethnic traditions that indicate some of the problems involved in the tacit assumptions employed by many engaged in the study of such materials. See, e.g., the remarks of E. Hobsbawm, "Introduction: Inventing Traditions," in *The Invention of Tradition* (ed. by E. Hobsbawm and T. Ranger; Cambridge: Cambridge University Press, 1983), pp. 1–14.

7 Though it is commonly asserted that the idea of nationality and nation-ness had its beginnings toward the end of the eighteenth century CE (cf. B. Anderson, *Imagined Communities: Reflections on the Origin and Spread of Nationalism* [London: Verso, 1983], pp. 12–14), I would maintain that during the period of the Israelite and Judahite monarchies in the Late Iron Age, the designations "nation" and "national" are appropriate for those petty dynastic monarchic states in Palestine defined by both geographic and dialectical linguistic distinctions.

8 The elements necessary for the formation of an "ideal-typical" ethnic group are outlined by Smith (*The Ethnic Origins of Nations*, p. 42).

symbolic universe that was constructed of myths, values, histories, etc., that defined the group and located it within the context of the larger world order. Finally, the various festivals and rituals that came to identify the religious life of the nation provided the means through which these defining symbolic expressions of Israelite identity could be transmitted. The deuteronomistic writer and the narrative construction of the "ideal" Israel that he produced may be understood as one of the essential elements in the production of an ethnic identity for this recreated Israel.

At the same time, however, the narratives of Joshua introduce a new level of complexity into the analysis of the materials due to the implicit claims of historicity embedded within the narrative form[9] chosen by the deuteronomistic writer.[10] However one chooses to read or analyze these materials, it is beyond dispute that the narratives themselves present an account of the way in which the united tribes of Israel under the leadership of Joshua, successor to Moses, fulfilled the commands of Deuteronomy and successfully conquered the land promised by Yahweh to their forefathers. In short, it purports to provide an account of past events in such a way as to make them meaningful to a present generation. To phrase this yet one further way, the narratives contain a claim that they represent a "shared" understanding of the past in a meaningful and significant manner. All of this is to say that the narratives of Joshua, like those of the remainder of the deuteronomistic corpus, constitute "history" in its broadest and most functional sense.[11]

Within the context of the social world construction of reality, the "past" that is narrated by the deuteronomistic historian becomes "real" when it is internalized and accepted as "reality." This basic process, i. e., the creation of a "real world" within which a particular group might function in a manner that fulfills some set or sets of particular expectations, also constitutes a major characteristic of religious literature. Implicit within the efforts of the deuteronomistic historian are not only the reconfirmation of the ethnic boundaries delineated by "Moses,"

---

[9] In literary terms, the deuteronomistic narrative clearly belongs to the genre "history." For a general definition of the genre, see B. Long, *1 Kings with an Introduction to Historical Literature* (FOTL 9; Grand Rapids: Eerdmans, 1984), pp. 250–51.

[10] On the general issue of the development of history writing in the ancient world, see J. Van Seters, *In Search of History: Historiography in the Ancient World and the Origins of Biblical History* (New Haven: Yale University Press, 1983).

[11] On the role and function of conceptual "fictions" as constructions designed to aid in the perception and understanding of the "real world," see Hans Vaihinger, *The Philosophy of 'As if': A System of the Theoretical, Practical and Religious Fictions of Mankind* (trans. by C. K. Ogden; New York: Barnes & Noble, 1935), p. 65.

reporting the commands of Yahweh in Deuteronomy, but also the reconstruction and creation of the traditions of the past into a form that would construct a consensus among those belonging to the group being defined.[12] Approached in this way, the deuteronomistic history is to be understood as belonging to the type of literature that functions to create a sense of cohesion in groups.[13] The effect of the socialization of individuals by way of the process of internalizing the narrated "realities" of the story as their own is to transform the "history" into the "historical."[14]

It is precisely this transformation that is critical to understanding the nature and functions of the deuteronomistic history, for it is with the internalization of the purported "events" of the past that the sense of antiquity, a concept essential to every ethnic, religious and national group identity, is created and maintained.[15] The fact that modern archaeological and anthropological reconstructions of the artifactual and cultural evidences from the Late Bronze/Early Iron transition period in Palestine give clear testimony that the "events" narrated in Joshua did not occur as presented by the historian does not directly affect the "reality" created by this ideological social world view. This phenomenon may be taken as a characteristic of religious literatures and world views in general: the paradigms and models which form the basis of such social worlds stand beyond the pale of confirmation or disconfirmation.[16]

---

[12] For the deuteronomistic writer, the imposition of the "all Israel" designation on the traditions concerning premonarchic Israel is a way of attempting to create such a consensus.

[13] On the use of nationalistic/ethnic literature to create such consensus, see W. Sollors, "Introduction: The Invention of Ethnicity," in *The Invention of Ethnicity* (ed. W. Sollors; New York: Oxford, 1989), p. xii.

[14] The performance of ritual activities, both at the narrative and societal levels, constitutes an important aspect in this transformation. As may be illustrated by the temporal and perspectival shifts within the narrative accounts of Deuteronomy and Joshua, the conscious decision to become a member of the group and to adopt the narrated "history" as a meaning-assigning fiction involves, or at least may involve, the ritual participation and transformation of the individuals concerned in either the action of the rite or the hearing of the presentation.

[15] The importance of a sense of continuity with the past has been emphasized by E. Hobsbawm ("Introduction: Inventing Traditions," p. 1): "'Invented tradition' is taken to mean a set of practices, normally governed by overtly or tacitly accepted rules and of a ritual or symbolic nature, which seek to inculcate certain values and norms of behaviour by repetition, which automatically implies continuity with the past. In fact, where possible, they normally attempt to establish continuity with a suitable historic past."

[16] An essential part of the cultural process of "universe maintenance" is based upon the stability and permanence of the accepted world view. What is most threat-

Despite the fact that there is little to indicate that any "ideal" peace or possession of Canaan ever occurred in historical terms, the deuteronomistic writer was nonetheless able to summarize the conquest of the land as follows:

> So Yahweh gave Israel all the land he had promised to give their ancestors. They took possession of it and dwelled in it. Yahweh gave them rest on all sides according to all he had promised their ancestors. Not a single one of all their enemies stood before them; Yahweh gave all their enemies into their power. Not a single thing failed from all the good word which Yahweh had spoken to the house of Israel. All of it happened (*hakkōl bāʾ*). (Josh 21:43–45)

Embedded in this idealized past, the "ideal" Israel is recreated in a new context.

Before proceeding to a consideration of the structure of Joshua and the ways in which Joshua contributes to the construction of such a world view, it is desirable to elaborate further on this process of paradigm construction, especially with regard to the efforts of the deuteronomistic writer. Though much about this author and his historical and social situation remains debated, several of his characteristics may be sketched out with some degree of assuredness. The author at no point in the narrative reveals his identity to the reader; instead, the final tradent speaks through selected characters in the narrative, e.g., Moses, Joshua, Yahweh, etc. Throughout the reporting and reported speeches of the deuteronomistic history,[17] important claims to authority are made by the writer via the choices of characters through whose personae the events are presented. The selection of characters presented, their importance to the narrative, and the surface contours that are described are all controlled by the deuteronomistic writer.

Yet, lest it be overlooked, this person did not produce the history in a vacuum, nor was it produced, in all probability, out of some arcane

---

ening to socially constructed world views is not change, but the inability to adapt to and incorporate possible contradictory or conflicting views while, at the same time, rejecting their influence on or significance to (if not their very occurrence) the previously accepted position. On the phenomenon of "universe maintenance," see P. L. Berger and T. Luckmann, *The Social Construction of Reality: A Treatise in the Sociology of Knowledge* (New York: Doubleday, 1966), pp. 92–128. Within the realm of religious communities, the concepts of canon and the authority attributed to it illustrate the contradictory position of an unchanged community despite centuries of radical changes.

[17] The importance of this literary device has been argued by R. Polzin, *Moses and the Deuteronomist* (New York: Seabury, 1980), pp. 25–72.

interest in "Israel's" historical past. Rather, this final edition of the deuteronomistic history stands as a compilation and editing of various traditions and interpretations of Israel's past[18] that have now, through a process of interactions on several social and cultural planes, taken a final narrative shape that functions so as to address a specific set of religious and cultural situations that existed within the context of the author and his audience. The compositional style of the deuteronomistic history creates a world of dialogue that involves the reader or hearer in the literarily constructed social world of the author as though the past were actually the present (or the present, past, depending on the perspective of the reader). Through a diachronic interpretation of selected traditions from Israel's past, a synchronic present is created by which the myths[19] and traditions recounting the past are interpreted and transformed into the history of the present generation.

In the case of the deuteronomistic writer, this tranformation is, in part, the result of the prophetic authority ultimately accorded the written work by the audience that adopted the view of reality constructed by the narrative. If truth and falsity were regarded in ancient Israel as a matter of correct or incorrect interpretation of the authoritative traditions,[20] then it is clear that the interpretive reconstruction of Israel's past produced by the deuteronomistic author eventually found acceptance as a correct rendering of the traditions of the past. How long it took for this prophetic voice[21] to gain this communally recognized authority is uncertain. It is clear, however, that the situation that engendered the creation of this narrative history shared the ideological views of reality that constitute the background for prophetic activity: the prophetic act of intermediation involves the beliefs in a supernatural realm which can affect, and be affected by, the human realm, a gap separating the two, and the perception of a need to bridge this separation.[22]

---

[18] For a discussion of some of the possible relationships between diachronic and synchronic approaches, see S. Boorer, "The Importance of a Diachronic Approach: The Case of Genesis-Kings," *CBQ* 51 (1989) 195–208.

[19] A provocative discussion of the use and misuse of the term "myth" by biblical scholars is presented by R. Oden in *The Bible without Theology: The Theological Tradition and Alternatives to It* (San Francisco: Harper & Row, 1987), pp. 40–91.

[20] B. O. Long, "Social Dimensions of Prophetic Conflict," *Semeia* 21 (1982) 32.

[21] On the prophetic nature of the deuteronomistic historian, see Polzin, *Moses and the Deuteronomist*, pp. 36–47.

[22] R. Wilson, *Prophecy and Society in Ancient Israel* (Philadelphia: Fortress, 1980), pp. 28–32.

If the above presuppositions are accurate, then the very process of the composition of the deuteronomistic history, when viewed as prophetic proclamation, requires consideration. One major problem area which has remained unaddressed by modern biblical scholarship concerns the literary nature of the deuteronomistic history and the attendant problems of audience, genre and function. Despite the application of various folklore methods to the field of biblical studies, there exists little evidence to suggest that the deuteronomistic history as a whole, or even its individual sections, e. g., Joshua, Judges, etc., ever existed or circulated in oral forms.[23] In other words, the deuteronomistic history as a whole appears to be a literary creation. Any analysis of this material must recognize the highly restricted audience in ancient Israel for which such a document might have been intended. The literary nature of the history itself and the restricted literacy of the general populace, especially with respect to a document written in an orthographic style which requires the reader to know the text in order to read it properly,[24] suggest several possibilities. First, the deuteronomistic history was produced for a rather elite and highly trained audience, one that would have had some knowledge of the language of the temple/court and of the traditions upon which the writer was drawing. More probably, some segment of the priesthood or temple/court personnel (including prophets [?]) would have constituted the primary literate audience among which this world view developed and was preserved.[25] As noted above, this would be a

---

[23] For a critique of those approaches that concentrate on the existence of such oral cycles of materials, see J. Van Seters, *Abraham in History and Tradition* (New Haven: Yale University Press, 1975), pp. 125–53. This is not to suggest that none of the component accounts was ever circulated as an oral tradition. Indeed, it is most probable that many of the traditions that the deuteronomistic writer utilized in shaping his own particular interpretation of Israel's past could be traced back to various orally transmitted accounts.

[24] The situation with the early Hebrew textual traditions is analogous to that of the early literary traditions of the Quran. Prior to the time at which the vowel indicators were added to the consonantal texts, the proper recitation of the materials was dependent upon a previous knowledge of the orally recited materials. Only with the addition of the vowel indicators did the texts themselves become "public property." On the role and function of orality in scriptures, and especially with respect to the situation regarding the Quran, see the comments of W. Graham, *Beyond the Written Word: Oral Aspects of Scripture in the History of Religion* (New York: Cambridge University Press, 1987), esp. pp. 79–95.

[25] Included in such a group would be members of the scribal schools or various scribal traditions. The exact composition and roles of such groups in the social and religious structures of ancient Israel remain obscure.

portion of the urban elite that claimed to control the traditions of the group.

Such an audience, enjoying some form of recognizable authority within the social system (possibly even state sanction prior to the exile), would constitute both the major group responding to the deuteronomistic message and interpretations of the Israelite traditions and the major source of disseminating the work, in whole or in part, among the more general populace. The injunction in Deut 31:10–13 that the *tôrâ* was to be read to the people at the festival of Sukkoth every seventh year provides at least an ideological base for the popularization of the major instructional portions of the deuteronomic corpus. In this way, "all Israel," men, women, children, and resident aliens, might learn "to do all the words of this *tôrâ*" (*laʿăśôt ʾet-kol-dibrê hattôrâ hazzōʾt*, Deut 31:12). It might not be unreasonable to suggest that along with this ritual reciting of the deuteronomic materials would be presented portions of the deuteronomistic interpretations of the law, a practice that might be suggested by Neh 8:1–8.[26] The officials who would use the materials and the populace who would participate in the ritual presentations and explication of the *tôrâ* would provide the setting for the public adoption and incorporation of these materials as part of Israel's official past. Though the available evidence is quite scanty, it would not seem unlikely that the origins of the practice of the recollection and recitation of various traditions might be found in the exilic communities, both in Babylon and in Palestine.

That this process is one of recreation and reconfirmation of group identity is suggested by the ways in which the particular ethnic boundaries formed so clearly in Deuteronomy are modified by the social world that is created and projected by the author of Joshua. Rather than simply to reiterate the traditions associated with Moses as though these had been followed to the letter, the narrative voice in Joshua interprets and modifies selected segments of those traditions.[27] Such modifications, a consideration of which will constitute the main portion of this chapter, focus upon the issues of the exclusion/inclusion of foreigners in the community, modifications of the rules of warfare, the question of the

---

[26] W. Holladay suggests that this public recitation of the law every seven years provides the proper chronological framework for the interpretation of the career and oracles of Jeremiah (*Jeremiah 1* [Hermeneia; Philadelphia: Fortress, 1986], pp. 1–10).

[27] Examples of the ways in which the deuteronomistic author has reinterpreted the "Mosaic" commands contained in Deuteronomy, especially in the materials contained in Joshua, are discussed by Polzin, *Moses and the Deuteronomist*, pp. 73–145.

extent of the occupation of the land, and the covenantal ceremonies by which the ethnicity of the group is refined via a process that might be called "monotheizing"[28] through social rituals and communal confession.

The fact that the deuteronomistic writer engaged in the ongoing interpretation of the Mosaic traditions (which had been, it must be remembered, recreated by the same author) introduces a more complex picture of the process of prophecy than is generally recognized. The realm of the supernatural, the "fictive" or mythological source of the prophetic revelations in such a world view, may have been regarded as eternal, but not static; nor was it beyond the influence of the prophetic or, indirectly, the prophetic audiences' responses. By readdressing and reapplying various aspects of the Mosaic pronouncements through the interpretive aspects of the "history" of the record of Israel's attempts at fulfilling the prophetic pronouncements commanded by the deity, the changing social, cultural, and historical situations produced the need for renewed interpretations that could be used to construct new visions of reality to address various perceptions of crisis. It is this supernatural aspect of the accepted world view that is perceived to be beyond the control of history that provides the possibility for the positing of a reality beyond, or in addition to, that which is the world as empirically known.[29] Concurrently, the renewed revelation produces the claim to authority to revise and reapply the interpretation to the public, whose changing situations have provided the setting for the shifting perspectives of the prophet *vis-à-vis* the supernatural.

In the case of the deuteronomistic writer, the production of a prophetic pronouncement in written form, despite the possibilities of editing and modification, implies on several levels the general stability of the interpretations produced.[30] Additionally, I would suggest, the continued appeals to prophetic figures, their announcements, and the

---

[28] See the comments by J. Sanders, "Hermeneutics in True and False Prophecy," in *Canon and Authority* (ed. by G. W. Coats and B. O. Long; Philadelphia: Fortress, 1977), pp. 40–41.

[29] R. Scholes and R. Kellogg, *The Nature of Narrative* (New York: Oxford, 1966), pp. 134–35. The manner in which such "feedback" may affect prophecy and the content of the prophetic proclamation is presented in T. Overholt, *Channels of Prophecy: The Social Dynamics of Prophetic Activity* (Minneapolis: Augsburg/Fortress, 1989), pp. 17–68.

[30] The survival of such layers of tradition within the narrative is a result of the cumulative aspects that are characteristic of materials produced over periods of time in literate societies (Van Seters, "Tradition and Social Change in Ancient Israel," p. 98).

fulfillment of those proclamations[31] constitute the overt claims to authority that are so necessary for the social acceptance of the prophetic message.[32] The "rehearsal" of such otherwise unattested traditions assigned to the past represents the possibility of the creation or invention of the traditions to which the author was appealing to support his own claims of authority and authenticity.[33] These "rehearsals," it should be noted, may be interpreted in terms of their literary and social functions within the narrative materials constructed and presented by the deuteronomistic writer rather than as historical accounts.[34] Likewise, the Mosaic authority of Deuteronomy and its boundary-forming aspects must be approached in a similar manner, for the great antiquity and authenticity attached to the traditions concerning Moses are derived from the Hexateuchal sources, all of which may be connected, in one form or another, with the deuteronomistic history.[35] The interpreter of the deuteronomistic history must recognize the possibility that neither the "history" that is narrated nor the "traditions" that are reported had any widespread acceptance, or even actual existence, prior to or apart from the production of the deuteronomistic history itself.

In short, the deuteronomistic writer was not only recreating the boundaries that should define and refine the ethnic identity of Israel and its members, but was also producing the authoritative traditions that supported and legitimized the claims made by the narrative and its prophetic author. This fictive way of presenting reality provides a basis for the creation of a new community out of the remnants of the people scattered and dislocated by the exile.[36] The crisis presented by the

---

[31] The classical statement of the structure of the deuteronomistic history around the notices of the fulfillment of prophetic announcements is that given by G. von Rad, *Studies in Deuteronomy* (SBT; London: SCM, 1953), pp. 74–91.

[32] Long, "Prophetic Authority as Social Reality," in *Canon and Authority*, pp. 3–20.

[33] As Hobsbawm points out, such "creations" occur most commonly at periods of rapid transformation of societies, which in turn weaken the abilities of the "old traditions" to interpret and make meaningful the present circumstances ("Introduction: Inventing Traditions," pp. 4–5).

[34] This is not to deny the possible historicity of the events that are recounted in the deuteronomistic narratives or the historical reliability of the traditions from which they were produced. It is, however, to suggest that before any attempt at ascertaining the possible historical referents of the traditions can be successful, the functions of the narrative must be explicated and understood.

[35] For a balanced summary of the present status of Pentateuchal studies, see Boorer, "The Importance of a Diachronic Approach," pp. 196–201.

[36] For examples of the creation of such traditions in tribal societies, see K. W. Whitelam, "Israel's Traditions of Origin: Reclaiming the Land," *JSOT* 44 (1989) 19–42.

Babylonian exile, the loss of the land, the dynastic state, and the religious rituals associated with the dynastic shrine in Jerusalem presented the possibility for the creation of a new set of traditions to anchor the newly envisioned people in the "primordial" times that provided the narrative foundations for the vision itself.[37] Not only does the deuteronomistic history construct the boundaries of this ethnic unit, but it also endows it with the mythic traditions that provide meaning and continuity with a past now protected by the narrative formation of the history itself. It is in this functional sense, i. e., as an interpretive effort to provide the exiles with a legitimizing statement for the retaking of the land from the indigenous non-Israelite inhabitants, that the deuteronomistic history operates in such a way as to transform myth into tradition, and subsequently, tradition into history. The effects which this has on understanding the narrative and the prophetic authority of the writer are important.

It is the realization that the deuteronomistic writer produces a "traditional" past and projects a form for the creation and maintenance of a new people and new state in the future for the scattered and exiled people of both Israel and Judah that elucidates the function and form of the narrative itself. This writer is clearly entitled to the designation "historian," not due in any manner to the accuracy or credibility of his work, but rather because of the authorial role that he adopted.

> Since Herodotus and Thucydides the *histor* has been concerned to establish himself with the reader as a repository of fact, a tireless investigator and sorter, a sober and impartial judge—a man, in short, of authority, who is entitled not only to present the facts as he has established them but to comment on them, to draw parallels, to moralize, to generalize, to tell the reader what to think and even to suggest what he should do. History from its beginning was closely allied with rhetoric, and the ancient *histor* knew that one of the first tasks of a speaker was to convince the audience of his authority and competence to deal with the subject at hand.[38]

That such adaptations commonly occur in situations of exile and deportation has been demonstrated by D. L. Smith, *The Religion of the Landless: The Social Context of the Babylonian Exile* (Bloomington, IN: Meyer Stone, 1989), esp. pp. 69–126.

[37] If the foundational elements of the Israelite traditions are interpreted as mythic and symbolic expressions of the origins of the people and the creation of its identity, then the primordial times, i. e., those of origin, would be contained within the narrative temporality created by the rehearsal and ritual repetition of those stories.

[38] Scholes and Kellogg, *The Nature of Narrative*, p. 266.

Obviously the deuteronomistic writer might displace Herodotus as the earliest known historian.[39] By creating a new selection and arrangement of traditions by which to interpret the past and to prepare for the future, the deuteronomistic writer serves as a strongly formative prophetic voice within the emerging written accounts of the formation and development of the ethnically defined group that designated itself as Israel/Hebrew/Judahite.[40] The boundaries that would set this entity apart from all others had been outlined in the presentations of the Mosaic speeches in Deuteronomy, accompanied by their covenantal and performative conditions. Yet, there, all was pressed into the future with the continual references to the obligations of the people "when you enter the land to take possession of it."[41] The purpose of the book of Joshua is to construct the tradition of this group's taking possession of the land from outside, thus creating a tradition that might address the audience of the writer of the narratives.[42]

With this interpretive material concerning the nature and function of the deuteronomistic writer having been presented, I shall now attempt to demonstrate how the narrative presentations of Joshua solidify the projections of the ethnic signifiers utilized in Deuteronomy by way of the narration of certain selected and mythic accounts of the actions of the ancestors of Israel who, under the leadership of the divinely designated successor to Moses, first seized the land and fulfilled the commands of the deity. The analysis of the materials must proceed from several differing perspectives, for the narratives created by the deuteronomistic writer to convey the concept of ethnicity, especially via the conquest and consolidation of the land and the adherence to the *tôrâ*, have blurred the

---

[39] Van Seters, *In Search of History*, pp. 209–48.

[40] The precise parameters of each of these terms remain somewhat unclear. Especially problematic is the term "Hebrew" as a designation of a national or social entity. On this term, see N. P. Lemche, "'Hebrew' as a National Name for Israel," *Studia Theologica* 33 (1979) 1–23.

[41] For references, see above, n. 4.

[42] As the considerations of the various portions of the deuteronomistic history will attempt to demonstrate, these narratives address the major motifs that constitute ethnic and national mythologies. Commonly, these myths address origins (spatial and temporal), ancestry, migration, oppression/liberation, a "golden age" and its loss, and the possibilities of rebirth (Smith, *The Ethnic Origins of Nations*, p. 192). It should be noted here that it is most conceivable that Israel/Judah already had traditions associated with the manner by which it had come to possess the land. The deuteronomistic writer has, however, utilized whatever traditions might have been available to him to construct his own particular interpretation of the "taking" of the land.

genres[43] of myth, legend, epic, and history, and have produced an extended narrative account that, while "history-like" in its presentation, blends various aspects of the other formal categories, especially with respect to content. In this way, the deuteronomistic author constructs a particular view of a "reality," the accuracy and acceptability of which rests upon the ways in which the audience addressed responds to the handling and interpretations given to the traditional and non-traditional materials used to construct this symbolic depiction of the world. Since the deuteronomistic construction of the "reality system" was dependent upon a particularly religious view of the world, it is natural that religious matters would constitute an important part of the identity being constructed for the people. Though the issue of conversion, especially within the context of emerging Israelite and Judahite national religions, remains debated,[44] some such consciously formed consensus on the correctness, or appropriateness, of the vision and interpretation of the social institutions, at least at the very initial stages, must be posited. Thus, it should be clear that the formation and composition of these narratives occurred within the complexities of the interweaving of social and cultural interactions and influences.

II. Identity through Covenantal Ritual Reenactment

For Joshua, the consensual nature of inclusion in and identity with the community is presented in the concept of allegiance to the *tôrâ*. The divine directions given to Joshua which open the narrative (1:1–9) make the entry into the land and the fulfillment of the promises to the patriarchs directly contingent upon the fulfillment of the commands given by Moses: "Only be strong and very courageous, being careful to do accord-

---

[43] On this concept, see C. Geertz, "Blurred Genres: The Refiguration of Social Thought," in *Local Knowledge* (New York: Basic, 1983), pp. 19–35.

[44] Compare the positions of Gottwald ("Religious Conversion and the Societal Origins of Ancient Israel," pp. 49–65) with those of Milgrom ("Religious Conversion and the Revolt Model for the Formation of Israel," pp. 169–76), referred to above in n. 5. The difference between the two positions is, in essence, one of definition of terms. A formal type of "conversion," as Milgrom argues, could not occur before the period of the Second Temple. Yet, as Gottwald has answered, the assimilation of disparate groups into the entity known as Israel implicitly assumes some type of conscious religious response that might be termed "conversion." Perhaps the designation of such actions as "communal bonding" or "religious socialization" might express the intended activities in a less confusing manner.

ing as all the law which Moses my servant has commanded you, not deviating from it at all in order that you may succeed in everything that you undertake."[45] After this opening section, no reference to *tôrâ* occurs until 8:31, in the first account of the covenantal ceremony on Mt. Ebal (8:30–35), a text which is a direct reference to the twice-repeated command for such a ritual in Deut 11:26–32 and 27:1–13. Despite the importance of this "written book" for the deuteronomistic historian, explicit references to it are rather infrequent in the history itself. In Deuteronomy, this book is referred to directly some seven times (28:58, 61; 29:19, 20, 26; 30:10; 31:26). Four times in the deuteronomistic history this book is referred to as "the book of the law" (*sēper hattôrâ*, Josh 1:8; 8:34; 2 Kgs 22:8, 11). Elsewhere in the history it is designated more specifically as either "the book of the law of Moses" (*sēper tôrat mōšeh*, Josh 8:31; 23:6; 2 Kgs 14:6) or "the law of Moses" (*tôrat mōšeh*, Josh 8:32; 1 Kgs 2:3). That this law is referred to as "the book of God's law" (*sēper tôrat ʾĕlōhîm*, Josh 24:26) should not go without comment, for this completes the identity of the law that was commanded both in Deuteronomy and in the opening address to Joshua (cf. vv. 7–8). For the narrator of Joshua, the law of God is to be identified with the book of the law referred to in Deuteronomy, i.e., the "book of the law of Moses," the precepts recorded in Deuteronomy itself. The requirements placed upon the people frame the events narrated within the book, as a comparison of Josh 23:6 with Josh 1:7 demonstrates: "And you will be very careful to observe to do all which is written in the book of the law of Moses, not deviating from it one way or the other" (23:6).[46]

The fulfillment of the precepts of Deuteronomy, and hence the formation and maintenance of the identity of this people as "Israel," is contingent, at least in part, on the conclusion of a prescribed covenant-making ceremony recorded in Deut 11:26–32 and 27:1–13. Deut 11:26–32 forms the conclusion of the first eleven chapters of that book and sets before the people the decision to choose obedience or disobedience to the laws that have been presented to them;[47] Deut 27:1–13 gives the specifics for the ritual actions that are prescribed upon entering into the Cisjordan area.[48] In parallel fashion, Josh 8:30–35 describes the ritual fulfillment of

---

45 *ḥăzaq weʾĕmaṣ meʾōd lišmōr laʿăśôt kĕkol-hattôrâ ʾăšer ṣiwwĕkā mōšeh ʿabdî ʾal-tāsûr mimmennû yāmîn uśmōʾwl lĕmaʿan taśkîl bĕkōl ʾăšer tēlēk*, 1:7.

46 *wahăzaqtem mĕʾōd lišmōr wĕlaʿăśôt ʾet kol-hakkātûb bĕsēper tôrat mōšeh lĕbiltî sûr-mimmennû yāmîn ûśmōʾwl*. Compare to 1:7; cf. n. 45.

47 Mayes, *Deuteronomy*, p. 217.

48 Ibid., pp. 340–43.

the commands given in Deuteronomy, while the account in Josh 24:1–28 describes the public ritual by which Israel chose to accept the stipulations of this covenant as binding upon them and as defining them as the worshippers of one particular deity, Yahweh, to the exclusion of other gods (cf. Deut 11:28b). Despite the clear conceptual connections between the parallel accounts in Joshua by which the people fulfill the commands of Deuteronomy, there is little to suggest that the narrative ever existed as a single unit, which has now been divided for rhetorical reasons.[49] Instead, the narrative arrangement of the materials parallels the double account of Deuteronomy and encloses the completion of the conquest of the land and its apportionment within the narrative accounts of the ritual by which Israel became the special people of Yahweh possessing the land promised to their ancestors.

As noted earlier, the manner in which these prescriptions of Moses are fulfilled indicates that the deuteronomistic writer has modified certain aspects of the commands. Rather than erecting the stones on which the law was to be written "on the day" that they crossed over the Jordan into the land (wĕhāyâ bayyôm ʾăšer taʿabrû ʾet-hayyardēn ʾel-hāʾāreṣ, Deut 27:2), the characters in the narrative do not perform these deeds until the end of the conquest of Jericho and Ai (Josh 6:1–8:29), a relocation and reinterpretation that are hardly coincidental. These stories describe, in quite clear fashion, the implications of the failure to follow the entirety of the Mosaic directions, especially with respect to the law of the ḥērem (Deut 20:15–18). At Jericho, the commands of Yahweh to Joshua regarding the manner by which the city would be taken were followed by the people. There was no military conquest involved; rather, Yahweh gave Israel the city as the result of the proper performance of the prescribed ritual (Josh 6:2–5; cf. Josh 1:2; 2:9; 5:6; Deut 4:21; 15:4; 19:10; 20:16; 21:23; 24:4; 26:1; etc.). In a manner similar to that used in the account of the crossing of the Jordan River,[50] the deuteronomistic writer has "ritualized" the narrative in such a way as to create a liturgical world different from that of the "real" world of the events.[51] The success of the

---

49 A standard view of modern commentators is that Josh 8:30–35 was originally an incipit for Joshua 24 or was derived from that chapter (cf. R. G. Boling, *Joshua* [AB 6; New York: Doubleday, 1982], pp. 246, 253). Notice that J. A. Soggin connects 8:30–35 so closely with Joshua 24 that he does not consider the passage in his commentary until after the discussion of chapter 24 (*Joshua* [OTL; Philadelphia: Westminster, 1972], pp. 220–44).

50 See the treatment of Josh 3:1–4:18, pp. 107–11.

51 Polzin, *Moses and the Deuteronomist*, p. 93.

taking of the land could be attributed to the proper performance of the ritual actions that provide the metaphoric content of the idea of the people "Israel" being created upon their entry into the land.

If, then, the correct performance of these public social events within the account might be interpreted as leading to the enactment of the "blessings" of the covenant (cf. Deut 11:26, 27, 29; 28:8; 30:1, 19), then the "curses" (cf. Deut 27:13; 28:15, 45; 30:1, 19) might be represented by the narrated violation of the ritual commands. Such a presentation is made explicitly in the continuation of the Jericho account which is connected with the story of the attempt to take Ai. Though the narrator confirms at the conclusion of the account concerning Jericho that "Yahweh was with Joshua and his fame was known throughout the land" (*wayhî yhwh ᵓet-yĕhôšūaᶜ wayhî šomᶜô bĕkol-hāᵓāreṣ*, 6:27; cf. 1:5; 3:7; 4:14), the continuation of the narrative offsets the impression that all the commands of the law had been fulfilled. Josh 7:1a begins with the notice that "the Israelites had committed a serious violation of the ban" (*wayyimᶜălû bĕnê-yiśrāᵓēl maᶜal bahērem*), a grievous matter which is then focused on one man, Achan (vv. 1b–26; cf. 22:22), whose misdeeds bring the curses of the covenant into reality.

Here, the account of the military attempt to conquer Ai, an attempt that met with initial failure (7:2–5), is interpreted within the ritual context of the Israelite efforts to avert the wrath of Yahweh that had been incurred as a result of Achan's violation of the *hērem* (7:1b). The explanation for the defeat is given by Yahweh to Joshua: "Israel has sinned and has broken my covenant" (*hāṭāᵓ yiśrāᵓēl wĕgam ᶜābĕrû ᵓet-bĕrîtî*, 7:11a). If Yahweh is to continue to be with the Israelites, then they must destroy the *hērem* that is in their midst (7:12; cf. 1:7–8). The ritual for the discovery of the guilty party is given to Joshua (7:14–15) along with the directions that the person and all that he has be burned in fire (*yiśśārēp bāᵓēš*). With the people ritually prepared for the ceremony, Joshua gathers "Israel" together and, in strict accordance with the directions given, detects and seizes the guilty party, Achan (vv. 16–24). Achan and all that belonged to him were taken by Joshua and "all Israel" (*kol-yiśrāᵓēl*) to the valley of Achor ("devastation"), and there "all Israel stoned him, burned them with fire, and stoned them" (v. 25).[52] In accord with Yahweh's

---

[52] Despite the problems in the versions with this series of verbs, it seems that the redundancy is a part of the earliest form of the text. Important to note is the etiological aspect of the materials here, for the name of the valley of Achor (*ᶜākôr*) is explained in v. 25 by Joshua's statement to Achan: "Why did you bring trouble on us? Today Yahweh brings devastation to you" (*meh ᶜăkartānû yaᶜkorkā yhwh bayyôm*

directions, then, the *ḥērem* was destroyed from the midst of the people (cf. 7:12). Conforming now to the covenantal demands of their god, Israel could engage in battle against Ai and be successful in the endeavor.

Following immediately upon the account of the conquest of Ai (8:1–29)[53] is the first portion of the account of the covenant ceremony prescribed in Deuteronomy. The disjunctive nature of the expression *ʾāz yibneh*, "then he (Joshua) built" (v. 30),[54] interrupts the narrative flow of the account of the conquest to recount the fulfillment of the commands contained in Deut 27:1–13 and in Deut 11:26–32.[55] An altar is erected "near Mt. Ebal" (*bĕhar ʿêbāl*, v. 30) as prescribed. Part of the significance of the placement of the account here is not simply the temporal dislocation, but also the geographical transposition that is involved. Joshua and "all the congregation of Israel, women, children, and the sojourner going in their midst" (v. 35),[56] have been relocated near Shechem, quite some distance from the sites of Jericho and Ai. The nature and extent of this public ceremony are critical for an understanding of the functional aspects of this account.

Josh 8:30–35 displays a direct literary dependence upon both Deut 27:1–13 and 11:26–32, yet does not recount a mechanistic fulfillment of

---

hazzeh). Though it might be argued that the etiological elements of the story are secondary additions to an already extant tradition (cf. B. O. Long, *The Problem of Etiological Narrative in the Old Testament* [BZAW 108; Berlin: de Gruyter, 1968], pp. 25–26), it might just as well be a part of the original composition.

[53] As Polzin has noted, the directions from Yahweh to Joshua concerning the conquest of the city involve a change in the interpretation of the *ḥērem* laws that had been in force with respect to Jericho (8:1–2), though he also argues that the covenant with Rahab and her family (2:12–14; 6:22–23) constitutes a reinterpretation of the law of the *ḥērem* contained in Deuteronomy 20 (*Moses and the Deuteronomist*, pp. 113–15). It is of interest to note that the LXX has transposed this section to follow the notice of the kings gathering to fight against Israel in 9:1–2.

[54] Boling notes that the similarly disjunctive *ʾāz yiqrāʾ* (Josh 22:1) that introduces the story concerning the altar on the banks of the Jordan connects these two stories in rhetorical terms (*Joshua*, pp. 246–47).

[55] The narrator has chosen to reverse the order of the fulfillment of the Mosaic commands concerning the ceremony in Deuteronomy. Here, the emphasis is upon the erection of the altar and the plastered stones (cf. Deut 27:1–8); the account in Joshua 24 is mainly concerned with the decision of the people to follow only Yahweh and to forsake other gods (cf. Deut 11:26–32). In this way, the narrator brings the people associated with Joshua into conformity with the ethnic boundaries prescribed by Deuteronomy.

[56] *kol-qĕhal yiśrāʾēl wĕhannāšîm wĕhaṭṭap wĕhaggēr hahōlēk bĕqirbām;* the LXX reflects a reading that adds "men" (*wĕhāʾănāšîm*) before "women." The word could easily have been lost by haplography.

the command. Rather, by way of a careful paraphrase, the deuterono-mistic author indicates that Joshua and all the components of Israel have kept the commission of Moses. The altar itself is patterned after the "blueprint" contained "in the book of the law of Moses" (v. 31), i. e., an "altar of whole stones upon which nothing of iron had been wielded."[57] Upon this altar they then sacrificed burnt offerings (ʿōlōt) and peace offerings (šĕlāmîm) to Yahweh (cf. Deut 27: 6b–7a). Joshua next "wrote a copy of the law of Moses upon the stones" (v. 32).[58] Here the author of Joshua has compressed the narrative to omit any reference to the erection of large stones which were to be plastered over and upon which the law was to be written (Deut 27:2–3), though, presumably, the erection of such stele is implied by the reference.[59]

In a similarly condensed manner, Josh 8:33–35 recounts the fulfill-ment of the injunctions concerning the recitation of the covenantal blessings and curses that are contained in Deut 11:26–32. Now the full cultic assemblage of "all Israel" (kol-yiśrāʾēl), both "resident alien and native born" (kaggēr kāʾezrāḥ, v. 33),[60] stood facing each other before Mts.

---

57 mizbaḥ ʾăbānîm šĕlēmôt ʾăšer lōʾ-hēnîp ʿălêhen barzel; compare with Deut 27:5: mizbaḥ ʾăbānîm lōʾ-tānîp ʿălêhem barzel; v. 6 describes the stones as ʾăbānîm šĕlēmôt.

58 wayyiktob-šām ʿal-hāʾăbānîm ʾēt mišnēh tôrat mōšeh; compare Deut 27:3, 8: wĕkātabtā ʿălêhen ʾet-kol-dibrê hattôrâ hazzōʾt. The notice that a "copy" of the book was written implies that the materials were already conceived of as being in written form.

59 Not to be overlooked in this connection is the mention of large stones invoked as "witnesses" to the covenant ceremony in Josh 24:26–27. The only unambiguous deviation from the Mosaic instruction is found in the failure of Joshua to construct this altar and to erect these stele "on the day" Israel crossed over the Jordan (Deut 27:2). As will be suggested below, this is a result of the deuteronomistic writer's separation of the accounts of the fulfillment of the ritual demands by various sections concerning the conquest of the land. The account of the erection of stones on the day on which Israel crossed over the Jordan is contained in the story of the ritual crossing into the land (Josh 3:4–4:24).

60 If this expression of inclusion in the covenantal community, kol-qĕhal yiśrāʾēl (v. 35), is considered seriously, then the composition of this group goes far beyond those who had just crossed over the Jordan and had taken part in the events narrated in the previous portions of Joshua. gēr stands as the common designation for someone who has taken up residence in a community or place not originally his own; ʾezrāḥ desig-nates persons indigenous to an area. When taken together, these would represent the complete population of the area, both the Israelite tribes entering with Joshua and the people encountered in the land. It might be reasonable to suggest that the "native born" inhabitants that would constitute such a group would include such figures as Rahab and her family, who had, like the Gibeonites would (9:3–27), entered into a covenantal alliance with the Israelites and had thus become consensual members of the community. The lack of any mention of the tribes, as listed in the ceremony in

Ebal and Gerizim for the presentation of the "blessing and the curse according as all which was written in the book of the *tôrâ*."[61] The notice that the "ark of the covenant of Yahweh"[62] was present further confirms the importance of these ritual recitals within the narrative and symbolizes the conclusion of a portion of the prescribed actions, for this is the final mention of this cultic object in the deuteronomistic accounts of Joshua. In fulfillment of "all which Moses had commanded" (v. 35), thus Joshua had done. The initial phase of the formation of a people Israel in the land of Canaan was completed by the reading and recording of the words of the *tôrâ* in fulfillment of the commands of Deuteronomy.[63]

Additionally, this narrative account of the assemblage of the people around the ark, which for the deuteronomic tradition was the repository of the tablets of the *tôrâ* (cf. Deut 10:1–5), reflects another important deuteronomic text regarding the reading of the law under the auspices of the "Levitical priests who carried the ark of Yahweh" (Josh 8:33; cf. Deut 31:9). As noted above, Deut 31:10–13 establishes the Mosaic legislation for the public reading of the law every seven years at the feast of Sukkoth. In Deut 31:9, the directive is given explicitly to the Levitical priests in charge of the ark and to the elders of Israel, two of the groups of officials gathered at the ceremony at Shechem. Though "the place which Yahweh would choose" (Deut 31:11) would finally be identified with Jerusalem, for the deuteronomistic historian it would be the presence of the ark that would signify this cultic location prior to David's establishment of the ark in Jerusalem (2 Samuel 6). For the narratives of Joshua, the last place that would be symbolized as Yahweh's choice by virtue of the presence of this cult object would be Shechem.[64]

Deut 27:12–14, further suggests that these two groups constitute the totality of the congregation.

[61] *habběrākâ wěhaqqělālâ kěkol-hakkātûb běsēper hattôrâ*; see above, pp. 100–2.

[62] *ʾărôn běrît-yhwh*; the "ark" is referred to also in Josh 3:3, 6, 8, 11, 13, 14, 15, 17; 4:5, 7, 9, 10, 11, 16, 18; 6:4, 6, 7, 8, 9, 11, 12, 13; 7:6; 8:33. With the exception of the notice in Judg 20:27 that the ark was at Bethel, this object does not appear in the deuteronomistic history again until its association with Shiloh in 1 Sam 4:3.

[63] In a similar manner, Josiah will reconstitute the covenant community by reading the *tôrâ* to all the people of Israel (2 Kgs 23: 2–3).

[64] I would argue that attempts to reconstruct an original Gilgal setting for this story have failed to understand that the deuteronomistic historian uses the location of the ark as one of the means by which the place for specified ritual activities might be identified. For the most detailed attempt at such a reconstruction of underlying traditions for these materials, see O. Eissfeldt, "Gilgal or Shechem?" in *Proclamation and Presence* (ed. J. L. Durham and J. R. Porter; Richmond: John Knox, 1970), pp. 90–101.

The completion of the ritualization of the narrative accounts of Joshua, and hence the creation and invention of the people "Israel," are located in two narrative descriptions of ritual enactments that provide literary frames encompassing the body of the activities noted thus far. Josh 3:1–5:12, which recounts the ceremonial crossing of the Jordan, the erection of memorial stones, the circumcision of males in the community, and the celebration of the Passover, sanctifies and prepares the community for the actual events of the conquest of the land. Likewise, Josh 24:1–28, the narrative of the ceremony at Shechem in which the people of Israel put away all other gods and devote themselves solely to Yahweh, concludes the liturgical frame within which is recreated a people consonant with, and identical to, those who heard the words of Moses on the plains of Moab. What the deuteronomistic historian has done by virtue of the structural arrangements of the narrative is to envelop the literarily stylized accounts of the seizure and allotment of the land of Canaan within a series of liturgical enactments and social dramas which interpret and define those who would belong to this group Israel.

III. The "Conquest" of the Land through Ritual Realization

The initial entry into the land, like the initial military conquest of Jericho, is couched in the form of a religious performance. Joshua 3–5 are here associated with the site of Gilgal,[65] which served as a base camp of military operations in the accounts in Joshua 1–12. The contents of the passage present obvious parallels to the accounts of the Passover and the crossing of the Reed Sea in Exodus 12–15.[66] In the Joshua account, most noticeably, the order of the "events" has been reversed: first the event at

---

[65] For an attempted reconstruction of a spring festival associated with Gilgal, see F. M. Cross, *Canaanite Myth and Hebrew Epic* (Cambridge: Harvard University Press, 1973), pp. 103–5 and the literature cited therein. The historical existence of such an organized cult at the period of Israel's development as a people remains conjectural.

[66] For a discussion of the complex literary problems associated with this section, see Soggin, *Joshua*, pp. 51–78, and J. A. Wilcoxen, "Narrative Structure and Cult Legend," in *Transitions in Biblical Scholarship* (ed. by J. C. Rylaarsdam; Chicago: University of Chicago Press, 1968), pp. 43–70. The issues of literary dependency or relationships between the Pentateuchal sources and the deuteronomistic history lie beyond the scope of the present work. The once solid foundations of the documentary hypothesis and the relative dating of the various sources have been seriously questioned, and the tendency seems to be to date many of the materials to the period of the exile and second temple.

the "Sea/Jordan"[67] is (re)enacted, and then the Passover is celebrated. It is with the commemorative stele and the participation in the Passover festival that the people of the "conquest" become, in ritual terms, identified with those who were delivered from Egypt. It is this type of infusion of metaphoric meaning into the narrated events that, in synchronic terms, ritually bridges the generations that have preceded and those that will follow. As the following discussion will attempt to demonstrate, this is part of the function and purpose of this type of narrative ritualization of communal traditions. It is precisely the "frozen" character of literary presentations that allows a responding community to participate, in psychological and ritual terms, in situations that no longer exist and to reconstruct their identities in terms of those events.

The account opens with the notice that "all the members of Israel" (*kol-běnê yiśrā'ēl*) journeyed from Shittim to the Jordan, where they lodged for "three days" (*šělōšet yāmîm*, v. 2) before actually crossing the river. The attempts to reconstruct a consistent chronology for the events from the temporal references that are contained in the narrative[68] have failed to recognize that the fivefold repetition of this "three day" period (1:11; 2:16, 22; 3:2) collapses the temporality of the narrated events into a contemporaneous whole that is then, by virtue of the structure of the storied events, presented as a series of unrelated vignettes. Hence, the preparations for crossing the Jordan (1:11) are contemporaneous with the events of the spies at Jericho (2:16, 22) and are projected into the lodging at the edge of the Jordan for three days (3:2). In order to participate, the people must prepare themselves ritually (*hitqaddāšû*, v. 5; cf. 7:13) and follow the lead of the "ark," for they were about to go on a path they had never before travelled (v. 4). Following a proclamation to the priests (vv. 6, 8), instructions are given for the selection of twelve men to represent the people (v. 12) in the events associated with the movement of the ark into the river itself. The symbolic procession stands to reinforce and reintroduce the initial address in 1:1–9, for the ritual crossing of the river will

---

[67] The parallels between "the Sea" and "the Jordan" in Ps 114:3, 5 present an interesting reflection of the ritual presented here:
  hayyām rā'â wayyānōs//hayyardēn yissōb lĕ'aḥôr...
  mah-lĕkā hayyām kî tānûs//hayyardēn tissōb lĕ'aḥôr
  When the Sea saw, it fled//The Jordan turned back...
  What is wrong with you, O Sea, that you fled; O Jordan, that you turned back?
  (vv. 3, 5; see also Ps 66:6)
[68] See, e.g., the efforts of Wilcoxen, "Narrative Structure and Cult Legend," pp. 60–61.

demonstrate the presence of the "living god" (*ʾēl ḥay*) in the midst of the people and the assurance that he would indeed dispossess "the Canaanites, the Hittites, the Hivvites, the Perizzites, the Girgashites, the Amorites, and the Jebusites" from before them (3:10).[69] This same listing of nations, with its minor variations of order and number, occurs at four other points in the book of Joshua and ties the entire series of conquests and battles together by noting that each major alliance of kings that is recounted within the narrative accounts included the rulers of these nations (9:1; 11:3; 12:8), all of whom gathered to battle against Israel at Jericho (24:11). Because of the importance given in the liturgical pronouncements of the narrative to these particular nations, the subsequent encounters with them are all interpreted by the promise of success in driving them out.

No clearer indication of the ritual "freezing" of narrative time could be provided than by the notice that when the priests carrying the ark dipped their feet in the edge of the water of the Jordan, the waters "stood in one heap" (*nēd ʾeḥād*, 3:16; cf. v. 13; Exod 15:8). With the flow of both the narrative and the river brought to a standstill, "the people crossed over before Jericho" (v. 16). Yet the ritual does not end with the simple crossing of the Jordan by "all the nation" (*kol-haggôy*, v. 17), for the priests will stand in the river until 4:18, at which time they will step out of the waters and the Jordan will resume its normal course. The erection of a national monument (4:1–8) is thus included in the ritualized crossing by the temporal freezing connected with the account of the location of the priests and the ark. Interestingly, the narrative seems to include a double account of the erection of a twelve-stone memorial to the event, the varying details of which frame and interpret the ritual of the crossing of the Jordan (4:1–8, 19–24).[70]

---

69 Boling (*Joshua*, p. 165) notes that this somewhat stereotyped list occurs some 21 times in the Hebrew Bible, and provides a list of occurrences. Most notably, these nations constitute those that are to be the specific object of the institution of the *ḥērem* according to Deut 7:1–6 and 20:17. In the former passage, which I have treated earlier (see above, chap. 3, pp. 64–67), these peoples are to be destroyed along with all their cultic apparatus, and any intermarriage is to be avoided so as to insure that the people do not stray after other gods.

70 It is most common to reconstruct a conflation of traditions and to argue that the deuteronomistic author has combined differing accounts of the erection of the stones and the interpretation of their meanings. See, e.g., the analysis by Soggin, *Joshua*, pp. 43–54. Utilizing a different approach, Van Seters argues that the basic deuteronomistic story of the conquest has been edited and expanded by the Yahwistic and Priestly tradents (*In Search of History*, pp. 324–31). Wilcoxen has correctly noted that

In the initial account of the erection of a memorial, the order to select twelve men is reiterated (4:2; cf. 3:12) and the purpose revealed: each is to take a stone from the Jordan and carry it to the place where they lodge for the night. The explanation of the act is given by Joshua in 4:5–7 in the form of a command: the twelve stones are to be a "sign" (ʾôt, v. 6) that would symbolize that the waters of the Jordan had been cut off when the ark, the symbol of the presence of Yahweh, had crossed over into the land and would be "a memorial for the members of Israel forever" (zikkārôn libnê yiśrāʾēl ʿad-ʿôlām, v. 7). In terms of community boundary formation, this memorial is meant not simply for the generation that had crossed over into the land, but for the future generations of the people who would see and ask the meaning of the monument.[71] It is important to note that the etiology here provided is one for the future participant in the ritual, not necessarily for any actual stone memorial at Gilgal or in the Jordan. The contrasting tradition of the location of a twelve-stone monument given in 4:9,[72] that is, "in the midst of the Jordan" (bĕtôk hayyardēn), suggests that the memorial(s) being referred to exist primarily in the narrative accounts and that the geographical ambiguity is a literary device employed here to connect the traditions about the erection of stone monuments with the events at the Jordan.[73] Significantly, it is only

---

the basic narrative framework of Joshua 1–6 may be used as a "datum for tradition and cultic history" ("Narrative Structure and Cult Legend," p. 59), though I would caution against an uncritical acceptance of the antiquity of such beyond the assignment to the "traditional" interpretation being created by the deuteronomistic writer.

[71] "When your sons ask you in the future what these stones mean...." (kî-yišʾalûn bĕnêkem māḥār lēʾmōr māh hāʾăbānîm hāʾelleh lākem, v. 6). Inclusion of community members not present at the ritual event is a part of the structure and function of the deuteronomic materials (cf. Deut 29:13–14).

[72] The LXX alleviates the ambiguity of the verse by reading "twelve other stones" (allous dōdeka lithous), thus creating a second set of actions by Joshua. While it is tempting to posit an haplography (ʾbn[ym ʾ]ḥr]ym; Boling, Joshua, p. 158), it seems more likely that the LXX is interpreting the Hebrew text in order to resolve the apparent textual discord.

[73] This ambiguity is an essential element to the narrative, for it allows the conceptual linking of this erection of stones with the command to do so "on the day you cross over the Jordan" (Deut 27:2–3) and the ritualized completion of that command in Josh 8:31–32. The erection of a "large stone" (ʾeben gĕdôlâ) by Joshua at the sanctuary of Yahweh in Shechem (Josh 24:26) is likewise to be associated with these ritualized activities that occur with the entry into the land.

after all of these acts that Joshua commands the priests carrying the ark to come out of the water (4:15–18).[74]

The second account of the stone memorial is presented in 4:19–24, i.e., immediately following the notice that the priests had finally exited the river. The similarity of this segment to that in 4:1–8 is confirmed by the observation that this section could be read after 4:8 without any signs of a gap or other literary problems.[75] Significantly, the narrative has separated the account of the erection of the monument to frame the movement of the priests and the ark. For the first time, the precise moment of the crossing and location of the encampment are noted: it was on the tenth day of the first month that the people came up out of the Jordan and encamped at Gilgal (4:19).[76] It was there that the memorial was erected (v. 20) and interpreted, but not in the same way as before. Whereas in 4:7 the stones symbolized that the waters of the Jordan had been "cut off" (*nikrĕtû*), here they stand for the fact that "Israel crossed over this Jordan on dry ground" (*bayyabbāšâ ʿābar yiśrāʾēl ʾet-hayyardēn hazzeh*, v. 22).[77] Now this reference to crossing over on "dry ground" provides an explanation synonymous with that given in 4:7 and, in part, elucidates the reason for the placement of stones in the middle of the river in 4:9: one memorial of stones symbolized the manner in which Yahweh had led his people out of Egypt and into Canaan.[78]

---

74 The fact that Joshua erects a platform for the priests carrying the ark *while* those actors are already standing in the river (4:9) suggests that the narrative should be understood as a ritual drama rather than as a description of any actual events. Also of note is the reference in 4:14 that "Yahweh magnified Joshua (*giddal yhwh ʾet-yĕhôšûaʿ*) in the eyes of all Israel on that day, and they revered him (*wayyirʾû ʾōtô*) as long as he lived, as they had Moses." This notes the fulfillment of the promises in 3:7 and in 1:5. This sense of reverence forms an essential part of the narrative in Josh 24:14, where the people are ordered to "revere/fear Yahweh" (*yĕrʾû ʾet-yhwh*).

75 Boling, *Joshua*, p. 185.

76 According to the pre-exilic calendar, the first month would be Abib; according to the exilic calendar, it would be Nisan. The cultic calendar of Deuteronomy (16:1–17:1) locates the celebration of the passover in Abib (16:1; see also Exod 13:4; 23:15). The location of Gilgal remains debated.

77 Note here the similarity in the forms by which the questions are asked in 4:6 (see above, n. 71) and 4:21: *ʾăšer yišʾālûn bĕnêkem māḥār ʾet-ʾăbôtām lēʾmōr māh hāʾăbānîm hāʾēlleh*; compare Deut 6:20.

78 The references to crossing over on "dry ground" are clear reflexes of the tradition contained in Exod 14:16, 22, 29; 15:19; and Neh 9:11.

This association of the "drying up" of the waters of the Jordan with those of the "Reed Sea" (*yam-sûp*, 4:23; cf. 2:10; 24:6)[79] provides a key literary connector between Rahab's confession of the *magnalia dei* (2:10–11)[80] and the reactions of the kings of the Amorites and the Canaanites in the following section (5:1–2), which serves as a brief transition back into "historical time." This social ritual does not return completely to "reality," but remains located in the temporal realm of the sacred. According to Rahab, the heart of the people had melted (*wayyimmas lĕbābēnû*, 2:11) when they heard how Yahweh had dried up the water of the "Reed Sea" and how he had defeated Sihon and Og in the region of the Transjordan. Similarly, when the Amorite and Canaanite kings heard that Yahweh had dried up the waters of the Jordan, "their hearts melted" (*wayyimmas lĕbābām*, 5:1). None of the people of the land could stand before the power of the Israelites,[81] a confirmation of the promise given in the opening statement of Yahweh (1:5a). The meaning of the memorial, however, is not limited to the future generations of Israel, but is intended as a demonstration of the might and power of Yahweh: "in order that all the peoples of the land (*kol-ʿammê hāʾāreṣ*) might know the power of the hand of Yahweh (4:24)."[82]

Now the stone memorials had been erected, the river crossed, and complete victory guaranteed. But before the actual physical seizure of the land could be recounted, the ritual possession of the territory had to be

---

[79] The Hiphil form of the root *ybš* occurs in only four places in Joshua (2:10; 4:23 [2x]; 5:1). Note that the reference to the events at the "Reed Sea" in Deut 11:4 does not reflect this tradition of the drying up of the waters or the passage through them on dry land. The deuteronomistic writer is either drawing upon other traditions here or creating a new one to serve as a bridge for the narrative reconstructions which follow.

[80] On the ideological significance of the confession of Rahab, see Polzin, *Moses and the Deuteronomist*, pp. 85–91.

[81] Compare the statement by Rahab with the report concerning the courage of the kings: "no longer does any man have courage because of you" (*wĕlōʾ-qōmâ ʿôd rûaḥ bĕʾîš mippĕnêkem*, 2:11) and "no longer did they have courage before the Israelites" (*wĕlōʾ-hāyâ bām ʿôd rûaḥ mippĕnê bĕnê-yiśraʾēl*, 5:1). The niphal form of the root *mss* occurs once more in Josh 7:5, this time in reference to the fact that when the Israelites were beaten back at Ai and lost a total of thirty-six soldiers, "the courage of the people melted and became water" (*wayyimmas lĕbab-hāʿām wayhî lĕmāyim*).

[82] The references to *magnalia dei* which appear in the speech by Rahab and are reflected in the notice of the kings of the Amorites and Canaanites are reiterated in the confessional recitation by Joshua in 24:2–13, within which the entire events of the "conquest" are summarized for the Cisjordan region by the reference to the defeat of the "lords of Jericho" (*baʿălê-yĕrîḥô*, v. 11).

concluded. In a purely paratactic manner typical of the deuteronomistic history, the account of the command from Yahweh to "circumcise the Israelites a second time" (*šûb mōl ʾet-bĕnê-yiśᵊrāʾēl šēnît*, 5:2)[83] is connected to the ritual actions by the vague temporal notice "at that time" (*bāᶜēt hahîʾ*). Despite the obscure origins of the practice of circumcision in Israel,[84] the rite is used here to note the fulfillment of the promise of Yahweh that "all the men of war" (*kōl ʾanšê hammilḥāmâ*, 5:4, 6; cf. Deut 2:14, 16) who had left Egypt would die without seeing the land of Canaan. Since, according to the explanation given in vv. 4–7, the generation that had been born in the wilderness had not been circumcised, the performance of this ritual was necessary.

In the context of the narrative of Joshua, the performance of this rite by Joshua, recounted in v. 8, has a threefold function. It serves as a dual etiology in the story, explaining the "Hill of Foreskins" (*gibᶜat hāᶜărālôt*, v. 3) and the name of the cultic encampment, Gilgal (v. 9).[85] Though the account provides no real etiology for either place, it does provide a further definition of Israel, for it was most explicitly the sons of those warriors who had gone out of Egypt that were circumcised and who now constituted the "nation" (*haggôy*, v. 8) Israel (cf. v. 2). Further, it would be those who belonged to that community who would be given this "land flowing with milk and honey" (v. 6),[86] a fact underlined by the use of the first person plural pronoun, "us," as the recipients of the land promised to their forefathers.

Most important, however, is the third function of this short ritual account: it prepares the people Israel to participate in the celebration of the feast of the Passover on the fourteenth day of the month. It is with the

---

[83] The LXX omits "a second time" and reads *šēb* instead of *šûb*, thus avoiding the sense of redundancy found in the Hebrew text. For differing interpretations of the possible meanings of this section, see Soggin, *Joshua*, p. 69.

[84] See the discussion in R. de Vaux, *Ancient Israel: Its Life and Institutions* (New York: McGraw-Hill, 1965), pp. 46–48. As de Vaux notes (p. 47), this practice took on special significance in Israelite religion, especially with the Priestly account of the covenant of circumcision with Abram in Genesis 17. On the practice of circumcision in the ancient Near East, see P. A. Mantovani, "Circoncisi ed incirconcisi," *Henoch* 10 (1988) 51–68.

[85] According to the text, the name *gilgāl* was given to the site because by the fulfillment of the command to circumcise the people, Yahweh could proclaim: "Today I have rolled away (*gallôtî*) the reproach of Egypt from upon you" (v. 9).

[86] Boling notes that this is the first occurrence of this phrase in Joshua (*Joshua*, pp. 189–90). He does not emphasize, however, that this is the *only* occurrence of the phrase in the deuteronomistic history. The phrase is common in Deuteronomy (6:3; 11:9; 26:9, 15; 27:3; cf. 31:20).

completion of this festival that Israel may be said to have possessed the land ritually. For the narrative presentation, the festival of Passover could be conducted only after the "reproach of Egypt" (*ḥerpat-miṣrayim*, 5:9) had been removed,[87] an effect here accomplished by the circumcision of all the males of the community.[88] There is no development of the specifics of the celebration of the seven-day ritual that was to be conducted in "the place where Yahweh would choose to make his name dwell" (Deut 16:1–8), nor does there seem to be any real division between the festivals of *pesaḥ* or *maṣṣôt*, though the two may have been originally separate (cf. Exod 12:15–20).

The central significance of the brief mention of the Passover celebration is to be found in the final two verses of this section, which provide a transition from the "period" of the wilderness (5:4–7; cf. Deut 1:19–35; 9:12–23), during which the people were fed with "manna" (Deut 8:3, 16; Exod 16:1–36), to the "period" of the consumption of the produce of the land. For the first time since crossing over the Jordan, the people "ate from the produce of the land" (*wayyōʾkĕlû mēʿăbûr hāʾāreṣ*, v. 11) on the day after the Passover celebration. It was this event, then, that ritually ended Israel's wilderness experiences, symbolized by the "manna," which came to an end on the day they ate from the produce of the land of Canaan (v. 12).[89] The sanctification of the people and the ritual entry into the land, led by the announcement of Yahweh and the ark of the covenant, now culminated in the ritual circumcision of all the males, who were then qualified as members of the community to celebrate the Passover meal. With the "reproach of Egypt" having been removed, the people could eat of the produce of the land, enjoying the benefits that

---

[87] The meaning of the "reproach of Egypt" is obscure, but it seems in the present context to refer to the rebellious actions of the people who had left Egypt and who had been condemned by Yahweh to wander in the wilderness and die without seeing the "land flowing with milk and honey."

[88] Notably, the Passover legislation contained in Exod 12:43–48 requires that any slave or resident alien who wishes to celebrate the Passover be circumcised. The section concludes: "No uncircumcised male shall eat it [the Passover]. There will be one law for native born and for the resident alien sojourning in your midst" (*kol-ʿārēl lōʾ-yōʾkal bô tôrâ ʾaḥat yihyeh laʾezrāḥ welaggēr haggār bĕtôkĕkem*, 12:48b–49). One might argue on the basis of this tradition that the requirement of circumcision was binding upon all who would participate in this ritual.

[89] The designation *ʾereṣ kĕnaʿan*, "the land of Canaan," occurs here in Joshua for the first time. Interestingly, it occurs only once in Deuteronomy (32:49), as a designation for the land which Yahweh is about to give to Israel as a possession. The phrase also occurs in Joshua in 14:1; 21:2; 22:9, 10, 11, 32; and 24:3.

were promised by Moses (Deut 6:10–11; 8:7–10).[90] With the initial conquests of the land having been completed (Josh 6:1–8:29) and the covenantal blessings and curses recounted (8:30–35), the prospect of the remainder of the land to be taken lay before them (9:1–12:24).[91]

The cycle of ritual formation of the people concludes with Joshua's rehearsal of the fulfillment of the words of Moses and a reminder of the blessings and curses incumbent upon the people (23:1–16). According to Deut 26:16–19, the acceptance of the covenantal standards involves the proclamation that Yahweh would be the god of Israel and that Israel would become his possession.[92] By way of a farewell speech to Israel, Joshua concludes a portion of the ritual narrative frame of the book by noting that Israel had followed the directives of Yahweh up to that day and that Yahweh had dispossessed the nations before them as he had promised (23:8–9; cf. 1:1–7). Joshua's warnings against mingling with the remaining nations and most explicitly against any intermarriage (vv. 12–14; cf. Deut 7:3) now reconfirm the boundaries constructed about the people to be included in Israel. The distinctions were not to be simply geographical or tribal; allegiance to Yahweh and Yahweh alone would constitute inclusion in the ethnic community to be known as Israel and distinguished from all others. For the deuteronomistic narrative of

---

[90] The following brief episode (5:13–15), the appearance of the "general of the armies of Yahweh" (*śar-ṣĕbāʾ yhwh*, vv. 13, 15), introduces the conquest stories that follow in chapters 7–12 and places them under the direct control of the divine. The conquest stories that follow constitute narrative accounts of social dramas that fall within the realm of myth rather than legend or history and present a liturgy of conquest rather than a recounting of historical events. This account constitutes the creation of a new story that, once it was accepted and internalized by those who participated in its narratives, became the tradition by which Israel understood its possession of the land of Canaan.

[91] The significance of the notices of Israel's failure to take all of the land and the manner in which it affects the possible interpretations of the narrative have been emphasized by Polzin (*Moses and the Deuteronomist*, pp. 126–34). It must be noted, however, that, as a whole, the book of Joshua stresses the powerful fulfillment of the promise of the land to be given to an Israel that would be obedient to the commands of the *tôrâ*. Joshua 13–21 contains the accounts of the allotment of the land to the various tribes. On the problems of dating the traditions contained in these chapters, see F. M. Cross and G. E. Wright, "The Boundary and Province Lists of the Kingdom of Judah," *JBL* 75 (1956) 202–26; and Y. Aharoni, "The Province-List of Judah," *VT* 9 (1959) 225–46.

[92] On this passage, see the treatment by M. Weinfeld, "The Emergence of the Deuteronomic Movement: The Historical Antecedents," in *Das Deuteronomium: Entstehung, Gestalt und Botschaft* (ed. N. Lohfink; BETL 68; Lueven: University Press, 1985), pp. 76–98.

Joshua, breach of covenant was to be equated with serving other gods, an essential concern for Deuteronomy and the deuteronomistic history[93] that has not yet been directly addressed in the ritual accounts of the book.[94]

The concluding chapter of Joshua is devoted to a stylized narrative account of the formation of the people by the fulfillment of the central commands of the deuteronomic corpus that they be officially and consciously dedicated to the worship of Yahweh alone. This story provides the concluding narrative frame that ritualizes and symbolically forms and, at the same time, defines, the parameters of membership in this community. Joshua 24 constitutes a second farewell speech of Joshua that culminates in a covenant-making ceremony at the site of Shechem. Contrary to the suggestions of most modern treatments, Joshua 24 need not be interpreted as a secondary ending or as an addition to the book.[95] Rather, in terms of the need to consolidate the identity of the social units that were envisioned and projected as constituting Israel, the ritually dramatic narrative presented is necessary for the conclusion of the covenant and the possession of the land.

"All the tribes of Israel" (*kol-šibṭê yiśrāʾēl*, v. 1) were assembled at Shechem, the city located between Mts. Ebal and Gerizim which had served earlier as the focus for the reading of the blessings and the curses of the covenant.[96] One element missing from the accounts of the reading of the *tôrâ* in the earlier ritual enactments, however, was the confirmation and acceptance of the covenantal stipulations by the people. It is precisely this process, the public proclamation of the acceptance of the demand to avoid the worship of "other gods" (*ʾĕlōhîm ʾăḥērîm*; see especially Deut 11:27–28), that defines the uniqueness of "Israel" and shapes the structure of that envisioned community. The narrative of Joshua 24 concludes the ceremony begun earlier in the narrative and brings to closure the dramatic ritual recreation of the possession of the land of promise.

---

[93] For the deuteronomistic warnings against the worship of other gods, see the materials gathered by M. Weinfeld, *Deuteronomy and the Deuteronomic School* (Oxford: Clarendon, 1972), pp. 320–21.

[94] The account of the building of an altar by the Transjordanian tribes in Joshua 22 touches upon the problem, but it is resolved when the altar is transformed into a memorial and a covenantal witness that "Yahweh is god" (22:34).

[95] On this point, see the standard commentaries on Joshua. Most agree, following the original analysis of M. Noth (*Überlieferungsgeschichtliche Studien* [3rd ed.; Tübingen: Max Niemeyer, 1967], p. 9), that this chapter is secondary and not an original part of the deuteronomistic work.

[96] See the treatment of Josh 8:30–35 above, pp. 104–6.

This final ritual action concludes the formation of the ethnic group Israel, defined now as the descendants of Abraham whom Yahweh had brought from "beyond the River" (*bĕʿēber hannāhār*, v. 2) and to whom he had shown the land of Canaan. This god had delivered the offspring of Jacob from Egypt, had brought the people to this place, and had given them this land as promised to their ancestors (vv. 2–13).[97] Those people assembled at Shechem, by participating in the events that follow this genealogical and ethnographic elaboration, would become "Israel." To become such, however, it was necessary for them to deliver the proper response to the demand for complete loyalty:

> Now, fear Yahweh and serve him in complete faithfulness (*bĕtāmîm ûbeʾĕmet*). Put away the gods whom your ancestors served beyond the river and in Egypt and serve Yahweh....Choose for yourselves today whom you will serve....I and my household will serve Yahweh" (vv. 14–15).

The *magnalia dei* recited to the people in vv. 2–13 present a challenge and a choice—to become a people dedicated only to Yahweh, i.e., to become Israel and to adopt this "traditional historical credo" as their own. The assent of Joshua and the dedication of his family to this ideal serve as the model for the response of the remainder of the people. The assembled people respond, "Yahweh is our god" (*yhwh ʾĕlōhênû*, vv. 17–18) and pledge to serve this powerful god who had led them out of Egypt and had driven out all the people living in the land from before them. It is precisely this conscious expression of dedication to the central covenantal command of devotion to Yahweh alone that recreates both the people and the boundaries by which they would be defined. But as the traditions of the past presented the "blessings" associated with such devotion to this god, so the warnings contained in the curses delineated the consequences of failing to adhere to the commands of the deity.

To emphasize this point to its fullest, Joshua presents another challenge to the group:[98] because Yawheh is a holy and jealous god who will

---

[97] Van Seters has noted the similarity of this narrative of events with the Yahwistic version of the Pentateuch (*In Search of History*, pp. 336–37). Whether this is sufficient to suggest that Joshua 24 is to be assigned to the Yahwistic writer, however, is a matter which demands more attention.

[98] D. J. McCarthy points out that this statement of Joshua notes that the fulfillment of the command is impossible and that such a choice assures that the group is doomed (*Treaty and Covenant* [2nd ed.; AnBib 21A; Rome: Biblical Institute Press, 1978], p. 236). Exactly such a position is anticipated in Deut 31:16–22 and might be

not forgive their transgressions or sins, they will not be able to serve him.[99] Further, should Israel serve foreign gods (*ʾĕlōhê nēkār*), Yahweh will destroy them (vv. 19–20). In summary form, then, the blessings and curses of 8:33–34 are presented as the warning before the conclusion of the ritual. The people answer the warning with resolution: "we will serve Yahweh" (*ʾet-yhwh naʿăbōd*, v. 21), and agree to stand as witnesses (*ʿēdîm*) that they had so sworn (v. 22). With this confirmation, the invocation to put away any foreign gods was greeted with the reaffirmation by the people that they would follow Yahweh and obey his commands (vv. 23–24).

Thus, Joshua concluded a covenant (*bĕrît*) with the people and wrote down the stipulations and ordinances "in the book of the law of god" (*bĕsēper tôrat ʾĕlōhîm*),[100] an act that immediately connects the ritual with the building of the altar and the recording of the *tôrâ* in 8:30–32. In addition, Joshua erected a "large stone" (*ʾeben gĕdôlâ*) to be a witness against the people "lest you deceive your god" (*pen-tĕkaḥăšûn bēʾlōhêkem*, v. 27). Thus, the stones stand as witnesses to the treaty promises and as a memorial to the consent of the people to follow Yahweh and Yahweh alone. As the stones taken from the Jordan and placed at Gilgal formed a memorial of the mighty deeds performed by Yahweh (4:1–8, 19–24), so this stele would contain the account of the response of the people to their god. The covenantal demands of Deuteronomy and the projections of the formation of a people Israel were now fulfilled. Israel was the possession of Yahweh, the god who had given them this land as their inheritance for faithful service. By virtue of the ritual participation of those who would identify themselves with this group and who would accept the responsibilities of the covenant demands, a people were both defined and created. The social dramas recounted in Joshua form a series of frames that encompass the shorter stories concerning the ways in which the land would be taken and the details of its allotment to the various tribes. But at all times the narrative reiterates that all is dependent upon the faithfulness of the people to the exclusive commands of the covenant. As the fulfillment of the projections of the ideals of Deuteronomy, Joshua forms a type of ethnogonic myth that brings together the whole of those who have chosen to internalize the traditions reformulated by this deuterono-

---

explained by the exilic audience with which the deuteronomistic writer was in conversation.

[99] *lōʾ tûkĕlû laʿăbōd ʾet-yhwh kî-ʾĕlōhîm qĕdōšîm hûʾ ʾēl-qannôʾ hûʾ lōʾ yiśśāʾ lĕpišʿăkem ûlĕḥaṭṭôʾtêkem*, 24:19.
[100] See above, pp. 100–2.

mistic writer. The consequences of the failure to adhere faithfully to these boundaries and guidelines is addressed in the book of Judges, and constitutes the subject matter of the next chapter.

5

JUDGES: FROM UNIFICATION AND IDENTITY TO CIVIL WAR AND COMMUNAL DISSOLUTION

I. Modifying the Perspective: The Recreation of a Context

The ritualized success of the conquest of Canaan by "all Israel," an impression created and maintained in Joshua 1–12, is deemphasized in chapters 13–21, which describe the territorial allotments to the individual tribal units. Passages like Josh 13:2–7, which recounts the "land that remains" to be conquered, or 22:9–34, which describes the near conflict between the Cis- and Transjordanian tribes after the allotment of the land, form the background for the presentation of the dissolution of the community that is developed in Judges. The peaceful resolution of this conflict and the communal ceremony of covenant dedication which concludes the book of Joshua offset such indicators, however, and reconfirm the "all Israel" emphasis that dominates the major portions of those narratives.[1] Despite this emphasis, these "negative" sections of Joshua

---

[1] The redactional history of the book of Joshua remains debated among commentators. M. Noth argued that neither Joshua 13–22 nor chapter 24 belonged to the original redaction of the history (*Überlieferungsgeschichtliche Studien* [3rd ed.; Tübingen: Max Niemeyer, 1967], pp. 8–9). In accord with this, Judg 2:6–3:6, which Noth accepted as the original introduction to Judges, originally followed directly upon the end of Joshua 23. If one follows this reconstruction, then Judg 1:1–2:5 is also

provide a foreshadowing of those events that could threaten Israel's existence if the nation were to fail to fulfill the obligations to which they had agreed and by which their identity in the land was defined. The narrativized rituals of the book of Joshua developed and encoded the communal aspects of the possession of the land and the determinant and liturgically appropriate covenantal identification of the group as the worshippers of one god, in accord with the ethnic ideals of Deuteronomy. The book of Judges depicts the narrative dissolution of that community through a series of vignettes that illustrate the dangers of failing to appropriate and maintain the ethnic boundaries established by Deuteronomy. As the book of Judges begins, there is little to indicate any communal coherence. Instead, the opening section of Judges recounts the attempts of the individual tribes to conquer and control their allotted portions of the land. One feature of the subject matter of Judges is the attempt to address a particular aspect of Israelite history— how Israel and Judah had nearly ceased to exist. The ability of "all Israel" to cooperate and avoid conflict expressed in the narratives of Joshua is paralleled by the inability of major portions of Israel to coexist peacefully with the other tribes as detailed in the stories of Judges.

In order to switch emphases so completely and yet retain a sense of continuity with the materials that have preceded, the deuteronomistic writer utilizes a number of sophisticated literary techniques. The opening chapter forms a literary bridge with the materials found both in Joshua and in the remainder of Judges that allows the writer to modify the con-

---

a secondary addition to the narrative whole. Since the stories of the judges themselves do not begin until Judg 3:7, Judg 1:1–2:5 and 2:6–3:6 are often interpreted as "double introductions" to the book. While this might be a reasonable reconstruction of the compositional process, and I have argued such elsewhere ("Judges 1:1–36: The Deuteronomistic Reintroduction of the Book of Judges," *HTR* 77:1 [1984] 33–54), for the present investigation a more productive approach is to interpret the whole of the narrative as it presently stands in the Hebrew text and to account for its purpose and function in this form. For the various reconstructions of the redactional history of Judges, see R. D. Nelson, *The Double Redaction of the Deuteronomistic History* (JSOTSup 18; Sheffield: JSOT, 1981), pp. 13–28, 42–53; W. Richter, *Die Bearbeitungen des "Retterbuches" in der deuteronomischen Epoche* (BBB 21; Bonn: Hanstein, 1964); W. Beyerlin, "Gattung und Herkunft des Rahmens im Richterbuch," in *Tradition und Situation: Festschrift A. Weiser* (ed. E. Würthwein; Göttingen: Vandenhoeck & Ruprecht, 1963), pp. 1–29; R. G. Boling, *Judges* (AB 6A; New York: Doubleday, 1975), pp. 29–38; and B. Halpern, *The First Historians: The Hebrew Bible and History* (San Francisco: Harper & Row, 1988), pp. 121–43. In contrast to these analyses, B. G. Webb argues for the literary integrity of the book in its present form (*The Book of Judges: An Integrated Reading* [JSOTSup 46; Sheffield: JSOT, 1987]).

cept of a unified conquest and to present the possession of the land from a radically different perspective.[2] Judg 2:11–13 notes that the generation after Joshua had forsaken the exclusive worship of Yahweh and had turned to other gods—a reversal of the situation created by the covenant ceremony at the end of Joshua. Notice is also given to the fact that the Canaanities had not all been driven from the land as prescribed by Deuteronomy (Judg 2:20–23; 3:1–6). The introductory materials in Judges provide the details needed to explain the failure of Israel to fulfill the commands of Moses as recounted in Joshua.

The book begins with a simple disjunctive statement, "After the death of Joshua…," which connects the following account of Israel's encounters with the indigenous inhabitants of the land[3] to the covenant ceremony that concluded the events associated with Joshua (Josh 24:27–31). The notice of Joshua's death is repeated in Judg 2:6–10, thus creating an interpretive frame for the materials narrated in 1:1b–2:5 and introducing a temporal continuity which seems, on the surface, to contradict the materials concerning the conquest.[4] Important to notice in this regard, however, is the way in which the writer has modified the account of

---

[2]   There are numerous parallels between Judg 1:3–36 and Joshua 14–19: Judg 1:4–7 and Josh 10:1–5; Judg 1:8, 21 and Josh 15:63; Judg 1:10–15, 20 and Josh 15:13–19 (cf. 14:6–15); Judg 1:18–19 and Josh 13:2–3; Judg 1:27–28 and Josh 17:11–13; Judg 1:29 and Josh 16:10; Judg 1:30 and Josh 19:10–16; Judg 1:31–32 and Josh 19:24–31; Judg 1:33 and Josh 19:32–39; Judg 1:34–35 and Josh 19:41–48. Though these passages are parallels, they are, at times, contradictory, e. g., Judg 1:18–19 and Josh 13:2–3.

[3]   Recent reconstructions of Israel's history suggest that Israel itself was indigenous to the land. See the arguments by K. Whitelam, "Israel's Traditions of Origin: Reclaiming the Land," *JSOT* 44 (1989), 19–42, and N. P. Lemche, *Early Israel: Anthropological and Historical Studies on the Israelite Society Before the Monarchy* (VTSup 37; Leiden: E. J. Brill, 1985), pp. 427–32.

[4]   Many commentators accept Judges 1 as both older and more historically reliable than the traditions in Joshua. See, e.g., the position of H.-W. Hertzberg, *Die Bücher Josua, Richter, Ruth* (2d ed.; ATD 9; Göttingen: Vandenhoeck & Ruprecht, 1959), p. 147. Against this view are those who adopt the position argued by G. E. Wright ("The Literary and Historical Problem of Joshua 10 and Judges 1," *JNES* 5 [1946] 105–14), which accepts the basic historical accuracy of the Joshua account. A summary and analysis of the major reconstructions of the conquest of Canaan and the ways in which the presentation of Judges 1 is incorporated into those views is given in R. de Vaux, *The Early History of Israel* (Philadelphia: Westminster, 1978), pp. 475–87. An extended critique of the internal rebellion models developed by G. E. Mendenhall and N. K. Gottwald is contained in N. P. Lemche, *Early Israel*, pp. 1–22, 411–35. The attempt to explain the emergence of Israel in Palestine by constructing a social-scientific model is exemplified by R. B. Coote and K. W. Whitelam, *The Emergence of Early Israel in Historical Perspective* (SWBA 5; Sheffield: Almond, 1987).

Joshua's final command to Israel in these two sections. In Josh 24:28, Joshua dismissed the people who had participated in the ceremony at Shechem "each to his inheritance" (*ʾîš lĕnaḥălātô*), a command that presumed the conquest and apportionment of the land. Judg 2:6, which reflects this same tradition, modifies it: "and the Israelites went, each to his own inheritance, to possess the land" (*wayyēlĕkû bĕnê-yiśrāʾēl ʾîš lĕnaḥălātô lāreśet ʾet-hāʾāreṣ*). The temporal placement of the events narrated in 1:1b–2:5 *after* the death of Joshua makes these events contemporaneous with the generations who "did not know Yahweh" (2:10) and who sinned against him, thus provoking his anger and his refusal to drive out the remainder of the inhabitants of the land (2:11–3:6).[5] The old leader, the *ʿebed yhwh*, was dead and would not be replaced by one who would be called "servant of Yahweh" until David emerged as the folk model for kingship.[6] The complete and final defeat of the "inhabitants of the land" would not occur until the successes of this new "servant," David, who would bring stability and direction to the newly formed people. The narratives of Judges suggest that the conquest of the land as ideally projected by Deuteronomy and enacted, at least in part, in Joshua, was never "historically" realized. The explanation of this "non-event" required a new ideological construct, and such is a function of the deuteronomistic version of Judges.[7]

As presented, Judg 1:1–36 provides the historical background for the condemnation of Israel by the messenger of Yahweh in 2:1–5. The latter presents a speech censuring Israel for having broken the covenant, an act which results in Yahweh's vow not to drive out the remaining nations (2:3). That such nations did indeed remain contrasts directly with the

---

[5] Though this overlapping narrative method creates chronological problems for the reconstruction of a consistent history, it nonetheless establishes a consistent temporal frame for the narrative which follows.

[6] In Judg 15:18 Samson, in a plea to Yahweh, refers to himself as "your servant" (*ʿabdĕkā*), but the title *ʿebed* is not applied to any of the other characters after Joshua in the deuteronomistic history in a direct address of Yahweh until its designation of David as such. The role of David as a folk model is not to be restricted simply to the status and understanding of the king. Rather, reflections of this model pervade the deuteronomistic history. On the influence of the model on the formation of the biblical narratives, see W. Brueggeman's *David's Truth in Israel's Imagination and Memory* (Philadelphia: Fortress, 1985).

[7] That the "conquest" might be termed a "non-event" in no way detracts from the importance such a concept might have within the belief system of a particular community, either as a future expectation or as an assertion about the past. On the application of this term, see J. Gager, *Kingdom and Community: The Social World of Early Christianity* (Englewood Cliffs, NJ: Prentice-Hall, 1975), pp. 43–49.

conquest traditions in Joshua 2–12 and expands upon those materials recounted in the allotment of the land in Joshua 13–21. It is also clear that this introduction does not attempt to present a complete picture of the conquest, for there is no reference to some of the tribes and their activities.[8] What is not certain, however, is whether the geographical details in the account of the allotment of the land west of the Jordan are to be understood as accomplished events or as ideals to be achieved in the future.[9] If, indeed, the latter is the case, then we have in Judg 1:1–36 an account that runs parallel to the version of the conquest in Joshua and presents another view of those narrated materials.

Whereas in Joshua the narrator concentrated on the ritualization of the taking of the land by the performance of certain divinely and/or prophetically prescribed actions, the concerns of the author in Judges turn to the details that led to the failure to realize the ideals presented in Deuteronomy. If the allotment of the land is understood as an ideal, then the final conquest of this ideal area would lie in the future, after the death of Joshua. Such a temporal emphasis is consonant with one of the major themes of Judges, the quest for legitimate leadership.[10] The need for such leadership provides an interpretive frame for the accounts of the judges, for twice in Judges Israel implores Yahweh for a leader (Judg 1:1b; 20:18). As with the completion of the conquest, consistent leadership and national unity would be ideals that would not be attained again until the accounts of the time of David.

---

[8] There is no mention of Reuben, Gad, or Issachar in this section, despite the fact that the account of the tribal allotments includes the apportionment of the land to these tribes (Josh 13:15–23, 24–28; 19:17–23). The failure to mention Reuben and Gad could be related to the fact that their holdings were in the Transjordan. No explanation, other than a lack of specific traditions regarding the tribe's settlement in the land, is apparent for Issachar.

[9] This point has been emphasized by R. Polzin (*Moses and the Deuteronomist* [New York: Seabury, 1980], pp. 127–31). The transition for this change in Joshua is provided in 13:1–6, which notes the land that remained to be conquered and which stands in contrast to the closing statement of this segment in 21:43–45. Between these two statements occur numerous references detailing land not yet possessed by Israel (Josh 14:12; 15:63; 16:10; 17:11–13, 14–18; 18:3–7, 8; 19:47).

[10] R. G. Boling emphasizes that the traditions in Judges are not clearly pro- or antimonarchical and that they must be understood as "essentially premonarchical" (*Judges*, p. 35). It should be noted that within the context of the deuteronomistic history as a whole, these stories illustrate the need for centralized leadership and provide part of the background for the rise of the monarchy. As such, they convey a decidedly promonarchical tone.

This account of the conquest, focusing as it does on the failures of Israel, constitutes a reinterpretation of materials selected from Joshua 13–21.[11] Likewise, these alterations of the basic data imply an intentional shift in the historical representation of the events and the possibility of the polemical intentions of the author.[12] The propagandistic aspects of the section may be detected throughout the introduction, which may be divided into three parts:[13] (1) 1:1–21: the southern tribes of Judah and Simeon; (2) 1:22–36: the northern tribes; and (3) 2:1–5: the messenger at Bokim. This abbreviated exposition of the conquest, which focuses upon the major failures attributed to the northern tribes (1:27–35), serves as the explanation for the troubled history of the northern tribes during the period being recounted and, by extension, as an introduction to the failures of the northern kingdom of Israel. Conversely, the emphasis placed upon the successes of Judah reveals a "patent Judean tendentiousness" on the part of the author[14] and contrasts the achievements of Judah with the failures of Israel.

The theme of Judahite primacy forms a framework for Judges in its final form, since it is the tribe of Judah that is twice divinely specified as the one to lead the tribal groups in battle. In both 1:1b and 20:18, query is made of Yahweh.[15] In each the question is the same: who would lead the assembled tribes in battle. In both instances, Yahweh answers that such

---

[11] A. G. Auld is correct in asserting that Judg 1:1–36 was derived, in part, from traditions contained in Joshua 13–21 ("Judges 1 and History: A Reconsideration," *VT* 25 [1974] 284). There is no compelling reason to postulate the existence of a common source from which both accounts were derived, as has been argued by E. O'Doherty, "The Literary Problem of Judges, 1,1–3,6," *CBQ* 18 (1956) 2, n. 8. J. Van Seters suggests that Judg 1:1–2:5, along with the accounts of the allotting of the land in Joshua 14–17, 18–19, is the work of the Priestly writer and, as such, comprises a late and secondary expansion of the deuteronomistic history; *In Search of History: Historiography in the Ancient World and the Origins of Biblical History* (New Haven: Yale University Press, 1983), pp. 335–42.

[12] On the general issue of the polemical tone of sections of Judges, see Y. Amit, "Hidden Polemic in the Conquest of Dan: Judges xvii–xviii," *VT* 40 (1990) 4–20.

[13] This division has been suggested by Hertzberg, *Die Bücher Josua, Richter, Ruth*, p. 147.

[14] M. Weinfeld, "The Period of the Conquest and of the Judges as Seen by Earlier and Later Sources," *VT* 17 (1967) 94–95, n. 1. Excepting the account of Othniel (Judg 3:7–11), which is generally accepted as a paradigmatic example of a judge (cf. Richter, *Bearbeitungen*, pp. 90–91), the tribe of Judah plays no part in any of the major narratives of Judges, a situation paralleled in the conquest stories of Joshua 1–12.

[15] In Judg 1:1–2, the gathering of Israel to inquire of Yahweh (*wayyišʾălû bĕnê yiśrāʾēl*, 1:1) assumes that the tribes have reconvened at a sanctuary sometime after having been dismissed by Joshua at Shechem (Josh 24:28).

leadership should belong to Judah. Not to be overlooked in the context of this inclusio signifying the supremacy of Judah is the radical shift in the enemy against whom battle was to be waged: in the first instance, it was the Canaanite, the inhabitant of the land, who was to be dispossessed and destroyed. In the second, it has become one of the Israelite tribes themselves, Benjamin, for its failure to hand over those who had participated in the outrage at Gibeah.[16] The consistency of the selection of Judah as leader is paralleled by the consistent demise of the unity of the groups displayed throughout the narratives of Judges.

The failure of the tribes to remain a unified group (i.e., "all Israel") is revealed in the following verses, for only the tribe of Simeon followed the lead of Judah (1:3–20); the remaining tribes attempted to conquer their territory independently of Judah (1:21–36) and, predictably enough, failed. The "Judean tendentiousness" of the deuteronomistic writer is clearly displayed by the differing manner of presentation in the stories that follow.[17] This contrasting style is apparent in the treatment of the traditions connected with Jerusalem in Judg 1:8 and 1:21. According to the former, Judah captured and burned the city of Jerusalem, a site located at one of the borders of Judah and identified in Josh 15:8 as Jebusite.[18] Josh 18:28 uses this same designation for Jerusalem as one of the cities of the tribe of Benjamin (also 18:16). Though Judg 1:8 places Jerusalem under the control of Judah, 1:21 states that "the Benjaminites did not drive out the Jebusites, the inhabitants of Jerusalem; so the Jebusite has dwelt with the Benjaminites in Jerusalem until this day." This statement is a clear adaptation of Josh 15:63, which states: "The

---

[16] On this incident, see the discussion below. There can be little doubt that the anti-Benjaminite theme that occurs in the account of the Gibeah story in Judges 18–21 carries an anti-Saulide edge. For a discussion of the antimonarchical tendencies of the book of Judges, see T. Veijola, *Das Königtum in der Beurteilung der deuteronomistischen Historiographie: Eine redaktiongeschichtliche Untersuchung* (Annales academiae scientiarum Fennicae, 198; Helsinki: Soumalainen Tiedeakatemia, 1977), pp. 100–14.

[17] For a detailed analysis of Judg 1:2–36, see my treatment in "Judges 1:1–36," pp. 46–53, and the literature cited there.

[18] Further Hebrew traditions, such as those contained in 2 Sam 5:6–9 and Judg 19:11–12, maintain that Jerusalem was not conquered until the time of David and that it did not belong to Judah during the period covered by the narratives of Judges (cf. de Vaux, *Early History*, p. 541). Boling attempts to resolve the historical problems by reconstructing the following events (*Judges*, p. 56): Judah was able to sack the unfortified southwest hill of Jerusalem, but the Benjaminites did not meet with the same degree of success. Thus, Jerusalem remained unconquered until the time of David. Interestingly, the traditions regarding the defeat of Adoni-Zedek (Josh 10:1, 3, 5, 23; cf. 12:10) say nothing about the defeat of the city.

Judahites were not able to dispossess the Jebusites, the inhabitants of Jerusalem; so the Jebusite has dwelt with the Judahites in Jerusalem until this day." By making only two changes, the redactor has rewritten the tradition contained in Josh 15:63: *běnê yěhûdâ* is replaced in Judg 1:21 by *běnê binyāmîn* in both clauses, and the verb clause in Josh 15:63a, *lōʾ-yākělû...lěhôrîšām* ("they were not able to dispossess them"), is changed in Judg 1:21a simply to *lōʾ hôrîšû* ("they did not dispossess"). The failure of Judah in Josh 15:63 has been transferred to the tribe of Benjamin in Judg 1:21. The illusion of success for Judah separates it from the rebuke delivered in 2:2, for the inability of Judah to drive out the Jebusites is transformed into the unwillingness of the Benjaminites to do so.[19] The ideological implications of the account are clear: the tribe selected by Yahweh successfully defeats the city that will belong to Yahweh.

The preeminence of Judah is developed further with the account of the victory of Othniel over the city of Debir (Kiriath-seper) in Judg 1:11–15 (cf. Josh 15:15–19). That the first deliverer of Israel would be associated with Judah is consonant with the introductory verses of this prologue.[20] In temporal terms, the repetition of the events purported to have taken place during the period of the allotment of the land in the context of the taking of the land collapses the distinctions between the two "periods." In ideological terms, the account of the destruction of Hormah (Zepath) focuses further attention on Judah, for the text notes explicitly that this city was placed to the ban (*ḥērem*) by Judah and Simeon (1:17).[21] Though this practice, required in Deut 7:2 and 20:16–18, was common to the narratives of conquest in Joshua,[22] it is noted only one other time in Judges (21:11), and there it applies to the Israelite city of Jabesh-Gilead. Only Judah of all the tribes fulfills the commands of Deuteronomy *vis-à-vis* the cities of the land in this retelling of the account of the conquest.

---

[19] Weinfeld, "The Period of the Conquest," p. 94. This same redactional change occurs with reference to Manasseh in Judg 1:27 (Josh 17:12).

[20] While it is often asserted that the name Othniel is a secondary insertion into the paradigmatic account of the first judge presented in 3:7–11 (W. Richter, *Bearbeitungen*, pp. 56–57, 136–37; see also Noth, *Überlieferungsgeschichtliche Studien*, p. 51, n. 1), it remains significant that the identification of the model for judgeship would be selected from the tribe of Judah.

[21] Num 21:1–3 contains the JE account of the destruction of Arad, which was put to the ban and renamed Hormah. The role of Simeon is unclear throughout Judg 1:3–20. While only in 1:3 and 1:17 is it noted explicitly that Simeon is an active party in the events, the plural verbs in 1:4–5 could be taken as indicators that Simeon was an active, if secondary, partner.

[22] Cf. Josh 6:21; 8:26; 10:1, 28, 35, 37; etc.

The pro-Judah emphasis of the author is continued in the concluding verses of this first section, which note that Judah successfully captured Gaza, Ashkelon, and Ekron, along with their territories (1:18).[23] Such overwhelming success is explained, and partially qualified, in the following verse, which notes that "Yahweh was with Judah" (1:19) as he had been with Joshua (cf. Josh 1:5, 9; 3:7; etc.). But the extent of the conquests of Judah was limited to the hill country: 1:19b notes that Judah "was not able[24] to dispossess the inhabitants of the plain, since they had iron chariots."

In contrast to this, and serving to provide a transition to the "negative conquest" account recorded in the traditions associated with the northern tribes (1:22–36), is the notice of the failure of Benjamin to drive out the Jebusites from the city of Jerusalem (1:21). As noted earlier, Benjamin simply failed to perform the required destruction of the indigenous population, and the deuteronomistic writer provided no explanation for that failure. The geographical location of Benjamin, i. e., "between the people of Judah and the people of Joseph" (Josh 18:11), supplies the literary link for the connection of the traditions regarding this representation of the conquest of the land. With this transition made, the conquest of Bethel by the house of Joseph is described. The account of the conquest of Bethel plays an important role in the present account of Judges, for it reappears in Judg 20:18 as a place of oracular inquiry and sacrifice by Israel. The anti-Bethel theme that develops at a later point in the deuteronomistic narrative (cf. 1 Kgs 12:28–33; 13; 2 Kgs 23:15) is absent in this account. Notably, the success of Joseph, as with Judah, is credited to the fact that "Yahweh was with them" (1:22b). But the successful conquest of Bethel is immediately offset by the accounts of the failure of the other northern tribes. Manasseh leads the account, for it "did not" drive out[25] the Canaanites living in Beth-shan, Taanach, Dor,

---

23 Both Josh 13:2–3 and Judg 3:3 note that the Philistine cities were not conquered at this time. Additionally LXX^{AB}, which adds Ashdod to this list, makes this a negative statement (cf. 1:19b). Since, however, Josh 15:45–47 allots Ekron, Ashdod, and Gaza, along with their towns and villages, to Judah, the present text of the MT should be retained. Whether these cities ever belonged to Judah remains open to question (de Vaux, *Early History*, p. 543).

24 The *lōʾ lĕhôrîš* of 19b is difficult. Read instead *lōʾ yākōl lĕhôrîš* with the versions. In either case, the explanation that follows in the text makes it clear that the failure of Judah was beyond its control.

25 The deuteronomistic writer has modified the account to make the failure one for which Manasseh may be held accountable. Judg 1:27 reads *lōʾ-hôrîš* in place of the *wĕlōʾ yākĕlû ... lĕhôrîš* of the parallel text in Josh 17:12.

Yibleam, or Megiddo, though Manasseh did subject them to "forced labor."[26] Ephraim, likewise, failed to dispossess the Canaanites from Gezer (1:29), as did Zebulun (1:30), Asher (1:31–32), Naphtali (1:33), and Dan (1:34–35).[27]

The final failure noted is that attributed to the tribe of Dan (1:34–35), a tribe that, like Judah (cf. 1:19), was unable to extend its holdings into the plain. Dan was restricted to the hill country by pressure exerted by the Amorites, who, like the other inhabitants of the land in 1:27–35, were eventually subjected to the *corvée*. In this case, the deuteronomistic author has divided his materials relating to the settlement of the tribe of Dan, presenting only the notice of Dan's failure in Judg 1:34–35. According to the allotment account in Josh 19:47–48, Dan eventually lost this territory and migrated to Leshem, which it conquered and renamed Dan. In Judges, however, this episode has been greatly expanded and recorded in chap. 18 as part of the account of the shrine of Micah (Judges 17).[28] By dividing the account in this way and by concluding this section with the notice that the house of Joseph did succeed in placing the Amorites under the *corvée* (1:35b), the writer has formed an inclusio with 1:22 that provides a clear indictment of the northern tribes. The house of Joseph did not possess the lands allotted them in the proper manner, as had Judah. Rather, they allowed Canaanite and Amorite to live among them, a situation providing for the condemnations and troubles to follow.

II. Reaction and Redress: The Establishment of a Pattern (2:1–3:11)

Lost at the very beginning of this new episode in the development of the identity of "Israel" is the ideal of unity. "Israel" would be defined by the way in which it fulfilled the Mosaic instructions in Deuteronomy for

---

[26] The *mas* (Judg 1:28, 30, 33, 35) was a specific form of compulsory labor to which certain conquered peoples were to be subjected (Deut 20:11). It did not, however, apply to the inhabitants of Canaan. On the development of this practice, see A. F. Rainey, "Compulsory Labour Gangs in Ancient Israel," *IEJ* 20 (1970) 191–202.

[27] In the allotment lists of Joshua 18–19, there is no mention of the failures of Zebulun, Asher, or Naphtali to drive out the inhabitants of the land. It seems clear, therefore, that the explicit references to such failures in the present context are to be attributed to the hand of the author of these materials.

[28] The account of the migration of Dan and its significance to the story will be treated in the next chapter.

the taking of the land and how closely it adhered to the covenantal obligations agreed upon at the conclusion of the ideal of conquest and allotment under Joshua. From the renewed perspective of the deuteronomistic development of the "actuality" of the conquest, "Israel" is now divided into individual tribal units with no apparent individual leadership. Masquerading on one level as a summary of Joshua 14–19, Judg 1:1–36 is, on closer inspection, a representation and recreation of the complete conquest of the land that is projected into the future as an ideal yet to be realized. The implications of the failures of "Israel" to fulfill the commands concerning the conquest of the land follow immediately upon the completion of the presentation of the tribal actions. In 2:1–5, a new figure and a pronouncement establish a new model by which the stories that will shape the community and prepare it for a different kind of leadership are presented. Without any introductory remarks, the narrator presents the *maləak yhwh*, "the messenger of Yahweh," to provide the indictment of Israel on behalf of Yahweh himself.[29]

Central to understanding the role and function of this passage is the recognition of the blurring of distinctions that occurs in this section *vis-à-vis* the manner in which the *maləak yhwh* appears and delivers the address.[30] This *maləak* "came up from Gilgal to Bokim," i. e., from the site of the tribal base camp in Joshua to the otherwise unknown place identified here only as "the weepers" (*habbōkîm*), and there delivered his message to "all the people of Israel" (*kol-běnê yiśrāəel*, 2:4). While it is common to identify the site of these events with Bethel,[31] the text itself makes no explicit identification. Instead, the reference to the site by this name anticipates the reactions of the people addressed and the etiology presented in vv. 4–5. In this way, the reference to Bokim provides a double inclusio—2:1–5 is both framed by and forms part of a frame with the

---

[29] The *maləak yhwh* does not occur in either Deuteronomy or Joshua. In Judges, the figure appears in three major narratives. The *maləak yhwh* functions as an intermediator who announces divine decisions affecting the human realm in 2:1–4; 6:11–12, 20–22; and 13:13–21. Within the contexts of the latter two, he is also referred to as "the messenger of god" (*maləak hāəělōhîm*, 6:20; 13:3, 6, 9).

[30] C. Westermann suggests that this figure serves as a transition form that differs from the figure of the prophet in that the *maləak yhwh* exists only for the duration of the delivery of the message (*Basic Forms of Prophetic Speech* (tr. by H. C. White; Philadelphia: Westminster, 1967], pp. 99–100).

[31] LXX[AB] adds "to the place of weeping and to Bethel and to the house of Israel." This identity is based, it would seem, on the identification of Bokim with the "oak of weeping" (*əallôn bākût*) associated with Bethel (Gen 35:8) and with the reference to Bethel as the location of the ark and of the assembly of "all Israel" in Judg 20:26–27.

later references to the "weeping" of Israel contained in Judg 20:23, 26 and 21:2.

With no introductory remarks, the *mal'āk* proclaims the actions of Yahweh in delivering Israel from Egypt (cf. Josh 24:17; Judg 6:8) and in bringing them to the land promised to their ancestors and concludes with a reference to Yahweh's promise never to break his treaty (*lō'-'āpēr běrîtî 'ittěkem lě'ôlām*, 2:1). The continuation of the address makes explicit the obligations that such divine assistance required: Israel was forbidden to make any treaty with the inhabitants of this land and was to tear down its altars.[32] The background for the indictment had been provided in the charter for the formation of the people in Deut 7:1–6 (see also Exod 34:10–16).[33] As indicated by the failure to eliminate the inhabitants of the land in 1:22–36, Israel has clearly failed to fulfill these commands. As a result, Yahweh (still via his *mal'āk*) proclaimed that he would not drive out the people from before Israel;[34] rather, they and their gods would remain as traps for Israel.

Because of its own failures, not Yahweh's, Israel would now face the task of community formation within the context of various competing cultural and religious influences. These will provide the possibilities for new ways of creating a distinctively Israelite ethnicity.[35] The reactions of "all Israel" reflect the immediate recognition of the shift in the model of the group. Their weeping and naming of the place for such indicates both an admission of their failure and an acceptance of the pronouncement. The offering of sacrifices provides a liturgical and a ritualized conclusion to this new chapter in the explanation and creation of the boundaries that would identify "Israel."

The modification of the old ideal offers the opportunity for the deuteronomistic writer to create a new paradigm that will serve as an intermediate step in the process of defining Israel.[36] This new model is

---

[32] *wĕ'attem lō'-tikrĕtû běrît lĕyôšĕbê hā'āreṣ hazz'ōt mizbĕḥôtêhem tittōṣûn*, 2:2.

[33] See above, chap. 3, pp. 63–67.

[34] This reaction, as noted by G. F. Moore (*Judges* [Edinburgh: T. & T. Clark, 1895], p. 59), reflects the statement in Josh 23:13 (see also Num 33:55).

[35] On the concept of the "invention" of culture and the ways in which it might be applied to the present narrative, see R. Wagner, *The Invention of Culture* (rev. ed.; Chicago: University of Chicago Press, 1981), pp. 71–132.

[36] It is important to stress that the formation of any group identity, regardless of the time frame or the manner by which it is undertaken, is, in cultural and historical terms, a process. Additionally, it is a process that is always in a state of reapplication and redefinition. The degree of flexibility of the symbol systems involved in the definition of the ethnic identity of a group is a significant factor in the ability of ethnic

provided in 2:6–3:11 with the description of the role and function of the figure of the "judge," an office that is the clear invention of the deuter-onomistic writer.[37] In addition to this office, the writer has also created a distinctive framework which has been employed throughout the central sections of the narrative and which invents a "period of the judges."[38] By creating and developing a form of leadership that by its very nature proved to be unsuccessful, the deuteronomistic writer presents a mythic past that is both credible and, once the history as a whole has been adopted by the community, authoritative.[39] As such, these stories could be incorporated as parts of the constituent elements from which the national monarchic state under David was built.[40]

---

communities to survive over periods of time (A. P. Royce, *Ethnic Identity: Strategies of Diversity* [Indianapolis/Bloomington: Indiana University Press, 1982], p. 7).

37 It is commonly maintained that the title "judge," which originally referred to an administrative position within the premonarchic tribal confederation, was "borrowed" from an earlier list, most often referred to as the "minor" judges, and was reapplied to the "deliverers," or "major" judges, with whom the larger narrative materials in the book are concerned. The figure of Jephthah, who bridged both functions, provided the connector for the writer. For the basic formulation of this idea, see Noth, *Überlieferungsgeschichtliche Studien*, pp. 47–50; "Das Amt des 'Richters Israels,'" *Festschrift Alfred Bertholet* (ed. W. Baumgartner; Tübingen: Mohr and Siebeck, 1950), pp. 404–17. For a differing interpretation of the manner in which these figures are treated, see my essay, "The 'Minor Judges': Some Literary and Historical Considerations," *CBQ* 44 (1982) 185–201.

38 For an analysis of the various parts of the framework which connect these materials, see W. Beyerlin, "Gattung und Herkunft des Rahmens im Richterbuch," *Tradition und Situation: Festschrift A. Weiser* (ed. E. Würthwein; Göttingen: Vandenhoeck & Ruprecht, 1963), pp. 1–2, and Halpern, *The First Historians*, pp. 121–24. As S. M. Warner has noted, once this framework is removed, "there exists no explicit evidence to establish either the order of the individual stories or the relationship of the period as a whole to the other phases of Israel's history" ("The Dating of the Period of the Judges," *VT* 28 [1978] 457). This is not to suggest that there was not a period of premonarchic tribal unification of some type during which there might have been a social office known as "judge." Rather, it is to assert that the "period" of such individual tribal "deliverers" that now constitutes a major portion of the book of Judges is the result of the deuteronomistic literary adaptation of the traditions which may have been employed.

39 On the classification of myth as a type of story that carries both credibility and authority for a particular social group and the ways in which such are essential for the formation of societal models, see B. Lincoln, *Discourse and the Construction of Society: Comparative Studies of Myth, Ritual, and Classification* (New York/Oxford: Oxford University Press, 1989), pp. 24–26.

40 As A. D. Smith argues, myth, history, and memory are necessary elements of the constitution and concept of nation (*The Ethnic Origins of Nations* [Oxford: Basil Blackwell, 1986], p. 2).

Coincident with the presentation of the new model of leadership, the author introduces a new generation in need of such. This is the function of Judg 2:6–10, which returns to the time when Joshua dismissed the people in Josh 24:28, and provides a "panoramic temporal overview"[41] of the period created and addressed by the book. The author distinguishes between those people who had belonged to the last generation, i.e., the contemporaries of Joshua, and those who would constitute the coming generations. The generation contemporaneous with Joshua "served Yahweh" so long as Joshua lived (2:7). Such faithfulness extended through the days of the "elders" who had seen "all of Yahweh's great work which he had done for Israel" (*kol-maʿăśēh yhwh haggādôl ʾăšer ʿāśâ lĕyiśrāʾēl*, 2:7; cf. Deut 11:7). This assertion both reiterates and reinforces Josh 24:31, stressing the faithfulness of the group that had entered the land.[42]

This new generation "knew neither Yahweh nor the work he had done for Israel" (2:10b), a contrast that is addressed and developed in 2:11–23, the section which defines and begins the narrative pattern for the remainder of the book. With no covenantal connections to Yahweh[43] and no knowledge of the ways in which Yahweh had provided for Israel, i. e., no direct knowledge of the *magnalia dei* referred to in 2:2, the generation was without the properly constructed boundaries by which it might differentiate itself from the populations and peoples within its midst. As a result, "the Israelites did what was evil in the sight of Yahweh"[44] (2:11a), rejecting the exclusive worship of their god and

---

[41] Polzin, *Moses and the Deuteronomist*, p. 151.

[42] Essential to understanding the invention of ethnicity through the process of narrative creation and representation of the past is the recognition of the ability of the author to recreate and reshape his own characters. While one would most certainly be correct in pointing to the numerous failures of the generation of Joshua, e. g., those enumerated in Judg 1:22–36, this is not the emphasis placed upon them by the final writer of these materials. Additionally, one might argue that the function of the narrative is not so much to exonerate the generation that is gone, but rather to differentiate and define the nature of the generation that would prove to be unfaithful to Yahweh.

[43] Such is directly implied by the use of the verb *yādaʿ*, the covenantal implications of which are well documented (cf. H. B. Huffmon, "The Treaty Background of Hebrew *Yādaʿ*," *BASOR* 184 [1966] 31–37).

[44] This is the introductory section of the frame that is used to provide the reason for the oppression and need for a deliverer (cf. 3:7; 3:12; 4:1; 6:1; 10:6; 13:1). In its present literary form, it exemplifies the perspective of the deuteronomistic writer, for it anticipates the manner by which judgment will be levied on the kings of Israel and Judah later in the deuteronomistic work. The expression "PN did what was

serving the Baals and Ashtaroth (2:13). In short, they became like the nations rather than separate from those other groups. Their identity as a people was in jeopardy.

The integrative dangers of this situation are characterized in a veritable explosion of standard deuteronomistic terms and phrases.[45] They abandoned the "god of their fathers, the one leading them from the land of Egypt" (2:12; cf. 2:1), and turned instead to these "other gods" (ʾĕlōhîm ʾăḥērîm). The result of such actions, as one would anticipate, given the warnings associated with the deuteronomistic ideal of covenant,[46] was the anger of the deity and the punishment of the people. The failure of the people resulted in Yahweh's withdrawal of his help. Now they were "no longer able to prevail over their enemies,"[47] for Yahweh had planned "evil" against them (2:15; cf. Josh 24:20) and had allowed them to be oppressed by those whom they had failed to dispossess.

At the same time, however, Yahweh would raise up a "judge," a šōpēṭ,[48] who, in turn, "would deliver them from their oppressors" (wayyôšîʿûm miyyad šōsêhem, v. 16). This establishes the pattern of apostasy, oppression, and deliverance that is repeated until the stories concerning Jephthah, who is only partially successful in his attempts to deliver Israel. Israel's response to the deliverance is not to repent; rather, according to the structure of the framework, the nation did not even obey its judges (2:17) and continued in its apostate ways. Yahweh's

---

evil/upright in the sight of Yahweh" occurs some 33 times in 1 and 2 Kings, but does not occur in this form in either Joshua or Samuel. Its only occurrence in Deuteronomy is found in 17:2b. The introduction of this phraseology here to judge the people based upon their adherence to certain patterns of religious practice provides the background for the extension of such judgment to the kings who would follow.

45 The terminology that characterizes the deuteronomistic materials is presented by M. Weinfeld, *Deuteronomy and the Deuteronomic School* (Oxford: Clarendon, 1972), pp. 320–65. Weinfeld also notes some nine concepts which dominate the deuteronomistic narratives: (1) the battle against idolatry; (2) centralization of the cult; (3) the themes of exodus, conquest, and election; (4) the monotheistic ideal; (5) the observance of the law and loyalty to the covenant; (6) the inheritance of the land; (7) retribution and material reward; (8) prophecy and fulfillment; (9) the election of the dynasty of David. All but the last of these are reflected in the narrative of Judges.

46 See, e.g., the curses of Deuteronomy 28 or the warnings of Joshua in the covenant ceremony at Shechem (24:19–20).

47 wĕlōʾ-yākĕlû ʿôd laʿᵃmōd lipnê ʿôyĕbêhem, 2:14. This presents an interesting contrast with the situation in 1:22–36, where, by implication, Israel had the *ability* to defeat the inhabitants of the land, but failed to use it. Now that ability has been taken away.

48 On the meaning of the root špṭ in the Semitic world, see W. Richter, "Zu den 'Rictern Israels,'" ZAW 77 (1965) 58–71.

actions in raising up one to deliver the people stand as a testimony to the deity's compassion at the "moaning" of the people being oppressed (2:18). The necessity for the judge, and the judgment implied by the title of the office itself, is the divine response to the failure of Israel to take the land and destroy all of the indigenous population as ordered. As soon as the judge died, the people would turn away from Yahweh, thus breaking the covenant and again angering him (2:18-20). In response, then, the pronouncement of the messenger in 2:3 was fulfilled: Yahweh would not dispossess the people remaining in the land (2:21).

The reason given for this particular type of punishment is "to test" the people (*lĕmaʿan nassôt bām*) to see whether or not they would observe the "way of Yahweh," as had their ancestors (2:22; cf. 3:4). The generations past are idealized and contrasted with the present generation[49] so as to develop a history to interpret the stories that would follow. The nations that were left (3:3) would test the Israelites who knew no war in Canaan (3:1) and would be the means for them to learn to fight (3:2), a skill that would be necessary for the subjugation of the land. As Deut 7:2-4 made clear, the failure to destroy the population of the land and their places of worship would lead Israel away from Yahweh and into relationships with other gods. Intermarriage, the ultimate form of dissemination for the deuteronomic school, would lead only to their destruction. Intermarriage and apostasy provide the final note of this elaborate introduction to the judges.

To complete this section, the deuteronomistic writer provided a parade example of the model constructed with the account of Othniel (3:7-11).[50] It is clear that the account is directly dependent upon the preceding description of the context in which this new generation of Israel was to reconquer the land. As for the actual content of the story, it is significant that apart from the names of the two characters, i. e., Othniel, the "judge" (3:9, 11), and "Cushan-rishatayim, king of Aram-naharayim" (3:8, 10), the material is practically all formulaic. No more perfect example of the workings of the new way could be presented; the complete and immediate success of the deliverer compassionately raised

---

49 Compare 2:12, 17, 20, 22.

50 The paradigmatic nature of this opening account is illustrated by the observation of J. A. Soggin: "...one firm point is the fact that it is not possible to find any kind of basis in history that we can recognize or that can appear probable" (*Judges* [OTL; Philadelphia: Westminster, 1981], p. 47). W. Richter (*Bearbeitungen*, pp. 23-26, 56-58) argues that this account is secondary to the history and is an addition at the latest stage of its composition.

by Yahweh in response to his direct oppression of the people because of their infidelity to him. The vicissitudes of historical memory, i. e., of conquest and oppression from outside, are narrated as remembered history, an important transformation in the development of a new group identity. Othniel, the only judge who was from the tribe of Judah (Judg 1:13; 3:9; Josh 15:17), is also the only judge who is so completely successful in delivering Israel. But this assurance of success is offset by the recognition that this paradigm is *not* what the upcoming stories are going to look like.[51] It represents potentiality and possibility; it presents an ideal. The implied clash between the institutions of "judgeship" and "kingship"[52] is resolved here until the appropriate point in the narrative formation of the community is reached. Before that, however, the deuteronomistic writer chose to represent the actions of the non-Judahite judges that created the background for one more structural recreation of the people.

III. The Initial Conflicts and their Results:
Ehud to Abimelek

The accounts of the judges that follow Othniel are developed as counter-examples to the paradigm that the deuteronomistic writer has developed for the presentation of the history of this new generation. From the ideal age of the Mosaic period, continued to the conquest in the heroic figure of Joshua, now is developed the background for the mythic expression of a period of decline.[53] Essential to the formation of ethnic identity is the creation of a sense of group solidarity. In this premonarchic period, the bonding is created through the sense of common oppression and subjugation that the people Israel experience at the hands of those "others" that surround them. In terms of the formation of ethnic boundaries, the experience of sharing the memories, real or created, of a common series of historical oppressions at the hands of outsiders provides an intensive differentiating principle by which Israel was able to define itself to itself in opposition to those outside its boundaries. In terms of religious ideology, the concept that such suffering was communally induced likewise bonded the people together via the narrative

---

[51] Polzin, *Moses and the Deuteronomist*, p. 156.
[52] Webb, *The Book of the Judges*, p. 128.
[53] As outlined by Smith (*The Ethnic Origins of Nations*, p. 192), this is the seventh of the eight elements that typically constitute myths of ethnic and national origins.

account of their common past. It is to this end that the deuteronomistic writer has presented the accounts of the judges.[54]

Significant to the present consideration of these stories are those elements occurring within the narratives that provide a contour for discerning the specifically Israelite characteristics from those qualities that are associated with the other nations. From the very outset, the position of the narratorial voice must be noted, for the author speaks and narrates from *within* the community of Israel. Descriptions of the oppressors and enemies create a sense of Israelite affinity and identity in response to those from outside the community. The struggles, both internal and external, that form the basis of the narratives that constitute the remainder of the book of Judges may be viewed as attempts to internalize, and thereby "objectify," the "conquest" of the homeland that the book of Joshua had presented as a ritualized ideal. Within the context of the community in exile, such an account could create bonds with that community of the "past" that had been delivered from outside oppressors by the actions of Yahweh.

In Judg 3:12–30, the exploits of Ehud, the first of Israel's deliverers, are presented. Because of the communal failure of Israel, its god had allowed Moab, with Ammon and Amalek as allies, to conquer and oppress Israel (3:12–14).[55] In the narrative, the shift from particular to universal transfers the significance of the account from a particular temporal or spatial location to a broader audience. Though Eglon, "king of Moab," defeated only the "City of Palms,"[56] Israel as a whole was subjected to him for eighteen years.[57] In response to Israel's cry, Yahweh provided Ehud as a deliverer for them (*môšîaʿ*, v. 15). Ehud is distin-

---

[54] For the present analysis, the distinctions between a redactionally secondary deuteronomistic framework and an older, traditional account of a tribal deliverer that might have been incorporated into the present book by way of the framework are not immediately relevant. For an extensive redactional analysis of Judges, see the work of W. Richter, *Traditionsgeschichtliche Untersuchungen zum Richterbuch* (BBB 18; Bonn: Peter Hanstein, 1966).

[55] An analysis of the major themes of the account is given by L. Alonso-Schökel, "Erzählkunst im Buche der Richter," *Bib* 42 (1961) 143–72. Major studies devoted to this passage are listed by J. A. Soggin, "'Ehud und 'Eglon: Bemerkungen zu Richter III 11b–31," *VT* 39 (1989) 99–100.

[56] This is commonly identified with Jericho (cf. 1:16), though such is not explicit in the text.

[57] The chronological references in Judges are problematic and are generally attributed to the framework created by the deuteronomistic writer. For an overview of the major approaches to the chronology of the book, see de Vaux, *The Early History of Israel*, pp. 689–93.

guished from the other actors in the story, for he is "the Benjaminite,"[58] i.e., a member of the tribe that bears the name "son of the right hand" but who was "bound/restricted in his right hand" (ʾiṭṭēr yad-yĕmînô), a condition that made him the appropriate choice to deliver tribute on behalf of Israel.[59]

This Ehud, however, would deliver more to Eglon than the required tribute, for the preparation of a special sword and the details of its concealment reveal that the deliverance of Israel from Moab's grip would come by way of violence. Ehud delivered the tribute to Eglon, described as "an extremely fat man," and then departed, only to return to address Eglon privately (vv. 17–19). In a scene that borders on the scatological, Ehud delivers a "matter of God" (dĕbar-ʾĕlōhîm) concerning Eglon—a double-edged sword to the stomach (vv. 19–22). The conflict between rival ethnic groups, Israelites and Moabites, is initially resolved by the stereotypical contrasts of conflict between two differentiated individuals—the stealthy Ehud and the overweight and rather nondiscriminating Eglon. The escape and flight of Ehud and the subsequent discovery of Eglon by his servants (vv. 24–25) draw a further distinction between Israelite and Moabite at the expense of the Moabites.

The account includes Israel as a whole in the conflict and provides a communal emphasis by extending this individual confrontation to a general war. In this way, the crisis begun by Ehud was resolved by Israel as a whole. Ehud blows the battle trumpet and Israel responds, coming down from the hill country and conquering the mighty warriors of Moab (vv. 27–30). This depiction of a victory by bĕnê-yiśrāʾēl extends the memory of the "deliverance" brought about by Ehud to one that was effected by the participation of the whole. Despite the positive nature of this representation for the bonding of the individual tribal units, it is important that the figure of the "judge" not be overlooked, for the existence of and actions by this individual stand as indictments of the people as a whole. Additionally, it is important to note the implications of the "success" brought about by the actions of the judge. According to 3:30b, "the land was at peace eighty years" (wattišqōṭ hāʾāreṣ šĕmônîm šānâ). This notice of peace and, by implication, freedom from any type of oppression

---

58 As Boling notes (Judges, p. 86), the use of the definite article here suggests that Ehud is being presented as a stereotypical Benjaminite.

59 The precise meaning of this phrase remains debated. It is used in Judg 20:16 to describe seven hundred crack Benjaminite troops. Halpern (The First Historians, pp. 40–43) argues that the phrase refers to the training principle by which Ehud learned to fight with his left, rather than with his right hand.

occurs three other times in Judges, and is associated with the figures of Othniel (3:11), Deborah/Barak (5:31),[60] and Gideon (8:28),[61] though in each of these cases, the period is only forty years long. What this implies is that the failures of Israel are not simply those of the "new generation" (cf. 2:10) that arose after the time of Joshua and his generation, but a continuing succession of failures that extended over a *series* of new generations. Each judge through Gideon "delivers" a different generation from its failure to learn from the mistakes of its predecessors.[62]

If the general interpretation of the biblical references to forty years as symbolic of the length of a generation is correct, then fully three generations had come and gone by the time of the successor to Ehud, Shamgar ben Anath. The account of this mercenary[63] intrudes into the narrative with neither formal introduction nor benefit of the structured framework that is now expected. Instead, the collective victory of Israel previously directed by Ehud dissolves into the individual exploits of Shamgar, who "came after him" (*wĕʾaḥărāyw hāyâ*, 3:31). There is no notice of the beginning or end of the oppression by the Philistines, nor even of the manner in which they came to threaten Israel. From the previous references to them, however, the Philistines were one of the unconquered groups that remained in the land (cf. Josh 13:2–3) who would test Israel in war and in its faithfulness to Yahweh (Judg 3:2–4). Disruptive though this account is, the details must be inferred from the frameworks that are given in the previous and subsequent accounts. What is brought into immediate focus by the account of Shamgar's exploits is that there remain internal threats to Israel. Though Shamgar "delivered Israel" (*wayyōšaʿ...ʾet-yiśrāʾēl*), no peace came to the land. Nor, it would seem, did the slowing of the Philistine threat, which will be renewed with the stories of Samson and not resolved until the wars of David, effect any change in Israel.

---

[60] 5:31 is commonly connected with the reconstructed "original" ending of the prose account of Deborah and Barak in Judges 4. Its present position makes it clear that the final redactor intends that Judges 4 and 5 be understood as parallel accounts.

[61] The references to the peacefulness following Othniel, Deborah/Barak, and Gideon are identical—"and the land was at peace for forty years" (*wattišqōṭ hāʾāreṣ ʾarbāʿîm šānâ*).

[62] That the land is not again described as being "at peace" after the account of Gideon is hardly accidental, for it is with the account of Gideon that the issue of kingship is raised explicitly. Likewise, as will be argued below, Gideon is the last of the judges to deliver the people completely from their oppressors.

[63] On the nature of this figure, see P. C. Craigie, "A Reconsideration of Shamgar ben Anath (Judg 3.31 and 5.6)," *JBL* 91 (1972) 239–40.

This threat of dissolution from inside the land is heightened in the double accounts of the exploits of Deborah, Barak, and Jael.[64] In order for the people to establish their ethnic and geopolitical identity in the land of Canaan, they would have to overcome such threats, and this they were able to do on a large scale under the leadership of the prophetess and judge Deborah. In this instance, however, the deuteronomistic author provides new insight into the only ways in which Israel can secure itself and its land by the actions of its deity on its behalf. The opening notice that "Israel continued to do what was evil" (*wayyōsīpû běnê yiśrā'ēl la'ăśôt hāra'*, 4:1) reveals that this particular "new" generation was no different from those that had preceded it, and the result was that Yahweh, god of Israel, gave his people into the power of Jabin, king of Canaan who ruled from Hazor, and his general Sisera, who, with their 900 iron chariots (cf. 1:19; Josh 17:16, 18), oppressed Israel for twenty years.

With the framing notices complete, the author introduces Deborah, a figure whose pronouncement of the divine word to Israel becomes a central focus of the story. Deborah was "a woman, a prophet" (*'iššâ nĕbî'â*) who was "judging (*šōpĕṭâ*) Israel at that time" (4:4). The Israelites would go up to her for judgment (*mišpāṭ*, 4:5), though no details of such are given by the text. Despite the similarities among this story and the others, similarities that are created primarily by the framework, Deborah occupies a role that is very different from that held by any of the other characters in Judges. That she is a woman signifies a change in the characteristic pattern of leadership that has been developed to this point in the deuteronomistic materials. That she is involved in the activity of "judging" and rendering some type of legal decisions also sets her apart from any of the other figures in Judges with whom narrative accounts

---

[64] Y. Amit ("Judges 4: Its Contents and Form," *JSOT* 39 [1987] 99–102) emphasizes the narrative balance of the roles of these three actors, as with the fourth, Sisera. As Amit notes, the real "saviour" in this story is Yahweh, not one of the human protagonists. Much debate has been devoted to the relationship of the prose account in chap. 4 and the poetic account in chap. 5. Halpern's arguments that the prose narrative is secondary to and dependent upon the poem are well conceived, but as he seems to admit, the same criteria may be used to argue the opposite (*The First Historians*, pp. 76–97). A literary analysis of the prose account is given by D. F. Murray, "Narrative Structure and Technique in the Deborah-Barak Story (Judges IV 4–22)," in *Studies in the Historical Books of the Old Testament* (ed. J. A. Emerton; VTSup 30; Leiden: E. J. Brill, 1979), pp. 155–89; literary evaluations of Judges 5 are presented by M. D. Coogan, "A Structural and Literary Analysis of the Song of Deborah," *CBQ* 40 (1978) 143–66, and A. J. Hauser, "Judges 5: Parataxis in Hebrew Poetry," *JBL* 99 (1980) 23–41.

are concerned.[65] But even more importantly, she is described as a prophet, a female *nābîʔ*,[66] the legitimate heir to Moses (cf. Deut 18:18–19). Since the deuteronomistic writer also assumes this role, the character of Deborah may be understood as the first of the prophetic figures that will play such a critical role in the formation of the remainder of the deuteronomistic history and the pronouncement of the divine word.[67]

In the past, Moses or Joshua had served as the human vehicle for the announcement of Yahweh's instructions for his people. At the beginning of Judges, the divine word was revealed either by divination (1:1) or by the appearance of the figure called the *malʔak yhwh* (2:1–5).[68] Now, however, the person of the prophet is introduced, one who will, like the *malʔak yhwh*, announce Yahweh's judgments on the people. In this case, however, the expected condemnation of the people for their continued failures does not materialize. Instead, the announcement takes the form of a guarantee of victory by Yahweh to Barak. In 4:6–7, Deborah relays the divine instructions and promise of victory over Sisera and the forces of Jabin, though an additional announcement by Deborah makes it clear that Sisera himself would be defeated by a woman, not by Barak (4:9). Despite the dominant patriarchal emphasis of the Israelite culture and society, the deuteronomistic writer is careful to include the female half of that society in the projection of this ideal ethnic community. Victory and prophecy could be realized through female as well as through male leadership.

As with the events associated with Ehud, the stories of the victory over Sisera move from the individual to the collective level. This is accomplished by the presentation of the "Song of Deborah" alongside the narrative account. In the prose narrative, Barak summoned the tribes of Naphtali and Zebulun to Qadesh to battle against Sisera (4:10), and there they defeated the forces of the Canaanites and destroyed them com-

---

[65] A possible exception to this could be the "minor judges" who are said to have "judged Israel," though the evidence that these figures actually served in some official legal capacity is open to question. See my evaluation of the traditions of the minor judges referred to above, n. 37.

[66] *nĕbîʔâ*, the feminine form of *nābîʔ*, occurs outside of this passage only in Exod 15:20; 2 Kgs 22:14; Isa 8:3; Neh 6:14; and 2 Chr 34:22.

[67] On the significance of prophecy and prophetic figures in the deuteronomistic history, see G. von Rad, *Studies in Deuteronomy* (SBT; London: SCM, 1953), pp. 74–91.

[68] Whether the *malʔak yhwh* is to be understood as a human or a divine figure is unclear from the texts. The appearance of the figure in conjunction with the prophet in Judges 6 and as a divine figure in Judges 13 seems to suggest that the author has blurred the distinctions between the two conceptual realms.

pletely (vv. 14–16). Only Sisera, the commander, escaped and fled to the tent of Jael, wife of Heber the Kenite, who was allied to the Canaanite king Jabin (4:17–18; cf. vv. 11–12). This event stands in an apparent tension to the prophetic announcement that had guaranteed that Sisera would be given into Barak's power (4:7, 9, 14). The tension is immediately resolved by way of Jael's brutal and somewhat treacherous murder of Sisera, an act that compares with the deed of Ehud, and by which Sisera is delivered to Barak and Israel (4:21–22; 5:24–27).

The completion of the victory through Jael's hand provides a transition back to the true "deliverer" of Israel, Yahweh. Jabin, the Canaanite king who had been used by Yahweh as punishment for his people, was now "humbled by God" until he was destroyed by Israel (4:23–24). Though Jael was not even an "Israelite,"[69] her deed led her to be hailed as "blessed among women" (5:24). From the individual actions of Jael, Deborah, Barak, and the tribes of Naphtali and Zebulun, however, the poem in Judges 5 recounts the actions in terms of both a collective Israelite battle and a cosmic ideal. The poetic expression of the individual battle against the general of the Canaanite forces is transformed into a cosmic conflict with Yahweh himself engaging in the fight (5:4–5), with the stars and constellations battling alongside (5:20) Israel. The list of those who came to fight on behalf of Israel (5:14–18), though not inclusive, contains a number of groups *not* mentioned in the prose narrative. This list provides a symbol of the communal effort by which Sisera had been defeated. By poetic metaphor, the individual actions that had been recounted could now be recast in cosmic, universal terms, thus creating an event that could be shared by all. Conversely, the failure to participate could bring a curse, as was exemplified by the sudden reappearance of the malʾak yhwh to deliver a curse on Meroz for "failing to come to the aid of Yahweh" (5:23). This curse stands in direct contrast to the blessing on Jael that follows (5:24), and further defines the community: those who belong to Israel are those who fight on Yahweh's behalf. Failure to do so can bring a curse and possible expulsion from the community.

---

[69] It is tempting to see in the story of Jael a commentary on membership in the community that is related to the issues raised in the earlier accounts regarding Rahab and the aid she gave Israel in its "conquest" of Jericho. A notable difference, however, is to be found in the fact that there is no Yahwistic confession associated with Jael, only an act of treachery by which she breaks the standard rules of hospitality. In this sense, the story anticipates some of the events that will be narrated in the account of the "outrage at Gibeah" in chap. 19.

Following the notice of another forty years of peace (5:31) and the implication that yet another generation had arisen, the author uses the standard framework to introduce the story of Gideon and to address the necessity of allegiance to Yahweh and to Israel. While the stories concerning Gideon's exploits and deliverance of Israel may be analyzed as a combination of various originally separate traditions,[70] in their final form they contrast the present generation of Gideon with the obedient generation associated with Joshua. As we shall show, the attempts by Gideon to challenge the ideology presented in the framework of the book serve instead to reinforce the recognition that the deliverance of Israel is the work of Yahweh alone. In its present form, the story of Gideon itself is presented as a series of interrupted and overlapping vignettes which comment on the nature and relationship of Israel, its religious practices, and its mode of leadership.

As a result of the seven-year oppression of the Midianites and their allies, Israel was in danger of losing possession of the land, the symbol of its existence as a people. Indeed, Israel was forced back into the hill country to hide in holes and caves in the face of the threats presented by the oppressors, who would destroy the produce of the land during their raids, forcing Israel again to cry out to its god (6:1–6).[71] Instead of simply moving directly to the notice of the raising of a deliverer (2:18; 3:9, 15), the narrative presents a prophetic "interlude" (6:7–10) that parallels the presentation of Deborah and the condemnation of Israel by the mal'ak yhwh in 2:1–3. The deuteronomistic writer has built upon these previous scenes to return Israel to the situation recreated at the beginning of the book of Judges. Here, several generations after the death of Joshua and the commands to conquer the land, the territory by which Israel identified and defined itself was still not conquered. Now, as earlier, the problem was the failure to obey the divine directives. In seemingly straightforward style, the author presents an unnamed figure, "a man, a prophet" (ʾîš nābîʾ, 6:8),[72] sent by Yahweh. Like the mal'ak yhwh of 2:1–3, this "prophet" first rehearses the acts of Yahweh in delivering Israel from

---

[70] On the complexity of the traditions contained in Judges 6–8 and an analysis of the various layers of materials, see Richter, *Traditionsgeschichtliche Untersuchungen zum Richterbuch*, pp. 112–246.

[71] This is the last time that Yahweh will respond favorably when the Israelites cry out (zʿq) to him (3:9, 15; 4:3; cf. 2:18). In Judg 10:10, the cry will bring an unexpected series of responses from Yahweh.

[72] Compare the phraseology with that applied to Deborah in 4:4, ʾiššâ nĕbîʾâ. These two particular expressions are unique in the Hebrew materials.

Egypt (6:8–9; 2:1) and then condemns Israel for its actions. The condemnation is identical to that given in 2:2b: Israel had failed to obey Yahweh's order (6:10).[73] Rather than remain loyal to Yahweh alone, an ideological precept that along with the concept of the possession of the land formed the core of the identity of the people, they had "feared the gods of the Amorites" (6:10), the very objects of worship their ancestors had agreed *not* to serve at the covenant ceremony at Shechem.[74] By means of a brief narrative description of a prophetic announcement, the people of Israel that had been formed by covenant and conquest in Joshua and which had strived through numerous generations to consolidate and preserve its identity were now returned to the beginning and threatened again with dissolution.

Gideon is introduced by way of another figure who speaks for the divine; as in 2:1–3, the *maḻʾak yhwh* arrives and appears to Gideon to announce that "Yahweh is with you, O mighty warrior" (*yhwh ʿimmĕkā gibbôr heḥāyil*, 6:12), an assurance of success, as demonstrated in the similar assurances given to various characters by the deuteronomistic writer. Gideon's response, however, separates him from others who had been assured of the presence and power of the deity, for Gideon answers with a challenge to Yahweh's power and presence: "Where are all his wondrous acts about which our ancestors have told us?" Further, he asserts that "Yahweh has abandoned us" (*nĕṭāšānû*) and for evidence cites the Midianite oppression (6:13). The generation represented by Gideon conformed to the new generations "who did not know" what Yahweh had done (cf. 2:10). Rather than accept the responsibility that the formation of a people would require, Israel now assumes that the oppression is the result of the desertion of the deity, not the fulfillment of the prophetic pronouncements presented.

In response to this challenge, Yahweh himself replaces the *maḻʾak yhwh* as the speaker,[75] a narrative shift that tends to blur any clear distinctions that might be made among the authority of the pronounce-

---

73 In each of these instances, the failure is clearly stated: "but you did not obey me" (*wĕlōʾ šĕmaʿtem bĕqōlî*).

74 The phrase "gods of the Amorites" (*ʾĕlōhê hāʾĕmōrî*) occurs only here and in Josh 24:15. On the connection of "fearing" and "serving" a deity, see Weinfeld, *Deuteronomy and the Deuteronomic School*, pp. 83–84, 332–33.

75 LXX^AB reads *maḻʾak yhwh* on the basis of 6:11 and the reappearance of this figure in 6:20–22, thus smoothing over the abrupt shift in speakers present in the MT. On the interpretation of this section of the account as a "call" narrative, see Van Seters, *In Search of History*, p. 256, n. 28, and the literature cited therein.

ments of the deity, his messenger, or his prophet. Yahweh himself confirms the announcement of the *malʾak* by asserting, "I will be with you" (*ʾehyeh ʿimmāk*, 6:16; cf. v. 12). Despite this assurance and its guarantee of victory over Midian, Gideon requests a sign (*ʾôt*), some indication that the speaker carries the power which he claims. What follows (6:18–23) amounts to the preparation of a food offering to the figure, intended perhaps as a gesture of hospitality to a visitor, but transformed in the narrative into a ritual expression of the power of the one to whom it was presented.[76] With the acceptance of the offering and the disappearance of the *malʾak yhwh*, Gideon recognized that things truly were as they seemed, and, in response, built an altar which he named "Yahweh is peace" (*yhwh šālôm*, 6:24), anticipating the outcome of this section of the narrative.

Apparently, then, Gideon had received and accepted as authoritative both the message and the sign given by the messenger of Yahweh. As a result, Yahweh (not the *malʾak yhwh*) commands Gideon to dismantle "the altar of Baal" (*mizbaḥ habbaʿal*) that belonged to his father and to cut down the asherah which was next to it (6:25).[77] In its place he is commanded to erect an "altar to Yahweh" (*mizbēaḥ layhwh*) and to offer a burnt offering upon it. The conflict with Midian, given the arrangement of the story, becomes also a battle against Baal; Gideon, as leader of the people, becomes a cultic reformer.[78] As is apparent from the story, both Gideon's father and the people of his hometown (cf. vv. 28–29) were accustomed to worshipping Baal at this cultic installation, and the interruption of the standard practices did not endear Gideon to the people. The interpretation of the conflict is clarified by the pronouncement of Gideon's father: though the people ask for Gideon's punishment because of his actions, his father insists that if Baal is a god, he should contend for himself (6:31). This singular episode introduces a theme into the narrative that will reemerge at various points to provide a basis for the deuteronomistic evaluation of Israel and its activities. At the conclusion of this section, Gideon is named Jerubbaal, a name that will connect the stories

---

[76] A similar scene will be recounted between the *malʾak yhwh* and the parents of Samson in 13:15–20.

[77] On the nature of the "asherah" in the Hebrew Bible, see Saul M. Olyan, *Asherah and the Cult of Yahweh in Israel* (SBLMS 34; Atlanta: Scholars Press, 1988), pp. 1–22.

[78] H.-D. Hoffmann, *Reform und Reformen: Untersuchungen zu einen Grundthema der deuteronomistischen Geschichtsschreibung* (ATANT 66; Zürich: Theologischer Verlag, 1980), pp. 275–78.

that follow,[79] for it would be Gideon/Jerubbaal who would lead the great victory against the Midianites (7:1) and whose son Abimelek (9:1–2) would claim kingship over Shechem (9:2–57), despite the rejection of such a possibility by his father (8:23).

The narrative now returns to the issue of the oppressive activities of the Midianites and the need for deliverance that introduced this series of accounts. If the foreign god could be overcome, then surely the foreign oppressor could also be defeated. Gideon, like Ehud earlier (3:27), sounded the war trumpet and sent envoys to Manasseh, Asher, Zebulun, and Naphtali. The conflict begins as though it would be a straightforward account of a confederated effort of several tribes against a common foe, as had been the victories of Ehud and Deborah/Barak. But Gideon was intent upon not letting success spoil him. In a further inversion of the deuteronomistic ideology, Gideon insists upon testing Yahweh to see if he would truly deliver Israel as he had spoken (6:36). According to the deuteronomistic writer (Judg 2:22; 3:1; cf. Deut 6:16), such was the purview of Yahweh, not of his people. The twofold test with the fleece and the dew reveals that Yahweh, who consented, was indeed in control of the natural forces, the realm that had been mistakenly attributed to Baal.

With the defeat of Midian foretold and guaranteed yet again, the narrator insures that the events in which Gideon and Israel will participate will be understood as the very "wonders" that Gideon had earlier questioned. Lest Israel think that it was delivered because of its power or strength, Yahweh gives a twofold test to the assembled soldiers and reduces their number to no more than three hundred. Yahweh proclaims that it will be with these that he will deliver Israel (7:7; cf. 4:7, 14). The actual battles stand only as demonstrations of his mighty deeds, actions comparable to the ways in which he led their ancestors out of Egypt (cf. 2:1–2; 6:13). With the forces of Israel reduced to a minimum, the narrator provides another brief vision into the actions of Yahweh, now by way of sending Gideon and his attendant into the Midianite camp and allowing them to overhear the dream of one of the Midianite warriors and its interpretation (7:9–15). The Midianite confession that the dream revealed that God had given them into the power of Gideon is reminiscent of the confession of Rahab that none could stand before the power of Yahweh

---

79 That Gideon and Jerubbaal are identified throughout the remainder of this complex is clear from Judg 7:1; 8:29, 35; 9:1–2, 5, 16, 19, 24, 28, 57; cf. 1 Sam 12:11. On the ways in which various traditions have been arranged to construct the present account, see H. Haag, "Gideon-Jerubbaal-Abimelek," *ZAW* 79 (1967) 305–14.

(Josh 2:9–11). Ironically, this provided the sign (cf. 6:17) sought by Gideon, for with this reassurance he assembled the people and routed the Midianite camp. With war trumpets blasting and torches burning, three hundred assembled Israelites cried: "A sword for Yahweh and for Gideon!" (7:20). In response to this ritualized attack, the Midianite camp dissolved, not unlike the walls of Jericho, before the cries and horn blasts at the end of that ritual (Josh 6:15–21).

The war, then, was won. All that remained was the mopping up operation, and for this, additional help was required. But, at the very point where one might expect the narrator to demonstrate the bonding of the community through the victory over the oppressors, a hint of discord intrudes. Gideon sent messengers to the hill country of Ephraim to employ them in the pursuit of Midian, and the men of Ephraim complied (7:24–25). After their success in capturing and executing Oreb and Zeeb, the Midianite commanders, they raised a challenge to Gideon for his failure to summon them in the initial battle (cf. 6:35). The challenge to the unity of the groups was avoided only by Gideon's skill at diplomacy (8:3). At the same time, the nature of the challenge raises the issue of combined tribal action on the part of the judges, for this is the first instance in which a group complains of being left out.[80] It does not resolve the issue, however, for as Gideon continues his pursuit of Zebah and Zalmunna, the Midianite kings, he and his men are refused aid by the inhabitants of Succoth and Penuel (8:4–8). In response, Gideon promises to punish each of the cities for their failure to provide him with aid (8:7, 9), and once he has captured Zebah and Zalmunna (vv. 10–12), he returns and fulfills that vow (8:13–17).

The contrast presented by the response of Ephraim and the refusal of Succoth and Penuel may be understood as indicative of the need for unified action on the part of all the people in order to provide for the protection of the group. The refusal of one or two cities to aid the exhausted forces of the leader of the tribal muster could have led to the failure of Gideon to capture the kings of the oppressing Midianites. The failure of the inhabitants of the city to understand that Yahweh had already preordained the success of Gideon (8:9) adds an additional comment to the nature of such tribal and regional assemblages. Unlike Ephraim, neither Succoth nor Penuel admits to any direct connection with the war being

---

[80] The Ephraimites will raise much the same complaint against Jephthah, but that incident will not be so easily resolved (12:1–7). The fact that Meroz had earlier been cursed for failing to come to the aid of Yahweh in battle (cf. 5:23) provides an interesting explanation for the Ephraimite actions here.

conducted. Thus, neither seems to have felt obligated to contribute to the effort. The lack of a strong unifying bureaucracy or of communal and familial ties among the disputants can create great problems for any type of protracted military engagement that requires support for an over-extended supply line. In the event of such failure to give aid, some type of public retribution was necessary to serve as an example to those who might entertain similar attitudes. Such would prove highly problematic for the development of a joint communal base, but could be overcome by way of the development of a shared history of oppression and deliverance.

The exploits of Gideon do not end, as would be expected, with the notice of the peacefulness and the eventual death of the judge immedi-ately following the account of the successful military exploits (3:11, 30; 5:31). Instead, the issue of kingship (i.e., of a permanent type of leader-ship over the tribal groups) is raised in explicit terms for the first time. Just as important is the offer of dynastic succession, for the Israelites request that Gideon, his son, and his grandson rule over them (*māšal bĕ-*), a proposal made in light of the Israelites' misunderstanding of their true deliverer. The request in 8:22 makes it clear that the offer is extended to Gideon and his family "because you have delivered us from the power of Midian" (*kî hôšaʿtānû miyyad midyān*). Conversely, Gideon's refusal of the offer, often taken to be a rejection of kingship,[81] is actually a refocusing of the issue: Yahweh, not he, had delivered Israel; therefore, "Yahweh shall rule over you" (*yhwh yimšōl bākem*, 8:23).

Had the account ended here, it could have formed a clearly focused point to reassemble the people and to rededicate them to the demands of Yahwistic expectations. But the deuteronomistic writer had further boundaries to describe. As the career of Gideon began with his failure to perceive the activities of Yahweh in Israel's history, so it would end with an accurate profession of that activity and an inappropriate and unac-ceptable response to it. Gideon requested that the people give him the spoil that they had taken and from it he fashioned an ephod (*ʾēpôd*), which he erected in his city of Ophrah. Whatever the intentions of this

---

[81] As would be imagined, this section of the narrative has received intense scrutiny by scholars attempting to determine whether the deuteronomistic writer was pro- or antimonarchical in the emphasis of his work. An excellent summary of the major treatments of this section is presented by G. E. Gerbrandt in *Kingship According to the Deuteronomistic History* (SBLDS 87; Atlanta: Scholars Press, 1986), pp. 123–29, and the literature cited therein. To this should be added the discussions of Veijola, *Das Königtum in der Beurteilung der deuteronomistischen Historiographie*, pp. 100–3.

action, the results are clear: the establishment of this golden ephod was a snare (*môqēš*; cf. 2:3; Deut 7:16) for the house of Gideon and became the object of all Israel's illegitimate worship.[82]

Midian was humbled, the threat was ended, and the land was at peace for 40 years (8:28). Not again in the book of Judges will this notice be given. Instead of the formation of a closely bonded people, united in its worship of Yahweh and in full possession of the land promised to their ancestors, the tribal units remained without single leadership and without full possession of the land. The discontinuity that pervades the narrative accounts of Gideon reflects the lack of correspondence between the ideal of the community and the actuality of the participants. Though Gideon receives enough indications that Yahweh is actively engaged in performing wondrous deeds on behalf of his chosen people, he and all the people of Israel fail to respond according to the deuteronomistic ideal. The death notice of Gideon (8:32) introduces the further disintegration of the people by way of the individualized actions of Gideon's son, Abimelek (8:31).

The complete failure of this next generation of Israel to recognize the basis of its common foundation is exemplified in the story of Abimelek's attempt to establish himself as the city-state king over Shechem (9:1–57). Whatever had been the nature of their unfaithfulness during the days of Gideon, Israel's failures became explicit after his death, for they "established Baal Berit as their god" (*wayyāśîmû lāhem baʿal bĕrît lēʾlōhîm*, 8:33).[83] Further, Israel is indicted for forgetting that it was Yahweh who had delivered them from their enemies and for failing to act faithfully with the family of Gideon/Jerubbaal (8:34–35). The specifics of these charges are developed in the account of Abimelek, son of Jerubbaal/ Gideon by his Shechemite mistress. At no point in the story that follows do *any* of the characters presented show any knowledge of Yahweh or any devotion to him.[84] With the failure to recognize the pivotal role of devotion to this one god in the formation of a people, it is not surprising

---

[82] The narrator notes explicitly that "all Israel played the harlot after it" (*wayyiznû kol-yiśrāʾēl ʾaḥărâw*, 8:27; cf. 2:17; 8:33; Deut 31:16). Another "ephod" will serve as an object of interest in the accounts of Micah's shrine and the Danite migration in Judges 17–18.

[83] On the identity of the deity Baal Berit and its connection with Shechem, see Boling, *Judges*, pp. 180–81. It is clear from the presentation that this non-Yahwistic epithet is intended by the deuteronomistic writer to designate an illegitimate object of Israelite worship.

[84] Polzin, *Moses and the Deuteronomist*, p. 174.

that the actions described by this story involve only Abimelek and the city and inhabitants of Shechem. At no point is there any attempt to involve the tribes or to offer this as a statement that creates Israelite unity.

Unlike the actors in the story, the deuteronomistic writer reasserted the role and position of Yahweh, for the key to understanding the movements within the narrative is provided not by the actions of the people but by the controlling works of Yahweh. The story is straightforward: Abimelek gained the support of the elders of Shechem based upon his kinship ties by way of his mother. Hiring mercenaries, he murdered his 70 brothers, missing only Jotham (9:1–6). As a result, the leaders of the city of Shechem "made Abimelek king" (*wayyamlîkû ʾet-ʾăbîmelek lĕmelek*, 9:6). In judgmental fashion Jotham emerged to stand on Mt. Gerizim, the mountain from which the blessings of the Torah were to be read (Deut 11:29; 27:12; Josh 8:30–35), and there delivered his famous "fable."[85] The application of this fable (9:16–20) becomes the basis for interpreting the actions that follow. The deuteronomistic writer reverses the expectation of a blessing announced from Mt. Gerizim and refers to it instead as "the curse of Jotham" (*qilălat yôtām*, 9:57), providing an inversion to the expected patterns that have been developed throughout the narrative to this point. Jotham does not become a righteous leader of the people, nor do the people emerge as a unit. Rather, Jotham pronounced his fable, interpreted it as it applied to Abimelek, and ran off to hide (9:21).

Despite the localized nature of his rule, Abimelek also served as the commander of Israel (*wayyāśar ʾabîmelek ʿal-yiśrāʾēl*, v. 22). This involves Israel indirectly in the actions and fate of this figure. But Abimelek's rulership over Shechem was short-lived, for the deuteronomistic author reestablishes the directing power of Yahweh by noting that God sent an "evil spirit" (*rûaḥ rāʿâ*, v. 23)[86] in punishment for his actions against his father's household. A native Shechemite, Gaal ben Ebed, challenged Abimelek's familial right to rule, but Abimelek overcame the challenge and reasserted himself over his city (9:28–49), a resurgence that led only to his death at Thebez at the hand of an unnamed woman (*ʾiššâ ʾaḥat*, v.

---

[85] On the highly antimonarchical tone attributed to this, see F. Crüsemann, *Der Widerstand gegen das Königtum: Die antiköniglichen Texte des Alten Testaments und der Kampf um den frühen israelitischen Staat* (WMANT 49; Neukirchen-Vluyn: Neukirchener Verlag, 1978), pp. 19–42.

[86] This provides a clear foreshadowing of the evil spirit which will be placed upon Saul by Yahweh (1 Sam 16:14–15).

53). The short-lived rule of Abimelek ended as ignominiously as it had begun. It would not be violence that would unite Israel or deliver it from its enemies. Rather it would be Yahweh who would bring about a just recompense on those who failed to fulfill his demands (9:55–56). Only in this way could Israel hope to preserve itself and to find a security in the land as a group united by its covenantal ties not to the gods of the people of the land, but to Yahweh alone. Thus, the story of Abimelek serves as an appropriate conclusion to the accounts of Gideon and his challenges to the ideologies of the deuteronomistic author. A common history and a mythic repertoire that would forge communal bonds would be one that recognized the exclusive sovereignty of Yahweh, the god who had chosen this people and bound them to himself by covenantal obligations. The continuation of the people who had failed to fulfill those obligations would be a result of the decision of the deity to be merciful rather than to exact the type of punishment that the people had earned. As the stories concluding with Abimelek illustrate, Yahweh was capable of either.

IV. The End of an Era: Tola to Samson

With the accounts concerning Samson, the elements of the deuteronomistic framework are no longer applied to individual figures,[87] and the narrative moves into a different arena—one of threats, both internal and external, to the existence of Israel as a people. In order to prepare the way for the abandonment of the episodic framework that has been utilized throughout to interpret the actions of the successive generations unable to obtain and establish their identity in the land and to confirm their allegiance to Yahweh alone, the deuteronomistic writer breaks his own pattern and prepares for the period of internal anarchy that will follow the career of Samson.

Prior to the presentation of the exploits of Samson are recounted the careers of six so-called "minor" judges.[88] Of these six figures (Tola [10:1–

---

[87] Though it is often noted that elements of the "judge" framework may be found later in the stories associated with Samuel, it is clear that the elements are applied in a different manner to that figure.

[88] The roles and functions attributed to these figures have received much discussion. See, for example, the treatments of A. J. Hauser, "The 'Minor Judges'—A Reevaluation," *JBL* 94 (1975) 190–200; A. D. H. Mayes, *Israel in the Period of the Judges* (SBT 29; London: SCM, 1974), pp. 55–67; Mullen, "The 'Minor Judges'"; H. N. Rösel, "Jephtah und das Problem der Richter," *Bib* 61 (1980) 251–55; K.-D. Schunck, "Die Richter Israels und ihr Amt," *Volume du congrès international, Genève 1965* (VTSup 15;

2], Jair [10:3–5], Jephthah [12:7], Ibzan [12:8–10], Elon [12:11–12], and Abdon [12:13–15]), a narrative account is attached only to Jephthah.[89] Though none of these figures is actually called a "judge," each is noted as having "judged Israel" (*wayyišpōṭ ʾet-yiśrāʾēl*, 10:2, 3; 12:7, 8, 9, 11, 13, 14; see also 3:10; 15:20; 16:31). Only in the case of Tola is there any reference to one of these figures "delivering" Israel, and in that case, there is no indication of the source of oppression from which this deliverance is intended (10:1). It seems most apparent, however, that no real separation of "offices" might be distinguished between the "major" and "minor" judges on the basis of the narrative traditions in Judges; rather, the distinction is useful only in differentiating the manner in which the traditions have been presented.[90]

What the accounts of these "minor" figures perform, in literary terms, is the quickening of the pace of the narrative. From the reign of Abimelek until the beginning of Samson's exploits, the passage of some 99 years is noted,[91] nearly two new generations. Unlike the accounts of the previous generations, however, these have more than one "judge" associated with them. If the appearance of the judge is related to the apostasy of the people, then the deuteronomistic narrative clearly suggests that Israel has only grown worse, not better, and that the people have not yet learned the lessons that were necessary. The narrative continues to emphasize that allegiance to Yahweh alone and complete adherence to his directions were the *sine qua non* for the survival of this people. Embedded in the narratives concerning Jephthah (Judg 10:6–12:7) are some of the major questions concerning the nature of Israel's

---

Leiden: E. J. Brill, 1966), pp. 252–55; and J. A. Soggin, "Das Amt der 'kleinen Richter' in Israel," *VT* 30 (1980) 245–48.

[89] The fact that Jephthah is a character in both the narrative accounts of the deliverers of Israel and the stylized account of the so-called "minor" judges is often cited as a major factor leading to the extension of the concept of "judge" to those figures who originally served only as "deliverers." According to the analysis by Schunk of the reports concerning the "minor" judges, the full form contains the following parts: (1) name and descent; (2) list of sons and daughters; (3) note of duration of judgeship; (4) death notice; (5) place of burial. The complete form is given only in the reports of Ibzan (12:8–10) and Abdon (12:13–15; "Die Richter Israels und ihr Amt," pp. 252–55). Notably, elements of the scheme also occur outside the lists, e. g., in the accounts of Othniel, Samson, Joshua, and Samuel.

[90] Hauser, "The 'Minor Judges'—A Re-evaluation," pp. 190–200; Mullen, "The 'Minor Judges,'" pp. 185–201.

[91] The reign of Abimelek (9:22), 3 years; Tola (10:2), 23 years; Jair (10:3), 22 years; Jephthah (12:7), 6 years; Ibzan (12:9), 7 years; Elon (12:11), 10 years; Abdon (12:14), 8 years; Samson (15:20; 16:31), 20 years.

relationship to Yahweh, and concomitantly, Israel's very identity and existence as a distinctive people. The brief, stylized accounts of Tola and Jair (10:1–5) speed the narrative forward to a new phase.

Though the beginning of the account of Jephthah appears to resume the cyclically episodic pattern set forth in Judg 2:11–23, such is not the case. Rather, what seems to have become predictable proves to be most elusive. The introduction to the Jephthah materials in Judg 10:6–16, a section in which deuteronomistic phraseology dominates, inaugurates a new era in the unfolding epic of Israel's sojourn in the land. That the people continued in their apostate ways was evident for each of the preceding generations, but 10:6 makes it clear that this generation had extended its unfaithfulness to a new degree. They not only worshipped the "baals" and "ashtaroth" (cf. 2:13), but also the gods of Aram, Sidon, Moab, Ammon and Philistia. In terms of religious identity, Israel had assimilated itself completely to the cultural practices of the people in whose midst it was settled. In response to this apostasy, Yahweh "sold them into the power of the Philistines and the power of the Ammonites" (10:7). The innovative feature here is the double oppression that is not like any of the previous punishments; Israel now was squeezed from two sides, and the new deliverer, Jephthah, would save Israel from the Ammonites only. The Philistine oppression would remain for Samson (Judges 13–16), whose efforts would fall short of any lasting success. Likewise, if this "double oppression" is taken seriously, then the judgeship of Jephthah must be understood as somewhat less than successful when compared to those of the deliverers who had preceded him.

The stage is set for the introduction of Jephthah with the notice that both the Trans- and Cisjordanian tribes of Israel were besieged by the Ammonites for eighteen years (10:8–9). As the continuation of the description of this new era, the deuteronomistic writer varies the reaction of Israel to this situation. Instead of crying out to Yahweh in response to the oppression, Israel confesses that it has sinned and repents for its misdeeds, going so far as to put away its foreign gods (10:10, 16).[92] Even more unexpected is the dialogue between Israel and Yahweh (10:10–15),[93] for Yahweh speaks directly with Israel, recounts his deeds of deliverance (vv. 11–12), and explicitly refuses to deliver them again: "Now you have abandoned me and served other gods. Therefore, I will no longer deliver

---

[92]   As Polzin emphasizes, at no other point in the book of Judges does Israel make such a reforming effort (*Moses and the Deuteronomist*, p. 176).

[93]   The unique nature of this speech has been underscored by Richter, "*Retterbuches*," pp. 88–89.

you" (*lākēn lōʾ-ʾôsîp lĕhôšîaʿ ʾetkem*, v. 13). The pattern of predictability established in 2:11–23 and repeated through the generations prior to the time of Jephthah is now broken. When Yahweh directs Israel to cry instead to the gods which they have chosen for themselves, Israel reasserts that it has sinned (vv. 14–15), and requests that Yahweh deliver its people yet one more time.[94] Israel puts aside its foreign gods, i.e., it does indeed repent of its apostate ways, but Yahweh makes no commitment in response.[95]

The era to be initiated by Jephthah, then, would not be governed by the episodic responses of deity or people that had been developed in the previous sections. Important to understanding the ideological view being developed by the deuteronomistic author is the recognition that people, ethnicity, and divine direction are all processes that go through various and often unpredictable changes. Ethnicity, like culture, is a conceptual ideal that is continually in the process of being reinvented and applied to changing situations. When this is done as a part of the reconstruction of a historical past, then for the community adopting this account as its own authoritative vision of its development, a number of options and viewpoints are elaborated. Clearly, the message being developed within the present context is that if Israel should continue to fail to devote itself to Yahweh, then Yahweh might cease to respond to Israel's cries for help. Whether Yahweh would, however, remained a question, for the story continues with the introduction of Jephthah.

The stories of this deliverer center upon a series of four dialogues (11:6–11, Jephthah and the elders of Gilead; 11:12–28, Jephthah [or messengers sent by him] and the king of Ammon; 11:35–38, Jephthah and his daughter; 12:1–4, Jephthah and Ephraim), which are connected by brief narrative reports. Each of these conversations refers back to and elaborates upon the dialogue between Yahweh and Israel in 10:10–16. Jephthah proves to be an unlikely choice as leader, for he was to some

---

94 An important theme is introduced in this section of the dialogue, for Israel implores Yahweh to "do to us as seems good in your eyes" (*ʿăśēh-ʾattâ lānû kĕkol-haṭṭôb bĕʿênēkā*, v. 15). This theme of "doing what is good or upright" in one's own opinion will be developed in the next chapter in the description of the complete breakdown of the unity of the tribes due to the lack of any legitimate form of leadership.

95 The deuteronomistic writer notes the divine response to Israel's request and actions: *yattiqṣar napšô baʿămal yiśrāʾēl*, v. 16. Webb renders this as "and he [Yahweh] became exasperated with the misery of Israel" (*The Book of Judges*, pp. 45–49). Polzin translates it "And he [Yahweh] grew annoyed [or impatient] with the troubled efforts of Israel" (*Moses and the Deuteronomist*, p. 177).

degree an "outsider": He was the son of a prostitute (11:1), driven from his family inheritance (11:2), and forced to live in non-Israelite territory (11:3). Such a personal situation paralleled that of the people he led: Israel had "played the harlot after other gods" (2:17; cf. 8:27, 33), lived in a land not originally its own (11:19–27), and was now faced with the loss of that land to Ammon. Though Yahweh had declared that he would not deliver his people, he placed his spirit upon Jephthah (11:29) and thus effected their delivery (11: 32–33). Ammon was subdued, but "Yahweh, the judge" (*yhwh haššōpēṭ*, 11:27) granted no peace to the land.

Prior to this story, the deliverance of Israel had been effected by Yahweh's mercy. Now, however, Israel repented and began to serve Yahweh (10:16). In their agreement with Jephthah, the elders of Gilead invoked Yahweh as witness (11:10) and Jephthah recited the *magnalia dei* to the king of Ammon, invoking Yahweh as judge between the two groups (11:15–27). To insure his victory over Ammon, Jephthah made a vow to Yahweh (11:30–31) which he refused to break, despite the implications of the fulfillment of that vow (11:35). On one level, it would seem that Jephthah represents the devotion to Yahweh that is required of Israel. But the nature of the vow taken by Jephthah serves as a condemnation of this relationship. Unwilling to trust that Yahweh would deliver him, Jephthah attempts to insure his victory with the promise of a burnt offering.[96] As a result of his oath, advertently or not, Jephthah promises Yahweh a human sacrifice (11:30–31), a deed that would constitute a direct violation of deuteronomic law (Deut 12:29–31). Still, Yahweh delivers Israel from the Ammonites, and Jephthah, after granting his daughter's special plea (11:37), fulfills his vow to Yahweh (11:39).[97]

The appearance of victory and deliverance, however, is superficial. Yahweh had not broken his vow not to deliver Israel. Instead, an internal

---

[96] These actions are comparable to those attributed to Gideon in Judg 6:36–40, where he tests Yahweh to determine if Yahweh would be with him. As noted above, "testing," at least in Judges, is reserved by Yahweh to ascertain the faithfulness of his people (2:22–23; 3:1, 4; cf. Deut 6:16).

[97] D. Marcus argues that the text is ambiguous and that a strong case might be made that Jephthah did not sacrifice his daughter, but rather dedicated her to remain a virgin in the service of the deity (*Jephthah and his Vow* [Lubbock, TX: Texas Tech Press, 1986]). I do not find his arguments on this issue to be persuasive. The severity of Jephthah's sacrifice is emphasized by the framing accounts of Jair, who had thirty sons (10:4); Ibzan, who had thirty sons and thirty daughters (12:9); and Abdon, who had forty sons and thirty grandsons (12:14). These references highlight the implications of Jephthah's sacrifice of his only offspring. On the debate concerning this section, see the comments of Soggin, *Judges*, pp. 215–19.

conflict arose that demonstrates the fragility of the tribal allegiances to each other. Ephraim, a tribe that had also been besieged by Ammon (10:9), confronted Jephthah for not summoning them to fight against Ammon and threatened to burn his house down on him (12:1), an encounter which hardly signifies a united Israel. Jephthah countered by accusing them of having failed to answer the call (12:2–3; cf. 5:23) and questioned their motives for coming up against him. The result was war that emphasized the differences between Gilead and Ephraim and which led to a major defeat for the Ephraimite forces (12:5–6).[98] Despite the fact that Jephthah is credited with having judged Israel for six years, there is little about his actions that can be seen as exemplary. Instead, when compared with Othniel, Deborah or Barak, or even with Gideon or Ehud, Jephthah seems more a caricature of a judge than a deliverer of the people. Though he did eliminate the threat by Ammon, Israel remained under the oppression of the Philistines (10:7).

It will be with Samson's exploits that the picture of the dissolution of the era of the judges will be completed.[99] The failure of Jephthah is amplified in the failures of Samson, which are, quite surprisingly, divinely ordained. The account of Samson[100] begins with a partial reversion to the cyclical scheme that was brought into question by the Jephthah narrative. Israel continued in its sins, demonstrating the lack of duration of the repentance in Judg 10:16, and fell to Philistine dominance (10:7). Despite the 40-year oppression,[101] the longest that is noted by the

---

[98] Contrast the use of diplomacy by Gideon in his potential conflict with Ephraim (8:1–3).

[99] The accounts of the judgeship of Ibzan (12:8–10), Elon (12:11–12), and Abdon (12:13–15) are presented in the form of narrative summaries like those of Tola (10:1–2) and Jair (10:3–5). The reports of these three figures confirm that Yahweh continued to be with his people, that there were no more peaceful interludes, and that there was no relief from the Philistine oppression.

[100] It is common to view Judges 16 as a later deuteronomistic addition to an older collection of deliverer stories associated with this figure which included chaps. 13–15. Hence, the reference to Samson's judging Israel in 16:31 is seen as a secondary redactional insertion based on the similar reference found in 15:20. On the literary style and structure of these stories, see J. Blenkinsopp, "Structure and Style in Judges 13–16," *JBL* 82 (1963) 65–76; J. L. Crenshaw, *Samson: A Secret Betrayed, A Vow Ignored* (Atlanta: John Knox, 1978); J. C. Exum, "Promise and Fulfillment: Narrative Art in Judges 13," *JBL* 99 (1980) 43–59, and "Aspects of Symmetry and Balance in the Samson Saga," *JSOT* 19 (1981) 3–29; J. A. Warton, "The Secret of Yahweh: Story and Affirmation in Judges 13–16," *Int* 27 (1973) 48–66.

[101] It is unclear how this is to be calculated. If the beginning of the Philistine oppression coincides with that of the Ammonite period, then the forty-year period

author, Israel does not cry out to Yahweh either from repentance or from oppression. Rather, the deuteronomistic writer depicts Yahweh as acting on his own initiative to demonstrate the need for adherence to a divinely prescribed set of social and cultural standards. Samson would serve to emphasize the need for such, if any sense of community or ethnic identity were to be formulated and maintained.

From his very conception Samson is set apart from the other characters in the story. In contrast to that of the chieftain Jephthah, the disinherited son of a prostitute, Samson's birth was announced by the appearance of the *malʾak yhwh*[102] to the barren wife of the Danite Manoah. She would bear a son who would be required to be a Nazirite (13:2–7).[103] In spite of this divine direction, he would not successfully free Israel from the Philistine threat; rather, "he will begin to deliver Israel from the power of the Philistines" (*wĕhûʾ yāḥēl lĕhôšîaʿ ʾet-yiśrāʾēl miyyad pĕlištîm*, 13:5). Hence, the Samson cycle of stories fits the scheme projected in Judg 2:11–23 no better than does the Jephthah cycle. Despite the havoc that he worked among the Philistines, the story ends with no notice of the defeat of the enemies at his hands or the hand of Israel, as was the case in the previous stories (3:10; 3:30; 3:31; 4:24; 8:28; 11:33). Simply put, despite his great individual exploits, Samson fails in his role as judge. Though twice

---

could overlap with the thirty-one years associated with Jephthah and the three "minor" judges who followed him. In that case, there would be only a seven-year span from the end of the judgeship of Abdon until the announcement of the birth of Samson. It is just as likely, however, given the schematic and sometimes obscure chronology utilized by the deuteronomistic writer, that "forty years" is simply the designation for the emergence of yet another new generation of Israelites.

[102] The way in which the figure of the "messenger of Yahweh" (*malʾak yhwh*) functions in the narratives of the deuteronomistic historian deserves further study. It is significant that this figure appears with the demise of the major human intermediaries for the divine will, i.e., Moses and Joshua, and before the standardization of the appearance of the prophets (*nĕbîʾîm*), beginning with Samuel. It is clear from the function of the figure in the history, however, that it serves to introduce divine pronouncements in those narrative situations wherein there was no immediately convenient figure to serve such a function.

[103] For the requirements of the vow, see Num 6:1–8. Judg 13:2–25 and 6:11–24 share so many parallels that it is clear that they come from the same literary tradition if not the same hand (Blenkinsopp, "Structure and Style in Judges 13–16," p. 67; on the parallels, see S. A. Cook, "The Theophanies of Gideon and Manoah," *JTS* 28 [1927] 368–83). The role of Manoah in not trusting the report of his wife and requesting the return of the *malʾak* to confirm her report (13:8–23) is similar to Gideon's testing Yahweh to assure the veracity of his pronouncement. On the problems associated with the name of the messenger, see D. Grimm, "Der Name des Gottesboten in Richter 13," *Bib* 62 (1981) 92–98.

the author credits him with having served in that capacity (15:20; 16:31), his victories were only local and personal. There is no group effort here, nor is there any sense of community for "Israel."

Still, with the blessing of Yahweh and endowed with his spirit (13:24–25), Samson would form a part of the picture of the past from which the deuteronomistic writer could begin to reconstruct a more durable and lasting concept of Israel. Samson's failures as a representative of Israelite society begin with the introduction of the actions of the lad himself.[104] His first deed as a Nazirite, i.e., as a cultic functionary dedicated to Yahweh (Num 6:8) intended as a type of religious model for the people, is to choose a Philistine woman as a wife (14:1–3). When his parents protest, asking if there is not instead a suitable woman from among his own people in contrast to a woman from the "uncircumcised Philistines,"[105] Samson insists that "she is pleasing to me" (*hî* *yāšĕrâ* *bĕʿênāy*, 14:3; contrast Deut 12:8). Marriage to those who lived in the land to be conquered, an act expressly forbidden in the deuteronomic charter because of the religious (and hence, ethnic) dangers involved,[106] becomes a focus of the stories of Samson. This one, vowed to Yahweh from his birth, chooses to ignore the divine dictates and pursue what is "good in his eyes" (cf. 17:6; 21:25).

---

[104] E. L. Greenstein has argued that the major themes of the book of Judges continue through the Samson narrative and that the figure of Samson serves as a type or symbol of the people Israel. The anomalous nature of the story creates a type of allegory that is without an exact parallel elsewhere in the biblical materials ("The Riddle of Samson," *Prooftexts: A Journal of Jewish Literary History* 1 [1981] 237–60). Samson, because of his anomalous nature, provides a fitting transition to the breakdown of the period of the judges.

[105] The issue of circumcision and the constant appellation of the Philistines as "uncircumcised" (*ʿārēl*; cf. Judg 15:18; 1 Sam 14:6; 17:26, 36; 31:4; 2 Sam 1:20; etc.) are noteworthy given the evidence that suggests that the Philistines may have practiced circumcision (P. A. Mantovani, "Circoncisi ed incirconcisi," *Henoch* 10 [1988] 57–60). Such distinctions among ethnic and cultural groups are often more a matter of accusation and belief than of actual practice. The appellation of the Philistines as "uncircumcised" is clearly intended to distinguish between Israelite "people" and the Philistine "creatures" and serves to establish a boundary that, at least from the standpoint of the ideals of the community, is not to be crossed. Against the assertion of Boling (*Judges*, p. 232) that the comment of Manoah has "nothing to do with ethnic dogma," I would stress that the issues of ethnicity and ethnic identity are precisely the implication of this comment.

[106] Deut 7:3–4; cf. Judg 3:6. On the importance of this in the formation of ethnic boundaries, see the discussion in chap. 2.

The deuteronomistic voice intrudes into the narrative at this point to demonstrate that Yahweh has not lost, nor will he lose control of his Nazirite, for Yahweh was secretly seeking an opportunity to engage the Philistines (14:4). The foreign wife, then, serves to provide the opportunity for such a confrontation, for Samson's initial actions against the Philistines were in response to the actions of this woman and her family. It was she who on threat of death (14:15) "betrayed" Samson's riddle to his companions (14:16–18).[107] Endowed again with the "spirit of Yahweh" (14:19), Samson responded by slaughtering thirty men in Ashkelon to pay his wager with the men of Timnah. Yahweh had created his opportunity; Samson had now engaged the Philistines, but he had lost his wife (14:20). In the next episode (15:1–7), Samson used the loss of his wife to another as the pretext for the destruction of the Philistine grain, a deed of which he proclaimed himself to be innocent (*niqqêtî happaʿam*, 15:3). In response, the Philistines burned his wife and her father, provoking Samson to execute "a great slaughter" by which he would avenge himself and after which he would cease (15:6–8).

By his actions, however, Samson had managed to provoke the Philistine and to alienate other elements of Israel. When the Philistines encamped against Judah for the express purpose of capturing Samson, Judah surrendered the Danite "hero" to the oppressors (15:9–13). But the "spirit of Yahweh" (15:14) again seized Samson, and he killed an entire contingent of Philistines with the jawbone of an ass (15:15; cf. 3:31), thus providing a victory for Yahweh over his enemies and an etiology for the place at which the events were localized. Connected to this was a second etiology, this one for the well in Ramat Lehi, for Yahweh had provided the thirsting Nazirite with water to revive his spirit (15:17–19). Thus, the deuteronomistic writer notes that Samson judged Israel twenty years "during the time of the Philistines" (*bîmê pĕlištîm*, 15:20), a period of judgeship that stood as an indictment of both the new generation of Israel and the office of the judge. The oppressor had not been overthrown, and Israel had not secured its land or constructed itself as a separate and holy people.

The final indictment of Samson and the individual exploits with which he would be remembered occur at Gaza, where he had once performed a mighty feat while mingling with a Philistine prostitute

---

[107]   The actions of both the Philistine wife (14:16–18) and Delilah (16:4–21) and their betrayals of Samson present interesting contrasts to the faithfulness of the Canaanite prostitute Rahab and her loyalty to the Israelite spies (Joshua 2).

(16:1–3). After falling in love with Delilah, yet another foreign woman who betrays him at the behest of her countrymen (16:4–21), Samson is finally captured by the Philistines. It is at the temple of Dagon in Gaza that the final deliverance to be attributed to this judge will occur. Blinded by the Philistines, used as a draft animal to grind grain, and prodded by their taunts to entertain them, Samson utters his final request of Yahweh. Rather than request the defeat of the enemy or the deliverance of Israel, Samson asks instead that Yahweh strengthen him this one final time in order that he might avenge himself against the Philistines for their having blinded him (16:28). His plea is purely personal and selfish. He seeks no deliverance—only vengeance. He requests to die with the Philistines (16:30), and his wish is granted. His judgeship ends with the burial notice and the second indication that he had indeed served as judge (16:31). This final reference, however, is in the past tense (šāpaṭ), indicating that both this figure and this period were at an end.

With Samson, then, the "office" of judge and deliverer, at least as a method of leadership of the people and as an organizing force that can provide for the identity of the group, is revealed as a failure. Though he was able to inflict numerous isolated victories against the Philistines, killing more by his own death than while he was alive (16:30), he was unable to provide a permanent solution to the Philistine aggression. This deliverance would not occur until the career of David. In almost every sense, Samson is the "polar opposite of Othniel."[108] The schematic style that characterized the narrative presentation is now abandoned by the deuteronomistic narrator.[109] No doubt the oppression of Israel and the concomitant fear of assimilation and loss of identity continued to build. Indeed, it would be the Philistine pressure that would provide the background for the upcoming stories of the complete breakdown of the community and its near self-destruction for want of competent, dependable leadership. The narrativized rituals of Joshua that had created the ideal for the people in the land are missing in Judges. There the ritual became the episodic succession of generations, each of which failed to be dedicated to Yahweh and each of which faced destruction by and assimilation into the people of the land. What was needed was the right leadership. But for the deuteronomistic historian, the time was not yet at hand.

---

[108] Webb, *The Book of Judges*, p. 170.
[109] For an analysis of the various characteristics of the "judge" formula that are found outside the book of Judges, see the analysis of Schunk, "Die Richter Israels," pp. 254–56.

6

THE NECESSITY OF KINGSHIP: THE FAILURES OF THE PAST

I. The Necessity for a New Order

With the end of the account of Samson and his term as "judge" over Israel (Judg 16:31), the deuteronomistic scheme of apostasy, oppression, cry, and deliverance that served to organize the stories of the judges (Judg 2:6–3:6) is broken and no longer provides a predictable pattern for the accounts that follow.[1] Instead, Judges 17–21 provides a series of loosely connected narratives that depict the near dissolution of the community that identified itself as "Israel." The complete lack of leadership and direction is illustrated by the notice that times were such that "each man would do what was right in his own opinion,"[2] an authorial comment that provides a frame for the materials presented (17:6; 21:25). The succession of judges from Othniel through Samson had failed to create

---

[1] Sections of the account of the career of Samuel (e.g., 1 Sam 7:2–17) include him among those figures to be counted as judges (M. Noth, *Überlieferungsgeschichtliche Studien* [3rd ed.; Tübingen: Max Niemeyer, 1967], p. 55). As will be apparent in the discussion that follows, such inclusion is appropriate on the conceptual level, but the role of "judge" is only one of several transitional roles that the deuteronomistic writer assigns to Samuel. On the variety of roles attributed to Samuel, see W. F. Albright, *Samuel and the Beginnings of the Prophetic Movement* (The Samuel H. Goldman Lectures; Cincinnati: Hebrew Union College, 1961), pp. 3–28.

[2] *ʾîš hayyāšār bĕʿênāyw yaʿăśeh*, 17:6; 21:25.

the ideological status for Israel that had been envisioned in the guidelines of Deuteronomy.

If the situation were to change in a positive fashion and Israel were to become a distinctive people devoted to Yahweh alone, then a new form of leadership would be necessary. The new interpretive frame that emphasized the anarchic situation also provided an indicator of the developments that would occur by noting that "in those days, Israel had no king."[3] This notice provides for the temporal construction of a period of transition that will recount several different attempts to fill this leadership void prior to the establishment of kingship recounted in 1 Samuel 8–12. This perspective recognizes that kingship was, for the deuteronomistic writer, a legitimate institution[4] that had played a highly significant role in the formation and preservation of Israel as a people and, under David, had constituted a "golden age" during which the ideals of the deuteronomic conceptualization of the nation had been realized.[5] The experiment with judges had clearly failed to produce the form of leadership that would provide the cohesive unity necessary to regain the territory that had been lost, but to which the community's identity remained connected.[6] The decisions concerning the future would have to

---

[3] *bayyāmîm hāhēm ʾên melek bĕyiśrāʾēl*, 17:6; 21:25; see also 18:1; 19:1. For T. Veijola, Judges 17–21 is original to the deuteronomistic history and provides a basis for understanding the positive evaluation of kingship that is presumed in the history; *Das Königtum in der Beurteilung der deuteronomistischen Historiographie: Eine Redaktionsgeschichtliche Untersuchung* (Annales academiae scientiarum Fennicae B 198; Helsinki: Suomalainen Tiedeakatemia, 1977), pp. 15–29. The majority of modern commentators, however, continue to follow the evaluation of Noth that these chapters were secondary additions to the history (*Überlieferungsgeschichtliche Studien*, p. 54, n. 2).

[4] The recent study of the deuteronomistic evaluation of kingship by G. E. Gerbrandt, *Kingship According to the Deuteronomistic History* (SBLDS 87; Atlanta: Scholars Press, 1986), provides an excellent investigation of the problems associated with the interpretation of kingship within the history. He concludes that kingship, for the deuteronomistic writer, was a legitimate form of government for Israel. Additionally, the role of the king was to lead Israel as its covenant administrator who would insure that Israel remained loyal to Yahweh alone (pp. 96–102, 189–94).

[5] Within the context of the formation of myths of ethnic descent, and hence the creation and formation of ethnic identities, the concept of a "golden age" during which the ideals of the mythic ideology were "actually" realized is a common phenomenon. On the importance of such symbolic representations in the formation of ethnicity, see A. D. Smith, *The Ethnic Origins of Nations* (Oxford: Blackwell, 1986), pp. 191–92. For a discussion of the application of the term "nation" to pre-modern, pre-industrial states, see Smith's discussion on pp. 6–18.

[6] The exilic community, no doubt, found itself in a position in which it was devoid of established and recognized forms of leadership and in grave danger of

be worked out through the evaluation of a variety of positions, all of which might have competed for dominance.[7] Royal, priestly, prophetic, and wisdom traditions were all preserved and reapplied to the new understandings of Israel that were being developed in the setting of the exile.[8] The first three of these traditions play a significant role in the deuteronomistic narratives presenting the transformation to kingship and the implications that such a development had on the identity and preservation of the people Israel, both past and future. The narrative creates a "social drama" that, by virtue of the breach of regular relations, precipitates a crisis that entails redressive action to resolve the situation that threatened the existence of the group.[9]

II. Priestly Failures: An Unknown Levite and the Destruction of Community

The initial story of this section introduces the themes of both the royal and the priestly traditions that permeate these materials. The account of Micah and his shrine and the story of the migration of Dan are connected by the figure and actions of the unnamed Levite who takes on the role of a priest.[10] In its present form, this story weaves together the

assimilation to the surrounding cultural groups. As A. D. Smith has asserted, myths of ethnic descent often represent the means of adapting to change and frequently emerge most specifically during periods of rapid and significant cultural shifts; "National Identity and Myths of Ethnic Descent," *Research in Social Movements, Conflict and Change* 7 (1984) 118–19.

[7] M. Smith has drawn attention to the existence of at least two major political positions that were influential in the formation of the materials constituting the Hebrew Bible; *Palestinian Parties and Politics that Shaped the Old Testament* (2nd ed.; London: SCM, 1981), pp. 75–95. The deuteronomistic writer clearly is to be associated with what Smith calls the "Yahweh-alone party."

[8] This more complex view of the competing traditions and visions that could shape the form of the community's future might be seen as indicative of the possibilities of variation within this "Yahweh-alone" position. The importance of these competing traditions during the exilic period has been noted by P. D. Hanson, "Israelite Religion in the Early Postexilic Period," in *Ancient Israelite Religion: Essays in Honor of Frank Moore Cross* (ed. by P. D. Miller, P. D. Hanson, and S. D. McBride; Philadelphia: Fortress, 1987), pp. 492–506.

[9] On the concept of "social drama," see V. Turner, *Dramas, Fields, and Metaphors: Symbolic Action in Human Society* (Ithaca: Cornell University Press, 1974), pp. 38–42.

[10] The account of the wandering Levite who is hired as a priest is generally interpreted as reflecting an "archaic" period before the standardization of the Levitical line of priests as an official part of the Israelite and Judahite cultus. See the

themes of cultic image, Levitical priesthood, and conquest to form a cultic etiology for the Danite shrine that has, quite undeniably, a pejorative character.[11] Additionally, another unnamed Levite appears as a central actor in chapter 19 and thus provides a connection between the accounts of the conquest of the city of Laish/Dan and the Israelite atrocities at Gibeah. In the absence of a king (17:6; 18:1; 19:1; 21:25), the stories concerning priestly and tribal forms of leadership come to the fore.

The episode begins quite simply: "There was (wayhî...) a man from the hill country of Ephraim named Micayah" (17:1; cf. 13:2; 19:1b; 1 Sam 1:1; etc.). Temporally the event continues the period of the judges, though no precise chronological reference is given. Spatially, the location of the events remains ambiguous, for the account notes only that this Micayah, "Who is like Yahweh?," whose name is shortened to Micah in 17:5, was from the hill country of Ephraim (har-ʾeprayim) and there built his shrine (17:8). Using a portion of the silver his mother had consecrated for the construction of an image, but that he had stolen and subsequently returned (17:2–3),[12] his mother commissioned the casting of a pesel ûmassēkâ, a "molten image," which was placed in the "shrine of Micayah" (bêt mîkāyĕhû, 17:4). In reply to the question embodied by his name, "Who is like Yahweh?," the central figure gives an answer—an image.[13] No particular form of the image is noted, nor need any particular shape be imagined. According to the deuteronomic code, anyone making such a thing is to be cursed, for such images are abominations to

---

discussion of A. Cody, *A History of Old Testament Priesthood* (AnBib 35; Rome: Pontifical Biblical Institute, 1969), pp. 52–61.

[11] M. Noth, "The Background of Judges 17–18," in *Israel's Prophetic Heritage: Essays in Honor of James Muilenburg* (ed. B. W. Anderson and W. Harrelson; New York: Harper & Brothers, 1962), pp. 69–71. For the deuteronomistic writer, the pejorative aspects are related to the polemic that was developed against the northern counter-cultus instituted by Jeroboam I (1 Kgs 12:28–33), and the fate of the Danite shrine (Judg 18:30b) anticipates the fate of the northern kingdom (2 Kgs 17:5–41); cf. M. Brettler, "The Book of Judges: Literature as Politics," *JBL* 108 (1989) 409.

[12] D. Marcus has suggested that Micah did not steal the money from his mother, but that he was simply bringing her the money that she had dedicated ("In Defense of Micah: Judges 17:2: He was Not a Thief," *Shofar* 6 [1987] 72–80).

[13] On the occurrences of the phrase *pesel ûmassēkâ*, see M. Noth, "The Background of Judges 17–18," p. 72. B. Halpern, in conjunction with the assertion that the shrine is to be located in Bethel, identifies the form of the image as that of a bull ("Levitic Participation in the Reform Cult of Jeroboam I," *JBL* 95 [1976] 36).

Yahweh.[14] Rather than a devoted Yahwistic act, it would seem that "Who is like Yahweh?" had constructed a counter-cultus.

This suspicion is confirmed in the very next statement, which makes clear the deuteronomistic writer's evaluation of the deed of Micayah, now called Micah, the proprietor of a shrine (*bêt ʾĕlōhîm*, 17:5; cf. 17:8). To complete his personal shrine, Micah constructs an ephod and teraphim (*ʾēpôd ûtĕrāpîm*)[15] and appoints one of his sons to be his priest.[16] The story demonstrates the individualization of the group that threatens to destroy the people. The mention of the ephod and teraphim, items along with the images that will be utilized in the construction of a tribal shrine by Dan (cf. 18:14, 17, 18, 20), reflects the deeds of an earlier figure, Gideon. The ending note to this first short narrative, that "each man" would act in accord with his conscience (17:6), demonstrates the danger implicit in the developing situation.

The deuteronomistic writer develops the narrative further by introducing a new character into the story, a Levite, a member of the preferred priestly group (cf. Deut 18:1–8). The ensuing section of the account shows how Micah attempted to legitimize his otherwise non-deuteronomic shrine by hiring one of these peripatetic hierophants to be his priest in place of his own son (17:7–13). The Levite is introduced as a sojourner from Bethlehem in Judah (17:7). He had left his home "to sojourn wherever he could find a place" (*lāgûr baʾăšer yimṣāʾ*), and it was his desire to "make his way" (*laʿăśôt darkô*) that had led him to come to the hill country of Ephraim and to the shrine of Micah (*bêt mîkâ*, 17:8). When Micah learned that this person was a Levite, Micah offered to hire him to remain with him as his priest (17:10), a position which the Levite

---

[14] *ʾārûr hāʾîš ʾăšer yaʿăśeh pesel ûmassēkâ tôʿăbat yhwh maʿăśēh yĕdê ḥaraš*..., Deut 27:15; see also Deut 5:8.

[15] The identification of each of these items of cultic paraphernalia remains uncertain, though it seems that the ephod refers to some type of priestly garment that might be connected with divination. In the present context, the teraphim seem to refer to a type of cultic image that might also be associated with divinatory practices; K. van der Toorn, "The Nature of the Biblical Teraphim in the Light of the Cuneiform Evidence," *CBQ* 52 (1990) 212–13.

[16] Contrary to the assertion of R. Boling, *Judges* (AB 6A; Garden City, NY: Doubleday, 1975), p. 256, this verse is hardly "anticlimactic." The account makes explicit the illegitimate nature of Micah's deeds. Likewise, the reference to the appointment of a priest from among his sons refers most explicitly to his family and is not a summary of the events that follow.

was willing to accept (17:11).[17] The result was that the Levite became "like one of his sons" (*kĕʾaḥad mibbānāyw*; contrast v. 5) and was consecrated as a priest, as had been one of Micah's sons earlier. Judg 17:13–18:1 forms a transition narrative that both concludes the present section and introduces the next. For Micah, the installation of the Levite as priest insured in his mind "that Yahweh will make things go well for me" (*kî-yêṭîb yhwh lî*, 17:13). The deuteronomistic concept of allegiance to Yahweh, observance of the Mosaic law, or adherence to the covenantal obligations (cf. Josh 24:20) had now been reduced to the level of personal actions. The lack of a king (18:1), the failure to install a covenant mediator who would see that Israel adhered to the covenant, is again recalled both to frame this episode (cf. 17:6) and to introduce the next.

Whereas the Levite was able to find a place to dwell and a shrine in which to work, the tribe of Dan, introduced in 18:1b, had not yet received an inheritance among the tribes. According to Joshua and Judges, Dan had received an inheritance, but had failed to take it. This contrasts with the Levite, who, in accord with deuteronomic ideals, was not supposed to receive an inheritance, at least according to the account given here.[18] In terms of narrative symmetry, however, this notice is important, not only in explaining the migration of the tribe of Dan, but also in returning the narrative movement to the failures noted at the beginning of the book of Judges. According to Judg 1:34–35, the tribe of Dan had been pressed by the Amorites into the hill country and did not allow Dan to dwell in the plain. The Amorites, it would seem, continued to live in the cities that had been allotted to Dan (Josh 19:40–46). According to the allotment lists in Joshua, Dan had been forced to migrate northward and to conquer a city known as Leshem, which it renamed Dan (Josh 19:47–48). In Judges, however, the author splits the allotment account and expands on the migration of the tribe and its conquest and renaming of Laish, which is

---

[17] Verse 10 ends with the note that "the Levite left" (*wayyēlek hallēwî*), which makes little sense within the context. It seems most likely that this is a dittography from the beginning of the next verse (cf. *BHS*).

[18] F. A. Spina has correctly noted the difficulties in reconstructing the history of the tribe of Dan, especially with respect to the contradictory nature of the sources. As he points out, Dan had no territory according to Josh 19:47 and Judg 18:1–7, but passages such as Josh 19:40–46 and 21:23–24 note that this was hardly the case ("The Dan Story Historically Reconsidered," *JSOT* 4 [1977] 60). Historical reconstruction is further hampered with the recognition that the story of the Danite conquest follows a basic narrative pattern used for "campaigns of inheritance"; A. Malamat, "The Danite Migration and the Pan-Israelite Exodus-Conquest: A Biblical Narrative Pattern," *Bib* 51 (1970) 1–16.

now connected with the shrine of Micah.[19] In this way, the failures of the northern tribes that dominate the introductory chapter of Judges are reemphasized and are associated with the religious failures accentuated in the story of Micah's shrine.

The deuteronomistic author does not simply separate these two types of failure, for in the ideological perspective formed by the narrative it is precisely the failure to adhere to the proper forms of worship that created the military and social failures on the part of the people "Israel." To emphasize this, the account of Micah's cultic trappings and the Levitical priest is intertwined with the account of the Danite slaughter of the people of Laish.[20] The cultic improprieties committed by Micah are extended to tribal proportions in a manner that stands in direct conflict with the more "official" Judahite traditions concerning the legitimate shrine (cf. 18:31).

In a manner reminiscent of a number of other biblical accounts, the tribe of Dan sends out spies to check their way.[21] Just as the Levite had come to the shrine of Micah in the hill country of Ephraim (17:8), so too do the spies from Dan (18:2). They recognize the Levite's voice and question him, learning that he had been hired as a priest by Micah, via a rather matter-of-fact rendition of the previous events (18:4). The only official functions performed by the Levite occur next in connection with the Danites rather than with Micah. At their request, he inquires of the success of their "way" (vv. 5–6) and receives a positive reply.[22] With this assurance, they continue on the journey to Laish and there find an unsuspecting, peaceful place.[23]

---

[19] On disparity in the city name Leshem or Laish, see Boling, *Joshua*, p. 466.

[20] It is notable that Leshem/Laish is not included by Josh 19:40–46 among the cities allotted to Dan. Though it must remain completely conjectural, the attack of Dan on the unsuspecting city in Judg 18:27–29 could be understood as a violation of the deuteronomic concept of holy war regarding cities that were distant from the lands listed in Deut 20:17.

[21] For an analysis of the literary structure of this chapter, see the discussion of B. G. Webb, *The Book of Judges: An Integrated Reading* (JSOTSup 46; Sheffield: JSOT, 1987), pp. 184–87. A number of these allusions are presented by Webb (pp. 185–86).

[22] Despite R. Polzin's notice of the possible ambiguity of this reply (*Moses and the Deuteronomist* [New York: Seabury, 1980], p. 198), it is apparent that the actors in the narrative all perceive it to have been a favorable one.

[23] 18:7 and 27 present a number of interesting problems to the interpreter. For a discussion of the major ones, see Boling, *Judges*, p. 263, and J. A. Soggin, *Judges* (OTL; Philadelphia: Westminster, 1981), pp. 272–73.

Neither the shrine of Micah, along with the molten image, the ephod, or the teraphim, nor the Levite whom he had hired as priest had acted in accord with the ideals prescribed for Israel. When the Danites received the report of their spies and journeyed forth on their path of conquest,[24] they too came to the hill country of Ephraim, to the shrine of Micah (18:13; cf. 17:8; 18:2). When they learned of the cultic installation there, they proceeded to the Levite's house and took the image, ephod, and teraphim (18:14–18). When the Levite challenged them, they simply enticed him into their service with a better offer than that proffered by Micah: "Which is better, that you should be priest to the household of one man or that you should be priest to a tribe, and a clan in Israel?" (18:19).

Neither religious propriety nor commitment to one's promises is featured. Rather, it is the individuality of the characters involved that takes precedence. The Levite goes with them and steals the cultic apparatus of Micah. When Micah pursues, pleading with the Danites that they had taken his god which he had made (18:22–24), his confession of his breach of what was to be understood as Israelite religious practice was brushed aside by a threat of violence that led him to withdraw (18:25–26). The Danites were now free to go on "their way" (*darkām*, 18:26; cf. 18:5; 17:8), a way that had been sanctioned by the Levite (18:6), whose own way now was part of theirs. For the deuteronomistic writer, however, the proper "way" (*derek*) was the "way of Yahweh," and the variety of travails that Israel had encountered had been presented by Yahweh to see if the people would follow along the "way of Yahweh" (Judg 2:22), one that could be assured only by observing "this book of the law" (*sēper hattôrâ hazzeh*, Josh 1:8). In both cultic and communal terms, Israel had failed.

As the Levite had predicted, the "way" of the Danites prospered, for they were able to capture and resettle Laish, renaming it Dan (18:27–29). Any connotation of success in obtaining an inheritance in Israel (cf. 18:1b) was quickly negated by Dan's own cultic impropriety. There they established the image which they had stolen from Micah, setting up their own shrine in their new city. Central to the deuteronomic code's presen-

---

[24] Embedded in the account of the migration of the tribe northward is an etiological note that Dan encamped in *qiryat yeʿārîm*, a city belonging to Judah, which was then renamed *maḥănēh-dān* (18:12). The reason for its inclusion at this point is obscure. It might be related in some way to the reading of the LXX in Josh 19:48, which recounts the conquest of Leshem, where the *běnê-dān* are replaced by the *běnê yěhûdâ*. On the problems associated with Josh 19:48, see Boling, *Joshua*, p. 463.

tation of the ideal form of Israel was the restriction of worship to "the place which Yahweh would choose."²⁵ The deuteronomistic writer gives no indication that Yahweh had provided any directions for the selection of this place. The narrative depicts quite the opposite situation, for it notes that they established "Micah's image" (*pesel mîkâ*) as the focus of their cult "all the time that the house of God (*bêt-hā'ĕlōhîm*) was in Shiloh" (18:31).²⁶ "The shrine of God" in Shiloh contrasts directly with "Micah's image" established in Laish and "a shrine" (*bêt 'ĕlōhîm*) that had belonged to Micah (17:5) and which had provided the cultic apparatus for this Danite shrine.²⁷ Of additional interest, especially for the accounts that follow, is the notice that a certain Jonathan, son of Gershom, son of Moses, i.e., a Mushite priest,²⁸ served there. This provided the shrine with an ancient and authoritative priesthood that traced its lineage back to Moses. Whether or not this Jonathan is the same as the Levite²⁹ is not made explicit by the narrator, and this might be taken as an indicator that the two figures ought not to be identified with each other.

This possibility is further suggested by the second section of the narratives concluding the book of Judges. Chapters 19–21 provide for the final dissolution of the community as Israel declares a holy war against one of its own tribal members for a crime committed against the concubine of a certain Levite who dwelled in the hill country of Ephraim (19:1b). Like the Levite of the previous story, he remains unnamed. Indeed, in this final section of Judges, all of the individual characters are

---

²⁵ *hammāqôm 'ăšer yibḥar yhwh*, Deut 12:5, 11, 14, 18, 21, 26; 14:23, 24, 25; 15:20; 16:2, 6, 7, 11, 15, 16; 17:8, 10; 18:6; 26:2; 31:11. For the deuteronomistic author, this place was ultimately identified with Jerusalem (1 Kgs 8:16, 44, 48; 11:13, 32, 36; 14:21; 2 Kgs 21:7; 23:27).

²⁶ Josh 18:1 notes that the whole congregation of Israel gathered at Shiloh and "set up the tent of meeting there" (*wayyaškînû šām 'et-'ōhel mô'ēd*). Shiloh remains the location of the "official" shrine throughout the accounts concerning Eli and Samuel (cf. 1 Sam 1:3, 9, 24: 2:22; etc.). On the nature and function of the tent of meeting, see R. J. Clifford, "The Tent of El and the Israelite Tent of Meeting," *CBQ* 33 (1971) 221–27.

²⁷ The negative evaluation of the shrine and the reference to the exile of Israel anticipate the Israelite establishment of a counter-cultus by Jeroboam and the later destruction of the northern kingdom by Assyria, ca. 722/1 BCE.

²⁸ For this reading, see F. M. Cross, *Canaanite Myth and Hebrew Epic* (Cambridge: Harvard University Press, 1973), pp. 197–98. For an expansion of this thesis concerning the Mushite priesthood and some of its possible implications, see the comments of B. Halpern, "Levitic Participation in the Reform Cult of Jeroboam I," pp. 31–42.

²⁹ Soggin, among others, identifies the two; *Judges*, p. 276.

unnamed.[30] Yet the identification of this Levite with the one of the previous narrative is suggested by the notice that he took a concubine for himself from Bethlehem in Judah (19:1), the home of the itinerant Levite who was seeking "his way" wherever he might find it (17:7–8). Since propriety has played so small a part in the activities of the actors to this point, to suggest that the Danites simply replaced the Levite with a priest from a more prestigious line would be consistent with the actions of the characters involved. If this is the case, then, the unnamed Levite of chaps. 17–18 appears in Judges 19 once again as a sojourner in the hill country of Ephraim and provides a narrative link between the episodes that otherwise might appear to have been unrelated.

In a series of remarkable events, the boundaries of proper social activity are trespassed, and the very existence of a portion of Israel is threatened. The initial section of the narrative, which might be divided into three parts,[31] centers around the events concerning the Levite, his concubine, and the actions of the men of Gibeah of Benjamin.[32] The story itself moves quickly, from the introduction of the Levite and his concubine to the initial movement, the concubine's desertion of the Levite and her return to her father's house,[33] an event that might be suggestive of the dissolution of the basic familial unit. In an effort to convince her to return, the Levite and his attendant (*na'ar*) go to her father's house, and

---

[30] P. Trible, *Texts of Terror: Literary-Feminist Readings of Biblical Narratives* (OBT; Philadelphia: Fortress, 1984), p. 66.

[31] The analysis here follows the divisions suggested by Trible, who divides chaps. 19–21 into three "acts": 19:1b–30: the story of the concubine; 20:1–48: Israel's wars against Benjamin; and 21:1–24: the efforts to secure wives for Benjamin (*Texts of Terror*, p. 87, n. 5). The narrative, quite obviously, can be divided in different ways. For example, Webb divides the narrative into four episodes: 19:1–28: the outrage at Gibeah; 19:29–20:11: preparation for war; 20:12–48: the war; and 21:1–24: post-war reconstruction; *The Book of Judges*, pp. 187–88.

[32] The most exhaustive treatment of Judges 19 is the literary analysis of H.-W. Jüngling, S. J., *Richter 19—Ein Plädoyer für das Königtum* (AnBib 84; Rome: Pontifical Biblical Institute, 1981). According to Jüngling, Judg 19:1–30a and 21:25 form an original unit to which chap. 20 was later added. Chapter 21 was an even later addition, according to his analysis (p. 285). For Jüngling, the narrative stands as a strong polemic directed against the Saulide house of Gibeah (p. 293).

[33] The reason for the concubine's abandonment of the Levite is unclear. The MT reads *wattizneh*, "and she committed harlotry/played the harlot," while LXX[A] seems to reflect a tradition that reads "she became angry at him." Perhaps the best solution to the problem is that suggested by Soggin (*Judges*, p. 284), to derive the verb from an otherwise unattested *zānâ* II, related to the Akkadian *zenû*, "to be angry" (*CAD* 21, pp. 85–86). All the versions agree that it was the woman who departed.

there the Levite experiences the epitome, if not the complete caricature of hospitality (19:4–9),[34] all of which provides a contrast with the events that are to follow.

Departing for home in the late evening, the Levite took his concubine and attendant and was forced to find a place to spend the night. He chose to bypass the city of Jebus, identified as Jerusalem, refusing to stay in a "city of foreigners who are not Israelites" (ʿîr nokrî ʾăšer lōʾ-mibbĕnê yiśrāʾēl, v. 12). Instead, he chose to go to Gibeah, a town which belonged to the tribe of Benjamin. While initially finding no one to offer him accommodations, he was finally welcomed by an old man who was coming back from working in the field (19:15–16). The dissolution of order and group identity is suggested by the identity of the old man: he was "from the hill country of Ephraim and was sojourning in Gibeah, but the men of that place were Benjaminites" (v. 16). The Levite and his entourage had found no help from the Israelite inhabitants of the town, but had been welcomed only by a fellow Ephraimite who was, like them, also separated from his home. The concept of Israel, a people composed of twelve tribes, had disintegrated into individual tribal units, none extending the proper hospitality to members of other tribal groups.

Following the meeting of the men and a brief conversation (19:16–21), the group accepts the invitation of the old Ephraimite and goes to his house. In contrast to the hospitality displayed by others in the text, "the men of the city, worthless men" (ʾanšê hāʿîr ʾanšê bĕnê-bĕliyyaʿal, v. 22) surrounded the house and demanded that the old man hand over his guest that they might "know him." Whatever the exact nature of their inhospitable demand,[35] it is interpreted by the host as nĕbālâ, "folly, sacrilege," which he urges them not to commit (vv. 23–24).[36] But the world

---

34 S. Lasine has noted that the context in which these actions are presented might be understood as an "inverted world" where the actions that are performed "are often ludicrous, absurd, and self-defeating" ("Guest and Host in Judges 19: Lot's Hospitality in an Inverted World," *JSOT* 29 [1984] 37). The issue of hospitality as an indicator of community and unity within the context of these stories has been emphasized by S. Niditch, "The 'Sodomite' Theme in Judges 19–20: Family, Community, and Social Disintegration," *CBQ* 44 (1982) 365–75.

35 As is the case with the parallel demand in Gen 19:5, the exact intentions of the group remain obscure. While the verb yādaʿ clearly can carry sexual connotations, the narrative does not demand that a homosexual interpretation be given to the text. What is clear from the response of the host in each of these parallel accounts is that the actions of the people of the town are in violation of the rules of hospitality.

36 Compare the use of the term in Deut 22:21; Josh 7:15; Judg 20:6; 2 Sam 13:12; Isa 9:16; 32:6; Jer 29:23; Job 42:8. While it is applied to sexual misconduct, it is also used

created by the author of the text becomes completely inverted with the actions that follow, for it becomes readily apparent that none of the expected social relationships that unite a people on either a group or an individual level is still operative. The host offers his virgin daughter and the Levite's concubine to the men with the invitation that they do to them "that which is good in your eyes" (*haṭṭôb bĕ⁽ênêkem*, v. 24),[37] but specifies that any sacrilege should be avoided. The events that follow, however, go far beyond any concept of "folly" or "sacrilege" that the term *nĕbālâ* might be understood as implying.

When the men proved unwilling to relent in their demands, "the man" (*hā⁾îš*, v. 25) seized "his concubine" (*pîlagšô*) and "sent her" out (*wayyōṣē⁾*) to the men. The focus shifts now to the Levite and his concubine; no mention is made again of either the daughter of the host or of the host. The course of the narrative has taken a deliberate and tragic turn. The "worthless men" (*bĕnê-bĕliyya⁽al*) then sexually abused the woman throughout the night, sending her away at daybreak. Able to make it back to the door of the house where her "master" (*⁾ădônêhā*) had remained, she collapsed. The totality of such a vicious crime that violated every social norm is recounted in the most laconic of fashions and is described in two brief verses (vv. 25–26).

But the depth of the crime and its communal aspects have only begun to be exposed by the deuteronomistic writer. If communities are united by common identities, values, and concerns, i.e., relationships, then it is clear that described here is a community that is in the gravest of dangers, for at every level both individuals and groups are unable to engage in any form of socially acceptable interchange.[38] For the deuteronomistic writer, this narrative reality displays the need for communal adherence to certain norms and standards that might be used as a method of redress for this social drama that threatens the existence of

---

in reference to other types of misdeeds. It is best to understand the reference as signifying the disintegration of an existing and socially proper relationship between groups; cf. the comments of A. D. H. Mayes, *Deuteronomy* (NCB; Grand Rapids: Eerdmans, 1981), p. 311.

[37] As Lasine notes ("Guest and Host in Judges 19," p. 55, n. 19), the events in Judges 17–21 illustrate that doing what is right in one's own eyes is often doing what is evil in Yahweh's eyes. In support of this he notes a movement within Judges from "doing what is evil in Yahweh's eyes" (2:11; 3:7, 12; 4:1; 6:1; 10:6; 13:1) to "doing what is right in one's own eyes" (14:3; 17:6; 21:25).

[38] The emphasis of these chapters on community and relationships has been convincingly demonstrated by Niditch in "The 'Sodomite' Theme in Judges 19–20," pp. 268–71.

this group. Even in terms of the ritualized activities of social dramas, however, redress does not always lead immediately to reintegration. Whether or not such might occur in this narrative remains to be determined.

Though the community of Benjaminite Gibeah failed in its responsibilities to provide hospitality to the Levite and his group, and though the host failed in his responsibilities to protect his guest, and though the Levite failed to respect or protect the concubine, and though the men of the city failed to respect the person or rights of the woman, none of these compares to the failure of the Levite to show responsibility, compassion, concern, or any other generally accepted human emotion for the woman, his concubine. The narrator notes simply that in the morning the Levite departed to go "on his way" (*darkô*, 19:27; cf. 17:8; 18:5, 26) and seemingly stumbled over the woman lying in the doorway, her hand on the door sill. His command to her to arise that they might be on their way, indeed the *only* words he speaks directly to her in the entire narrative,[39] defies belief. But the Levite proves able to act in an even more discreditable fashion. Paying no attention to the state or welfare of his concubine, he places her upon his ass and returns home (vv. 27–28). Upon arriving at his house, after an unspecified passage of time and distance, instead of attending to the needs of his concubine, either in terms of health care or burial preparations (the text does not explicitly note whether or not the woman was dead),[40] he hacks the woman's body into twelve pieces, which he sends through all the borders of Israel.[41] Israel reacts with unanimity: "All who saw exclaimed: Such a thing as this (*kāzōʾt*) has not happened or been seen from the time that Israel came out of Egypt until this day" (v. 30a).[42] The abomination, *kāzōʾt*, ambiguous as it is, brought about the need for consideration and action, i.e., communal redress.

---

[39] It is interesting that the Levite's concubine never speaks to him in the narrative. As Trible has noted, only the men speak in this story; *Texts of Terror*, p. 66.

[40] Polzin has emphasized the ambiguity of the text here and suggests that the Levite's hacking into pieces the still-living woman constitutes "the most outrageous thing of all" (*Moses and the Deuteronomist*, p. 200). The LXX adds "for she was dead" after the notice in v. 28 that the woman did not answer when the Levite told her to get up. Boling (*Judges*, p. 276) suggests that the proper reading is that of the LXX, the MT having suffered a haplography (ʿnh [ky mth]). It is noted by the Levite, when he testifies before the assembled people, that the woman was already dead (Judg 20:5).

[41] Compare the actions of Saul (1 Sam 11:7) and Ahijah (1 Kgs 11:30–39).

[42] LXXA contains a lengthy addition at the end of v. 30 that recounts instructions given by the Levite to the men he sent throughout Israel, and it is these who are to ask the Israelites if such a thing had ever before happened and to implore them to

In response to the mandate to take counsel and speak (v. 30b), all Israel came together "like one man" at Mizpah, a group that was identified as "the congregation of the people of God" (*qĕhal ʿam hāʾĕlōhîm*, 20:1–2). In response to the individual actions that had led to the present situation, now Israel responds in a manner appropriate for the deuteronomistic ideals. They assemble together as a single community before their god, an identification that forms the very content of their ethnic identity. In order to correct the situation that threatens to dissolve the community, all Israel convenes for holy war.[43]

Not since Judg 2:1–5 have "all the Israelites" (*kol-bĕnê yiśrāʾēl*, 20:1) gathered together.[44] In a seemingly parenthetical manner, the narrative notes that the Benjaminites (*bĕnê binyāmīn*, 20:3) heard that Israel (*bĕnê-yiśrāʾēl*) had assembled at Mizpah. But such an aside is critical to the developments in the community, for the distinction between Israel and Benjamin is maintained throughout these stories. Because a thing like this had not happened since Israel had been in the land, the assembly inquired as to the cause of the atrocity. The Levite, identified now as the "husband of the murdered woman" (*ʾîš hāʾiššâ hannirṣāḥâ*, v. 4), testifies that the Benjaminites of Gibeah, who had sought to kill him, had abused and killed his wife, whom he then dismembered and sent throughout Israel. His action, he claims, was in response to the "wickedness and sacrilege" (*zimmâ ûnĕbālâ*) which *they* had committed (v. 6). In a manner reminiscent of the response to the circulation of the mutilated corpse, now the Levite invokes the collected people of Israel to take counsel and respond.[45]

---

consider these things. For a discussion of the textual problems involved, see Soggin, *Judges*, p. 289, and Boling, *Judges*, p. 277; Jüngling (*Richter 19*, pp. 246–51) interprets v. 30b, and hence the problem presented by the Septuagint's reading, as a secondary expansion, added to the text to connect chaps. 19 and 20.

[43] Niditch notes that the Benjaminites' actions have broken the demands of behavior expected of all Israelites, and compares this situation to the deuteronomic concepts expressed in Deut 13:13–19 ("The 'Sodomite' Theme in Judges 19–20," p. 372).

[44] As Boling notes, "all Israel" is also referred to in Judg 8:27, where they failed by "committing harlotry" after the cultic creations of Gideon (*Judges*, p. 283).

[45] On the manner in which the Levite intentionally distorts his testimony, see Lasine, "Guest and Host in Judges 19," pp. 48–49. Perhaps the most telling point of the Levite's presentation of the "facts" is that the "worthless men" (*bĕnê bĕliyyaʿal*, 19:22; cf. 20:13) who committed the crime are transformed into the "nobles of Gibeah" (*baʿălê haggibʿâ*, 20:5).

The desire to respond is a form of social redress, and here Israel proceeds in a manner that is filled with ritual elements. The entire episode concerning the war against Benjamin and the restoration of the remnant of the tribe is described within the parameters of the ritual fulfillment of the oaths taken by the members of the united tribal group whose standards and social boundaries had been violated. All Israel assembles (v. 11), and men are sent throughout the tribe of Benjamin, requesting that the guilty men, the *bĕnê bĕliyyaʿal*, be handed over so that they might be put to death. In this way, according to the narrative, Israel might be able "to exterminate the evil" from its midst.[46] If this were done, then the commands associated with Deut 13:13–19 might be fulfilled and Israel might do "that which was upright in the eyes of Yahweh your god" (*hayyāšār bĕʿênê yhwh ʾĕlōhêkā*, Deut 13:19). Such activity might be able to exonerate the type of *ad hoc* political policies that had delivered and united Israel to this point. If Israel could cooperate and agree to fulfill the commands of the Mosaic laws under the guise of a sacral confederation, then a tribal form of political governance might be justifiable, the priesthood being the medium through which the divine will would be known to the assembled people.

This type of action, however, requires the cooperation of all the tribes, a community from which the narrator has already excluded Benjamin. In response, the Benjaminites refuse "their brothers" (*ʾăḥêhem*, 20:13) and assemble themselves for war (20:14; cf. 20:11). With the sides drawn up, the troops are mustered, and final preparations for the resolution of the social schism are made (20:15–17). Since the Benjaminites have chosen not to hand over the guilty parties, the only recourse is the implementation of the strictures of holy war, i.e., the complete eradication of the offending city of Gibeah. But the battle is not so confined, for as Gibeah belonged to the tribe of Benjamin, so the conflict becomes one that unites the entire tribe against the remainder of the larger group, "Israel." For Israel to reestablish its social balance according to deuteronomistic ideals, Benjamin, the tribe refusing to participate in the "purification" of the larger communal group, would have to be destroyed.[47]

---

46 The phraseology here (*bʿr hrʿ mqrbk/ myśrʾl*) is thoroughly deuteronomic. See M. Weinfeld, *Deuteronomy and the Deuteronomic School* (Oxford: Clarendon, 1972), pp. 355–56.

47 The importance of warfare to the formation and maintenance of ethnic identity and group cohesion should be noted here. As the battle lines are here drawn, conscious decisions are implied *vis-à-vis* the group with whom one chooses to be

The attempt at resolution continues in its ritualized form with the inquiry of God made by Israel at Bethel (20:18).[48] The question posed to the oracle is nearly identical to that which opened the book in 1:1, only now Israel's battlefield enemy is no longer the Canaanites, but the Benjaminites. In a very important sense, the insider, Benjamin, by its failure to uphold the standards of the larger tribal community, has become an outsider. The leader against the new enemy would be Judah, the only successful group in the initial chapter of Judges. The deuteronomistic writer has now brought the story of the "period" of the Judges full circle. Without stable leadership (i.e., a king and dynastic succession), Israel is not only unable to defeat its enemies; it is also unsuccessful at maintaining the unity of the group itself. Israel suffers through two defeats at the hands of the Benjaminites (20:20–28), each time engaging in various oracular and ritual ceremonies to insure the proper performance of the war. It is not until the third battle against Benjamin, one which has numerous parallels with the ritualized narrative of the conquest of Ai in Joshua 8, that Israel is successful.[49]

The ritualization of the narrative account becomes clear through the intrusion of the divine into the battle account. This was not simply a battle of warring tribes: "Yahweh defeated Benjamin" (*wayyiggōp yhwh ʾet-binyāmīn*, 20:35). Israel fulfilled the dictates of holy war by putting the city of Gibeah to the sword (Deut 13:16), destroying it completely (20:37–40), and by attempting to destroy the towns remaining to Benjamin (20:48). But the complete destruction of Benjamin failed, for some six hundred men were able to escape and hold out at the "Rock of Rimmon" (*selaʿ hārimmôn*) for four months (20:47). Of the tribe of Benjamin only 600 warriors remained. Despite the widespread warfare, the issue had not yet been resolved. Or had it?

The opening statement of the final chapter recalls, in parenthetical manner, an oath that Israel had taken at Mizpah (cf. 20:1, 3): "No man from us will give his daughter to Benjamin for a wife" (*ʾîš mimmennû lōʾ-*

---

identified. On the role of war and ethnic formation, see A. D. Smith, "War and Ethnicity: The Role of Warfare in the Formation, Self-Images and Cohesion of Ethnic Communities," *Ethnic and Racial Studies* 4 (1981) 375–97.

[48] The idiom "to inquire of god" (*šʾl bʾlhym*) is standard for such proceedings (cf. 1:1; 18:5; 20:27) and no doubt required the presence of specialized divinatory priests trained in such matters.

[49] It is generally agreed that at least two sources recounting the defeat of Benjamin have been combined in 20:29–48 to produce the present narrative. On the problems involved in attempting to untangle these sources, see the discussion of Soggin, *Judges,* pp. 293–96.

yittēn bittô lĕbinyāmīn lĕʾiššâ, 21:1). The fulfillment of this vow would, in effect, force the survivors of Benjamin to find women from outside Israel, thus, in ideal terms, becoming outsiders themselves (cf. Deut 7:3–6; Josh 23:11–13; Exod 34:15–16). Again, however, Israel inquires of Yahweh, this time asking why it has happened that a tribe from Israel has been lost (21:3), a question that should be redundant in light of the incredible breach of the social contract that gave rise to the present dilemma (19:30; 20:3). Rather than to give explicit recognition to the nature and import of the events that had transpired, Israel returned to the performance of its standard ritual (cf. 2:1–5). Rather than repent and change its ways, Israel "felt sorry" for Benjamin (21:6) and concocted a way to resolve the dilemma and preserve the tribe of Benjamin. Evidently two oaths had been taken at Mizpah: one concerning the withholding of Israelite women from the Benjaminites and the other, the "great oath" (*haššĕbûʿâ haggĕdôlâ*, 21:5), concerning the punishment for any tribe that failed to participate in the assemblage of the people. Anyone who failed to participate would be put to death (*môt yûmāt*). Since no one from the city of Jabesh Gilead had come to the assembly (vv. 8–9), the entire city, save the 400 virgin women found there, was put to the sword. The *ḥērem*, instituted here for failure to come to the aid of the confederacy (cf. 5:23), was directed against this city, and the virgin women were taken to Shiloh.[50]

This reference to Shiloh provides a connection with the two accounts that follow. Despite the efforts of the Israelites to provide wives for the remnant of Benjamin and avoid the implications of the oath they had taken and the ideology to which they were to adhere, they were still 200 women short. To resolve this conflict, a second source of available women was sought.[51] The answer is found in the fact that there was an "annual feast of Yahweh in Shiloh" (*ḥag-yhwh bĕšílô miyyāmîm yāmîmâ*, 21:19), a reference that clearly anticipates the introduction of the stories of Samuel and Eli that follow (1 Sam 1:3). Likewise, Judg 18:31 has already noted that "the house of God" was in Shiloh, giving this city a position of sacral authority within the narrative. Yet, for Israel, the resolution of the problem of obtaining 200 women for the remnant of the Benjaminites was to overcome any concern with the sanctity of a Yahwistic feast or shrine. Rather, the collected congregation instructs the

---

[50] The exaggerations in the story are obvious, given that Jabesh Gilead appears in 1 Samuel 11 as a thriving town. Whether this contains an anti-Saulide polemic is difficult to determine, though the connections between Saul and this town will be emphasized in the accounts of the rise and fall of Israel's first king (cf. 1 Samuel 31).

[51] It is clear that 21:16–24 is a parallel account of 21:1–15.

Benjaminites to set an ambush and to seize the young women who have come out to participate in the festival (21:20–21). Thus, Israel, giving assurance to Benjamin that it would protect them from any accusations that might arise (21:22), insured that Benjamin would remain a viable tribal unit and that its marriage alliances would all remain endogamous. With tribal sanctions, the Benjaminites were able to seize the needed women and to return to their land and rebuild their cities. The issue had been resolved. Benjamin had been reintegrated into the larger tribal confederation. At the same time, a severely negative polemic had been directed at the tribe of Benjamin, which cannot help but provide a negative background for the introduction of the first king of Israel, Saul, the Benjaminite,[52] that will be recounted in the continuation of the story. In contrast stands the leadership role of Judah, the tribe designated by God. That David would come from Judah and find himself in conflict with Saul of Benjamin is already prepared for by the narrative. The social drama had reached its narrative denouement. Problematically, the Israelites had failed to fulfill the demands that the evil be purged from their midst. Rather, each man of this reconstituted "Israel" returned to his tribe and clan; each went to his inheritance (21:24). Israel, despite its best intentions, had proven unable to adhere to the deuteronomic code; instead, "each man did what was right in his own eyes" (21:25b). So long as its people failed to conform to what was right in Yahweh's eyes, Israel would fail to unite itself as a separate people, as Yahweh's personal possession. The experiment with both *ad hoc* and non-dynastic priestly leadership had failed. Might an established priestly family provide the necessary stability?

III. From the Priestly to the Prophetic:
Eli and Samuel

The events associated with the itinerant Levite had proved disastrous for the tribal association, leading to the near extermination of one of the primordial "Israelite" groups, the Benjaminites, and causing the tribal confederation to destroy one of its own towns and to seize the women from another. Though directed at another group, the plea of the host in Judg 19:23–24 that the men of the city refrain from committing a social breach (*nĕbālâ*) had gone unheeded. Without consistent and dependable leadership that would stabilize the group and maintain the

---

[52] See above, n. 32.

boundaries of its ideological foundations, i.e., its special covenantal relationship with Yahweh, the existence of the community called "Israel" would be endangered. Such an account has obvious emotive and cognitive appeal to a group attempting to create and maintain its own special identity within a crisis situation.

The narratives introducing Eli, the priest of Shiloh, and Samuel, his attendant and the prophetic voice of the premonarchic ideals of community, are connected with the preceding materials by a number of threads.[53] There is no apparent stylistic or temporal break with the stories which are continued by the opening chapters of the first book of Samuel. Instead, the narrator introduces a certain Elkanah of Ramathaim in the same paratactic manner that characterizes the presentation to this point: "Now there was a certain man from Ramathaim...and his name was Elkanah" (*wayhî ʾîš ʾeḥad min-hārāmātayim ... ûšĕmô ʾelqānâ*, 1 Sam 1:1; cf. Judg. 13:2; 17:1; 17:7; 19:1). This Elkanah not only resided in the "hill country of Ephraim" (*har ʾeprayim*), the setting of much of the material at the end of Judges, but he also went on a yearly pilgrimage (*miyyāmîm yāmîmâ*; cf. Judg 21:19) to the Yahwistic shrine at Shiloh, where Hophni and Phineas, the sons of Eli, officiated.[54] Hence, the reference to a com-

---

[53] Modern scholarly consensus concerning the composition of the books of Samuel, as with the other portions of the deuteronomistic history, remains elusive. It is most common to argue that the final form of the text is the result of the redactional combination of various hypothetically reconstructed narratives, such as the history of David's rise, the Ark Narrative, or an even earlier prophetic history. Convenient summaries of the various theories may be found in R. W. Klein's *1 Samuel* (WBC 10; Waco, TX: Word, 1983), pp. xxv–xxxiii; P. K. McCarter's *1 Samuel* (AB 8; Garden City, NY: Doubleday, 1980), pp. 12–30; and A. F. Campbell's *Of Prophets and Kings: A Late Ninth-Century Document (1 Samuel 1–2 Kings 10)* (CBQMS 17; Washington, DC: The Catholic Biblical Association of America, 1986), pp. 1–16. An insightful review essay concerning some of the major recent works on 1 Samuel that is highly critical of the more traditional approaches, such as those represented in the works just noted, is R. Polzin's "1 Samuel: Biblical Studies and the Humanities," *RelSRev* 15 (1989) 297–306. On the competing voices that are evident in the text of 1 Samuel 1–15 when read as a whole, see J. S. Ackerman, "Who Can Stand before YHWH, This Holy God? A Reading of 1 Samuel 1–15," *Prooftexts* 11 (1991) 1–24.

[54] The traditions associated with Shiloh in the Samuel materials indicate that there was a "temple" of Yahweh (*hêkal yhwh*) located there (1:9; 3:3; cf. *bêt-haʾĕlōhîm* of Judg 18:31). Whatever the historical circumstances of the development of Yahwistic religion might have been, it is clear that the deuteronomistic writer is asserting in the present context that the cultus at Shiloh was an authentic Yahwistic shrine and that the priesthood there had claims to legitimacy. It is possible that Eli and his priestly line, like that of the Mushite Jonathan of Dan (Judg 18:30), traced its lineage back to Moses; cf. Cross, *Canaanite Myth and Hebrew Epic*, pp. 196–203.

mon shrine in a common location and the implication of a continuing common festival connect this otherwise new episode with the stories that have been presented thus far.

Along with such continuities, some new aspects that contribute to the process of transition are introduced. Elkanah had two wives, Peninnah, who had sons and daughters, and Hannah, who was barren (1:2, 6). The narrator focuses attention on Hannah and presents her, not her husband, as a central figure in the story of the birth of the lad Samuel. It was Hannah who, at the annual festival, went to the shrine of Yahweh to pray and, in her distress over her childlessness, to make a vow. This, however, is hardly the only shift that is presented in the account, for the patriarchal priest, Eli, is introduced into the narrative couched in *royal* terminology (1:9b),[55] a device most fitting for the continuation of the question of the role of the priesthood in the leadership of a nation which lacks a king. Would it be this levitical priest of the Mushite line and his sons who would establish a line of succession that might stabilize the community?

Hannah's vow was a very simple, straightforward one: if Yahweh would give her a son, then "I will give him to Yahweh all the days of his life" (*ûnětattîw layhwh kol-yěmê ḥayyāyw*, 1:11). Additionally, the vows of a Nazirite are offered by Hannah in her request.[56] The uprightness of Hannah is contrasted, quite directly, with the somewhat bumbling manner of the "royal" priest Eli, who is able to watch the entire event from his "throne" and then misunderstand it. Hannah prays silently, her words heard only by Yahweh (and the reader/hearer of the account), yet with her lips moving. Eli, not recognizing the prayers of the woman, considers her to be drunk (1:13) and even directs her to put away her strong drink (1:14). Most telling is the correction that Hannah gives to Eli, for she implores him not to include her among the "worthless women" (*bat-běliyyāʿal*, 1:16), a term which should bring to mind the *běnê*

---

[55] R. Polzin, *Samuel and the Deuteronomist: A Literary Study of the Deuteronomic History, Part Two: 1 Samuel* (San Francisco: Harper & Row, 1989), p. 23.

[56] Cf. Judg 13:5, 7; Num 6:1–21. It seems likely that the text has suffered from haplography and that a portion of the Nazirite vow has been lost. The text-critical problems associated with the books of Samuel are numerous and will be noted only where they might have an effect on the interpretation being presented. Both S. R. Driver, *Notes on the Hebrew Text and the Topography of the Books of Samuel* (2nd ed. [a reprint of the 1912 Oxford edition]; Winona Lake, IN: Alpha, 1984) and H. P. Smith, *The Books of Samuel* (ICC; Edinburgh: T. & T. Clark, 1969 [first printed 1899]) remain valuable for text-critical issues. The more recent commentaries of McCarter (*1 Samuel*) and Klein (*1 Samuel*) make use of readings from the scrolls from Cave 4 at Qumran.

běliyyaᶜal of Gibeah. Properly chastised, Eli invokes a blessing on her request.[57] The distinction between impropriety and sobriety is clearly too elusive for Eli to grasp.

The narrator compresses the return home, the impregnation and entire pregnancy of Hannah, and the birth and naming of Samuel into two verses (1:19–20). These events comprised exactly one year, so Elkanah and his family immediately returned to Shiloh for the annual festival (1:21). Both the aspects of piety, in the sense of dedication to a tradition of worship, and pilgrimage, in the form of allegiance to a recognized holy site, form an essential part of the patterning of the presentation of this chapter. Hannah, however, remained behind until the child was weaned, a request that received the blessing of her husband, thus giving his consent to her earlier vow. When this had been accomplished, she took the lad, along with an appropriate sacrifice, to Eli in Shiloh and announced that Samuel was the child that she had requested and that Yahweh had fulfilled her vow (1:27; cf. 1:17). The entire event of the vow and its fulfillment is ritualized by the narrative account of pilgrimage, prayer, and sacrifice, and defines a mode of conduct that has been absent since the "days" of Joshua. Such ritualized presentations are designed to endorse both the private, individual aspects of the pious worshipper, in the prayer and vow made by Hannah at the shrine, and the public aspects of devotion to the deity, with the acts of pilgrimage and sacrifice.

The communal and public nature of the private narrative of the birth and dedication of Samuel is emphasized by the brief but evocative "Song of Hannah" (2:1–10).[58] This hymn, suitable for use as a song of thanksgiving in the cultus, is placed on the lips of the pious Hannah, whose

---

[57] The story of the birth of Samuel is filled with allusions to requesting or asking, words related to the root *šaᵓal*, which occur in 1:17, 20, 27, 28, and 2:20. The name Samuel, according to the implications of the text, is related to this root. For a discussion of the meaning of the name Samuel and its probable form, see McCarter, *1 Samuel*, pp. 62–63. The numerous textual differences between the MT and the LXX in 1 Samuel 1 are treated by S. D. Walters, "Hannah and Anna: The Greek and Hebrew Texts of 1 Samuel 1," *JBL* 107 (1988) 385–412.

[58] While this poetic passage is generally regarded as an independent composition (cf., e.g., the remarks of H. W. Hertzberg, *I & II Samuel* [OTL; Philadelphia: Westminster, 1964], p. 29), it is now integrated completely into the surrounding narrative and introduces a number of themes that will be developed in the accounts of the emergence of kingship in Israel.

presentation of the hymn creates a "chorus" of voices,[59] each drawing the reader or hearer into the communal setting being created by the narrative preparation for the consolidation of the land under a new form of leadership. Emphasized throughout the hymn are the magnificence of Yahweh (2:2, 8, 10), the elevation of those who had been reduced in status (2:4–5, 7–8), and the invocation that Yahweh give strength to his "king" and "messiah" (2:10). Such references imply the end to possible leadership by the priesthood. Instead, the leader would be a "king" (*melek*), who would distinguish the coming days from those tumultuous ones during which "Israel" had failed to free itself from the oppressors who surrounded the nation (Judg 17:6; 18:1; 19:1; 21:25). The enemy confronting Israel now continued to be Philistia, a force introduced within the context of the stories of the judge Jephthah (Judg 10:7), who were the object of the bellicose activities of Samson (Judg 13:5, etc.) but had not yet been defeated.

Eli, Samuel, and Saul would each be involved with the Philistine menace in differing ways and degrees. The stories about them provide numerous transitions within the structuring of the identity of the community by the changes that are realized within the narrative itself. The overlapping of the activities and careers of Eli and Samuel and Samuel and Saul[60] allows the author of the history to deliver direct commentary on the nature of each of the figures and the traditions which they typify. The royal imagery applied to Eli, however, will not be continued by his line. The house of Eli will be destroyed because of its failure to adhere to the covenantal demands placed upon it. The description of the actions of Eli's sons presents the background for the double rejection of his line. There is no ambiguity in the nature of Eli's sons or their prospects for assuming any leadership role in Israel:[61] the author categorizes them as

---

[59] Polzin has noted that at least three voices are to be heard in this hymn: those of the rejoicing Hannah, the exultant king, and the deuteronomistic narrator, each of whom provides a differing perspective on the meaning of the text (*Samuel and the Deuteronomist*, pp. 30–39). In addition to the voices embedded in the text, I would emphasize that there are the voices of those utilizing these materials for instruction and the formation of an identity for the community.

[60] A most significant overlap in the narrative development of these communal structures and ideals is provided in the so-called "history of David's rise" (1 Samuel 16–31), where the rise of David is presented within the context of the demise of Saul. On these materials, see below, chap. 7.

[61] The concept of dynastic succession in the ancient Near East was a standard part of kingship and was an integral aspect of the culture of the age. On the role of dynastic monarchy and the national state, see the discussion of G. Buccellati, *Cities*

"worthless men," *běnê běliyyaʿal,* just like those who had committed the outrage at Gibeah (2:12; Judg 19:22; 20:13). Their failure to know Yahweh was exemplified by the manner in which they conducted the sacrificial cult (2:13–17) so as to "parody" the customs of the priesthood dictated in Deut 18:1–8.[62] Such actions are judged a "great sin" (2:17) and place these worthless sons, who refused the directions of their father (2:25) as well as those of Yahweh, in contrast to Samuel, who continued to prosper due to Yahweh's blessing (2:21, 26).

To indicate the absolute judgment that would be exacted on the recalcitrant priesthood represented by the sons of Eli, the deuteronomistic writer notes that "Yahweh desired to kill them" (*kî-ḥāpēṣ yhwh lahămîtām,* 2:25). To proclaim this judgment, the author introduces an anonymous figure, "a man of god" (*ʾîš-ʾĕlōhîm,* 2:27),[63] whose announcement reconfirms the rejection of Eli and his line. But the nature of this announcement goes beyond its simple implications for the priestly line of Shiloh. This "pivotal" deuteronomistic passage[64] presents a preview of the history of the "legitimate" priestly line that will not be fulfilled until much later in the narrative itself. Further, the very act of failing to assign a name to this prophetic figure allows for the "intrusion" of the narratorial voice and, in public usage, that of the community leader, into the story to deliver a commentary on the nature of the actions and to provide a vision for the future.[65]

---

and Nations of Ancient Syria (Studi Semitici 21; Rome: Istituto di Studi del vicino Oriente, 1967), pp. 125–30.

[62] P. Miscall, *1 Samuel: A Literary Reading* (Bloomington, IN: Indiana University Press, 1986), p. 17. The proscriptions for the handling of the sacrifices in Deut 18:3 differ from those delineated in Lev 7: 28–36.

[63] On the expression *ʾîš (hā)ʾĕlōhîm* and its usage in the deuteronomistic materials, see W. E. Lemke, "The Way of Obedience: 1 Kings 13 and the Structure of the Deuteronomistic History," in *Magnalia Dei: The Mighty Acts of God* (ed. F. M. Cross, W. E. Lemke, and P. D. Miller, Jr.; Garden City, NY: Doubleday, 1976), pp. 313–14.

[64] R. A. Carlson, *David, the Chosen King: A Traditio-Historical Approach to the Second Book of Samuel* (Stockholm: Almqvist & Wiksell, 1964), pp. 44–46.

[65] On the role of prophecy in the deuteronomistic narrative, see G. von Rad, *Studies in Deuteronomy* (SBT; London: SCM, 1953), pp. 78–93, and W. Dietrich, *Prophetie und Geschichte. Eine redaktionsgeschichtliche Untersuchung zum deuteronomistischen Geschichtswerk* (FRLANT 108; Göttingen: Vandenhoeck & Ruprecht, 1972). One of the major functions of the introduction of such prophetic "predictions" within the structure of the history that has gone unrecognized is the ability to "suspend" the temporal aspects of the narrative and to allow any number of sub-plots to be presented, all of which are constantly reinterpreted by the seemingly "final" and "irrevocable" divine will announced earlier. In ideological terms, this device also

The prophetic announcement provides a divine assurance that Israel would not be led by a priestly line. Most instructive about the present passage is the manner in which the concepts of divine promise and fulfillment are presented via the oracle. With the spoken words attributed to Yahweh, and with the unnamed prophetic voice privy to those very words, the divine will becomes textually accessible. Even though Yahweh had promised (ʾāmôr ʾāmartî) that the house of Eli would "walk before me forever" (yithallĕkû lĕpānay ʿad-ʿôlām, 2:30), the situation was to be changed. It would seem that the concept of eternity, at least as applied to the promises made by Yahweh, might be subject to qualification. In this instance, the misdeeds of Eli and his sons (2:29) could offset a promise that had originated in the days of the Exodus (2:27–28). Such qualifications placed upon the divine promise create a degree of uncertainty about the absolute stability of any concept of succession, be it priestly or otherwise.[66] The conditionality of even the unconditional is expressed in the explanation given for the actions: "I will honor those who honor me, but those who despise me will be cursed" (mĕkabbĕday ʾăkabbēd ûbōzay yēqāllû, 2:30). No clearer reminder could be given that the commands of the Mosaic law, the boundary manifesto for the deuteronomistic writer, were binding upon all; failure to follow the way of Yahweh could, and possibly would, negate any prior agreements. The announcement of such was not addressed to Eli alone, but to the community for whom dependence upon divine promises formed an important support in times of crisis.

This decision did not constitute a rejection of the priesthood; rather, it was the rejection of a certain priestly line and the subjugation of the priesthood to a new organizational ideal. Yahweh would establish a "faithful priest" (kōhēn neʾĕmān) and would establish a "sure house" (bayit neʾĕmān) for him, but the final fulfillment of this prophecy would

---

allows the writer to insure the reader or hearer that the actions which occur are not random, but are rather part of a divine purpose that is, quite obviously, within the purview of the author. The importance of this method of structuring the narrative will be developed more fully in the discussions of the accounts in the books of Kings.

[66] This qualification placed on the absolute nature of the divine word will be developed even further in the consideration of the divine promise of eternal dynasty given to David in 2 Samuel 7 but "conditionalized" in its announcement to Solomon (1 Kgs 9:1–9). The idea of the possible revocation of the divine promise is reflected also in both Exod 32:7–14 and Num 14:11–12, where, because of the failure of the people to follow the divine will, the promises to Abraham (cf. Gen 12:1–2, etc.) are nearly transferred to Moses.

remain quite distant from the time of its delivery.[67] This new priest would, according to Yahweh's decree, "walk before my anointed forever" (*hithallēk lipnê-mĕšîḥî kol-hayyāmîm*, 2:35). It would be an anointed king (cf. 2:10) who would stand at the head of this people, served by a trustworthy priesthood of a line other than that of Eli. The sign (*hā'ôt*) that this was assured would be that both of Eli's sons, Hophni and Phineas, would die on the same day (2:34; cf. 4:11).

With the notice of the rejection of the priesthood as the appointed leaders of the community, the way was opened for the institution of the kingship. But for the deuteronomistic writer, kingship would not be an institution which would arise in and of itself without the need for a mediator and director. A conscience was needed to guarantee that the king never failed to fulfill the ways of Yahweh guaranteed in the "law of the king" (Deut 17:14–20). For the deuteronomistic author and for the vision of community and identity being created within his narrative, only a prophet would be able to provide the guidance necessary for the future. The lad Samuel, who continued to serve Yahweh (3:1), would provide for the creation and definition of this role. As defined by Deut 18:18, the *nābî'* would be a person whom Yahweh himself would raise up and on whose lips he would place his word (*wĕnātattî dĕbāray bĕpîw*). It would be the prophet who would serve as intermediator between the divine and human realms and who would bridge the gap between the divine will and human perception in times of crisis.[68]

The significance of the position of Samuel is emphasized in the narrative of his establishment as Yahweh's prophet. Unlike the sons of Eli, he did not inherit this position; rather, he was elevated to it on the initiative of Yahweh alone.[69] The deuteronomistic author reorganizes the

---

[67] The obvious parallels here with the promise to David (2 Sam 7:12–16) are neither accidental nor unintentional. It is generally accepted that the "faithful priest" is to be identified as Zadok. The narrative explicitly notes the fulfillment of the prophecy in 1 Kgs 2:26–27, 35. It is significant to note also that this prophetic announcement might serve as the explanation for what seems to be the change in the status of the Levites within the "reform" efforts of Josiah (2 Kgs 23:8–9; cf. Deut 18:1–8).

[68] On the applicability of the term intermediator to the biblical prophet and the social prerequisites that support intermediation, see R. Wilson, *Prophecy and Society in Ancient Israel* (Philadelphia: Fortress, 1980), pp. 28–88.

[69] For an analysis of 1 Samuel 3 as a "prophetic call narrative," see M. Newman, "The Prophetic Call of Samuel," in *Israel's Prophetic Heritage* (ed. by B. W. Anderson and W. Harrelson; New York: Harper & Row, 1962), pp. 86–97. On the general topic of the "call narrative," see K. Baltzer, "Considerations Regarding the Office and Call

structure of the group so that it might function in accord with the means envisioned as appropriate by the writer. In order to do this, he must establish some authority structure.[70] For the deuteronomistic writer, it would be the prophet, not the priest, who would provide the leadership for the transition to a monarchy, but only by way of the direction provided by the pronouncements of Yahweh. The conceptual setting for the elevation of Samuel is provided in the opening verse of 1 Samuel 3: "Now the word of Yahweh ($d\check{e}bar$-$yhwh$) was scarce ($y\bar{a}q\bar{a}r$) in those days; there was no frequent ([?] $nipr\bar{a}\d{s}$) vision" and no $d\check{e}bar$-$yhwh$ to provide direction to the community. The initiation of Samuel into the prophetic role itself is depicted as a distinct change in the young man's social status; prior to these events, "the word of Yahweh had not been revealed to him" ($w\check{e}\d{t}erem\ yigg\bar{a}leh\ {}^{\textgreek{}}\bar{e}l\bar{a}yw\ d\check{e}bar$-$yhwh$, 3:7).

By virtue of the appearance of Yahweh, Samuel was recognized by all Israel as the successor to Eli. The initial pronouncement given to the new prophet was a reconfirmation of the rejection of the house of Eli (3:11–14),[71] which confirmed that its fulfillment was imminent. Most important for the development of the narrative and the organizational implications for the community is the reaction given by Eli when Samuel, at the old priest's insistence, revealed Yahweh's words against him (3:16–18). Eli replied simply: "He is Yahweh. May he do what is good in his eyes" (3:18). The representative of the priestly line acknowledges the judgment of Yahweh and the elevation of Samuel. The deuteronomistic writer reconfirms the new status given to the young man in 3:19–4:1a, a passage that establishes the ideal figure of the prophet.[72] It would be

---

of the Prophet," *HTR* 61 (1968) 567–81; N. C. Habel, "The Form and Significance of the Call Narrative," *ZAW* 77 (1965) 297–323; and W. Richter, *Die sogenannten vorprophetischen Berufsberichte* (FRLANT 101; Göttingen: Vandenhoeck & Ruprecht, 1970).

[70] As A. Cohen has noted, the effective operation of social interest groups is dependent upon the development of boundaries (or the perception of distinctiveness), communication, decision-making procedures, ideology, authority structure, and socialization; "Introduction: The Lesson of Ethnicity," in *Urban Ethnicity* (ed. A. Cohen; New York: Tavistock, 1974), pp. xvi–xvii. The manner in which the deuteronomistic history fits into this scheme should be apparent.

[71] On these verses and the way in which they are commonly related to the previous announcements of the judgment against the house of Eli in 2:27–35, see T. Veijola, *Die ewige Dynastie. David und die Entstehung seiner Dynastie nach der deuteronomistischen Darstellung* (Annales academiae scientiarum Fennicae B 193; Helsinki: Suomalainen Tiedeakatemia, 1975), pp. 35–39.

[72] Campbell, *Of Prophets and Kings*, p. 66.

through Samuel, established now as Yahweh's prophet, that the *dĕbar-yhwh* would continue to be revealed to "all Israel" (3:21b–4:1a).[73]

With a new order envisioned by the author and established within the narrative context, the story returns to the external problems threatening Israel in punishment for its failure to fulfill the word of Yahweh (cf. Judg 10:6–7). It is the Philistines, whom Samson only "began" to defeat (Judg 13:5), who now not only provide a threat to Israel's ability to hold the land, and hence to preserve one of its major elements constituting its self-identity, but also threaten to remove one of the central religious symbols of Yahweh's presence with his people. These threats to the existence of the group Israel are addressed in 1 Sam 4:1b–7:1a, an account commonly designated as "the Ark Narrative"[74] because it involves the cult symbol designated as the "Ark" (*ʾărôn*).[75] At the same time, the Philistine threat provides the external background for the transition from the *ad hoc* leadership of the judges to the emergence of a more permanent form of leadership, a transition that would be accomplished under the auspices of the prophet Samuel. Hence, it is only fitting that this story be interwoven with the account of the emergence of this new figure and his function in Israel's "history."

Since the "Ark Narrative" is an integral portion of this larger account, it should be possible to illustrate the ways in which it func-

---

73 Though the ending of 3:21 is commonly accepted as a secondary expansion to the text (cf. *BHS*), the mention of *dĕbar-yhwh* forms a very tight inclusio with the opening notice in 3:1.

74 The classic formulation of the theory of a pre-deuteronomic independent narrative concerning the Ark is that of L. Rost, *Die Überlieferung von der Thronnachfolge Davids* (BZWANT III/6; Stuttgart: W. Kohlhammer Verlag, 1926 [*The Succession to the Throne of David*, trans. by M. D. Rutter and D. M. Gunn (Historic Texts and Interpreters in Biblical Scholarship 1; Sheffield: Almond, 1982)]). The exact extent and function of this postulated text remain debated. For the different positions, see the recent treatments of the narrative by A. F. Campbell, *The Ark Narrative* (SBLDS 16; Missoula, MT: Scholars Press, 1975) and P. D. Miller, Jr., and J. J. M. Roberts, *The Hand of the Lord: A Reassessment of the "Ark Narrative" of 1 Samuel* (Baltimore: Johns Hopkins University Press, 1977). From the standpoint of literary criticism, as exemplified by the study of Miscall, for example, it is clear that the story of the Ark now forms an integral part of the narrative whole and cannot be separated from its present position in the narrative without much of the fabric of the narrative itself being destroyed (*I Samuel*, pp. 26–40).

75 The biblical materials themselves give differing interpretations of the function of the Ark. In the present context, it is clear that the Ark is regarded as the symbol of the presence of Yahweh among his people. For a brief discussion of the "Ark," see Klein, *1 Samuel*, pp. 41–42.

tioned to define and identify "Israelite" identity and religion over against that of its neighbors. It is the story of the Ark that serves as an introduction to the request for a monarchy, an institution that would, in the words of the elders and people, make Israel "like all the nations" (1 Sam 8:5, 20; cf. Deut 17:14). To maintain a concept of Israelite uniqueness within the context of those nations, however, the deuteronomistic historian uses the narrative account of the Ark[76] to compare and distinguish the Israelite and Philistine religious and ethnic identities. As a result, the descriptions of the Philistine practices recounted within the story of the Ark may be viewed as functionally negative characterizations rather than as accurate accounts of the ways in which the Philistines responded to an actual crisis presented by having taken the Ark of Yahweh in battle.[77] As such, this portion of the narrative serves, as does the deuteronomistic national history as a whole, as a form of theodicy that explains the existing inequalities of both power and privilege and legitimizes the particular social order that is under scrutiny.[78]

The "Ark Narrative" might be summarized as follows: in response to an attack by the Philistines that led to an Israelite defeat, the Israelites decided to take "the Ark of the covenant of Yahweh of hosts who is enthroned upon the cherubim" (ʾărôn běrît-yhwh ṣěbāʾôt yōšēb hakkěrūbîm, 1 Sam 4:4; cf. 2 Sam 6:2)[79] into battle (1 Sam 4:1b–5). The Philistines heard

---

[76] The story of the Ark belongs to a narrative genre well represented within the ancient Near East that describes the carrying off and returning of a conquered nation's gods. Such materials are attested from Hittite and Mesopotamian sources from the Old Babylonian period through the end of the Neo-Babylonian era. The major comparative materials are presented and summarized by Miller and Roberts, *The Hand of the Lord*, pp. 9–16, 76–87.

[77] R. Oden, in his consideration of the issue of "cultic prostitution" in ancient Israel, points out that the biblical denunciations of sacred prostitution "perhaps …ought to be investigated as an accusation rather than as a reality"; *The Bible Without Theology* (San Francisco: Harper & Row, 1987), p. 132. I suggest that a similar situation exists here with the characterizations of the Philistine religious practices.

[78] On the nature of theodicy in the process of social world construction and maintenance, see P. Berger, *The Sacred Canopy: Elements of a Sociological Theory of Religion* (Garden City, NY: Doubleday, 1967), esp. p. 59. In the production of the final edition of the work sometime during the period of the exile, the crisis would have been understood as both external, i.e., conquest and exile at the hands of the Babylonians, and internal, i.e., the necessity of explaining the cognitive tension between the established theology that provided an interpretive frame for the national religious institutions of the people and facts of the conquest and destruction of those institutions.

[79] It is possible that this reflects a liturgical name for the Ark; Cross, *Canaanite Myth and Hebrew Epic*, p. 69.

the battle cry of the Israelites and immediately knew that the Ark had been brought into the field. Interestingly, the Philistines here refer to the battle camp of Israel as "the camp of the Hebrews" (*maḥănēh hā'ibrîm*, 4:6), a reference that serves to name and thus differentiate the groups involved.[80] Despite the recognition on the part of the Philistines that the Ark represents the presence of the deity who had performed such mighty deeds against the Egyptians, an aspect of Yahweh's abilities that seems to be forgotten with regularity by the Israelites, they still fought and defeated Israel, seizing the Ark as part of their spoil. In the same battle, Hophni and Phineas, the priests who had carried the Ark into the battle camp, died (4:11b; cf. 2:34). The story immediately signals that it is concerned not only with the fate of the Ark, but also with the fulfillment of the promises of Yahweh.

News of the defeat is taken back to Shiloh with a twofold effect. When Eli, still seated on his "throne" (*kissē'*, 4:13; cf. 1:9), received the word that his sons had been killed and the Ark had been taken, he fell backwards, breaking his neck. To demonstrate that the transition in social formation was still far from complete, the writer adds the notice that Eli had "judged Israel for forty years" (*šāpaṭ 'et-yiśrā'ēl 'arbā'îm šānâ*, 4:18b). But the earlier prophecy was not yet completed, for within this context is also recorded the birth of a son to the widow of Phineas, one who bore the name Ichabod (*'î-kābôd*, 4:21–22), "Where-is-the-Glory?," a lament for the loss of the symbol of the presence of Yahweh among his people.

The distress felt by Israel was extended to the Philistine captors of the Ark who placed the captured object before the image of Dagon in their shrine in Ashdod. Soon they discovered the power of this symbol, for twice they found the statue of Dagon fallen from its pedestal, the

---

[80] It is well documented that the term "Hebrew" (*'ibrî*; see also 1 Sam 4:9; 13:3, 7, 19; 14:11, 21; 29:3) is most often used in the Hebrew text as a designation of an Israelite from the perspective of a non-Israelite within the narrative. For a discussion of the term, see McCarter, *1 Samuel*, pp. 240–41. Though it is clear that the term is intended as an ethnic ascriptor, it is most unclear exactly what traits it was intended to convey or at what historical period it came to be applied as a self-description by those who considered themselves Israelites or Judahites. What is important in the present context, however, is the recognition that the act of naming, i.e., of designating a group by a single descriptive term, is an important part of the act of erecting and maintaining social boundaries and identities. On this function, see H. R. Isaacs, "Basic Group Identity: The Idols of the Tribe," in *Ethnicity: Theory and Experience* (ed. N. Glazer and D. P. Moynihan; Cambridge: Harvard University Press, 1975), pp. 46–52.

second time suffering severe breakage. Such provided the etiology for the Ashdodite practice of not stepping on the threshold of the shrine to Dagon (5:1–5; cf. Zeph 1:9). But not only did Yahweh strike down the image of Dagon; he also afflicted the Ashdodites with a plague of "tumors" (*ʿĕpōlîm/ʿŏpālîm*, 5:6),[81] which led the Ashdodites to assemble the Philistine rulers and have the Ark sent elsewhere (5:6–8). The plague followed the journey of the Ark to the Philistine cities of Gath and Ekron (5:9–12), leading the Philistine leaders, after having had possession of the Ark for seven months (6:1), to seek the advice of their own holy men. The Philistine priests gave the details of the ritual that must be followed to determine the cause of the plague and to placate the offended deity (6:3–9). A "guilt offering" (*ʾāšām*) which was to consist of images of "five golden tumors and five golden mice" for the plague that had afflicted them (6:4)[82] was to be returned with the Ark. The Philistine lords followed the directions precisely and returned the Ark to Beth Shemesh and to Israelite territory (6:10–12). The people of Beth Shemesh rejoiced to see the Ark and offered sacrifices for its return, but a plague broke out among them also, leading to the Ark's being taken to Qiryath-Jearim, where it would remain until taken into Jerusalem by David (6:13–7:1).[83]

The crisis described by this narrative and the threat to the Israelite social world construction should be obvious. The possible symbolic reapplications of the story, likewise, should be apparent. The way in which this author presents the Philistines in very non-Israelite ways and, as a result, distinguishes between Philistine and Israelite practice functions to confirm the correctness of all that is Israelite. Though it does not play a role in this story, the deuteronomistic characterization of the

---

[81] The vocalization of the word is uncertain because the MT, in each instance, vocalizes it as though it were the word *ṭĕḥōrîm*, which is intended as a gloss on *ʿplm.* For various conjectures on the nature of the plague, see L. I. Conrad, "The Biblical Tradition for the Plague of the Philistines," *JAOS* 104 (1984) 281–87, and J. Wilkinson, "The Philistine Epidemic of I Samuel 5 and 6," *ExpTim* 88 (1977) 137–41.

[82] The textual problems concerning the point of the introduction of the mice into the story, introduced along with the first mention of the plague tumors in 5:6 in the LXX, and the exact number of "mouse images" that are to be returned (contrast 6:4 with 6:17–18a) do not affect the interpretation of the role and function of the story within the larger narrative. For attempted solutions to these problems, see the commentaries.

[83] Polzin's analysis of this section draws upon the parallels between the account of the movement of the Ark in 1 Samuel 4–6 and the story of David's taking of the Ark into Jerusalem in 2 Samuel 6 (*Samuel and the Deuteronomist*, pp. 68–71) and provides an additional indication that the account might be indicative of the transition in leadership that would be completed only with the reign of David.

Philistines as the ʿărēlîm, the "uncircumcised,"[84] to define the non-Israelite character of this group further explicates the boundary-forming aspects of these materials. The style chosen by the writer is quite clearly satirical in part, for even though the Philistines attempt to placate the offended deity with their reparations, attention to the story itself shows them to have been completely inept. Though the narrator presents a very straightforward account of the Philistine concern with the collection and dedication of the "guilt offering" (ʾāšām), the facetious character of the presentation has been almost completely missed by modern commentators.

At some point what might be called the "situational incongruity"[85] created within the story as related by the narrator is important to consider. While scholarship attempts to resolve the number of images returned with the Ark and the nature of the plague afflicting the Philistines, a rather obvious absurdity is missed: what would an image of a plague-boil, tumor, or hemorrhoid look like?[86] Though various uses and representations of mice are attested in the ancient Near East,[87] plague boil symbols are of a different category. How would golden tumor images appease an angered deity? Though the Philistines attempted to influence what they identified as an angered deity, as the Israelite author presents the story, they did everything in such a way as

---

[84] Cf. Judg 14:3; 15:8; 1 Sam 14:6; 17:26, 36; 31:4; 2 Sam 1:20. Interesting also is Ezekiel's use of ʿărēlîm as a designation of the inhabitants of the underworld. The ideological import of this categorization is even more apparent when the possibility is considered that the Philistines, like many other groups within Syria-Palestine, did indeed practice circumcision. For the evidence, see P. A. Mantovani, "Circoncisi ed incirconcisi," *Henoch* 10 (1988) 51–68.

[85] This phrase is borrowed from J. Z. Smith's discussion of the approach to interpreting mythological materials; *Imagining Religion: From Babylon to Jonestown* (Chicago: University of Chicago Press, 1982), pp. 90–101. Though the present usage differs somewhat from that intended by Smith, I would argue that the application of this idea to the present context is appropriate.

[86] Few scholars have accepted the suggestions of O. Margalith that the phrase ṣlmy ʿkbrym refers to "images of the mouse god" and, by analogy, ṣlmy ʿplym should be translated "images of Apollo," referring to the worship of Apollo Smintheus. According to Margalith, the correction of ʿplym to ṭḥrym reflects the later efforts of the editors of the Hebrew Bible to eliminate the names of foreign deities from the text ("The Meaning of ʿplym in 1 Samuel v–vi," *VT* 33 [1983] 339–41). As ingenious as this solution might seem, it should be noted that it fails to account for the retention of the name of the foreign god, i.e., ʿplym, in all but two cases in the text.

[87] See the study of such uses by B. Brentjes, "Zur 'Beulen' Epidemie bei den Philistern in 1. Samuel 5–6," *Altertum* 15 (1969) 67–74.

to show themselves and their practices as completely unacceptable to the Israelite conception of proper worship.

An analysis of 1 Samuel 5–6 from this perspective provides a different view of the events from that presented by historical-critical or literary approaches. After the disastrous (and, as noted above, somewhat humorous) events precipitated by placing the Ark of Yahweh in the temple of Dagon in Ashdod, an event which itself was credited with producing a rather strange ritual behavior,[88] the Philistines sent the Ark to Gath and then to Ekron, bringing a plague of tumors on the inhabitants of each city. The presence of the Israelite holy symbol in foreign territory had led to the recognition of the necessity of returning it to its place to avoid the slaughter of the people (*wĕyāšōb limqōmô lĕlōʾ-yāmît ʾōtî wĕʾet-ʿammî*, 5:11).

After seven months of such suffering and affliction, the Philistine lords summoned their priests (*kōhǎnîm*) and diviners (*qōsĕmîm*) to provide instructions for the proper return of the Ark, a situation that should have engendered at least the raising of an eyebrow on the part of the reader or hearer. The deuteronomic condemnation of the use of divination (*qōsēm qĕsāmîm*) that occurs in Deut 18:10 renders the entire Philistine enterprise ritually suspect. The reply of these diviners and priests in vv. 3–9 further displays the inappropriateness of the ways of the Philistines, for the reparation is to be made in the first instance, it should be noted, with "images" (*ṣĕlāmîm*) to be fashioned from gold. The injunction against image-making in Deut 5:8 (cf. Exod 20:4) clearly marks this activity as inappropriate for Yahwistic practice, yet at the same time characterizes the Philistines as image makers. If the ambiguity of the form of Dagon[89] depicted in the story creates conceptual problems for the reader, the specification of the form of the *ʾāšām* as images of "golden tumors and golden mice" is even more ludicrous.

The depiction in the narrative of the forms by which the Philistines, at the advice of their priests and diviners, chose to symbolize themselves compounds the severity of the characterization of the Philistines and underscores the depth of the ethnic, cultic, and religious separation that was asserted by the author. Verses 10–18 confirm that the Philistine rulers took great care to follow the instructions of their holy men.

---

[88] On the sometimes happenstance situations that can intrude into and become part of ritual performances, see Smith, *Imagining Religion*, pp. 53–65. That such a situation should be reconstructed for the present text, however, is questionable.

[89] On the problem of the nature of the god Dagon, see the comments by McCarter, *1 Samuel*, pp. 121–22.

Consequently, returned with the Ark was the golden image of a plague tumor to represent each of the Philistine cities. On one level, most certainly, the tumor-images are symbols of the "one plague" that was on all the Philistines. On another, the Philistines have chosen to represent themselves and their cities as nothing other than "anal swellings." The inclusion of the images of the mice, symbols of all that belonged to the Philistine rulers, represented the people of Philistia as pestilence-carrying rodents which were, in Israelite terms, ritually unclean (Lev 11:29).

The presence of those symbolic characterizations in the text, a set of representations chosen to display the non-Israelite ethnic and religious aspects of the Philistines, illustrates the role that a narrative might play in the construction and maintenance of a specifically Israelite world view. Faced with the threat of foreign domination and the loss of central religious symbols and institutions, the deuteronomistic writer compiled a national history that could maintain and legitimize those social structures that defined his particular version of the Israelite world view. Within the context of the exile, with the concomitant loss of land and temple and the threat to the monarchy, an even greater threat was experienced. The dissolution of the boundaries that had created the ethnic social unit identified as Judah and the absorption of the individual Judahite members into the surrounding cultures became, in empirically undeniable terms, a reality that threatened the very plausibility structure that had maintained the Judahite world view. Against the threat that this people would become "like the nations," the history reestablishes the boundaries that were, in the historian's world construction, to be maintained.

The ways in which the Philistines are depicted within the account of the narrative of the Ark confirm the ethnic and religious boundaries that distinguish between Judah and the "others," portrayed here as the conquering Philistine lords. Yet conquerors they are not, for the recounting of their victory is a presentation of their ultimate defeat. Despite their efforts to placate the deity viewed as responsible for the plagues afflicting them, they are depicted as powerless against him. Despite the defeat of Israel and Judah by outsiders, groups who were not a part of their ethnic or social religious world views, the narrative recreates a world that reverses the defeat in the past and promises a similar reversal in the present or future. For the deuteronomistic historian, the covenantal schema developed within this prophetically interpreted past define, maintain, and project a vision of the future identity of the people "Israel" and create the perception of the present as the fulfillment of commitments and promises made in the past. Such reflective reconstructions are also able to project the present as promise and the fulfillment as future.[90] The story of the Philistine capture and return of the Ark might be understood in terms of its functional ability to distinguish the ethnic and religious character of the social world envisioned by the deuteronomistic historian as that which should be externalized and maintained. This social crisis, both as created within the narrative and as realized in the historical situation which provided the background within which it was composed and presented, remained in a transitional state that required some type of redress and reincorporation into the community structure.

IV. The Transition to a New Order: Samuel and Saul

The first task toward the recreation of stability and the restructuring of the community and its ethnic distinctiveness would fall to the prophetic figure of Samuel, the successor to the now defunct priestly line of Eli. The return of the Ark had not brought any apparent indication of blessing or victory to Israel. Rather, it had resulted in a disastrous plague that displayed the power of Yahweh against his own people as well as against his enemies (6:19–20). The narrative indicates that for some twenty years, while the Ark remained in Qiryath-Jearim, the Israelites "lamented"[91] after Yahweh, a notice that introduces a change in the situation of Israel that is about to be given ritual significance in the text. It is with this transitional passage, 1 Sam 7:2–17, that the old pattern that characterized the period of the judges (cf. Judg 2:6–3:6) is concluded and a new period, characterized by adherence to the Mosaic law and an emphasis upon absolute obedience to Yahweh is initiated. The obligations are placed upon both the new king and the newly conceived people.

The career of Samuel concludes the old era and initiates the new. This is performed by way of a call to repentance and the performance of

---

[90] This view of the reflection on the past as promise is presented by T. L. Thompson with respect to the development of the stories of Abraham in the pentateuchal stories; *The Historicity of the Patriarchal Narratives: The Quest for the Historical Abraham* (Berlin: Walter de Gruyter, 1974), p. 329.

[91] The precise meaning of the verb in 7:2 is debated and, following the differing readings of the versions for this verse, has led to numerous suggested emendations. Given the context in which the verb appears, the idea of lamentation following the plague at Beth Shemesh and the continued Philistine harassment seems quite appropriate.

a communal penitential ceremony (7:3–6). Samuel's invocation of the assembled "Israel" emphasizes the conditional nature of this new era. Deliverance would depend upon undivided loyalty to Yahweh:

> If it is with all your heart that you are returning to Yahweh,[92] then put away the foreign gods in your midst, the ashtaroth, and establish your heart on Yahweh and serve him alone (wĕᶜibdūhû lĕbaddô), so that he might deliver you (wĕyaṣṣēl ʾetkem) from the Philistine power (7:3).

Israel, in response to Samuel's entreaty, put away its foreign gods and "served Yahweh alone" (wayyaᶜabdû ʾet-yhwh lĕbaddô, 7:4), thus complying with the requirements of the Yahwistic covenantal demands (cf. Josh 24:23).

This narrative actualization of the exclusive worship of Yahweh, the key factor in the deuteronomistic writer's presentation of Israelite identity, is reinforced by the public profession of sin by the collected group. In Judg 10:10–16 Israel had implored Yahweh to deliver them from the Ammonite threat and admitted that it had sinned by serving other gods. There, however, the nature of the "reform" on behalf of the people was clearly tied to one single situation, and the continuing narrative made it clear that this penitent attitude did not last. In the present context, however, the repentance is in response to Samuel's announcement of the required actions that would result in deliverance from Philistia.[93] Samuel's role does not end here, for he gathers the Israelites together and announces that he will intercede with Yahweh on their behalf (7:5), a confirmation of one of the roles that will be played by this emergent prophetic model in the context of the development of the monarchy.

Israel's performance of libations and fasting leads to a public profession of its sin: "We have sinned against Yahweh" (ḥāṭāʾnû layhwh, 7:6; cf. Judg 10:10, 15). One of the most striking aspects of the presentation of Israel's public confession and ritual performance is the concluding notice in 7:6: "Samuel judged the Israelites (wayyišpōṭ šĕmûʾēl ʾet-bĕnê yiśrāʾēl) in Mizpah." In contrast to the "judgeship" of Eli (cf. 1 Sam 4:18), which had resulted in cultic misconduct, defeat by Philistia, and the loss of the Ark, Samuel's career as "judge" resulted in a national ceremony of repentance

---

92 On the deuteronomic nature of this phrase, see Weinfeld, *Deuteronomy and the Deuteronomic School*, p. 335.

93 It should not be overlooked that the "oppressors" who were responsible for Israel's admission of guilt in Judg 10:10–16 were, at least in the present form of the account, both the Ammonites and the Philistines. No deliverance of the Philistines has yet been recounted in the narrative.

and a victory over the Philistines (7:10). As such, the account may be understood as a parallel and "counter-point" to the narrative of the Ark that preceded it.[94] But in drawing the cyclical accounts of the failures of Israel and its leaders, which began in Judg 2:6–3:6, to a close, it presents a new beginning within which Israel's story might be understood. This Israel that had repented so that "Yahweh's power was against the Philistines all the days of Samuel" (7:13) was now in a position to continue in the way of Yahweh and become his personal possession, i.e., a holy nation, or it could choose to become "like the other nations," a deed that would be an abrogation of the ethnic ideals that had given rise to its very creation.

Now an Israel which had repudiated the ways of its past that had led to its oppression at the hands of the foes surrounding its borders was once again, within the unfolding narrative presentation of the deuteronomistic historian, ready to conquer the land promised as its possession. In order to do this, however, the proper king who would lead them in accord with the covenantal demands of the position would be required. Samuel, the prophet who also acted as Israel's "judge" throughout his life (7:15), would be instrumental in the rise of this new form of leadership. For such to occur, all that was needed was the initiative on the part of one of the parties in the story. The impetus to action was provided by the issue of succession and continuity of leadership, this time in the guise of the sons of Samuel.

As with each major movement within the narrative, the inauguration of a new epoch in Israel's story of its identity is introduced by a solemn assemblage of the people, now in the guise of the elders (8:4). The reason for the gathering was the perversity of Samuel's sons, Joel and Abijah, who had failed to uphold justice and had not walked in the way of their father (8:1–3).[95] The public assembly of elders at Ramah officially ended any aspirations that Samuel might have had toward a succession of his own family or to reinstitute the "ideals" of judgeship that he had been able to maintain in his own career. Instead, with little introduction, the elders command Samuel: "Now appoint us a king to judge us like all the nations" (śîmâ-lānû melek lĕšopṭēnû kĕkol-haggōyīm, 8:5). The demand was straightforward and simple; the implementation of the request would

---

[94] Miscall, 1 Samuel, p. 36.
[95] D. Jobling notes that the attempt to make the institution of judgeship permanent through heredity brings itself to an end and that the people's request for a king is a rebuff of Samuel's own initiative; The Sense of Biblical Narrative: Structural Analyses in the Hebrew Bible, II (JSOTSup 39; Sheffield: JSOT, 1986), p. 63.

require a readjustment of the basic identity of the people's self-percep-
tions. These readjustments are begun in the narrative accounts contained
in 1 Samuel 8–12.[96]

The complexities of viewpoints that are embedded within these
chapters reveal a number of issues critical to the formation and reformation of Israelite self-identity. The most perplexing of these problems is
represented by the institution of kingship itself. It must be emphasized
that the Israelite demand for a king was in complete accord with
deuteronomic legislation.[97] According to the "Law of the King"
contained in Deut 17:14–20, kingship was envisioned as the legitimate
form of government for Israel in the land of Canaan.[98] This "law" places
certain particularly "Israelite" qualifiers upon the type of king that might
be accepted. As such, it stands as a divine response to Israel's "later"
decision: "Let me set a king over me like all the nations around me"
(ʾāśîmâ ʿalay melek kĕkol-haggôyîm ʾăšer sĕbîbōtāy, Deut 17:14). On the surface, it would appear that the demand for a king given to Samuel would
be in accord with this very charter. Yet the ensuing narrative makes it
clear that while the concept of kingship might be acceptable, the *request*
for such was not.[99] The key to understanding this is embedded in the
nature of the request and the issue of the concept of "judgeship," for
"judging" is not a part of the deuteronomic ideal of "kingship;" rather,
the act of "judging" in the deuteronomistic history belongs only to
Yahweh and his appointed leaders.

---

[96] The literary history of these chapters remains debated among scholars, and
there seems little reason to envision a consensus emerging on these issues. There is
agreement that the final deuteronomistic structuring of the materials combines both
pro- and anti-monarchical sentiments, but whether such ambiguities may be used to
separate the texts into corresponding sources, as is the standard analytical practice, is
much less certain. For an example of the way in which these materials are commonly
divided, as well as a review of the major competing theories, see Halpern's analysis
of 1 Samuel 8–12 in *The First Historians*, pp. 181–93. Recent efforts to approach these
chapters in terms of their literary unity are reviewed by Polzin in *Samuel and the
Deuteronomist*, pp. 238–45. I am more inclined to agree with the observations of Van
Seters that 1 Samuel 8–12 reflects the combination of "free composition" and the
formation of "redactional links" between independent units to produce the present
materials, a process that he characterizes as "the basis of historiography in Samuel
and Kings" (*In Search of History*, p. 258).

[97] Miscall, *1 Samuel*, p. 47.

[98] On the role of Deut 17:14–20 as a part of the deuteronomic charter, see the
discussion above in chap. 3, pp. 73–74.

[99] Gerbrandt, *Kingship According to the Deuteronomistic History*, p. 145.

That the request for a king was regarded as a sin and as a rejection of Yahweh is made explicit within the narrative account from the responses of Samuel, Yahweh, and the people. Though Samuel regarded the request as evil (8:6; cf. 12:17), it was Yahweh's reply to Samuel that characterized it as a rejection of Yahweh's prerogatives: "It is not you they have rejected, but me whom they have rejected from ruling over them" (*kî lōʾ ʾōtěkā māʾāsû kî-ʾōtî māʾăsû mimmělōk ʿălêhem*, 8:7b). This judgment is further confirmed in the account of the ritual selection of Saul at Mizpah, when Samuel proclaims that in the demand for a king, Israel had rejected its god, who delivered them (*ʾăšer-hûʾ môšîaʿ lākem*) from their troubles (10:19). Finally, in the ceremony of the renewal of the kingship at Gilgal, the people themselves admit to the sinfulness of their actions: "For we have added evil to our sins in requesting a king for ourselves" (*kî-yāsapnû ʿal-kol-ḥaṭṭōʾtênû rāʿâ lišʾōl lānû melek*, 12:19). Why this request is regarded as evil and as a rejection of Yahweh is a matter that is not made explicit in the narrative. The answer to this problem might be discovered in the final notice of Samuel's response to the people, commonly referred to as "the manner of the king" (*mišpaṭ hammelek*, 8:11–18). Samuel provides a rather realistic view of the power and prerogatives of the king and the manner in which the king will subject the people and their property to his own use. Such resulting "oppression" might be taken as an indicator that the institution of kingship might prove to be less than an "unmitigated success."[100] The consequences of kingship might be so far-reaching that the people as a whole would cry out for relief from their chosen king, but Yahweh would not answer them (8:18).[101] Such a series of events would, if fulfilled, make Israel "like the nations," i.e., destroy the very distinctiveness that the concept of a chosen people ruled over by their god, Yahweh, was envisioned to embody. Only if the king were to fulfill the demands of Yahweh and his *tôrâ* could this new ideal persist.

---

[100]   D. M. Gunn, *The Fate of King Saul: An Interpretation of a Biblical Story* (JSOTSup 14; Sheffield: JSOT, 1980), p. 61.

[101]   The literary contrasts here between the concept of Samuel as "judge" (esp. 7:2–12) and the custom of the king are numerous. Likewise, the custom of the king parallels the custom of the priesthood that introduced the sins of Eli's sons, leading to Yahweh's rejection of his house. The literary connections also establish analogies between the various types of hereditary leadership (i.e., by priest or by judge) and lead to a negative evaluation of hereditary leadership as a principle. For an analysis of the literary structures and parallels leading to these conclusions, see the work of M. Garsiel, *The First Book of Samuel: A Literary Study of Comparative Structures, Analogies and Parallels* (Ramat Gan, Israel: Revivim, 1985), pp. 58–75.

While the request for a king may be understood as the beginning of a new "judge" cycle,[102] it is more accurately interpreted as a distinct break with that period. Israel had failed to understand that it was Yahweh who had been its deliverer, i.e., that it was Yahweh alone who could act as "judge" (cf. Judg 11:27). As a result, Samuel the prophet stood before Israel to pass judgment on them for their request and to remind them that despite the fact that they had continually failed to serve Yahweh alone, he had been responsible for delivering them from their enemies on every side (12:7–11). Despite this, Yahweh consented to the request and commanded Samuel to give Israel a king (8:7), though it is clear that this king represented a power that required special attention and control. Israel's future relationship with Yahweh would now be determined not only by Israel's faithfulness to Yahweh, but also by the faithfulness of the king who would rule over and represent the people.[103] Samuel's announcement of "the manner of the king" failed to sway the people's resolve (8:19), so what remained was to institute the kingship and to incorporate it into the structure of the Israelite social world. The ambiguities and redundancies that result from the variety of views represented in 1 Samuel 8–12 might be related to the very ambiguities faced by the community pondering the identity it might attempt to create and retain within the context of a changing political and social world. It is the ritual recounted in 1 Sam 12:16–25 that serves to incorporate kingship as a part of the covenantal,[104] and hence conditional, nature of Israel's self-understanding of the manner by which it was to stand in relation to Yahweh and his demands.

Despite the common assessment that the materials in 1 Samuel 8–12 were originally composed independently and were only secondarily edited into their present form,[105] the arrangement of the final narrative whole represents a very specialized concept of the nature of Israelite kingship that is to be incorporated into Israel's world view. Contributing to this presentation are the three ritual enactments recounted in associa-

---

[102] Jobling, *The Sense of Biblical Narrative, II*, p. 65.

[103] This interpretive factor becomes evident in the narrative with the evaluations of the deeds of the individual rulers that begin with Solomon (1 Kgs 11:1–6) and which are presented for nearly every ruler over Israel and Judah. On the importance of this for understanding the structure and presentation of the period of the Hebrew kingdoms, see the discussions in chap. 8.

[104] D. J. McCarthy, "The Inauguration of Monarchy in Israel: A Form-Critical Study of I Samuel 8–12," *Int* 27 (1973) 412.

[105] See, e.g., the analysis of A. D. H. Mayes, "The Rise of the Israelite Monarchy," *ZAW* 90 (1978) 1–19.

tion with the establishment of kingship which provide a unique perspective on both the monarchic and the prophetic office from the particular viewpoint of the deuteronomistic author. That the deuteronomistic writer seems to have envisioned his own narratorial voice as bearing prophetic authority and himself as the heir to the Mosaic traditions helps to explain the manner in which the presentation interweaves the traditions concerning Samuel and the selection of the first king.

The "Law of the King" (Deut 17:14–20) provides the following qualifications on the nature of acceptable Israelite kingship and provides a set of controls over this figure: (1) the king would be one chosen by Yahweh from among the Israelites; there could be no foreign kings; (2) he should not multiply horses, wives, or silver and gold for himself; (3) he should not return the people to Egypt; and (4) he must make a copy of the law for himself and must live by it. This final qualification is noteworthy, for it places the king under special restrictions. It would be the duty of the king to make a "copy of this law" (*mišnēh hattôrâ hazzōʾt*, Deut 17:18) and to "observe all the words of this law and all these statutes and to do them" (*lišmōr ʾet-kol-dibrê hattôrâ hazzōʾt wĕʾet-haḥuqqîm hāʾēlleh laʿăśōtām*, 17:19). If such a king would follow the teachings of the book of Moses, deviating in no way from its directions, then "he might lengthen the days upon his kingdom, he and his sons, in Israel" (*yaʾărîk yāmîm ʿal-mamlaktô hûʾ ûbānāyw bĕqereb yiśrāʾēl*, 17:20). In short, for the deuteronomic ideals of Israel, kingship may well be an acceptable institution, but the duration of the rule or dynasty of any individual king was conditional upon the fulfillment of the demands of the *tôrâ*.

It is at this point that the matter of the relationship between king and prophet comes into play in the development of the account of Saul's rise. If the king to be appointed is to meet all of the directions of the law, then he will require some type of interpretive leadership in following Yahweh's *tôrâ*. Such leadership was provided in the prophetically inspired figure of Samuel and, by analogical extension, the voice of the deuteronomistic writer who was addressing the concerns of a community in exile, one which was in the process of identifying a model for its identity that would allow it to endure the problems it faced. The role and functions assigned to Samuel in the institution of the monarchy illustrate this prophetic role within the narrative and attempt to create a similar relationship between the community and its perceived understandings by way of the correctives and directives given by the prophet, especially *vis-à-vis* the king. The function fulfilled by the unnamed "man of god" in

2:27–36 is now replaced by the prophetically commissioned Samuel (3:11–21).

The public ceremony in which Israel's request for kingship is granted by Yahweh through Samuel (8:4–22) is followed by the account of the meeting between Samuel and Saul and the subsequent anointing of Saul as ruler (9:1–10:16).[106] The young Saul is introduced in a manner to demonstrate clearly that he fulfills the requirements for kingship outlined in the "Law of the King." He is an Israelite of the tribe of Benjamin. At no point in his career will he be accused of trying to increase his status by acquiring wives, horses, or money, nor will he be accused of returning the people to Egypt. The only question remaining to legitimize the selection of Saul is his choice by Yahweh (cf. Deut 17:15), an action that would require the services of both a prophet and a ritual assembly, at least in this particular instance.[107] The answer is provided through the actions of Samuel, as might be guessed, who serves as the vehicle through which the divine choice is made.[108]

When the young Benjaminite Saul, who had been sent in search of his father's lost asses, discovered that they were nowhere to be found, his attendant suggested that they consult the highly respected "man of god" (ʾîš ʾĕlōhîm, 9:6) who lived in a nearby city. Upon determining that they had the appropriate fee with which to procure such special help in locating their quarry,[109] they entered the city and eventually encountered none other than Samuel (9:14). It would be the prophetic voice of Samuel which would exceed the expectations of Saul's attendant, who had voiced the following simple hope in consulting this ʾîš ʾĕlōhîm: "Perhaps he will tell us our way on which we have embarked" (ʾûlay yaggîd lānû

---

[106] For an example of the traditional approach to these materials, see B. C. Birch, "The Development of the Tradition on the Anointing of Saul in I Sam 9:1–10:16," *JBL* 90 (1971) 55–68. Though it is commonly held that Samuel's anointing of Saul is a secondary interpolation into the text, in its present form it is an essential part of the narrative structure.

[107] The issue of whether Saul will fulfill the demands of the Yahwistic *tôrâ* and thereby lengthen his reign and the succession of his sons (Deut 17:18–20) belongs to the next chapter, which addresses the creation of the model of the proper king.

[108] As R. E. Clements has noted, the concept of Yahweh's choice and designation of a king is of critical importance to the deuteronomistic writer; "The Deuteronomistic Intepretation of the Founding of the Monarchy in I Sam. VIII," *VT* 24 (1974) 398–410.

[109] The notation in 9:9 that the *nābîʾ* was formerly called a "seer" (*rōʾeh*) allows the writer here to connect several different traditions in the person of Samuel. Embedded in the text of 9:7–8 is what seems to be a popularized explanation of the term *nābîʾ*. Cf. the observations of J. B. Curtis, "A Folk Etymology of *nābîʾ*," *VT* 29 (1979) 491–93.

ʾet-darkēnû ʾăšer-hālaknû ʿālêhā, 9:6b). Little might this unnamed attendant of Saul have known that the way on which they had come would lead to kingship, the formation of a monarchic state, or the threat of dissimilation in a foreign land, but such would be the full account told, not to Saul, but to those who would listen to the story told by the voices of the prophetic interpreters appearing throughout the narrative. Not only would Samuel inform Saul that the lost asses had been found (9:20), but he would also make known to him "the word of god" (dĕbar ʾĕlōhîm, 9:27).

Embedded in the context of this story is the notice to Samuel that this Saul was the one who would serve as the king requested by Israel. On the day before Saul's appearance in the city, Yahweh told Samuel of his arrival and gave these instructions to the prophet: "You will anoint him prince over my people Israel" (ûmĕšaḥtô lĕnāgîd ʿal-ʿammî yiśrāʾēl, 9:16).[110] Saul would be designated to deliver Israel from the Philistines, for Yahweh had heard Israel's cry of distress (9:16). While on one level this appears to be a continuation of the traditions associated with the "judges," two important changes are instituted here. Now the deliverer would be ritually anointed by a prophetic figure. The ideological background presented in Judg 2:6–3:6 which had served to interpret the activities of the deliverers is here transformed into a public ritual of selection and presentation. With Samuel's fulfillment of the divine command in 10:1, the older "office" of the judge was rendered obsolete.

But this new form of leadership would not break completely with the ideals of the past, for the power and support of Yahweh would be the ultimate foundations upon which the ideology of Israelite kingship would rest. To provide confirmation of the pronouncement's validity, Samuel related three signs to Saul (10:2–7), the fulfillment of which would signify the transformation in both Saul and Israel. The extent of the change taking place is symbolized by the fact that when the third sign would occur, the "spirit of Yahweh" (rûaḥ yhwh) would rush upon him and he would become "another man" (ʾîš ʾaḥēr, 10:6; cf. also 10:10; 11:6). The significance of the notice that rûaḥ yhwh would take possession

---

[110] The precise meaning of nāgîd as distinct from melek remains both elusive and debated. It is clear within the context of the present deuteronomistic account, however, that nāgîd is used as a synonym for melek. For discussions reflecting the variety of opinions on the distinctions between these two terms, see T. N. D. Mettinger, King and Messiah: The Civil and Sacral Legitimation of the Israelite Kings (Lund: C. W. K. Gleerup, 1976), pp. 152–84, and B. Halpern, The Constitution of the Monarchy in Israel (HSM 25; Chico, CA: Scholars Press, 1981), pp. 1–11.

of Saul is to be discovered in both the past deuteronomistic notices of such (e.g., Judg 3:10; 6:34; 11:29; 14:6, 19; 15:14) and the future notice concerning David (1 Sam 16:13). As with the figures of the judges, this possession would indicate Yahweh's presence (10:7). Unlike the change that will occur with David, however, it is not necessarily constant. The prophet then directed the king-designate to go to Gilgal and wait for Samuel to come and offer sacrifices once these signs had come to pass (10:8).

The direction and development of the kingship would come at every stage through Yahweh's directions. With this firmly established within the context of the narrative, it was provided a public and ceremonial setting. The special nature of Saul is made public with the fulfillment of the third sign, for Saul's "spirit-directed" prophesying occurred in public and included the notice of people who had known him previously (10:11–13).[111] The private representation of the choice of Saul, revealed not even to his uncle (10:14–16), becomes public with the account of the assembly at Mizpah (10:17–25). Following the prophetic proclamation that the request for a king was a rejection of Yahweh (10:18–19; cf. 8:7), Samuel proceeds with the ritual selection of Saul from among the gathered tribal groups (10:19–22). Saul, who for unstated reasons had attempted to hide from the people, was found and presented to them. Samuel proclaimed: "Do you see the one whom Yahweh has chosen? There is none like him among all the people." Israel responded: "Long live the king!" Despite the warnings concerning the dangers of instituting kingship and the ideological interpretation of its results, including a second warning concerning the "custom of the kingdom" (10:25; cf. 8:11–18), the people were not to be dissuaded. The deuteronomic requirements for kingship had been met: Yahweh had selected one of the men of Israel to be king over his people. Further, this people had gone so far as to devote themselves completely to Yahweh (7:3–4), thus creating the potential for a new era in the life of Israel.

Only one ideological question remained: how well would Saul fulfill the requirement that he obey the Mosaic *tôrâ*? This requirement is

---

[111] The meaning of the saying "Is Saul also among the prophets?" remains quite disputed. It is repeated in an extremely different context in 1 Sam 19:24. It seems clear, as noted by Gunn, that in the present passage it is intended as a positive confirmation of status (*The Fate of King Saul*, p. 63). For attempts at interpreting this maxim, see V. Eppstein, "Was Saul among the Prophets?," *ZAW* 81 (1969) 287–303, and J. Sturdy, "The Original Meaning of 'Is Saul Also among the Prophets?' (I Samuel X 11, 12; XIX 24)," *VT* 20 (1970) 206–13.

confirmed in the public reconfirmation of Saul as king. After Saul was able to lead Israel against the Ammonites who had attacked Jabesh-Gilead (11:1–11),[112] demonstrating in no uncertain terms that he represented the type of leader that was needed for the crisis that had occurred, Samuel reassembled the people at Gilgal to "renew the kingship" (11:14–15). With this third public assembly, the institution of kingship became official. Israel now had a king; the ritual performances for the institution of the office had been completed. But it is noteworthy that throughout the account the warning that kingship might not be the best course of action had been sounded. The reasons for this are more complex than a simple historical memory on the part of the deuteronomistic writer. But the deuteronomistic writer now makes clear through a covenantal assembly that the implications of this action are serious. As part of his farewell speech to Israel, Samuel challenges them to find any fault with his leadership, acknowledging that he has grown old and has been replaced by a king (12:1–5). This is followed by a brief rehearsal of the acts by which Yahweh had delivered the people from their oppressors and the continued failures of the people to remain faithful to their god (12:6–13). The new events, however, lead to a new covenantal stipulation. If both the people *and* their king follow Yahweh's commands and do not rebel against them, then all will be well. If, on the other hand, the people (or king) fail to obey all of Yahweh's *tôrâ*, then the hand of Yahweh will be against them (12:14–15).

The covenant that would form the ideological foundation of the self-understanding of the community would be one that would require the king to follow the same code as the people (cf. Deut 17:18–20). This pronouncement is likewise confirmed by a sign (12:16–18) that leads the people to confess their sins and to implore Samuel to continue as their intercessor (12:19, 23; cf. 7:5; 8:6). The continued roles of both prophet and king were provided for by the ritualized narrative presentations of the deuteronomistic writer. For Samuel, all that remained was to implore the people to serve Yahweh alone and not to turn away from their god. Both they and their king would be swept away if they failed in this task (12:20–25). The king and people had only to be obedient to Yahweh's covenantal demands to which they had given their full consent. If they were able to do what they had failed to do at any other stage of their nar-

---

[112]   According to McCarter, the 4QSam[a] scroll contains a long passage that is to be inserted in 10:27b and that provides a reason for the Ammonite attack (*1 Samuel*, p. 199).

rated past, then they would be delivered by their god. If they continued in their rebellious ways, then they could expect to be destroyed. This new epoch includes a new responsibility, for now the fate of the people could rest upon the faithfulness of one man, the king. The successes and failures of this figure would be announced by the prophets. If the king failed and the people were destroyed, it would be the prophetic voice that might explain how and why these things had occurred, reminding the people that if this path were chosen again as the basis of a new community, the same covenantal demands might remain in force.

7

THE GOLDEN AGE CREATED:
THE IDEAL REALIZED

I. The Symbol of Kingship

With the establishment of a permanent form of leadership that accompanied the institution of the monarchy under Saul,[1] the deuteronomistic writer embarked on a new epoch in the development of Israel's self-identity. From this "ambiguous" start, a "golden age" would be created, and a portion of Israel's past would be applied in such a way as to recreate and redefine the very concept of Israel as a national monarchic state governed by a divinely appointed king. The folk model of David, the ideal ruler of this state, would dominate the remainder of the history of the people who incorporated it as a part of their past,[2] at least

---

[1] There is ample evidence suggesting that the political and structural developments under Saul indicate that the term "chiefdom" is a more accurate designation for Saul's realm than kingdom. For the characteristics of chiefdoms and the role of warfare in their development, see R. L. Carneiro, "The Chiefdom: Precursor of the State," in *The Transition to Statehood in the New World* (ed. G. D. Jones and R. R. Kautz; Cambridge: Cambridge University Press, 1981), pp. 37–79. For the application of this model of social formation to early Israel, see F. Frick, *The Formation of the State in Ancient Israel* (SWBA 4; Sheffield: JSOT, 1985), pp. 71–97.

[2] On the variety of views of David that are presented in the biblical texts, see W. Brueggemann's *David's Truth in Israel's Imagination & Memory* (Philadelphia: Fortress, 1985).

according to the deuteronomistic writer's presentation. Concomitant with this "memory" of a "golden age," an essential element in the development of both an ethnic and a nationalistic identity, was also the recognition that this age had been lost.[3] The remainder of the books of Samuel and Kings is devoted to the extended explanation of the reasons for the loss of this ideal period from the past and ways in which the present community, so apparently separated from that past, might reincorporate and recreate its identity in a new, yet continuous form.

The narratives describing the monarchic states of Judah and Israel are structured by the contrasting of individual figures and nations, compared not only to each other but to their loyalty to the deuteronomic *tôrâ* as interpreted by the deuteronomistic writer. In this way, these figures from the past, recreated in the history of the Israelite state, were allowed to "speak" to the community hearing and incorporating a structured vision of how the present "Israel" must reconstitute its life and identity if it were to survive the loss of such essential self-defining ideals as king, land, and temple. Through this prophetic eye, and scrutinized and interpreted at all points by such deuteronomic vision, the "rustic" charismatic rule of Saul would be replaced by the glory of the more "polished" David, the figure who provides the model for many of the future ideals of the group. This change would be accomplished by way of the presentation of divine choice and human accountability to the prophetic interpretation of the *tôrâ*.

Important to understand in the deuteronomistic presentation of the narrative of Israel's past is the creative function that it serves. The narrative is not simply mimetic (i.e., historical), nor is it solely didactic (i.e., instructional), though each of these constitutes a portion of what I understand as a major functional aspect of the deuteronomistic narrative. In addition to these functions, the narrative is creative; it constitutes an ideological vision of reality that renders both the past and the present meaningful to those who adopt it as their own.[4] In so doing, the narratorial voice underlying the text identifies itself as a (or, from the deuteronomistic writer's perspective, *the*) prophetic voice that has the authority to

---

[3] As A. D. Smith points out, the "loss" of the "golden age" is an essential element in the formation of ethnic groups and national identities; *The Ethnic Origins of Nations* (Oxford: Blackwell, 1986), pp. 191–200.

[4] For an extended discussion of the positive roles of ideologies, see C. Geertz, "Ideology as a Cultural System," in *The Interpretation of Cultures* (New York: Basic, 1973), pp. 193–229. As Geertz points out, ideologies serve as "maps of problematic social reality and matrices for the creation of collective conscience" (p. 220).

present and direct the interpretation of that past for the present. The power of these ideological narratives provides a form of redress to the social crises faced by the exilic community. This prophetic interpretation mediates between the memories of the lost "golden age" and the hope for a future "exodus from bondage," a new "conquest" of the land, and the consequent rebirth of identity. A successful effort would result in the recreation of the basic core of the group's self-perception; i.e., it would be able to form an ethnic boundary for the people "Israel."

The continuation of the narrative revolves around three figures who will be determinant for the future construction of Israel's identity—Saul, Samuel, and David. By Samuel's prophetic leadership, the concept of kingship has been ritually incorporated into the ideology of Israel's social world.[5] Though Saul had been empowered as king, he was a ruler who would enjoy few successes and no favorable memory in the history recounted by the deuteronomistic author. Instead, he would serve only as a transition, a negative example that would introduce the central figure of David into the account. Rather than establish a new form of leadership and insure that the people were loyal to their covenantal obligations to Yahweh, Saul would act more like the earlier "judges," leading the people in an *ad hoc* fashion against their enemies, the Philistines. For Israel's active historical memory, Saul's kingship provided Yahweh with the opportunity to select a king who represented the choice of the deity, not of the people.

This dialectic of choice and rejection, played out between the two figures of David and Saul, comprises the basic theme of 1 Samuel 13–15.[6] It is in the very interplay of these characters, mediated at critical points

---

[5] This is not to suggest that kingship was some form of alien institution, a judgment that has often characterized interpretations of Israel's history. Rather, as more recent studies have shown, kingship was the standard form of state governance in the ancient Near East from the Bronze Age onward. In the deuteronomistic account of Israel's past, kingship had not been incorporated into the covenantal and societal structure until this point. On the way in which this incorporation was achieved, see above, pp. 206–7.

[6] J. P. Fokkelman, "Saul & David," *BibRev* 5 (1989) 26. For an intensive investigation of the literary characteristics of the materials dealing with Saul and David, see Fokkelman's *Narrative Art and Poetry in the Books of Samuel, Volume II: The Crossing of Fates (I Sam. 13–31 & II Sam. 1)* (SSN 22; Assen, The Netherlands: Van Gorcum, 1986). These chapters introduce the section of the narrative referred to as "the history of David's rise," which is commonly regarded as an independent literary tradition that is now found in 1 Samuel 16 through 2 Samuel 5. For bibliography pertinent to that section, see N. P. Lemche, "David's Rise," *JSOT* 10 (1978) 18–19, n. 1, and P. K. McCarter, *I Samuel* (AB 8; Garden City, NY: Doubleday, 1980), pp. 42–44.

by the figure of Samuel, that the deuteronomistic writer presents a number of important ideological assertions regarding the nature of the relationship between Yahweh and his people. These insights are likewise mediated through a succession of prophetic figures, first Samuel, then Nathan and Ahijah, followed in the history by a series of inspired voices, each of which interprets Israel's adherence to Yahweh's commands by way of the narrative presentation. By concentrating on those points in the story where these important figures make their pronouncements, one might better understand the overall structure and import of the deuteronomistic presentation of the histories of the kingdoms and the ways in which they influence the form and concept of the community for which they were produced.

Despite the textual problems associated with the verse, 1 Sam 13:1 represents a new beginning in the narrative presentation of Israelite history.[7] The major portions of the story are placed in chronological order by similar regnal formulae that focus the events to be narrated on the actions of one person and use the king as a personification of the people at large. This identification of the acts of the people with the acts of the kings is critical to the development of the remainder of the history, for it is precisely this narrative device that allows the deuteronomistic writer to hold both king and people directly responsible for their fate.[8] Now the narrative turns to the deeds of Saul, who "ruled as king over Israel" (*mālak ʿal-yiśrāʾēl*, 1 Sam 13:1). This was the young man supplied by Yahweh at the request of the people and proclaimed by the prophet Samuel as the one Yahweh had chosen (10:24; cf. 9:15–17). For the deuteronomistic writer, the fate and fortune of Saul and the united Israel that he

---

[7] The numbers giving Saul's age at the beginning of his reign and, quite possibly, the number of years he served as king, seem to have been lost from the text. The versions present a variety of attempts to resolve the problem, but no agreement. What is clear is that the structure of the regnal formula indicates a definite shift from the past narrative style and functions to signify the beginning of a new era in Israel's history.

[8] This explicit judgment of the people passed with reference to the deeds of the individual kings begins with the end of Solomon's reign (1 Kgs 11:1–10) and occurs in conjunction with the regnal formulae at the beginning of the reign of each new ruler. In a sense, these judgments, given in the narrative prior to the account of the actions of any ruler, interpret the events that are presented. The particular slant placed on the reign of each king is important to the development of the deuteronomistic account.

led[9] were directly related to the degree to which the new king would follow the *tôrâ*.

The critical importance of Saul for the progress of the narrative is suggested by the fact that he was the first publicly recognized leader of all Israel since Joshua. Just as Joshua's success in the conquest of the land was interpreted against the backdrop of the people's fulfillment of the law (Josh 1:1–9), so now Saul's successes would be decided by the degree to which he conformed to the law of Yahweh. One contrast was evident, however. Whereas Joshua served as both Yahweh's appointed leader and the one responsible for the interpretation and enforcement of the covenantal demands upon the people (Josh 23:6–13; 24:14–28), Saul's role would be much more restricted. Such would be the case with the subsequent rulers who would sit upon the throne of Judah and/or Israel. While each leader would be responsible for the enforcement of the covenant, the interpretation of the covenantal commands of the deity would be relayed by Yahweh's designated prophetic interpreter. For the deuteronomistic writer, this would be accomplished through the pronouncements of a prophet like Samuel or Moses or, in their absence, through the prophetic voice of the deuteronomistic narrator himself. In developing the ideal parameters by which "Israel" would be recreated, the deuteronomistic writer circumscribes all monarchic powers and prerogatives by subjugating them to the will of the deity manifested through the prophetic intermediary. In terms of social position, then, for the deuteronomistic history, the prophet occupies a central position in the social structure.[10] Through the model of Samuel, the groundwork for this position is laid.

It was Samuel who had recognized that the request for kingship was tantamount to a rebellion against Yahweh and a breach of the basic covenantal agreements, though such a judgment could be rendered only

---

9 Despite the historical probability that Saul was recognized as king by only a portion of the northern tribes, those that would later comprise the independent monarchic state of Israel as separate from that of Judah, such a distinction is not developed by the deuteronomistic writer in the narrative. Rather, from the standpoint of the author, all Israel is viewed as being under the rulership of Saul. On the possible historical kingdom ruled by Saul, see J. M. Miller and J. H. Hayes, *A History of Ancient Israel and Judah* (Philadelphia: Westminster, 1986), pp. 138–41.

10 Prophetic figures are commonly regarded as "peripheral" to the dominant social structures. On the social location of prophetic figures, see R. R. Wilson, *Prophecy and Society in Ancient Israel* (Philadelphia: Fortress, 1980), pp. 38–39, 66–83. The deuteronomistic writer, in attempting to restructure and recreate Israelite society, is actively placing the role of the "true" prophet at the center of this social unit.

with the knowledge and insights of the exilic position of the deuteronomistic writer who controlled the perceptions of the prophetic character of
Samuel. Similarly, it was Samuel who gave Israel the king it requested, in
obedience to the command of Yahweh; it would be this same Samuel
whose pronouncements would, at the direction of Yahweh, remove Saul
from the throne. Within the context of the religious traditions that form
the basis for Israel's "new" self-understanding as the chosen people of
Yahweh, one of the most central questions would center upon the degree
of Yahweh's allegiance to his people. Would or could Yahweh abandon
them completely and let them be destroyed? If so, what would be the
conditions that might bring this about? Since the events that produced
the exile had rendered questionable much, if not all, of the religious
symbol system that had bolstered the national religions of Israel and
Judah,[11] the question of Yahweh's trustworthiness with respect to the
promise of the land and the establishment of "his" people would require
redress. To provide answers to these questions and to give new
emphases to the symbols that provide the supports for the identity of the
group,[12] the deuteronomistic writer utilized various expressions from
Israel's past to connect the present with that ideal of historical continuity.

Quite naturally, kingship became the focus of much of this symbolic
recreative activity, for as Judah and Israel had originally formed a unit
known as "Israel" for a brief time, it occurred only by virtue of the power
of a monarchic presence.[13] Within the biblical literature and most especially within the deuteronomistic narrative, the person and function of
the king occupied the most critical of positions. As the history was

[11]   R. Klein, *Israel in Exile: A Theological Interpretation* (OBT; Philadelphia: Fortress,
1979), p. 5.

[12]   As A. P. Royce emphasizes, no ethnic group survives for any period of time
without benefit of a flexible symbol system; *Ethnic Identity: Strategies of Diversity*
(Bloomington: Indiana University Press, 1982), p. 7.

[13]   As noted in the discussion of Deuteronomy as a "manifesto" of ethnic identity
(chap. 3), the concept of "Israel" is an exilic construct that draws upon a variety of
ways in which "Israel" is used in the biblical materials. At least four different applications of the term may be identified in the Hebrew Bible: "Israel" is used for the
geographic region in the northern section of Palestine, for the "tribal confederation"
that seems to be presupposed for the narrative in Deuteronomy through 1 Samuel,
for the "united monarchy" under David and Solomon, and for the monarchic kingdom that later occupied that same area and that lost its political identity with its
conquest by Assyria in ca. 722 BCE. For the deuteronomistic writer, this new "Israel"
would be a recreation of portions of all of these past symbolic designations for the
people. On the differing uses of the term "Israel" in the Hebrew Bible, see G. W.
Ahlström, *Who Were the Israelites?* (Winona Lake, IN: Eisenbrauns, 1986).

developed in detail, the king came to represent the "body politic," and his moral activities and health were direct indicators of those of the populace at large.[14] With the person of the king taking on such a central determining role for the welfare of the people, the concept of the choice or rejection of a particular king by Yahweh had implications that reached beyond the matters of dynastic stability or monarchic collapse; rather, the rejection of a king would be at least potentially tantamount to the rejection of the people themselves. Through this particular ideological concept, the interpretation of the coincidence between the selection and rejection of Saul and the choice and anointing of David might be made more understandable to those who would define their present situation and project their future on the bases laid by these events.

II. The Rejection of Saul and the Choice of David

The fate of both king and people was emphasized by the deuteronomistic writer and ritually introduced into the structure of the narrative and the social world of the participants by way of the covenantal ceremonies that marked the end of Samuel's public career before all Israel (1 Sam 12:13–15, 24–25). Within this ideological context, the fate of the people is interconnected with the demise of the Benjaminite Saul and his hopes for succession and the exaltation of David and the insurance of his southern Judahite dynastic house. As Judah would, through the choice of David, become the ruler of "all Israel," so the remnants of Judah would become the inheritors of the symbol "Israel" for their future identity. Before this would occur, however, Saul had to be rejected and David selected. To illustrate the manner by which the historian created a new understanding for the people who would inherit Saul's "kingdom," four "events" may be selected for investigation. The first is the initial "rejection" of Saul in 1 Sam 13:13–14. This refusal to establish Saul's dynasty is followed by the account of Saul's aborted oath (14:23–46), an elaboration on the theme of faithfulness to the word of Yahweh. The third selection to be investigated, 1 Sam 15:10–35, is an intriguing text recounting the second "rejection" of Saul and the "repentance" of Yahweh for having designated him as king. Finally, the "secret" selection of David as Yahweh's choice for king provides the resolution for this section of the drama rehearsed by the narrator. The process of the inte-

---

[14] J. Rosenberg, *King and Kin: Political Allegory in the Hebrew Bible* (Bloomington/Indianapolis: Indiana University Press, 1986), pp. 193–95.

gration of this ideal leader into the narrative simultaneously creates and reinforces the recognized schism with the older order.

In 1 Samuel 13 the era under a new form of leadership requested by the people is introduced. In accord with their "sinful" request (8:7; 12:19), Saul had been coronated to "judge" the people like the other nations (8:5, 20). Despite his success in rallying the tribal muster and defeating the Ammonite Nahash (11:1–11), Saul would not succeed in delivering Israel from the Philistine threat. Instead, he would battle against them throughout his entire life (14:52), eventually dying at their hands in the battle on Mt. Gilboa (31:1–6). The very failure of Saul to succeed as either king or judge and to establish his dynastic line on the throne introduces a number of questions that do not receive fully developed answers in the continuation of the narrative.[15] Instead, as with the development of the characters and plot within the narratives themselves, numerous questions and their proposed answers remain "fraught with background,"[16] seeking to impose upon the listener or participant both a judgment and a response, always requiring, at least ideally, an interpretation. Within this account, the authority of interpetation belongs to the prophetic figure of Samuel alone. It would be he who would pray on behalf of Israel and who would instruct them in the good and upright path (12:23; cf. 9:6b). While the king may have taken the powers and prerogatives of war leader, the word and way of Yahweh belonged to Samuel alone.

The introductory account of Saul's reign as king contains also the explicit rejection of Saul's family as the one to establish a dynastic line in Israel and the divine decision to select another (13:13–14).[17] This text is important because of the information it does not provide as well as for that which it does. The narrative introduces Saul about to do battle with the Philistine forces at Michmash (13:2–7) and confronting a most diffi-

---

[15] It might be argued from the beginning that the underlying problem, at least on an ideological plane, is the perennial question of theodicy. That the deuteronomistic writer, with his emphasis upon retributive justice and an absolute correspondence between the demands of *tôrâ* and its fulfillment, does not always provide consistent or satisfying answers to the modern commentator may be attributed to the basic paradoxical nature of the structure of religions in general.

[16] On the implications of this term for the biblical narratives, see E. Auerbach, *Mimesis: The Representation of Reality in Western Literature* (Princeton: Princeton University Press, 1953), pp. 8–23.

[17] The ambiguity of the reply has been noted by D. Gunn, who emphasizes that the rejection contained here could be taken to mean that Saul's kingship could come to an immediate end, since a successor had already been chosen, at least by implication; *The Fate of King Saul* (JSOTSup 14; Sheffield: JSOT, 1984), p. 67.

cult internal situation. Not only was he about to engage a powerful enemy force, but he was also plagued with the problem of desertion from his base camp at Gilgal. To complicate the issue further, he was attempting to comply with the earlier commission of Samuel that he was to go to Gilgal, where Samuel would come to offer sacrifices: "You shall wait seven days until I come to you and I shall make known to you what you are to do" (10:8). Saul seems to have been willing to obey this command of the prophet. Indeed, he waited the full seven days (13:8), but Samuel did not come, and the army continued to scatter. In response, Saul took upon himself the right to offer the sacrifices which had been mentioned by Samuel (13:9).[18] Predictably, the prophet appears and questions Saul with respect to his actions and receives an open and accurate explanation (13:11–12). The prophetic command, however, was not something that Samuel would allow to be changed on the basis of military or monarchic expediency.

The results of Saul's deeds and the interpretation of their implications are announced immediately by Samuel. Of note is the fact that there is no account of a divine speech; instead, only the prophetic notice appears that it was he who could announce Yahweh's decisions. Because Saul had not followed the precise instructions of Samuel, he was condemned for having failed to follow the command of Yahweh: "You have not observed the command of Yahweh your God that he gave you" (lōʾ[19] šāmartā ʾet-miṣwat yhwh ʾĕlōhêkā ʾăšer ṣiwwāk, 13:13). The import of this terrible gaffe on Saul's part was that it cost him any hope of dynastic continuance. His kingdom would not be established "forever" (ʿad-ʿôlām), a possibility that had not been mentioned before, but that seems to be suggested by Samuel's address. Instead, Yahweh had sought out a man to replace Saul, though the narration of that choice will not be given until 16:1–13. This newly selected ruler, called here nāgîd as Saul had been (9:16), would be a "man of his own choosing" (literally, "a man according to his own heart" [ʾîš kilbābô], 13:14).

---

[18] Whether or not such sacrifices were a standard part of the concept of "holy war" in ancient Israel and were to be offered only by a prophet (B. Birch, *The Rise of the Israelite Monarchy: The Growth and Development of I Samuel 7–15* [SBLDS 27; Missoula, MT: Scholars Press, 1976], p. 84) is not, in my opinion, an issue in the present text. Rather, arbitrary though it might seem, the issue is introduced in the speech of Samuel that follows to condemn Saul's monarchy.

[19] We retain here the reading of the MT. Some commentators suggest reading lû(ʾ), "if, if only," for the negative lōʾ of the MT, but this is not necessary for the context.

The future of Saul's kingship, then, is no longer in doubt within the narrative. Rather, only the time of Saul's replacement is left open to consideration. In no uncertain terms, the remnant of Saul's reign would be played out against the background of the rise of David, who is here envisioned as the king "chosen" by Yahweh in contrast to Saul, who was the king abandoned by Yahweh.[20] It is clear from the presentation of the deuteronomistic writer that it was Yahweh who chose a ruler to replace Saul while Saul still lived and battled on behalf of Israel. The reasons for the change are unambiguous. Saul failed to follow the commands of Yahweh as interpreted by Samuel,[21] a failing that will be demonstrated even further in the following two sections. As it would be Yahweh who would support David's attainment of the throne,[22] so too would it be the deity who would cause the downfall of his initial choice as king. Though Saul might be defended for trying to maintain the integrity of Israel's defenses and for operating within what *he* might have interpreted as the "spirit" of Yahweh's command, Samuel stood as the authoritative representative of the deity who could claim that only a strict and complete adherence to the command would suffice. The power and authority wielded by the prophetic voice underlying this narrative and directed at its selected audience project upon them the importance of obeying the commands of Yahweh precisely as the Yahwistic prophet might interpret them. In the formation of a communal identity, this would place tremendous formative powers in the hands of those who might be regarded as prophets by the communities that would constitute their support groups.

Having declared that Saul had been replaced by Yahweh, Samuel departed, leaving Saul to continue, unaided by prophetic guidance. This is precisely what Saul did; he continued in his battle against the Philistines as though nothing had changed (13:16–14:46), while in ideological terms determinant to the narrative and its implications, everything was now very different. Two points come to the foreground concerning the manner in which Saul continued his efforts: not only had Saul failed to obey the prophetic command, but his actions indicate that he had not understood that his position as king of Israel was one that was dependent upon adherence to those demands. It was against overwhelming odds that Saul and his son Jonathan continued in the struggle

---

[20] McCarter, *1 Samuel*, p. 28.

[21] Miscall, *1 Samuel*, p. 114.

[22] Lemche, "David's Rise," p. 3.

against the Philistines,[23] odds that were insurmountable, unless some change on the part of the deity were to be effected.

Saul's failures continued as he attempted to engage the Philistine forces and to insure Yahweh's aid in his endeavor. The background for the second depiction of Saul's inability to conform to the divine will is provided by the actions of Jonathan, who decided to press the battle against the enemy without informing his father of his actions (14:1; cf. 13:3). While his son carried the battle to the Philistines, Saul remained at Gibeah with about 600 men (14:2). Most important, however, is the priest with whom Saul is associated: Ahijah, great-grandson of Eli, was with Saul and was in charge of the ephod and, presumably, oracular consultations (14:3). Ironically, the dynasty of Saul, now represented by his son Jonathan, had been rejected as had that of Eli, embodied now in Ahijah (cf. 2:27–36; 3:11–18). Ultimate victory would belong to neither house unless there were a change in the divine decree. While the full implications of this possibility will not be developed until the next episode (15:1–35), the prophetic position announced by Samuel is important to note at this point: "The Eternal One of Israel does not lie, nor does he repent (wĕlōʾ yinnāḥēm), for he is not a human that he should repent (lĕhinnāḥēm)" (15:29).[24] For the prophet Samuel, the fates of Saul and Eli are not to be changed. Neither will establish a dynastic line in Israel; each will be replaced by another family chosen by Yahweh as theirs had been.[25]

---

[23] The reference in 13:19–23 to the lack of a smith in Israel and the need for Israel to go to the Philistines to have its farming implements sharpened is generally interpreted as reflecting a Philistine monopoly on iron. The notice in v. 22 that only Saul and Jonathan had a sword or spear is an effective way of stressing the degree to which Israel found itself oppressed by the Philistine power. In metaphorical terms, the exile of the leading elements of Judahite society might also make "Israel" devoid of both "smiths" and weapons. Within this context also is the designation of the Israelites as "Hebrews" (ʿibrîm, v. 19; cf. 4:9; 13:3, 7) by the Philistines (called "uncircumcised" [ʿărēlîm, 14:6]), a clear attempt at distinguishing between ethnic groups within the narrative account.

[24] As will be developed below, this response on Samuel's part stands in direct contrast to the narrated fact that Yahweh did indeed "repent" (15:11, 35), i.e., change his mind about what he had done. This particular meaning for the Niphal of nḥm occurs some 33 times in the Hebrew Bible. The tension that this produces in the account of the final rejection of Saul is critical to understanding the attempts of the deuteronomistic writer to provide internal boundaries for the development of the community that is being created.

[25] On the use of the verb bāḥar, "to choose," in these contexts, see the discussion below.

Jonathan and his armor bearer were able to create a general distur-
bance in the Philistine camp (14:6–15). In response, Saul called a muster
to determine who was missing from the camp and learned that it was
none other than Jonathan (14:16–17). Having determined this, Saul
summoned his priest to bring the ephod[26] so as to inquire of Yahweh,
most probably with respect to the manner in which the battle might be
conducted (cf. Judg 1:1; 20:18, 23, 27). When Saul noticed that the distur-
bance in the Philistine camp continued to escalate, he inexplicably
ordered Ahijah to stop the inquiry (14:19b) and proceeded to rally his
men and attack the Philistine camp. The opportunity of the moment
commanded Saul's attention more than did the completion of an inquiry
to Yahweh. This fact is unfortunate, for the next time that Saul attempts
such an inquiry, he will receive no answer (14:37; cf. 28:6).

This ritual failure on Saul's part did not result in an immediate
setback on the battlefield. Instead, Saul was able to regain the support of
a number of "Hebrews" who had earlier defected to the Philistine side
(14:21).[27] Nonetheless, credit for the success would not be attributed to
either Saul or Jonathan. Rather, "Yahweh delivered Israel on that day"
(14:23). This statement serves as a clear ideological reminder that Saul
and Jonathan fulfill symbolic roles in the social world created by the
deuteronomistic narrative. This reality, defined around the deuteronomistic interpretation of covenantal obligation and fulfillment, would
require an unyielding loyalty to the divine word by those who would
bear the responsibilities of leadership. Such ability seems to have been
beyond the capacities of Saul. This impression is strengthened by the
next series of events. As the fighting against the Philistines continued,
Saul made the army he had gathered take an oath:[28] "Cursed be the man
who eats food before evening comes and I have taken vengeance on my

---

[26] Reading here with the LXX against the MT's "ark of god" (*ʾărôn hāʾĕlōhîm*).

[27] McCarter's distinction between "Hebrew" as an "ethnic" rather than a "religio-
political" designation (*1 Samuel*, p. 240) creates a division that is out of place in the
present context.

[28] There is the possibility that a significant haplography has occurred at the end of
v. 23 and the beginning of v. 24 in the MT. Based on the reconstruction of S. R. Driver,
it is possible to read the following at the end of v. 23: "And all the army (*hāʿām*) was
with Saul, about ten thousand men, and the battle was scattered into the hill country
of Ephraim. Now Saul committed a great error (*wĕšāʾûl šāgâ šĕgāgâ gĕdōlâ*) on that
day...."; *Notes on the Hebrew Text and the Topography of the Books of Samuel* (2nd rev. ed.
[reprint of 1912 Oxford edition]; Winona Lake, IN: Alpha, 1984), p. 112. Despite the
general acceptance of this reading, Klein notes that there is no convincing explanation for this haplography (*1 Samuel*, p. 132).

enemies" (14:24). The illogic of such an act is exemplified by the response that Jonathan gives upon learning of this requirement. Jonathan, who had not heard the oath sworn by the army, ate some honey and was quickly informed of his misdeed by one of the soldiers (14:25–28). His response was quite pointed: "My father has brought trouble on the land" (ʿākar ʾābî ʾet-hāʾāreṣ, 14:29). It is tempting to read in this reply a veiled reference to the violation of the ḥērem by Achan (Josh 7:25; cf. 6:18), a deed which "brought trouble" on Israel and upon himself and which might anticipate the problems that Saul will have with the ḥērem in the next chapter. Jonathan's insubordination, both in terms of his denouncement of his father and of his actions, borders on treason. Saul's curse had been accepted by the army (14:24) and broken by Jonathan. Would it be by Saul's own hand that the apparent heir to the kingdom would perish?

The deuteronomistic writer moves quickly to illustrate the continuing failures of Saul as a competent leader for Israel. Philistia was defeated that day (14:31). Was Saul responsible for the victory? Had his oath induced Yahweh to fight for Israel? Had this even been the purpose of the oath? Surely, if Saul were to provide a model for future leaders, then such questions would demand answers. The narrative provides them in a rather unflattering manner. Saul's troops, no doubt quite famished from having honored their leader's oath, began to slaughter the captured animals and eat the meat without draining it of the blood. Deut 12:23–27 (cf. Lev 19:26) clearly forbids that the blood be eaten with the flesh; rather, it is to be poured out on the ground or on Yahweh's altar. The army of Israel, by virtue of its actions, breaks one of the primary dietary restrictions that serve as identifiers of the community. Saul's response to the situation is both immediate and appropriate: he prepares a place for the proper slaughter of the animals so that the dietary misdeeds of the army might be stopped (14:33–34). Ironically, Saul acts to resolve a group-threatening action that was caused by his own inexplicable oath.[29] Thus far in Saul's career at least four different versions of proper action have been presented. Saul seems quite uninhibited in carrying out those actions that he feels are appropriate to resolve conflicts arising within his social world; the people with Saul seem quite adept at

---

[29] The episode ends with the notice that Saul built an altar for Yahweh there and that this was the first of the altars that he built (14:35). Earlier in the narrative, Samuel also constructed an altar (7:17). It is possible that Saul here usurps one of the prerogatives of the prophet, though such is not exploited by the narrative. In its present form, the story suggests that Saul's actions, however well intended, simply fail to satisfy the requirements of the position.

acting in whatever ways they deem acceptable; Samuel, though ostensibly bound by the decrees of Yahweh, freely acts to counter Saul's deeds, identifying the actions of the army with those of the king; and, finally, Yahweh's concept of correct behavior, presented through the narrative account of the deuteronomistic author, is conveyed in different ways within the story.

Yahweh's response to these events comes in an unexpected manner that leads to Saul's discovery that Jonathan had not obeyed the oath sworn by the army. The divine response to Saul's actions is directly implied in Saul's second effort at an oracular inquiry. When Saul proposed to continue in the pursuit of the Philistines at night in an effort to destroy them completely, the army responded: "Do whatever is good in your eyes!" (kol-haṭṭôb bĕʿênêkā ʿăśēh, 14:36b). The army was willing to place their fate in Saul's hands and judgment. As though reminding Saul that there were certain requirements for doing what was "good," the priest suggests that they inquire of Yahweh (14:36). When Saul asked if they should pursue the enemy and if God would give them victory, he received no reply (14:37).[30] The refusal of an answer stands as Yahweh's indication that some obligation had not been fulfilled by the people. Saul's response illustrates his awareness of the implications of Yahweh's failure to answer, for he assembles the people and casts lots to find the one responsible for the sin of the people (14:38–42), again in a manner reminiscent of the selection of Achan for his violation of the ḥērem (Josh 7:16–21). Jonathan freely, perhaps even defiantly, admits to his deed and to his willingness to die; on his own life, Saul confirms that Jonathan must die for his act (14:43–44; cf. vv. 39–40). Saul, in his effort to fulfill an ill-advised oath, now faces the prospect of annihilating his own dynastic line.

Since the army had twice given Saul their consent to do "the good" in his opinion (vv. 36, 40), the fate of Jonathan seemed fixed. But what turned out to be the "good" in Saul's eyes was not the fulfillment of his vow but rather his accession to the protestations of the army. The army proclaims instead, by its own invocation of Yahweh, that Jonathan, who had led them in their victory over the Philistines, would not die. No comment is recorded for Saul. Jonathan had been rescued by the same army that had given Saul complete freedom to do as he saw fit and then

---

[30] For the practice of inquiring of Yahweh before going into battle, see Judg 1:1; 20:18, 23, 27; 1 Sam 23:2, 4; 28:6; 30:8. In 1 Sam 28:6 Saul will inquire of Yahweh once again and receive no answer, either by dream, lot, or prophecy. Saul, by that point, correctly perceived that Yahweh had abandoned him (28:15b).

refused to follow him when he made his decision. For the development of the story, Saul appears unable to fulfill his obligations, even those which were self-imposed,[31] with or without the benefit of prophetic guidance. But the ultimate victory over Philistia was not to belong to Saul. Having failed to fulfill his oath, he broke off his pursuit of the enemy (14:46); since Yahweh had refused any direction, he chose not to take the initiative into his own hands. Instead, it appears that Saul had lost the opportunity to defeat Philistia (14:52) as he had lost the loyalty of his own troops.[32]

The final episode in the development of the reasons for the rejection of Saul and the justification for that same rejection is narrated in the next chapter. The preceding events had provided a general depiction of Saul as a well-intentioned leader whose perceptions of reality were often in conflict with those of Samuel (or of the deuteronomistic narrator). Now Saul was to be evaluated by the divine, an event that would supply for the deuteronomistic writer's audience an important insight into the demands of the deity and the concept of eternal verities. As suggested in the last chapter with respect to the promises to Eli, the conditionality of the unconditional creates a tension that allows for the explanation of a broad range of typical and atypical events.[33] The deuteronomistic writer creates within this account of the second rejection of Saul what may be called the "divine paradox": though Yahweh neither changes his mind nor breaks his promises, he also does not tolerate disobedience to his commands. The basic paradox is created within the religious realm by the recognition of the reality of divine retribution and the opposite insistence on the necessity that that belief be suspended.[34] Not only does this

---

[31] In this, Saul provides an interesting contrast to Jephthah, who was able to fulfill his vow despite its implications.

[32] Saul was not depicted as a complete failure as a military leader, for 14:47–48 accords a number of victories to him. It is clearly stated in 14:52, however, that he was not able to gain a complete victory over Philistia.

[33] By no means is this to suggest that the deuteronomistic author held a relativistic view of the divine or of divine truth, for such positions are modern creations. I do mean to suggest, however, that the deuteronomistic writer may have understood the divine truths to be "relational," that all knowledge occurs within the context of a particular position. On the importance of this distinction, see P. Berger and T. Luckmann, *The Social Construction of Reality: A Treatise in the Sociology of Knowledge* (New York: Doubleday, 1966), p. 10.

[34] For this analysis of the basic dialectic inherent in the deep structure of religious traditions and moral reasoning, see R. Green, *Religion and Moral Reason: A New Method for Comparative Study* (New York: Oxford, 1988), pp. 3–23.

viewpoint justify the rejection of Saul and the coinciding choice of David, but it also provides the ideological basis for the eventual loss of the kingdoms and the destruction of the national states of Israel and Judah. At the same time, this paradox provides the basis for the reconstitution of the community from the traditions of the past cast now in this interpretive light.

The sudden appearance of Samuel alongside Saul in 1 Sam 15:1 serves to remind the king that it was Yahweh who had commissioned his anointing (9:16) and that Yahweh's prophet was never far from the side of the king to cause him to remember the commands of the *tôrâ*. With formal prophetic introduction, Samuel pronounces Yahweh's commands to Saul. The king is to destroy the Amalekites, the ancient enemies of Israel (Deut 25:17–19; Exod 17:8–13). As with Joshua's conquest of Jericho (Josh 6:17–19), Saul was to institute the custom of the *ḥērem*: "You shall show him no pity" (*lōʾ taḥmōl ʿālāyw*, 1 Sam 15:3); every living thing belonging to Amalek was to be killed. On the surface there was no ambiguity in Yahweh's directive to Saul as given by Samuel. The problem arose when Saul took the opportunity, as he had earlier, to interpret the prophetic command.[35] Saul attacked Amalek as directed, and he put the people and the spoil that was not of the highest quality to the ban. However, "Saul and the army showed pity" (*wayyaḥmōl šāʾûl wĕhāʿām*), and they captured Agag, king of Amalek, allowing him to live, and also seized the best of the livestock. The explanation provided in the narrative is straightforward: "for they were not willing to devote them to the *ḥērem*" (*wĕlōʾ ʾābû haḥărîmām*, 15:9). As presented, this is neither a simple failure nor an inadvertent action. Rather, Saul and his men simply were not willing to carry out the order as expected.[36] The Amalekites were attacked and defeated, but the required ban was instituted only partially. Saul and the army had asserted themselves as the interpreters of the prophetic decrees.

---

[35] Miscall notes the interesting dilemma that the text presents. If both Yahweh and Samuel are allowed to interpret the precise meaning of Yahweh's command, why is this prerogative denied to Saul (*1 Samuel*, p. 100)? As suggested above, for the deuteronomistic vision of the structure of communal authority, the interpretive powers belonged to the prophet, not to the king.

[36] As with the story of Saul's failure to fulfill the commands of Samuel in chap. 13, it is possible to argue that since Saul intended to sacrifice these materials that were to be devoted to Yahweh (cf. 15:12–21), the actual breaking of the command is ambiguous. Any possible ambiguity of meaning is removed by the replies of Yahweh and Samuel to Saul's actions.

That the implications go beyond any simple human prophetic jeal-
ousy over status or power is revealed in the scene that follows the report
of Saul's failure. Yahweh addresses Samuel: "I repent that I have made
Saul king for he has turned away from following me and he has not fulfilled my commands" (niḥamtî kî-himlaktî ʾet-šāʾûl lěmelek kî-šāb měʾaḥăray
wěʾet-děbāray lōʾ hêqîm, 15:11; cf. v. 35). From the standpoint of the interpretation of the divine, there is no doubt that Saul had failed. His failure
had been so severe that Yahweh now chose to change his mind about
having made Saul king. One portion of the "divine paradox" is in
place—Yahweh can and does change his mind. This forms an interpretive frame for the encounter between the king and the prophet and
removes any doubt of the divine prerogatives. The second half of the
paradox is embedded in the confrontation between Samuel and Saul
(15:12–33).[37] Samuel again finds Saul in Gilgal, having just finished offering sacrifices (cf. 13:8–14).[38] This time, Saul was apparently pleased to see
Samuel, blessing him and exclaiming upon meeting him: "I have fulfilled
the command of Yahweh" (hăqîmōtî ʾet-děbar yhwh, 15:13). Saul's self-
evaluation, based on his interpretation of Samuel's account of the divine
decree to institute the ḥērem against Amalek, places him in direct conflict
with Yahweh's own perspective (15:11).

Samuel and Saul then engage in a revealing exchange of words, for
Samuel had heard not only the sounds of the animals that had not been
slaughtered (v. 14), but also the decree of Yahweh that had already
passed judgment on the recalcitrant king (v. 16). What Saul had done had
been assessed as "evil in the eyes of Yahweh" (hāraʿ běʿênê yhwh, v. 19).

---

37 Two narrative texts outside of the deuteronomistic corpus emphasize Yahweh's
repentance in a similar manner. In Exod 32:7–14, a text commonly associated with the
deuteronomic style (M. Noth, A History of Pentateuchal Traditions [Englewood Cliffs,
NJ: Prentice-Hall, 1972], p. 31, n. 113), Yahweh decides to destroy his people and
make a nation of Moses, thus negating his promise to Abraham. In response to the
intercession of Moses (32:11–13), Yahweh "repented" (wayyinnāḥem yhwh) from doing
so (v. 14). Likewise, in Gen 6:6–7, a text commonly associated with the Yahwist
(Noth, p. 28), Yahweh "repented" for having made humankind and decided to
destroy them. According to Judg 2:18, Yahweh "repented" at the sound of Israel's
groaning under the oppression that was the punishment for having followed other
gods. Finally, in 2 Sam 24:16, Yahweh "repented" and stopped his messenger from
carrying out the decreed destruction on Jerusalem. That Yahweh was depicted in
Hebrew literature as capable of "repenting" is well attested both within and without
the deuteronomistic materials.

38 The end of v. 12 or the beginning of v. 13 has suffered a haplography which,
according to the LXX, contains the reference to Saul's sacrifice of burnt offerings. For
a reconstruction of the Hebrew text, consult the commentaries.

Saul's only defense is that he had *intended* to complete the *ḥērem* and that he had spared the cattle at the behest of the army (*hāʿām*, vv. 20–21). As in the case of the broken oath, the voice of the people had taken precedence over the command of Yahweh. Protest his innocence as he might, Saul had failed to recognize his obligations to obey Yahweh's commands and to accept his responsibility for the actions of the people. It was this that led to the final prophetic pronouncement concerning Saul's kingship: "Because you have rejected Yahweh's command, so he has rejected you from being king" (*yaʿan māʾastā ʾet-dĕbar yhwh wayyimʾāsĕkā mimmĕlōk* [with LXX], v. 23b). The reaction of Yahweh announced by Samuel makes it clear that not simply Saul's dynasty but his kingship had now been rejected by Yahweh, the god who had appointed him as king and commanded his actions (vv. 17–18). Saul's rejection was not solely because of his failure to follow the commands of Yahweh as interpreted by Samuel,[39] for the narrative itself reveals that it was *Yahweh's* evaluation of Saul's deeds that was the reason for the rejection. Samuel served simply as the intermediary of these commands.[40] As the integrity of Samuel was evaluated, so, by implication, was the reliability of the deuteronomistic narrator.

When his dynasty had been rejected, Saul had not spoken even a word of recognition. He did not remain quiet now that his kingship (and presumably he himself) had been rejected. His reply to Samuel is insightful; Saul admits that he has sinned, and admits the nature of that sinfulness. Rather than to obey the command of Yahweh, he had listened to the desires of the people (v. 24). When Saul asked Samuel to forgive his sin and return with him that he might prostrate himself before Yahweh, Samuel refused and reiterated the announcement of Yahweh's rejection (vv. 25–26).[41] In attempting to force the prophet's endorsement, Saul seized Samuel's robe and tore it, which became a symbolic act in the pronouncement of Samuel: as Saul had torn his garment, so Yahweh had

---

[39] *Contra* Miscall, *1 Samuel*, p. 114.

[40] In terms of literary critical analysis, the question of the reliability of the narrator is often an issue. In the case of the deuteronomistic historian, the complete reliability of the narratorial voice is often open to question, e.g., in the two accounts of the death of Saul or the conflicting references to the killer of Goliath. While such issues are important for the modern literary analysis of the texts, they remain peripheral to the present study. On the significance of the "unreliable narrator," see W. C. Booth, *The Rhetoric of Fiction* (2nd ed.; Chicago: University of Chicago Press, 1983), pp. 158–59, 295–96.

[41] The realization of sin and proclamation of repentance after final judgment has been announced are reminiscent of Israel's actions in Judg 10:10–16.

torn the kingdom from Saul and had given it to his neighbor (v. 28; cf. 13:14; cf. 1 Kgs 11:29–39). The pronouncement had been made and reiterated; there would be no retraction or change. The second half of the "divine paradox" was now in place. Samuel declares that Yahweh neither lies nor repents, for Yahweh is not a human (15:29; cf. Num 23:19). Clearly, the statement of Samuel cannot be reconciled with the divine pronouncements in vv. 11 and 35, where it is noted that Yahweh does in fact repent. The tension between the two statements is not reduced, nor can it be. The narrator objectified the facticity of the divine act and defended the authority of the prophetic announcement as two related authoritative voices within the community that are to be understood as the only proper sources for the interpretation of the *tôrâ*. It is the fulfillment of the obligations of the *tôrâ*, no matter how ambiguous or difficult it might be, that provides the interpretive bridge between the two seemingly conflicting positions. For the deuteronomistic writer, the role of the interpretation of *tôrâ* belonged by divine decree to the prophet alone (cf. Deut 18:18–22). When Saul admitted a second time that he had sinned and implored Samuel to return and honor him before Israel, Samuel consented, but the rejection was not revoked. Indeed, Samuel symbolically strips Saul of his authority by slaying Agag himself (15:32–33), thus fulfilling the command concerning the *ḥērem*.

If rejection (*m²s*) is the antonym of choosing (*bḥr*),[42] then it is appropriate that the account that begins with the rejection of Saul as king does not conclude until it details the choice of David (16:1–13), a narrative generally associated with the stories of David's accession to the throne.[43] Though Samuel might mourn over Saul's situation (15:35–16:1), such was not Yahweh's intention. He had changed his mind about Saul and had announced that the kingdom had been given to another. Such prophetic pronouncements provide the interpretive keys to the deuteronomistic narrative and the vision for the community. The prophet would be known by the fulfillment of his decrees, for they bore the authority of Yahweh. In this manner, the decrees provided by the deuteronomistic narrative would also find their narrative fulfillment within the account itself. The presentation of the kingdom to David is developed through an extended narrative account that begins with the story of Yahweh's choice of David as the new king, a choice that could be revealed because of the

---

42 Klein, *1 Samuel*, p. 153; McCarter, *1 Samuel*, p. 268.

43 The intricacies of the narrative development of the "history of David's rise" lie beyond the parameters of the present study. See above, n. 6, for bibliography.

rejection of Saul. It is important to note that in its present form, the story of David's accession to the kingdom makes no overt efforts to legitimate his claims. From the deuteronomistic viewpoint, the claims had already been legitimated by Yahweh's anointing of David as his chosen ruler; no other legitimation was required. The power of Yahweh to choose and change presents a challenging perspective of the divine to a community in crisis.

The narrative involving the selection of David is presented in a short, direct manner. Samuel is directed to go to the house of Jesse in Bethlehem, and there he is to anoint the one that Yahweh will designate (16:3b). In the proper prophetic manner, Samuel did as Yahweh had commanded (v. 4) and, under the pretext of a sacrificial ritual, proceeded to Jesse's house. There he viewed the sons of Jesse (cf. 1 Chron 2:13–15), but none of those present was chosen by Yahweh (*lōʾ-bāḥar yhwh*, 16:8–10). Just as Yahweh did not repent the way humans did, so also he did not see like humans—"Yahweh looks at the heart" (*wayhwh yirʾeh lallēbāb*, 16:7; cf. 13:14). Unlike Saul, who had been requested by the people and then announced as Yahweh's choice (10:24), the paradigmatic king would be the sole choice of Yahweh. When David was summoned from the fields to come before Samuel, Yahweh made his selection, directing Samuel, "Arise, anoint him, for he is the one" (*qûm mĕšāḥēhû kî-zeh hûʾ*, 16:12b).[44] When the act was completed, "the spirit of Yahweh rushed upon David from that day onward" (*wattiṣlaḥ rûaḥ-yhwh ʾel-dāwid mēhayyôm hahûʾ wāmāʿlâ*, 16:13). Concurrently, the "spirit of Yahweh" that had from time to time seized Saul (10:6, 10; 11:6) left him, replaced now by "an evil spirit from Yahweh" (*rûaḥ rāʿâ mēʾēt-yhwh*, 16:14).

Yahweh's choice had been made. Saul had been replaced as Yahweh's king by one on whom Yahweh's spirit would rest continually. But would this choice also be liable to change? If the divine could reject one king, what about another? This could be answered only by appeal to the manner in which the newly chosen king would fulfill the obligations of the divine command. To this end, the remainder of Saul's life would serve as a direct contrast to David's. In the deuteronomistic author's final analysis, Saul's kingship was a disastrous failure. The slogan that had

---

44 The choice of David is reiterated at several places within the narrative (2 Sam 6:21; 1 Kgs 8:16; 11:34). It is interesting to note that after the accounts of the choice of David, the verb "to choose" (*bāḥar*) ceases to be used in the language describing the establishment of a king; H. Seebass, "בָּחַר (*bāchar*)," *Theological Dictionary of the Old Testament* (Vol. II, rev. ed., ed. G. J. Botterweck and H. Ringgren; Grand Rapids, MI: Eerdmans, 1977), p. 77.

framed the transition period from the judges to the monarchy, "In those days there was no king in Israel; each man did what was upright in his own eyes,"[45] was put to the test with the early reign of Saul and found to be an inaccurate characterization of the needs and actions of the people. Under Saul, the people continued to "do what was right in their eyes," going so far as to ignore the sacrality of solemn oaths, the essential dietary restrictions that separated them from the "uncircumcised," and the strictures of the *ḥērem*. Quite clearly, the deuteronomistic writer's ideological perspective required not simply a king, but a model of kingship, one initiated and selected by Yahweh. Saul, as interpreted by the author, was not this figure; he was unable to defeat the Philistine enemies and was ineffective at leading the people in the way of covenantal faithfulness. Under Saul, the people remained disunited. All this would be reversed by David, the model of kingship. In the deuteronomistic construction of that model, a confirmation of the role of the prophet would also be presented.

III. David and Saul: From Rejected Prototype to Recreated Model— The Symbolic Integration of the Ideal Israel

With the account of the selection of David and the consequent rejection of Saul, the deuteronomistic writer shifts the focus of the narrative to the central figure in the account of the kingdoms of Israel and Judah. In terms of the literary structure of the narrative, the accounts concerning David are at the very center of the deuteronomistic history and represent a climax of that history in a very important sense.[46] It is under David that the land is completely conquered; it is after David that the same land will be lost. David quite clearly occupies a pivotal role in the development of the deuteronomistic ideology that would supply the conceptual boundaries of the new ideal of "Israel." It was with the figure of David that the deuteronomistic writer created the integrative symbol that reversed the failures of the past and provided both an explanatory model for the disasters of the present exilic community and a hope for a future restora-

---

45 Judg 17:6; 21:5; cf. 18:1; 19:1.
46 G. E. Gerbrandt, *Kingship According to the Deuteronomistic Historian* (SBLDS 87; Atlanta: Scholars Press, 1986), p. 158. Gerbrandt also points out that some 40 chapters of the history (1 Samuel 16–1 Kings 1) portray David as the major character, while the remainder of the history of the two kingdoms occupies only 46 chapters (1 Kings 2 through 2 Kings 25).

tion of the "golden age" once obtained.[47] The figure of David and the stories narrated concerning his life and deeds provide the legitimation for the institutional forms presented in the deuteronomistic vision of "Israel."[48]

Though the literary history of the stories of David remains debated, it is clear that in their present form these accounts are dependent upon the stories of Saul.[49] By contrasting the careers of these two early rulers, the deuteronomistic writer unifies the various political, administrative, and religious roles that had constituted the older "tribal" order and creates a unified state under the leadership of David.[50] Whether a state would ever have developed under Saul or whether David actually accomplished this deed is not relevant to understanding the importance of the narrative. What is at stake is the unification of an acceptable and commonly accepted account of a social past that may be internalized by a new generation that had not directly experienced the "glories" that had belonged to the old regime. What Saul had begun, David would fulfill. Saul, the transition figure, would yield to David, the model. Within these stories are cast the outlines of the ethnic "nationalism" that would be forged as "Israel" in the visions of the deuteronomistic history.[51]

---

[47] As Smith notes, such ancient heroes are important for developing ethnic and national consciousness because they symbolize a past "golden age" which provides focus and comparison with the present. What is important about these figures "is their ability to evoke a lost splendour and virtue, and to act as stimuli and models for a national self-renewal today. Hence, that hero and that golden age which can, at any juncture, best conjure up the appropriate vision and exert the greatest leverage on the majority of the literate classes will be most sought after and will have the greatest influence in shaping the moral direction and tone of the national revival"; *The Ethnic Origins of Nations*, pp. 199–200.

[48] On the necessity of universe maintenance and legitimation, see Berger and Luckmann, *The Social Construction of Reality*, pp. 92–128.

[49] J. Van Seters, *In Search of History: Historiography in the Ancient World and the Origins of Biblical History* (New Haven: Yale University Press, 1983), p. 270.

[50] A generally accepted definition of "state" remains debated. For the purposes of the present work, the definition offered by R. L. Carneiro is sufficient: "A state is an autonomous political unit, encompassing many communities within its territory and having a centralized government with the power to draft men for war or work, levy and collect taxes, and decree and enforce laws" ("The Chiefdom: Precursor of the State," in *The Transition to Statehood in the New World* [ed. G. D. Jones and R. R. Kautz; Cambridge: Cambridge University Press, 1981], p. 69). By the end of the account of David's reign, an Israelite "state" will have come into existence.

[51] While it is common to argue that the emergence of "nations" and "nationalism" is a modern, post-industrial development (see B. Anderson, *Imagined Communities: Reflections on the Origin and Spread of Nationalism* [London: Verso, 1983]), a strong

For the deuteronomistic writer, it is the replacement of Saul that leads to the ultimate unification of the two major political divisions that would constitute the new monarchic state, Judah and Israel.[52] Only through the political maneuvering of David would these two groups be united under a single polity, the development of which would last throughout the reign of this integrating symbol himself. At nearly every point the voice of the deuteronomistic narrator provides the necessary prophetic sanction for the actions followed by the prototype of monarchic leadership, thus constructing a divinely sanctioned form of polity by which this unity "Israel" would conceive of itself. Before we proceed to the manner in which this was accomplished, one central issue in the deuteronomistic structure of the history should be addressed. If it is accurate to conclude that the "reality" of kingship was viewed by the deuteronomistic writer as an ultimate failure and, by his own narrative, as a rebellion against Yahweh, why did the writer give it such a prominent place in his account of Israel's past? The answer to this lies in the basic dialectic that constituted the "divine paradox" that characterizes the deuteronomistic interpretive development of the founding deuteronomic charter.

In order for communities and their foundational identity structures to compete and survive conditions of crisis and stress, the basic symbols upon which the social worlds are constructed must be flexible enough to be adapted to new situations. At the same time, it is also important that

---

argument might be made that many of the elements that constitute the "nation" may be found in much earlier periods (Smith, *The Ethnic Origins of Nations*, pp. 6–18). Most helpful in the present context is the twofold definition of "nation" provided by E. Gellner. A nation supports a commonly shared culture, i.e., a system of ideas, signs, association, and values that constitute an accepted way of life. Such a national consciousness, or social world view, creates individuals who are able to recognize others of their nation by way of voluntary assent to certain norms of action; *Nations and Nationalism* (Ithaca, NY: Cornell University Press, 1983), p. 7. In this way, the "nation" coincides closely with the concept of "ethnic group." It is this that the deuteronomistic writer uses to consolidate his narrative. Whether such common cultural awareness ever existed in the populace of ancient Israel or Judah prior to the exile or restoration is open to question.

[52] The reconstruction of the history and relationships of the various clan and tribal groups that formed these larger units is beyond the parameters of this study. For discussions of the history and problems associated with such efforts, see N. K. Gottwald, *The Tribes of Yahweh: A Sociology of the Religion of Liberated Israel, 1250–1050 B. C. E.* (Maryknoll, NY: Orbis, 1979), and the extensive critique by N. P. Lemche, *Early Israel: Anthropological and Historical Studies on the Israelite Society before the Monarchy* (VTSup 37; Leiden: E. J. Brill, 1985).

some essential claims to continuity with the past be maintained by the developing traditions, or else the legitimation of the institutions supporting them and supported by them may be called into question. This would be especially important in those situations where a new generation, one that had not directly experienced many of the "realities" symbolized in the emerging narrative description, was being addressed. This has clear structural implications for the deuteronomistic writer's presentation of his materials. As the historian has structured his narrative, a basic relationship has been established between the roles of prophet and king. The development of the institution of kingship throughout the narrative provides an institutional support and explanation for the continuing role of the prophet. Such legitimation would be especially important within the context of a new social situation wherein kingship was no longer to be an active component of the society.[53] With this relationship between the two institutional aspects of the "Israelite" world posited, the maintenance of the institution of kingship became a necessity for the author's own authority structure to be continued. This constituted one way in which the author could attempt to maintain a social base of support for his position within the changing social order.[54] The emergence of the prophet and priest as institutionally recognized roles and as established parts of the social world of ancient Israel is

---

[53] Ezekiel's visions of restoration seem to "demote" the king to the role of "prince" and to find the major communal leadership role to be embedded in the Aaronide priesthood. While there is a connection with the past traditions, there is also a clear development from them in a different direction. Ezekiel's own role as a member of the temple priesthood clearly influenced the manner by which the prophetic was subsumed by the priestly. In contrast, the prophetic visions of restoration recorded in deutero- and trito-Isaiah envision a much more egalitarian restoration community wherein leadership is by some noninstitutionalized authority. For discussions of these two contrasting and competing ideals, see P. D. Hanson, *The Dawn of Apocalyptic* (Philadelphia: Fortress, 1975), pp. 32–208; 228–40. As I have suggested at other points in this work, the deuteronomistic historian presents yet another competing and contrasting view of the possibility of a restoration and revival of community, this time in terms of an ethnic polity known as "Israel." The observation that "...the institution of prophecy appeared simultaneously with kingship in Israel and fell with kingship...." (F. M. Cross, *Canaanite Myth and Hebrew Epic* [Cambridge: Harvard University Press, 1973], p. 223) might be understood as a view created by the narrative constructions of the deuteronomistic writer and furthered by the community adopting this world view as its own.

[54] As suggested by T. Overholt, it was precisely the loss of such a social support base that ultimately led to the demise of prophecy as a culturally accepted form of religious expression; "The End of Prophecy: No Players Without a Program," *JSOT* 42 (1988) 110.

clearly associated by the deuteronomistic writer with the emergence of the monarchy. Likewise, the traditions of the monarchy were too essential not only to the recent past, but also to the general cultural milieu, to be omitted by one attempting to recount that past in meaningful terms for the present.

For both traditional and ideological reasons, then, the writer maintained kingship as an essential interpretive symbol of the social order that had led to the present cultural crisis. A restored community might define itself in terms of a monarchic state, but the ideal model of such would be one that would find its design in the figure of David. At no point in the narrative would the *institution* of kingship be condemned by the writer; the concept of a divinely chosen king who would act in accord with Yahweh's will formed a part of the basic charter of the community's self-identification (Deut 17:14–20). The very dialectic this position created is played out in the narrative tension developed by the transposition of the careers of Saul and David—Israel's selection and Yahweh's choice. The divisions that characterize these two figures, one permanently endowed with the spirit of Yahweh and the other periodically possessed by an evil spirit sent from Yahweh, are emblematic of the internal rifts that symbolized an Israel divided in its visions of its future and its relationship with its god.

At the time David was anointed, "Israel" was politically united only by its dependence upon Saul to deliver it from the Philistine threat. By the end of the account of David's rise to power, Saul will have proved himself to be a complete failure at all of the necessary aspects of kingship and dynasty. Instead, all of these will be fulfilled in David. David would come to Saul's court and become his armor-bearer. It would be David who would soothe Saul when the king was possessed by the evil spirit (16:14–23). It would be David who would win Saul's love (16:21). On the other hand, David would be the ostensible source of Saul's madness, provoking Saul so that he would twice attempt to kill David (18:10–11; 19:8–10), and would pursue him as though he were a common bandit (19:18–31:13).[55] David, in contrast, would refuse to harm Saul, the

---

55 A number of aspects of David's career suggest a connection with "social banditry." For a discussion of these, see M. Chaney, "Ancient Palestinian Peasant Movements and the Formation of Premonarchic Israel," in *Palestine in Transition: The Emergence of Ancient Israel* (ed. by D. N. Freedman and D. F. Graf; SWBA 2; Sheffield: Almond, 1983), pp. 77–83. On the broader issues of "social banditry" and its implications for various social groups, consult E. Hobsbawm, *Bandits* (rev. ed.; New York: Pantheon, 1969).

"anointed of Yahweh," though twice given the opportunity (24:1–7; 26:6–12). Throughout the narrative, the two figures are developed as opposing characters. The distinguishing feature is the position taken by Yahweh with respect to each. The narratorial voice of the deuteronomistic writer controls throughout the manner in which each of these kings influences the visions of the future "Israel."

It is the presentation of Yahweh's position *vis-à-vis* David and Saul that provides an interpretive crux in the deuteronomistic ideology of divine activity. The perspective of the author clearly requires of Israel an absolute allegiance to the proper performance of the commands of Yahweh. Israel is required by the deuteronomic ideal to "love Yahweh," a command requiring an unqualified obedience and providing the basis of the covenantal relationship.[56] Yahweh, who had initiated the covenantal bond as a result of his love of Israel (Deut 7:8, 13; 10:15; 23:6), could still "repent" of his decisions and change the manner in which he responded to his subjects. Though such "changes" occur only in response to Israel's failure to fulfill the covenantal obligations that defined and sustained it, this characteristic of divine activity in the ideology of the deuteronomistic writer prevents the ways of the divine from being reduceable to a predictable formula of action. It is also this structural element that necessitates the attempt to provide some assurance of security for those who internalize this religious world view. This, I would argue, is precisely the role played by the deuteronomic ideal of the divine choice. Yahweh had chosen Israel as his people, and the choice had obligated the people to meet Yahweh's covenantal demands. The people themselves had willingly accepted these obligations, which defined them in terms of their god and a commonly shared past (Josh 24:2–27). Now Yahweh had chosen David, but had not placed any special covenantal obligations on his king beyond those that had been imposed upon Saul and which would be placed on all David's successors.[57]

---

[56] W. L. Moran, "The Ancient Near Eastern Background of the Love of God in Deuteronomy," *CBQ* 25 (1963) 78. For the variety of deuteronomic terms used to express these obligations of Israel in response to the demands of Yahweh, see M. Weinfeld, *Deuteronomy and the Deuteronomic School* (Oxford: Clarendon, 1972), pp. 332–39.

[57] Cf. Deut 17:18–20. As will be demonstrated in the next section of this chapter, the model of obedience that is formed by the presentation of David will become the basis for a monarchic covenant that will be applied equally to the kings of Judah and those of Israel.

Whereas Saul was depicted as earnestly attempting to interpret and act in accord with Yahweh's commands, failing at the critical points to follow the leadership of Samuel, David is portrayed in a very different manner. With David's early career the issue of the *tôrâ* and its proper interpretation does not arise. Further, the manner in which David gains the support of the various factions depicts him as somewhat less than reflective on the nature and implications of many of his deeds. All of this suggests that operating in the stories of David is this element of the divine paradox that confirms the predictability of Yahweh's actions: because Yahweh has chosen David, David succeeds in all that he attempts. For David, obedience is not a focus of concern until he has established himself on the throne and united the various aspects of the monarchic structures under his person. Once a new covenantal bond is invoked (2 Samuel 7), the matters of obedience become a central focus, and David the primary actor. As will be developed in the accounts of the kings to follow David to the throne of Judah, it would ultimately be Yahweh's allegiance to David and/or Jerusalem that would determine their fates rather than the deeds that they performed.[58] David's career illustrates the Yahwistic confession: "With Yahweh on my side, I do not fear; what can a man do to me?" (Ps 118:6).

That Yahweh was "with David" (1 Sam 18:12, 14, 28; 2 Sam 5:10) and determined his successes is exemplified by the way in which the institutionalized roles of dynastic heir, prophet, priest, military, and landed gentry would all be simultaneously forfeited by Saul and collected by David. David would gather under his control not only the various roles necessary for the formation of a political state, but also the affection and requisite loyalty of the major actors within the narrative. David gained the "love" (*ʾāhēb; ʾahăbâ*) not only of Saul (16:21), but also of Jonathan (18:1, 3; 20:17), Michal (18:20, 28), and "all Israel and Judah" (18:16). The loyalty of subject to king[59] is expressed to David long before he accedes to the throne, a narrative expression of the depiction of David's rise as clearly under the blessing of Yahweh,[60] a symbolic expression of the

---

58 1 Kgs 11:12, 13, 32, 34, 36; 15:4; 2 Kgs 8:19; 19:34 (cf. Isa 37:35); 20:6.

59 On this generally recognized political connotation of the Semitic concept "to love," see Moran, "The Ancient Near Eastern Background of the Love of God in Deuteronomy," pp. 78–79.

60 On the redactional presentation of David as "under the blessing" and "under the curse," see R. A. Carlson, *David, the Chosen King: A Traditio-Historical Approach to the Second Book of Samuel* (Stockholm: Almqvist & Wiksell, 1964), pp. 20–37.

manner in which those chosen by Yahweh might hope to succeed when the demands of the deity were fulfilled.

Though David's selection was by the prophetic actions of Samuel, the guidance of his early career was by the permanence of the Yahwistic spirit that enveloped him at his anointing (16:13). The legitimation of the reign of David is never an issue in the present arrangement of the deuter-onomistic history;[61] Yahweh had selected David as his legitimate king for his chosen people. What remained was to demonstrate how David was able to accomplish for Israel what Saul had failed to do and for which failure he had been rejected. A major factor in the presentation of David's rise to kingship over a united kingdom of Judah and Israel is that of public recognition. Though the anointing of David was recounted in 1 Sam 16:2–14, there is no public recognition of David's kingship until after the death of Saul (2 Sam 2:4) and Ishbosheth (2 Sam 5:1–3). The narrative process that details David's rise to the throne constitutes a part of the objectification process of the social world created by the deuteronomistic writer; the manner by which David is depicted as unifying "all Israel" provided the common past through which the "descendants" of that Israel could understand both their present and their future.

Like Saul, David is depicted as an accomplished warrior. His first great deed is the defeat of the Philistine champion Goliath (17:1–58),[62] an accomplishment symbolic of his successful leadership against this nemesis that had not been defeated since its appearance in Judg 10:7. It is David's military prowess that provides the very vehicle by which he becomes the agent to bring about the complete conquest and pacification of the land (2 Sam 8:1–14; cf. Deut 12:10) and to gain the public recogni-

---

[61] The description of the "History of David's Rise" as a type of court apology, as is common, rests upon the presupposition that the document had a prehistory inde-pendent of the present context. For an exposition of the major themes that might constitute such an apologetic purpose, see P. K. McCarter, "The Apology of David," *JBL* 99 (1980) 489–504.

[62] It is commonly recognized that the present account of the defeat of Goliath reflects two differing traditions that have been combined to form the present story. The shorter textual account of LXX[B] is taken by some to suggest that the story in the MT has been supplemented at a later point and by others to suggest that the LXX has been shortened and simplified (see McCarter, *1 Samuel*, pp. 306–9). A detailed expo-sition of the differences between the MT and the LXX is given by E. Tov in "The Composition of 1 Samuel 16–18 in the Light of the Septuagint Version," in *Empirical Models for Biblical Criticism* (ed. J. H. Tigay; Philadelphia: University of Pennsylvania Press, 1985), pp. 97–130. The tensions produced in the story reinforce the complexity of the figure of David that is developed by the deuteronomistic author.

tion of his role in the life of Israel. Saul, despite his individual successes against Philistia, was never able to free Israel of their oppression (1 Sam 14:52). David, at every point, won only praise and recognition for his abilities: "Saul has slain his thousands, and David his tens of thousands" (18:7; 21:12; 29:5). The military successes of David brought him the adoration and allegiance of the people. It was David who was placed by Saul at the head of the army (ʿal ʾanšê hammilḥāmâ) and who was successful in every mission given him by his commander-in-chief (18:5). The actualization of military success in the career of David led to the public recognition of the obedience and respect that David was to receive: "Now all Israel and Judah loved David, because he went forth and came in before them (from battle)" (18:16). The symbolic power of David's victories unified the people of both Israel and Judah under his leadership.

This recognition of his powers extended beyond that of the general populace. A major obstacle to David's public claims to the throne is presented by the fact that Saul already had an heir to his throne in his son Jonathan. That Saul also hoped to establish a dynasty seems most probable and is confirmed in the deuteronomistic narrative (1 Sam 20:31). In political terms, the legitimation of succession within the family is dependent upon public recognition,[63] and the narrative makes it clear throughout that this belonged to David. David's public presumptions to the throne were further legitimated by his initiation into the family of Saul. By marriage to Saul's daughter Michal, David became a potential legitimate heir to the throne (18:20–27).[64] Yet the power of David extended beyond normal expectations, for his fate was governed throughout by the divine word; he would be the next ruler of Israel (13:14), not Jonathan. This fact is recognized by Jonathan, who entered into an

---

[63] G. Buccellati, *Cities and Nations of Ancient Syria: An Essay on Political Institutions with Special Reference to the Israelite Kingdoms* (Studi Semitici 26; Rome: Istituto di Studi del Vincino Oriente,1967), p. 196. That Saul's monarchy must be understood as dynastic in principle seems beyond reasonable dispute (pp. 195–200). Notably, the first rejection of Saul by Yahweh presumes that the dynastic principle was operative (1 Sam 13:13).

[64] The account concerning Saul's elder daughter Merab (18:17–19) may have been originally connected with the promise of Saul in the narrative concerning Goliath (17:25); H. W. Hertzberg, *I & II Samuel* (OTL; Philadelphia: Westminster, 1964), pp. 159–60; McCarter, *1 Samuel*, pp. 306–9. While the biblical text seems to downplay the possibility, it has been suggested that David also married Saul's wife Ahinoam, a move that would have strengthened his claim to the throne; J. Levenson, "1 Samuel 25 as Literature and as History," *CBQ* 40 (1978) 27–28.

alliance with David and even endowed him with his robe (18:4), a symbolic transfer of the right to succession.[65] In addition, Jonathan announces to David that it will be David who will be king (23:17), a fact later acknowledged by Saul himself (24:21). Recognition of David's potential claims to the throne extended into Philistia (21:12), where he was forced to flee from the attacks of Saul (27:1–28:2; cf. 21:11–16).

The manipulative side of David figures actively in the procurement of his authoritative status in the eyes of his contemporaries. While fleeing from Saul, David went to Nob and sought provisions for his men from the Eliade priest Ahimelech (21:2–10). In a deceptive manner David lied to the priest in order to gain his help (21:3–4). The results of this were twofold: the priestly family there was slaughtered at Saul's command (22:6–19), and its lone survivor, Abiathar, joined David (22:20–23), thus giving him the control and cooperation of the priesthood. This deceptive side of David's character is exonerated by the fact that it provides the vehicle for the actualization of the prophetic pronouncement against the Eliade line of priests (1 Sam 2:27–36; 1 Kgs 2:26–27). In symbolic terms, the figure of David now possessed control of the rights to dynastic succession, control over the the Saulide line (20:14–16; 24:21–22; 2 Sam 9:1–13), and control of the priesthood and the apparatus for divine inquiries (23:2–4; 30:7–8; 2 Sam 2:1; 5:19, 23). Slowly but surely, the narrative consolidation of both political and religious institutional roles under the purview of David was achieved.[66]

In addition to such symbolic possession of the rights to the throne, some base of political support would be necessary if David were to establish himself as successor to the throne. Three texts give ample support to his abilities to procure this foundation. As a "social bandit" with a motley band of followers pursued by the crown, David lacked a stable base. This factor is illustrated by the "protection" money demanded of the wealthy Calebite landholder Nabal, who refused to acknowledge any status or support for this "servant" who had rebelled against his master (25:10). But such failure to recognize and support the one who had been divinely selected to succeed to the throne had dire consequences; to such

---

[65] T. N. D. Mettinger, *King and Messiah: The Civil and Sacral Legitimation of the Israelite Kings* (Lund: C. W. K. Gleerup, 1976), p. 34.

[66] The account of the slaughter of the priesthood at Nob is divided by the account of David with Achish of Gath (21:11–16), the notice of his gathering of an "outlaw group" (22:1–2), and the story of his relocation of his parents in Moab (22:3–5). Each of these furthers the extent of David's recognition, and each displays the ingenuity and ability of David to succeed no matter what the obstacles.

treatment David took offense and vowed immediate action (vv. 13, 21–22), but was prevented by Abigail, the wife of the offending party, from incurring bloodguilt (vv. 26, 33). Embedded in her plea to David for restraint was the assurance that Yahweh would provide him a "sure house" (*bayit ne²ĕmān*, v. 28; cf. 2 Sam 7:16), a statement that applied not only to the situation that was unfolding there, but to the future establishment of his dynastic line. It would be Yahweh who would fulfill David's vengeance for him. David would not become the "master of his fate,"[67] at least not at this point in the narrative. Nabal, the "fool," would die as the result of Yahweh's actions (v. 38), and David would take his wife Abigail as his own (vv. 40–42), procuring at the same time a base in Judahite territory.

When David is forced to flee to Achish of Gath to seek asylum from Saul among the Philistines (27:1–28:2; cf. 21:11–16), he is able to manipulate the situation to his own advantage. For his services, David received the city of Ziklag (27:6) as his own and was appointed as Achish's permanent bodyguard (28:2). As when he was in the service of Saul, David met with success in all his military exploits, though they were not what the Philistines had conceived. By attacking and destroying Israel's traditional enemies, e.g., the Geshurites and Amalekites (27:8–12), and redistributing the booty among the landholders of Judah (30:26–31), David gained the support of the Judahite landed gentry. Rather than support his Philistine masters, David gained a solid Judahite support base for himself. All that remained for him to provide for was the continued loyalty of his military forces. While the booty from the raids supplied part of this, there was one additional action that aided the young aspirant to the throne. In a battle against Amalekite raiders (30:1–31), an event that took David out of the Philistine attack against Saul (31:1–13), David created a rule and ordinance for redistributing the spoils of war among both combatants and non-combatants in his following (30:25–30), insuring the loyalty of all who aided David in his successes.[68]

Thus David was able to procure the support of the landed gentry of Judah and to marry into the wealth of the area himself. All that stood in his way was Saul, the "anointed of Yahweh," whom he refused to kill.

---

[67] Hertzberg, *I & II Samuel*, p. 204. It is notable in this regard that this section of the narrative began with the notice of the death of Samuel (25:1), "David's theological mentor" (Klein, *1 Samuel*, p. 253). Despite the loss of this prophetic power, David's career would not falter until after the "new order" had been established.

[68] On the relationship of this passage to the account of Moses' distribution of the spoils in the battle against Midian (Num 31:25–31), see Klein, *1 Samuel*, p. 284.

This obstacle was removed on Mt. Gilboa in a battle whose outcome had been announced by the shade of the dead prophet Samuel (28:16–19). Nowhere can the deuteronomistic view of the power of the prophetic voice be seen more clearly than in the "resurrection" of Samuel by the necromancer at En-dor.[69] Samuel's pronouncement returns to the condemnation of Saul in 13:13–14 and reconfirms that Yahweh had indeed torn the kingdom from Saul and given it to his neighbor. This time, however, David is explicitly named. Saul's impending death is announced and, on the next day, realized. David stood on the threshold of the realization of the divine establishment of his kingship, yet he would take care to see that it would be Yahweh's and not his own or any other human hand that would procure the kingdom for him. The reward given the Amalekite who brought him the royal insignia of Saul was death (2 Sam 1:14–15). David was directed to Hebron by Yahweh himself (2:1–3). There he became king over Judah, a position he would hold for seven and one-half years (2:4, 11).

The final integrative function that remained to be performed by David's kingship was the unification of the two kingdoms. The chronology is collapsed by the narration techniques to bring this about as quickly as possible. Saul was succeeded by his son Ishbosheth, supported by Saul's general, Abner (2:8–10), resulting in hostilities between the two regional monarchies (2:12–3:1), with David emerging as the stronger of the two parties. It was through the efforts of Abner that the political groundwork for the unification of the two states was laid (3:6–19). The rallying cry for such was the proclamation that David was Yahweh's choice to deliver Israel from the continuing Philistine threat (3:18; cf. 1 Sam 9:16). Quite clearly, David would be the legitimate successor to the failed experiences of the judges and the failure of Saul to unify the country and to institutionalize the monarchy. Not surprisingly, Abner was killed by David's general Joab as the result of a blood feud, or so the text relates (3:20–30). The resulting denunciation of Joab by David for this deed (3:31–39) continues the depiction of the new king as one completely

---

[69] Polzin suggests that Samuel's rise and Saul's fall form a "parabolic *inclusio*" concerning the nature of kingship in the exilic community; *Samuel and the Deuteronomist*, pp. 223–24. The revivification of the prophetic figure of Samuel, I would argue, says more about the deuteronomistic view of prophecy than about the nature of kingship, especially with respect to the Davidic ideal that is developed. As I interpret the deuteronomistic history, kingship, though it may not have been a successful enterprise, was nonetheless an important element in the identity of the community and its understanding of its potential restoration.

free of any wrongdoing or bloodguilt. The final obstacle, Ishbosheth, was violently removed from the scene, but again those responsible for such actions found no reward from David (4:1–12).

The path to the unification of Israel and Judah was open. The symbolic integration of the kingship and the nation was about to be completed under the leadership of David. In recognition of Yahweh's proclamation that David should "shepherd" his people (5:2), the tribes of the northern kingdom came to David at Hebron and entered into a covenant with him and anointed him as their king (5:3). Now David stood as the anointed ruler of both Israel and Judah. The land and people were united. With the conquest of the old Jebusite city of Jerusalem and the establishment of it as his capital (5:6–10),[70] the city that Yahweh had chosen[71] belonged to this united people. With the transfer of the Ark to Jerusalem and its establishment in a tent-shrine (6:1–19), David had effected the unification of the religious symbols of the tribal units.[72]

The entirety of the account of David's rise stands as the narrative fulfillment of the prophetic pronouncement that had sealed the fate of Saul for his failure to follow the instructions of Samuel: "Yahweh has sought out for himself a man according to his own heart and has commanded him to be *nāgîd* over his people" (13:14). David was the one sought out and chosen, for to Yahweh belonged the power to look into the heart (16:7). The private anointing of David provided the narrative base for the presentation of the social legitimation of the institution of the Davidic dynasty as the model for the unification of Israel and Judah into one state, Israel, centered in the political and religious capital, Jerusalem. The deuteronomistic writer could consider this portion of the prophetic word fulfilled and begin the construction of the religious legitimation of the successors to David by the establishment of a new covenantal assurance. This new divine promise completes the model of kingship envisioned with the rule of David.

---

[70] As McCarter notes, the verses detailing the taking of Jerusalem "contain obscure references that have exercised the ingenuity of interpreters since ancient times"; 2 *Samuel* (AB 9; Garden City, NY: Doubleday,1984), p. 137.

[71] For the deuteronomistic usage of this phrase, see Weinfeld, *Deuteronomy and the Deuteronomic School*, pp. 324–25.

[72] The importance of these innovative actions has been emphasized by Cross, *Canaanite Myth and Hebrew Epic*, pp. 230–32. The exact end of the "history of David's rise" remains debated. For a discussion of some of the major positions, see A. A. Anderson, 2 *Samuel* (WBC; Waco, TX: Word, 1989), pp. xxvii–xxxvi.

IV. David and Nathan: The Unconditional
Promise of Perpetuity

With David, the deuteronomistic author developed an integrating symbol by which a politically and religiously united "Israel" could be defined. Through some of the most skillful narrative developments contained in the Hebrew Bible, this writer provided a careful depiction of the power of Yahweh's choice and blessing on those he favored. Such an integrating symbol stood as a clear indicator of hope for the community seeking to retain and recreate a sense of identity from the debacle of the exile and the loss of political independence and ancestral homeland. It was David and his successes that provided a focus for the developing identity system that would find its expression in the realization and creation of a "people" that would define itself as "Israel."[73] The symbolic power of David and the 400-year dynasty that he would establish[74] created an *axis mundi* around which the Israelite world could be rebuilt and its boundaries reconceived.

The divine confirmation and legitimation of this newly formed entity are expressed in the royal grant[75] to David that is narrated in 2 Sam 7:1–17, a text that initiates a new epoch in the creation of an "Israelite" identity that is fulfilled with the establishment of the succession of Solomon on the throne and the erection of the temple during his reign. Since the introduction of Samuel as the prophetic intermediary who proclaimed Yahweh's decisions, and thus affected the development of Israel's future, the fulfillment of such prophetic pronouncements, as defined in Deut 18:21–22, provided a structure for interpreting the mate-

---

[73] We follow here the definition of "people" suggested by E. H. Spicer: "...a determinable set of human individuals who believe in a given set of identity symbols." Important to understanding such systems is the recognition of the importance of the beliefs about historical events that integrate the experiences of the individuals who are formed by such systems; "Persistent Cultural Systems," *Science* 4011 (1971) 796.

[74] Whether the claims to such dynastic succession are historically correct is not relevant to the present investigation. What is essential is the recognition of the ideological expression of descent and continuity that is symbolized by the narrative presentation of this dynasty. On the problems associated with the biological descent of Jehoash, see above, chap. 2, pp. 29–31.

[75] On the concept of the royal grant in the ancient Near East and as it applies to this text, see M. Weinfeld, "The Covenant of Grant in the Old Testament and in the Ancient Near East," *JAOS* 90 (1970) 184–203.

rials presented by the deuteronomistic historian.[76] At the same time, this narrative, like those that have preceded it, intentionally creates a dialectic in the manner by which it recreates this Israelite past within the context of its continued history.

While this dynastic promise to David provides the culmination of the construction of David's symbolic appropriation of the kingship and unification of "Israel," the version of the promise in 2 Sam 7:1–17 is not the only, nor is it the more common, expression of the relationship between royal dynasty and Yahwistic blessing.[77] The dynastic oracle to David, with its unconditional promise of a sure house and dynastic perpetuity, a promise that would not be revoked even if his successors were to fail to follow after Yahweh (7:14–16), reconstructs one pole of the dialectic of the deuteronomistic ideology. It provides for the aspect of hope within the context of the development of an ideology of divinely guaranteed retributive justice (cf. Deut 28:1–68). Standing in constant tension with this view of dynastic stability and divine support are a series of passages that contain a conditionalized form of the promise (1 Kgs 9:2–9; cf. 2:4; 3:14; 6:11–13; 8:25–26), thus reemphasizing the equally unconditional deuteronomic demand of obedience to *tôrâ* and comprising the other part of this dialectic.[78] For a proper understanding of the

---

[76] The manner in which the dynastic promise provides a structural norm that explains the later historical developments has been noted by D. J. McCarthy, "II Samuel and the Structure of the Deuteronomic History," *JBL* 84 (1966) 131–38. Both the literary unity and the historical development of the "Davidic covenant" remain debated among scholars, and it is doubtful that agreement will be reached on either matter. For a convenient summary of the variety of positions and pertinent bibliography, see Anderson, 2 *Samuel*, pp. 109–16. Despite the modern tendency to date the dynastic promise to the period of Solomon and to interpret it as an effort to legitimate Solomon's empire, the assertion of T. Veijola that the Davidic dynasty required no theological legitimation so long as the Davidides remained on the throne might suggest that the exile provided the time for the formulation of this particular idea; *Verheissung in der Krise: Studien zur Literatur und Theologie der Exilszeit anhand des 89. Psalms* (Annales academiae scientiarum Fennicae 220; Helsinki: Soumalainen Tiedeakatemia, 1982), p. 94.

[77] Expressions of the unconditional nature of this covenant are found in 1 Chr 17:1–15, 2 Sam 23:1–7, and in Pss 89:19–38 and 132:11–12. The dating and relationships of these texts to each other remain a matter of debate. For a discussion of these problems, see Veijola, *Verheissung in der Krise*, pp. 47–118.

[78] As J. Levenson has emphasized, there is a plurality of theological positions expressed within the Hebrew Bible; "The Davidic Covenant and its Modern Interpreters," *CBQ* 41 (1979) 217–19. While the differing covenantal formulations may "originally" have belonged to separate redactional strata, with the composition of the

composition and purpose of the deuteronomistic history, both poles must be recognized as essential elements in the structure of the narrative. The tension created by the two extremes is both functional and instructive at the level of communal self-identification. Though people and rulers might fail to fulfill their obligations to Yahweh, Yahweh would not fail to watch over his chosen people. At the same time, such watching over might result in severe chastisement (7:14), but hopefully not in the complete removal of the divine loyalty as had occurred with Saul, the king who belonged to the old era of Israelite memory.

As important as the unconditional nature of this dynastic oracle promising that David's scion would build a temple for Yahweh and that Yahweh would establish his throne forever (7:12–13) is the manner in which the pronouncement is given: it is delivered by Nathan the prophet (*nātān hannābîʾ*), who declares that Yahweh is with David (7:2–3). With the expression of a new element within the narrative characterization of "Israel's" emerging identity structure, a prophetic figure appears as though from nowhere (cf. Judg 6:7–10; 1 Sam 13:9–10) to introduce the word of Yahweh. Not since the ominous appearance of the shade of Samuel declaring the fulfillment of his prophetic pronouncements against Saul (1 Sam 28:16–19; cf. 13:13–14; 15:22–28) had a prophet figured prominently in the presentation of the narrative.[79] The power to interpret and to intermediate the will of Yahweh belonged to this figure. Nowhere could this be more clearly demonstrated than in the role and figure of Nathan and his pronouncements in the reign of David and the problems of the succession to the throne. It would be through the powers of this prophet that David's line would be guaranteed (7:1–17), judged and sentenced for wrongdoing (12:1–15), and finally properly established on the throne (1 Kgs 1:11–48). While the deuteronomistic writer envisioned Yahweh's choice as the determinant factor in David's success, the directions of that kingly career and its implications would be guided by the power of the prophetic word.

---

deuteronomistic history in its present form, they represent a reformulation that now belongs to the same level of meaning and significance.

[79] The prophet Gad is also associated with David and is the figure who directed David not to remain in Moab but to return to Judah (1 Sam 22:5). The same figure appears at the end of the account of David's reign in the story concerning David's census of Israel and Judah (2 Sam 24:11–19). The role of this prophet, however, is not further developed in the deuteronomistic account. He is referred to as the "seer of the king" (*ḥōzēh-hammelek*) as distinguished from Nathan "the prophet" (*hannābîʾ*) in 2 Chr 29:25.

When the king expressed the desire to build Yahweh a temple, it was Nathan who first gave him permission, then, upon receiving a revelation, revoked that permission (7:2–3, 4–7). Nathan announced that Yahweh would make a "house" for David (7:11). Further, it would be David's offspring who would be placed on the throne and who would build for Yahweh a temple (7:12–13). The throne of his kingdom would be established forever (7:13, 16). The oracle is completely unconditional; for the faithfulness of the past, David was awarded the guarantee of an eternal dynastic line that Yahweh would never abandon (7:14).[80] This oracle constitutes one of the major themes of the remainder of the history of Israel and Judah: Yahweh's promise of faithfulness to David and his dynastic line.[81] Additionally, it demonstrates the power of the prophetic pronouncement in both political and narrative terms. The prophet, at Yahweh's command, is able to contradict the wishes of the king; notably, David obeys the prophetic directions not to build a temple. The distinction with Saul is clearly drawn. In the proper relationship, the prophetic pronouncement took precedence over the royal prerogatives for the deuteronomistic author.[82]

In narrative terms, the fact that the fulfillment of this prophetic announcement does not occur immediately is another characteristic of the manner in which the historian uses prophetically related materials to structure the remaining history. Prophecy-delay-fulfillment comes to characterize the structure of the history and constitutes an important part of the ideology that is at the foundation of the authority of both the narrative presentation of the concept of "Israel" and the deuteronomistic author creating it. The fulfillment of the prophetic pronouncement is the guarantee that the prophet spoke the word of Yahweh (Deut 18:21–22), an important distinguishing factor in a setting where multiple voices compete for the rights to interpret and reformulate the major symbols for the reestablishment of the community. By emphasizing the fact that the prophetic word was not always fulfilled immediately, the deuterono-

---

[80] The oracle of Nathan is commonly viewed as a composite of two originally separate oracles, one regarding the construction of a temple and the other regarding the promise of offspring to David. See, e.g., the analysis of T. Veijola, *Die ewige Dynastie: David und die Entstehung seiner Dynastie nach der deuteronomistischen Darstellung* (Annales academiae scientiarum Fennicae 193; Helsinki: Soumalainen Tiedeakatemia, 1975), pp. 68–79.

[81] Cross, *Canaanite Myth and Hebrew Epic*, pp. 281–82.

[82] The didactic aspects of this text should not be overlooked, for the "explanatory and exhortatory" are important aspects of both universe construction and maintenance; Berger and Luckmann, *The Social Construction of Reality*, p. 109.

mistic writer provided a structural guide for major portions of his history and grounded his own authoritative claim within that narrative construction. The history of Israel and Judah would repeatedly demonstrate that the prophetic ideals espoused by the writer were confirmed by "historical realities."[83]

In light of the continued deuteronomistic insistence on allegiance and obedience to the *tôrâ*, the most striking of the concepts presented in the promise to David is that contained in 7:14–16: if David's successors should do wrong, he would be punished but not rejected. This creates a tension not only with the deuteronomic ideal of covenantal obedience, but also with the deuteronomistic incorporation of the institution of kingship into the social world of Israel (1 Sam 12:20–25). By the power of the narrative presentation of strategically placed prophetic pronouncements, the deuteronomistic historian recreates within his account of Israel's past a structural dialectic that enables him to control his presentation of the materials and to reenvision the significance of both the past and the present. This past that the narrative orders, explains, and objectifies is directed to a generation in danger of losing its identity and its past in the midst of the assimilatory pressures presented by its spatial and temporal dislocation from its own social world. In order to combat the threats presented by the competing symbol systems encountered in the exile, the deuteronomistic writer created a uniquely Israelite version of history that recreated and maintained Israel's religious identity in the face of its own failure to adhere to the basic presuppositions of that same identity. The entirety of Israel's history, for the deuteronomistic presentation, could be interpreted by this basic dialectical relationship between Yahweh and his chosen people "Israel:" the eternal verity and reliability of the divine promises and their fulfillment are conditioned by the deity's response to Israel's obedience or disobedience to the requirement

---

[83] As will be demonstrated in the next chapter, this principle is essential to the presentation of such events as the loss of Israel by Solomon, Jeroboam's loss of dynasty, the postponement of the destruction of Ahab's dynasty, the "limited royal grant" to Jehu, and the condemnation of Judah for the deeds of Manasseh. It was introduced in the extensive narrative delay between the condemnation of Saul's reign (1 Sam 13:13–14) and the consolidation of the kingdom under David (2 Sam 5:1–3). This narrative device also allowed the writer to structure his account in such a way as to be able to incorporate extensive interpretive materials, like the "Ark Narrative," the "History of David's Rise," or the "Succession Narrative" into his account for didactic and illustrative reasons.

that they be a holy people, separate and different from the nations.[84] In the deuteronomistic version of the Israelite social world, it is the role of the prophet to intermediate between Yahweh and Israel and to announce Yahweh's plans to his people.

With the new element of the promise to David introduced as an operative component of the deuteronomistic ideology, the deuteronomic promises to Israel of rest from their enemies and the complete possession of the land are proclaimed to have been fulfilled (7:10; cf. Deut 12:9; Josh 21:43–45). As the entry into the land had created a new epoch through the ritual narrative rehearsals (Joshua 1; 24), the establishment of kingship had required an equivalent ritual incorporation (1 Samuel 12). The fulfillment of the promises to Israel and the unification of the people under the king established on the dynastic throne who had been chosen by Yahweh were marked by a new expression by the divine (2 Sam 7:1–17). It is only to be expected that the account of this new covenantal relationship should be followed by the notice of David's conquest of all the surrounding areas, thus establishing his kingdom and insuring the security of his people (8:1–14). The monarchic state was established, and a new paradigm of "Israel" had received expression. Under the integrative symbol of the Davidic ruler, the tribes of Israel and Judah were united as one people, "Israel" (2 Sam 8:15).

But as was no doubt known to those in exile, this "golden age" ideal kingdom did not endure. After only one successor, Solomon, the ideal of a unified people had disintegrated. Further, the northern kingdom of Israel had long since ceased to exist as a political entity. If Yahweh's promises to David and to the ancestors of Israel were true, then how is this to be understood? Clearly, the loss of the land and temple were indicators of divine displeasure and punishment, but how might such failures be utilized to construct an identity for an exiled group? Such a period of social stress and threatened change called for a prophetic vision, and the deuteronomistic author possessed just such a constructive symbol set. To David Yahweh had announced, "If he does wrong, I will chastise him with the rods of men...." (7:14b). The veracity of this promise, as well as its implications for the future of the kingdom and

---

[84] Because this tension is basic to the deuteronomistic author's version of Israel's history and religion, it is natural that the narrative contains a number of differing voices expressing variations of perspective and evaluations of events and figures. Against attempts to reduce these narratives to a single unambiguous voice, see R. D. Nelson, "The Anatomy of the Book of Kings," *JSOT* 40 (1988) 39–48.

people, is exemplified in the manner in which it is applied not just to David's successors, but to David himself.

8

THE GOLDEN AGE LOST:
THE PARADOX RECREATED

I. David and Solomon:
The Unconditional Conditionalized

The well-known sin of David's illicit affair with Bathsheba and the murder of her husband Uriah (2 Sam 11:1–27a)[1] reintroduces the prophet Nathan to the story and provides an instructive application of Yahwistic punishment for the failure to do what was upright.[2] As such, this story provides the pivotal narrative for the introduction of the consequences of failure to fulfill the commands of Yahweh, even if the actor is his chosen king. A complete model should be able to support all of the realities of

---

[1] The relationship of this section to the materials known as the "Succession Narrative" (2 Samuel 9–20 + 1 Kings 1–2) remains a matter of debate. On the various theories regarding the "Succession Narrative," see the discussions in P. K. McCarter, *2 Samuel* (AB 9; Garden City, NY: Doubleday, 1984), pp. 9–13, and in A. A. Anderson, *2 Samuel* (WBC 11; Waco, TX: Word, 1989), pp. xxvi–xxxvi. A discussion of the various positions concerning the "Succession Narrative" from the standpoint of modern literary critical theory is provided by J. S. Ackerman, "Knowing Good and Evil: A Literary Analysis of the Court History in 2 Samuel 9–20 and 1 Kings 1–2," *JBL* 109 (1990) 55–60.

[2] For the role of this story in the section concerning David "under the curse," the second portion of the presentation of David, see R. A. Carlson, *David, the Chosen King: A Traditio-Historical Approach to the Second Book of Samuel* (Uppsala: Almqvist & Wiksell, 1964), pp. 146–62.

life, and so David himself would provide the structural parameters for interpreting the remaining historical narrative. The Bathsheba event illustrates that Yahweh will remain loyal to his promises: he will not abandon David, nor will he allow his misdeed to go unpunished. The entire episode with Bathsheba and Uriah reveals a different picture of David than the one that had been developed previously. Here, the king acts on his own behalf and in his own interests; he attempts to take hold of his own fate.[3] Such efforts, for the king and for Israel, would inevitably prove to be futile according to the deuteronomistic ideology, since the activities of the king were at all times to be governed by the book of the *tôrâ* (Deut 17:18–20). Whenever the need might arise, Yahweh would raise up a prophet to pronounce his judgment (Deut 18:16–18). "But the thing that David had done was evil in Yahweh's eyes" (*wayyēraʿ haddābār ʾăšer-ʿāśâ dāwīd běʿênê yhwh*, 11:27b). This narrative judgment disrupts the ideal of security that had been established with the promise to David (7:10–11) and reintroduces the possibility of turmoil that had preceded the formation of the kingship (cf. Judg 17:6; 21:25; cf. 18:1; 19:1). Into the crisis was sent Nathan, who confronted the king with a parable (12:1–7a) that elicited not only David's self-condemnation but also the pronouncement of divine judgment against the king and his house (12:7b–14). Both the contents of the judgment and the responses to it are significant, for they establish a pattern that will be repeated in the narrative and will provide a model for repentance that is directed at the community.[4] David immediately acknowledged that he had sinned against Yahweh (12:13a) and was informed by Nathan that Yahweh had forgiven his sin (v. 13b). Yet in light of the covenantal ideals of the deuteronomistic writer and in accord with the promises to David him-

---

[3] This action is reminiscent of the events that characterized David in the account of the conflict with Nabal in 1 Samuel 25. There it was the woman, Abigail, who interceded and kept David from murdering Nabal for his failure to give David what he wanted. Instead, Yahweh had acted on David's behalf. Here, David receives no such aid from Bathsheba. Instead, he incurs the bloodguilt that he had managed to avoid throughout his rise to power.

[4] A parallel to this is presented in 1 Kgs 14:7–16, where Jeroboam's wife sought out the oracle of the prophet Ahijah concerning the fate of their son, who had become sick. The corresponding prophetic response condemned not only the child, but also the dynasty of Jeroboam. An obvious difference in the account is Jeroboam's failure to acknowledge his sin before Yahweh, an essential part of the pattern being established in the narrative.

self, punishment was still required.[5] In immediate terms, the life of the child born of the illicit union was taken (12:14, 19). In terms of the longer narrative history to be presented, however, the more important part of the judgment was the one that would not be completed by the historian: because David had despised Yahweh by acting in this manner, "a sword will not depart from your house forever" (*lōʾ-tāsûr ḥereb mibbêtĕkā ʿad-ʿôlām*, v. 10a). While the following two verses specify one aspect of this judgment, preparing the way for the turmoil and bloodshed that would ravage the Davidic house until the succession of Solomon was established (1 Kgs 2:46b),[6] they also convey a deeper structural significance for the deuteronomistic ideology of the kingdom. Just as Yahweh's steadfastness would not turn away from David's household (7:15), a dynastic line that would last "forever" (*ʿad-ʿôlām*, 7:16a), because of David's lack of obedience, neither would the threat of the sword and violence be absent. Such a structural tension as this provides a basis for both the assurance of stability, for Yahweh will never abandon his chosen, and also the guarantee of retribution for failure to be obedient, an obligation placed upon all Israel, including the Davidic ruler.[7]

The punishment on David was exacted, the retribution on his household announced. The narrator now recounts the birth of Solomon, proclaimed Jedediah, "beloved of Yahweh," by Nathan (12:24–25). It would be Solomon who would fulfill the succession promised to David and build Yahweh's temple (2 Sam 7:13–14; 1 Kings 6–8) and, concurrently, provide the impulse for the dissolution of the ideal that had been created. As David had accumulated for himself all of the institutional roles that constituted the paraphernalia of the state (2 Sam 8:15–18), Solomon ascended the throne with the support of the critical personnel, including both Nathan the prophet and Zadok the priest. The purges that consolidated his kingdom (1 Kgs 2:1–46) eventually led to the development of a full administrative complement for the operation of the state (1

---

5 As McCarter has noted, some degree of atonement was required for the deed (2 *Samuel*, p. 301).

6 12:11–12 is fulfilled in the narrative with Absalom's public acts in 16:21–22. On the contents of the "Succession Narrative," see the works cited above in n. 1.

7 While it is possible to interpret the "Succession Narrative" and the problems associated with Solomon's accession to the throne as anti-Davidic (cf. J. Van Seters, *In Search of History: Historiography in the Ancient World and the Origins of Biblical History* [New Haven: Yale University Press, 1983], pp. 287–91), this approach overlooks the balanced structure in terms of social world construction that the deuteronomistic narrative functionally creates. On the modification of this curse, see the treatment of 1 Kgs 11:39 below.

Kgs 4:1–19).[8] With Solomon, Israel reached the pinnacle of statehood; the "golden age" initiated by David found its fulfillment with Solomon. But just as this period completed the integration of all the previous disparate elements that had led to the formation of the state, it also began the dissolution of that same epoch. As presented by the deuteronomistic writer, Solomon's reign is contained in 1 Kings 1–11, a narrative that displays a high degree of literary and contextual symmetry.[9] Most significantly, the end of the account of Solomon's reign contains the report of the prophetic announcement of Ahijah the Shilonite to Jeroboam proclaiming that Yahweh was about to strip the majority of the kingdom from Solomon and give it to him (11:26–39). The covenantal promise offered to Jeroboam, however, was explicitly conditioned by the obligation to be obedient to Yahweh's *tôrâ* (vv. 38–39). As such, a second type of dynastic covenant was introduced into the narrative by the deuteronomistic writer.[10]

The background for the introduction of this conditionalized promise that removes a major portion of the kingdom from the Davidic line under the authority of a divinely directed prophetic action is laid by the reign of Solomon. It is in the account of his reign that the deuteronomistic writer places conditions on the dynastic grant and uses these to construct a didactic emphasis in the history that is guided throughout by religious and ideological factors. The narrative of Solomon's reign may be divided into two distinct parts: the period prior to the building and dedication of the temple (chaps. 3–8) and the period following the dedication of the temple (chaps. 9–11). Each of these sections concludes with a narrative summary that depicts Solomon's attitude toward God.[11] The first such

---

[8]   On the development of this state bureaucracy, see T. N. D. Mettinger's study, *Solomonic State Officials. A Study of the Civil Government of Officials of the Israelite Monarchy* (Lund: C. W. K. Gleerup, 1971).

[9]   For a literary analysis of these chapters, see K. I. Parker, "Repetition as a Structuring Device in 1 Kings 1–11," *JSOT* 42 (1988) 19–27; cf. B. Porten, "The Structure and Theme of the Solomon Narrative (I Kings 3–11), *HUCA* 38 (1967) 93–128.

[10]   As with most issues involving the composition of the deuteronomistic history, the redactional relationship of the conditional and unconditional forms of the covenantal promises, including those to Jeroboam, remains debated. Which version might have been "original" to some reconstructed stage of the process of the composition of the books of Kings is irrelevant to the present interpretation. What is of import is that both forms were incorporated into the account that was constructed by the deuteronomistic writer in the exilic situation and that the creation of a symbolic interpretive tension must be understood in light of its functions in the present narrative. On the promise to Jeroboam, see the discussion below.

[11]   Parker, "Repetition as a Structuring Device in 1 Kings 1–11," p. 27.

expression depicts Solomon in the proper devotion to Yahweh (chaps. 6–8); the second portrays Solomon allowing the worship of other gods by his foreign wives (11:1–13). Similarly, each of the sections depicting his reign is introduced by a theophany in which Yahweh directly addresses the king, whose attitude is portrayed differently in the narrative. 1 Kgs 3:3a notes that "Solomon loved Yahweh, walking in the ordinances of David his father" (*wayyeʾĕhab šĕlōmōh ʾet-yhwh lāleket bĕḥuqqôt dāwīd ʾābîw*); in contrast, 1 Kgs 11:1 begins with this notice, "Now Solomon the king loved many foreign women" (*wĕhammelek šĕlōmōh ʾāhab nāšîm nokrīyyôt rabbôt*). There can be no doubt as to the contrasting purposes of the author in the presentation of the reign of Solomon: because of his promise to David, Solomon his son would establish his dynasty and construct the temple; because of Solomon's actions, the unification of the people about that symbolic axis would be lost.

The first section introduces Solomon in the proper relationship to Yahweh. But within the narrative transfer of the throne from David to Solomon, a shift in the covenantal grant occurs. In his final instructions to Solomon, David implored the heir to the throne to follow in the ways of Yahweh "as written in the *tôrâ* of Moses" (1 Kgs 2:3). This would be necessary so that Yahweh would fulfill his promise to David: "'If your sons watch over their ways, going before me in faithfulness with all their heart and soul, then none of your sons will be cut off from the throne of Israel'" (2:4). These instructions constituted the "ordinances of David his father" (3:3) that Solomon followed.[12] At the same time, they placed a condition upon the promise of dynasty that provided the governing ideological presupposition for the remaining presentation of the history of the kingdoms. Allegiance to Yahweh's *tôrâ* and the worship of Yahweh alone was mandatory for the rulers of Yahweh's people. From the perspective of the exilic setting of the deuteronomistic writer and his intended community, the remainder of the history itself provides a commentary and midrash on this very principle. If there exists a single foundational assertion within the deuteronomistic social world as expressed in these narratives, it is that the *tôrâ* of Yahweh, despite its need for continued prophetic interpretation and application, demanded of "Israel" complete and unceasing devotion. Devotion to Yahweh alone and to the fulfillment of his commands was the ideal ethnic identifier of this people.

---

[12] S. J. DeVries, *1 Kings* (WBC; Waco, TX: Word, 1985), p. 51.

The nature of the punishment for the failure to follow Yahweh's commands is also important for an understanding of the "history," for it is with the fulfillment of this threat that the "golden age" is lost. The ideal period was the result of the unification of both Judah and Israel under the Davidic monarchy. The failure to follow Yahweh's word would result in the dissolution of this group, i.e., of the ideal "Israel." To distinguish too sharply between the concept of the loss of Israel and the loss of the Davidic dynasty[13] would be to overlook the consequences of the failure to follow Yahweh. Any division of the country would constitute a return to the pre-conquest days, a symbolic retrogression to the time before Joshua, when the land had not been conquered and unified by "all Israel." If the Davidic successors failed to fulfill the word of Yahweh and lost even a portion of the kingdom, then the "golden age" would come to an end. The conditionalization of the covenantal promise provided an explanation for the events that would transpire. Further, the dialectic established by the transposition of both conditional and unconditional promises within the same narrative provides an interpretive possibility that would be restricted somewhat were only one to be present. As it stands within the structure of the deuteronomistic ideology, the tension produced by the two forms of the covenant creates and maintains the possibility of divine choice within the face of human activities.

Within the context of the conditionalization of the promise, the first theophany to Solomon is described (1 Kgs 3:1–15).[14] The description of the location of the theophany is essential to the narrative, for the deuteronomistic writer points out that the site of Gibeon "was a great high place" (hî' habbāmâ haggĕdôlâ, 3:4). This is immediately preceded by two related notices: "However the people were sacrificing at the high places

---

[13] R. E. Friedman has argued that the "throne of Israel" does not constitute a part of the promise to David, which referred only to the throne of Judah; "From Egypt to Egypt: Dtr[1] and Dtr[2]," in *Traditions in Transformation: Turning Points in Biblical Faith* (ed. B. Halpern and J. D. Levenson; Winona Lake, IN: Eisenbrauns, 1981), pp. 175–76. Following this interpretation, B. Halpern argues that there is "no substantive contradiction" between the two forms of the covenant; *The First Historians: The Hebrew Bible and History* (San Francisco: Harper & Row, 1988), p. 173. Such attempts to alleviate the tension in the narrative and to attribute it to redactional activity overlook the structural importance of this type of dialectic in the ideology of the writer himself as expressed in the final form of his work.

[14] An extended analysis of this passage is presented by H. A. Kenik, *Design for Kingship: The Deuteronomistic Narrative Technique in 1 Kings 3:4–15* (SBLDS 69; Chico, CA: Scholars Press, 1983).

(*babbāmôt*) because a house for the name of Yahweh had not been built prior to those days" (3:2) and "Solomon loved Yahweh, walking in the ordinances of David his father; however he would sacrifice and offer incense at the high places" (*babbāmôt*, 3:3b). Three times reference is made to a "high place," a type of cultic installation whose exact nature remains unclear.[15] What is clear within this context, however, is that the "high place" is presented as a legitimate site of Yahweh worship at this time. The notice in 3:2 provides a qualifier to this, however, by noting that the temple had not yet been built. The deuteronomic ideal of the centralization of all worship in one location (Deuteronomy 12) would not be invoked until the establishment of the temple in Jerusalem (1 Kings 8). Prior to that time, Samuel could be associated with the *bāmôt* (1 Sam 9:12, 13, 14, 19, 25), and the people and king could offer sacrifices at them with no implied condemnation. Yahweh even appeared at the "great high place" at Gibeon and there granted Solomon wisdom and wealth. In addition, he promised that if Solomon would follow all his precepts (cf. 2:3–4), then he would grant him a long life (3:14). This represents a further conditionalization of the promise, this time by the deity himself, for there is no mention of eternal stability or a geographic locale as the blessing for faithfulness to the covenant; instead, a long reign is promised.

This theophany is balanced, in literary terms, by the second and final appearance of Yahweh to Solomon. This occurs in 1 Kgs 9:1–9 and forms the epilogue for the account of the construction and dedication of the temple.[16] Embedded in the narratives concerning the temple are two

---

[15] The evidence regarding the *bāmâ*, though scanty, suggests that this installation should be understood in architectural terms either as a temple-type structure in which certain activities were performed (W. B. Barrick, "What do we really know about 'high-places'?," *SEÅ* 45 [1980] 50–57) or as a structure similar to an altar in design and function (M. Haran, *Temples and Temple Service in Ancient Israel: An Inquiry into Biblical Cult Phenomena and the Historical Setting of the Priestly School* [Oxford: Clarendon, 1978; reprinted Winona Lake, IN: Eisenbrauns, 1985], pp. 15–25). What is clear, however, for the deuteronomistic author is that after the construction and dedication of the temple in 1 Kings 8, any cultic activity performed at a *bāmâ* is regarded as illegitimate and in violation of the deuteronomic ideals of worship. The text in 1 Kgs 3:2 constitutes the basic text in the deuteronomistic history to which numerous references to the *bāmôt* that connote the author's evaluations of the individual monarchs are to be compared; H.-D. Hoffmann, *Reform und Reformen: Untersuchungen zu einen Grundthema der deuteronomistischen Geschichtsschreibung* (ATANT 66; Zürich: Theologischer Verlag, 1980), pp. 336–37.

[16] For an analysis of the four major addresses that constitute the dedication of the temple in Jerusalem in 1 Kgs 8:1–66, see J. Levenson, "From Temple to Synagogue: 1

additional references to the promises to David, both of which provide a background for the contents of the second theophany at Gibeon. In 1 Kgs 6:11–13 Yahweh speaks directly to Solomon and promises him that if the king follows all of his commandments, then he will fulfill his promise to David and will dwell in the midst of Israel and never abandon his people.[17] In the context of the fulfillment of the promise in 2 Sam 7:13 that David's scion would build his temple, Yahweh conditionalizes both his dwelling in the temple and his allegiance to his people upon the king's fulfillment of his ordinances. This brief passage radically modifies the security of the ideal state from that which was implied in the unconditional promise to David. This conditional form of the promise is further confirmed by Solomon's prayer of dedication. In 8:25–26 Solomon implores Yahweh to fulfill his promise to David that not one of his sons would be cut off from the throne of Israel. This particular phraseology refers back to the conditionalized form repeated to Solomon in 1 Kgs 2:4 (cf. 3:14) and not directly to the promise in 2 Sam 7:1–17.

Yahweh's response to Solomon's prayer is contained in the account of the second theophany at Gibeon (9:1–9). Of immediate import is the fact that Gibeon is not referred to here as a "high place," nor is there any reference to either the king or people sacrificing at such cultic installations (contrast 3:2–4). Rather, this section both confirms the deuteronomic ideal of cultic centralization (Deuteronomy 12) and combines the conditional and unconditional versions of the Davidic grant in order to produce a conditionalized one that is consonant with the deuteronomistic concepts of covenantal allegiance. As in 6:11–13, the obedience of the king is singled out as the primary factor in the divine-human drama that is being constructed. The establishment of monarchy and state had provided public symbols under which the deuteronomistic author consolidated and integrated the life of the whole. The fate of the temple, the

---

Kings 8," *Traditions in Transformation*, pp. 143–66. In its present form, the temple dedication is clearly exilic in composition. It is of note that the deuteronomistic writer emphasizes that the temple was of Solomonic rather than Davidic origin (contrast the emphasis of the Chronicler). While this may reflect an historically accurate observation, it is also helpful in explaining the destruction of the temple and the vision of a restored community that is focused upon the prophetic understanding of *tôrâ* rather than on priestly rituals and temple services.

[17] These verses are commonly regarded as a secondary expansion of the text because they interrupt the description of the building of the temple and they are missing from the LXX. For a discussion of these verses, see E. Würthwein, *Die Bücher der Könige: 1. Könige 1–16* (ATD 11/1; Göttingen: Vandenhoeck & Ruprecht, 1985), p. 65.

land, and the people, those very elements that constituted the essence of the ideal "Israel," was directly related to the actions of their kings in response to Yahweh's demands.

It is also notable that this shift from the unconditional dynastic grant to David to the conditionalized form confirmed to Solomon, one whose contents have implications far beyond that of dynastic succession, is given by way of a direct theophany of Yahweh to the king. There is no prophetic intermediary operative in the story; rather, it is the prophetic hand of the deuteronomistic writer that shapes the contours of this new covenantal grant given directly by Yahweh to the successor of David. Yahweh answers Solomon in the first instance with the assurance of the acceptance of the temple and the establishment of his name there (9:3). The address then turns to the issue of Solomon and his dynastic successors (9:4–5) and combines elements from both forms of the promise. In 9:4 the condition is placed upon Solomon that if he should go before Yahweh in complete uprightness as had his father David and do all of Yahweh's commands, then Yahweh would establish the throne of his kingdom over Israel forever (ʿal-yiśrāʾēl lĕʿōlām) as he had promised David (9:5). The promise to David that is referred to here, however, is the one recounted in 1 Kgs 2:4, 6:11–13, and 8:24–26. Solomon's request that Yahweh fulfill his promise to David was now guaranteed, but only in its conditionalized form.

The continuation of the response presents the implications of the covenantal responsibility on the king and the manner in which it will affect the people.[18] In 9:6 the address shifts from the second person singular to the second person plural: "But if you or your sons should turn away from following me...." (ʾim-šôb tĕšūbûn ʾattem ûbĕnêkem mēʾaḥăray), thus radically altering the perspective of the address. No longer is it simply Solomon, but rather the entire Davidic line that would occupy the throne that is being addressed.[19] The test of faithfulness that is explicitly mentioned is the very characteristic that separates Israel in ideological terms from the other nations—allegiance to Yahweh alone. The establishment of the temple and the succession under Solomon provide the opportunity for the complete incorporation of kingship into the

---

[18] There is little debate that these verses, like the final form of Solomon's prayer of dedication, presuppose the exile and the destruction of the temple. For a discussion of this oracle, see Würthwein, Die Bücher der Könige: 1. Könige 1–16, pp. 104–6.

[19] Contra the interpretation of DeVries (1 Kings, p. 127) that the plural designates Israel rather than Solomon. Israel is addressed in the third person plural and is introduced in 9:7.

fabric of the nation (cf. 1 Sam 12:20–25). For the king and his successors to fail to follow Yahweh's commands and to "go after other gods to serve them" would constitute a breach of the original charter that defined Israel (cf. Deut 6:14; 11:16; 17:3; etc.) and bring disastrous results upon both monarchy and people.

If the kings of Israel were to follow after other gods and thus make Israel "like the nations," the result would be more than just a punishment of the monarch. Instead, Yahweh would "cut off Israel from upon the face of the ground that I have given them" (9:7) and would destroy this temple that he had sanctified for his name (9:7–8). Most importantly, the reason for his actions would not be hidden, but would be known by all who might pass by. Because the Israelites abandoned Yahweh and served other gods, Yahweh enacted these punishments against them (9:9). The failure of the kings to follow Yahweh could lead to only one result: Yahweh's allegiance to his covenantal obligations would force him to destroy his temple, his land, and his people. The side of the divine paradox requiring absolute justice and the cosmic security it provided demanded that some such assurances be instituted. But the varieties of religious traditions also reveal the human desire that they might not always be forced to carry the responsibilities for their actions. Though the dynastic promises to Solomon had been completely conditionalized, the unconditional grant to David had not been cancelled. This provided the possibility of divine decisions against enforcing the covenantal curses and gave the deuteronomistic author a sub-theme for the presentation of the history of the kingdoms that would allow him to construct a social world in which complete and total obedience was demanded, but might not always be required. But, then again, it might.

II. Solomon and Jeroboam: The Power of the Paradox— History and Ideology

Even though 1 Kgs 11:1–43 formally completes the account of Solomon's reign, it also introduces the prophetic announcement of the division of the kingdoms and the conditional dynastic promise to Jeroboam, the first king of the northern state of Israel. As such, these verses provide the ideological groundwork for understanding the historical division of the kingdom that had been formed by covenant under David and developed into a genuine monarchic state by Solomon. Yahweh's love for Solomon (2 Sam 12:24–25) could be tempered by the

manner in which Solomon's activities clashed directly with the deuteronomic provisions for kingship (cf. Deut 17:17–18). Indications of the way
in which Solomon had fulfilled these charges are provided by the notices
of the wives, wealth, and horses he accumulated (10:14–15, 23–29; 11:1–
8). The continuation of Solomon's empire, however, would be determined by the religious implications of these very events. The ideological
evaluation of the reign of Solomon is stated in 1 Kgs 11:6: "And Solomon
did evil in the eyes of Yahweh (*wayyaʿaś šĕlōmōh hāraʿ bĕʿênê yhwh*) and
did not go completely after Yahweh like David his father."[20]

Solomon had failed in explicit terms to follow Yahweh's injunction
against marrying foreign women (11:2; 3:1; cf. Deut 7:3–4; Josh 23:12), a
deed that threatened the ethnic distinctiveness demanded by the ideal
construct of Israel. In his old age, his heart had been turned "after other
gods" (*ʾaḥărê ʾĕlōhîm ʾăḥērîm*, 11:4), those of his foreign wives.
Additionally, he built "high places" for the gods of his wives (11:7), thus
providing places around Jerusalem for their worship.[21] This angered
Yahweh, for it was a direct violation of his command, a breach of his
covenant (11:10–11; cf. 9:6). Punishment was required and given, but not
in the manner one might suspect. Rather than the destruction of Israel
from upon the face of the land, as implied by the pronouncements in 9:7–
9, only the "kingdom" (*hammamlākâ*) would be taken from him and given
to his "servant" (*lĕʿabdekā*, 11:11). The similarities in both language and
content with the rejection of Saul (1 Sam 15:28) are obvious, for these
events constitute an important element of the patterns that were created
by the deuteronomistic writer within his presentation of Israel's past.[22]
Divine pronouncements demanding obedience were not optional; the

---

[20] As Hoffmann notes, this is the first occurrence of the evaluation formula that
will be used in the presentation of nearly every king of Israel and Judah (*Reform und
Reformen*, p. 49).

[21] For the deuteronomistic history, these actions of Solomon provide a constant
"negative" theme that will be developed to one degree or another in narratives of all
the kings to follow until Josiah. These illegitimate high places will continue to exist
until removed by Josiah as part of his reform efforts (2 Kgs 23:13). Hezekiah is said to
have removed them (2 Kgs 18:4), but they were reestablished by Manasseh (2 Kgs
21:3).

[22] Whether or not there exist patterns in history stands quite beyond the realm of
the verifiable. When the differing perspectives of individual historians are compared,
it would seem most evident that the patterns that are discovered are supplied by the
basic conceptual paradigms or models that form the social worlds internalized by
those historians. The interpretation of the past is ordered and explained by these
concepts, which then acquire the appearance of objective existence.

covenantal blessings and curses were divinely guaranteed. The timing and implementation of each, however, were not predictable. The possibility of delays in fulfillment of such pronouncements is part of the structure of this narrative world. In the case of Solomon, the loss of the kingdom would not occur in his days, but in the days of his son (11:12). Further, not all of the kingdom would be taken away; one tribe would be left to the Davidic line "for the sake of David my servant and for the sake of Jerusalem which I have chosen" (11:13; cf. 11:32, 34, 36; 2 Kgs 8:19; 19:34; 20:6).

Here is revealed the interplay between the tensions created by the contrasting forms of the dynastic covenant as the deuteronomistic writer developed it. Because of Solomon's sins and those of his sons, the kingdom would be lost, but not entirely. Because of Yahweh's promise to David, the kingdom would endure, though not in its "ideal" form. The divine word and the prophetic pronouncements provide the foundations of the structure of this past. Though Solomon enjoyed a long reign as Yahweh had promised (11:42; 3:14), the sword had not departed from the house of David (2 Sam 12:10). In Solomon's own day trouble was faced from Hadad of Edom, Rezon of Damascus, and one of his own servants, Jeroboam (11:14–28). Solomon's sin had brought about the divine announcement of the dissolution of the ideal "Israel" that had been created under David. What had been established by Yahweh's faithfulness was about to be lost because of human disobedience.

That this new segment of the history of Israel should be introduced with a new prophetic figure, Ahijah, who is modelled after the patterns of Samuel and Nathan, should occasion no surprise. Likewise, that this new epoch in the people's history should bring together history and ideology in a dialectic and creative way should also be predictable. This servant of Solomon would be the one to receive the kingdom from the hand of Solomon's son. Such would be declared and insured by the actions and words of Ahijah, the prophet (nābîʾ) from Shiloh, who appears in the narrative as suddenly as Nathan had. In a symbolic gesture that recalls Samuel's pronouncement to Saul concerning his loss of kingship (1 Sam 15:27–28), he seized his new garment and tore it into twelve pieces, offering ten to Jeroboam (11:29–31). The prophetic repetition of the divine word interprets the acts: Yahweh was about to tear the kingdom from Solomon, and ten tribes would be given to Jeroboam. One tribe would remain in the hand of Solomon's son, "for the sake of David and Jerusalem" (11:31–32).[23] Ahijah likewise explains to Jeroboam the reasons that the kingdom is being taken away (11:33–35): Solomon had gone after other gods in violation of Yahweh's ordinances. Consequently, Jeroboam would be "king over Israel" (*melek ʿal-yiśrāʾēl*, 11:37). Though the Davidic line might retain a portion of its kingdom, it would not be the only one that could receive a "sure house." Yahweh extends the possibility of dynastic security to Jeroboam and his successors. All they need to do is to obey Yahweh's statutes as David had done and as Solomon had failed to do. If they did these things, then Yahweh would establish for Jeroboam a "sure house" (*bayit-neʾĕmān*) just as he had for David (v. 38; cf. 2 Sam 7:16). The law of the king and the obligations of the covenant were extended to Israel as they had been to Judah under Solomon. With the announcement of this punishment, the patterns for the presentation of the history of Judah and Israel were nearly constructed. What remained to be provided was the counterbalance to the deeds of Solomon.

Upon Solomon's death and the accession of his son Rehoboam, the ideal kingdom, appropriately represented as a "new garment," was torn apart, never again to be united in this form. Just as the deeds of David and those of his successor Solomon provided the basis for understanding the relationship of Yahweh with Judah and the Davidic line, so the actions of Jeroboam would be developed by the deuteronomistic writer to guide the presentation of the history of Israel. Rather than renew the covenantal agreement that had bound Israel to the throne of David and Judah, Jeroboam was selected as king, leaving Rehoboam only the tribe of Judah, as the prophet Ahijah had proclaimed (1 Kgs 12:1–24). The division was guaranteed by the oracle of a "man of god," Shemiah, whose announcement ended Rehoboam's plans to reunite the kingdoms through military action (12:21–24). But more is being developed within this narrative than a structural manner in which to present a series of historical events. Rather, the structures of a social world are under construction within the implied comparisons and contrasts that will be developed to present the futures of these two Yahwistic states. A point not to be overlooked is that those for whom the final form of this history

---

[23] The mathematical problem of ten plus one equalling eleven is alleviated by the LXX, which notes that two tribes rather than one would be given to David. It is possible that Benjamin was to be included along with Judah as the tribe(s) relegated to the Davidic line. Verse 36 reiterates this idea by noting that David would have an eternal "inheritance" (*nîr*) in Jerusalem. For this meaning, see P. D. Hanson, "The Song of Heshbon and David's *Nîr*," *HTR* 61 (1968) 297–300.

was addressed were well aware of the fates of these two national monarchies: each had been destroyed and the populations displaced, if not
totally assimilated into the surrounding cultures. This "history" presents
the past associated with these two monarchic states in a manner that
provides a prophetically sanctioned structure for the development of a
new ideal "Israel" from the ruins of those older, defunct political entities.
The episodes composing the "history" became object lessons for those
who understood the stories as a meaningful rendition of their own past.

Solomon's failure to follow Yahweh's demand for exclusive worship
had led to the loss of a major portion of the kingdom. Now it was
Jeroboam's opportunity to develop integrative symbols for the
consolidaton of his state, Israel. For the deuteronomistic narrative, the
integrative figure was David. Jeroboam, like Solomon and his successor
Rehoboam, would be presented as disintegrative powers in the development of the community and people. To keep the people of his newly
created state from defecting to Jerusalem to worship, Jeroboam made calf
images and placed them at Dan and Bethel (1 Kgs 12:28–30); he
appointed non-levitical priests at his high places (12:31; 13:33) and
established a rival festival to that which was held in Jerusalem (12:32).[24]
From the viewpoint of the deuteronomistic writer, these actions constituted the basis for establishing Jeroboam as a counter-symbol to that
created in David. 1 Kgs 12:28–29 makes it clear that the bull images are to
be understood as gods, which could mean only gods other than Yahweh.
His deeds were so heinous that they "became the sin of the house of
Jeroboam" (wayhî...lĕḥaṭṭaʾt bêt yārobʿām) to destroy and annihilate it from
upon the face of the land (13:34). An unnamed prophet, "a man of god
from Judah" (13:1), was introduced into the context of the dedication of
these new cultic sites to proclaim the destruction of the altar at Bethel by
a coming Davidic king, Josiah by name (13:2).[25] The implications of

---

[24] In doing so, Jeroboam may have been instituting a different calendar; S. Talmon,
"The Cult and Calendar Reform of Jeroboam I," *King, Cult and Calendar in Ancient
Israel: Collected Essays* (Leiden/Jerusalem: E. J. Brill/Magnes, 1986), pp. 113–39. On
the numerous textual problems within the traditions regarding Jeroboam, see J.
Debus, *Die Sünde Jerobeams: Studien zur Darstellung Jerobeams und der Geschichte des
Nordreichs in der deuteronomistischen Geschichtsschreibung* (FRLANT 93; Göttingen:
Vandenhoeck & Ruprecht, 1967), pp. 55–92.

[25] This clear case of a *vaticinium post eventum* forms a literary backdrop against
which the remainder of the history of the kingdoms is presented. If the prophetic
word is regarded as immutable, and the deuteronomistic writer certainly seems to
present it in this manner, then the future of the Davidic line is guaranteed at least
until the time of Josiah. On the literary structure and the significance of this story in

Jeroboam's actions extended much further than the future of his own dynasty; these sins, if not corrected, would result in the future destruction of the northern kingdom (2 Kgs 17:20–23). The covenantal curse directed to Solomon and Judah in 1 Kgs 9:6–9 would be applied to Israel and would provide an objective demonstration of the retributive aspects of the divine covenant.

Notable about the manner in which the deuteronomistic writer develops Jeroboam and his deeds as a counter-theme to those concerning David is the fact that of all the kings of Israel, only Jeroboam is compared to David.[26] The theme of the everlasting fidelity to David, however, constituted an element not found in the covenantal promise to Jeroboam. In a flagrant violation of Yahweh's commands, Jeroboam instituted the worship of "other gods."[27] For this sin, he would pay with the destruction of his family and dynastic line. Predictably enough, the announcement of this punishment, like that on David for his sin and Solomon for his, would come from the lips of a prophet. In a manner reminiscent of the deuteronomistic presentation of David, Jeroboam's counter-image, the author conveys the account of the condemnation of Jeroboam through a narrative concerning the illness of his son.

I Kgs 14:1–20 contains the final narrative account concerning Jeroboam's rule.[28] It begins with the notice that his son, Abijah, had fallen ill. Jeroboam then instructed his wife to disguise herself and go to the prophet Ahijah, who would tell her the fate of his son (vv. 1–3). Jeroboam's actions seem to indicate a recognition on his part that he had

---

the deuteronomistic history, see W. E. Lemke, "The Way of Obedience: 1 Kings 13 and the Structure of the Deuteronomistic History," in *Magnalia Dei: The Mighty Acts of God* (ed. by F. M. Cross, W. E. Lemke, and P. D. Miller, Jr.; Garden City, NY: Doubleday, 1976), pp. 301–26.

[26] F. M. Cross has argued that Jeroboam's sin constitutes a major theme in the deuteronomistic history that finds its climax in the peroration over the fall of Samaria in 2 Kings 17; *Canaanite Myth and Hebrew Epic* (Cambridge: Harvard University Press, 1973), pp. 279–81. In its present form, however, the theme is not resolved until the account of the fall of Jerusalem in 2 Kings 24–25.

[27] What Jeroboam's intentions might have been in establishing a cultus separate from that in Judah is not pertinent to the manner in which the deuteronomistic writer had developed his materials. What is important is that Jeroboam violated the covenantal agreement (1 Kgs 11:38) by setting up these calf images and proclaiming them to be gods (12:28–29).

[28] These verses are missing from LXX[BL], though portions of them are preserved at 12:24g–n. This section is generally understood to have undergone extensive editorial expansions. For a discussion of the various redactional strata, see Würthwein, *Die Bücher der Könige: 1. Könige 1–16*, pp. 172–79.

failed, though unlike David (2 Sam 12:13a), Jeroboam would make no such admission. Rather than to interact directly with the prophet, Jeroboam sent his wife as his messenger. Ahijah, who was unable to see, had received instructions from Yahweh about what was about to occur (cf. 1 Sam 9:15–16), so that immediately upon the arrival of Jeroboam's wife, he could pronounce Yahweh's judgment on Jeroboam. Because Jeroboam had failed to be like David, Yahweh's servant (v. 8), and because he had made "other gods and molten images" (*ʾĕlōhîm ʾăḥērîm ûmassēkôt*, v. 9),[29] his line would be completely destroyed (vv. 10–11). As a sign that the prophetic pronouncement would be fulfilled, the child would die as soon as the woman would reenter the city (vv. 12–13).

Because he had failed to follow Yahweh's commands like David, his son would die. But unlike David, whose son was also required (2 Sam 12:14–19), the entirety of Jeroboam's house would perish (1 Kgs 14:10–11). This was Yahweh's decree; this was the prophetic pronouncement. Though it would not be fulfilled until the death of his son and successor Nadab (1 Kgs 15:27–30), the divine judgment would be executed. Even more important, Jeroboam's deeds here become the basis for the destruction and exile of Israel. Ahijah announces that Yahweh would "pluck up Israel from upon this good ground he had given to their ancestors and he would scatter them beyond the Euphrates" (14:15). The loss of Israel would be attributable to one thing: "the sins of Jeroboam which he sinned and which he caused Israel to sin" (14:16).[30] All the kings of Israel would follow in the footsteps of Jeroboam. There would be no revocation of the divine pronouncement. Though Jeroboam had started his reign with the same dynastic possibilities as Solomon,[31] he

---

[29] B. Halpern has argued that the term *massēkâ* constitutes a euphemism for Jeroboam's calf images in the deuteronomistic history; "Levitic Participation in the Reform Cult of Jeroboam I," *JBL* 95 (1976), 36. The use of the plural form here clearly reflects the author's interpretation of the calf images as images of other gods (see 2 Kgs 17:7).

[30] The phrase *ḥaṭṭôʾt yārobʿām ʾăšer ḥāṭāʾ waʾăšer heḥĕṭîʾ ʾet-yiśrāʾēl*, "the sins of Jeroboam which he sinned and which he caused Israel to sin," is a standard phrase for the deuteronomistic condemnation of the kings of Israel (cf. 1 Kgs 15:26, 30; 15:34; 16:19; 16:26; 16:31; 22:53; 2 Kgs 3:3; 10:29; 13:6; 13:11; 14:24; 15:9; 15:18; 15:24; 15:28). For a detailed analysis of these judgment formulae as applied by the deuteronomistic writer, see H. Weippert, "Die 'deuteronomistischen' Beurteilungen der Könige von Israel und Juda und das Problem der Redaktion der Königsbücher," *Bib* 53 (1972) 301–39.

[31] B. O. Long, *1 Kings with an Introduction to Historical Literature* (FOTL 9; Grand Rapids: Eerdmans, 1984), p. 157.

had forfeited the future of the entire kingdom. The remaining history of the northern monarchy, then, serves to illustrate in vivid terms the deuteronomistic assurance of the efficacy of the prophetically pronounced word. Time might pass before its enforcement, but the announcements of Yahweh's prophets would be actualized.

In historical terms, the kingdom of Israel and Judah, united by covenant with David and developed into a full-scale state under Solomon, dissolved into two separate geographic and political entities after Solomon's death. Rehoboam, son of Solomon, continued the Davidic line on the throne of Judah; Jeroboam, an Ephraimite, took the throne of Israel. His dynasty, unlike that of David, would not continue. Rather, it would end in a palace revolution after the brief reign of his successor. Such instability would characterize the two-century history of Israel,[32] providing a clear contrast with the stability associated with the Davidic line. In the hands of the deuteronomistic writer, such matters provided the foundations for the construction of the symbolic ideal known as "Israel." Jeroboam had failed to receive a "firm dynasty" (11:38) because he had committed a sin in pursuing other gods (12:28–29; 13:34). The fact that none of his successors to the throne would rectify this situation would lead to Yahweh's decision to destroy Israel (2 Kgs 17:20–23; cf. 1 Kgs 9:6–9). If divine justice is consistently retributive, then the kings of Judah might take an object lesson from the fate of the apostate rulers of the North. The structured manner in which the deuteronomistic author develops the remainder of the history of the two kingdoms confirms the interplay of this ideological interpretation of the outlines of the events of the past as they form a social world that can identify and unite those who participated in it.

---

[32] No fewer than nine usurpations of the throne are recounted in the narratives concerning the kingdom of Israel. T. Ishida posits three reasons for the large number of dynastic changes: the failure of the king in military affairs; intertribal rivalries; and antagonism among the classes; *The Royal Dynasties in Ancient Israel. A Study on the Formation and Development of Royal Dynastic Ideology* (BZAW 142; Berlin: de Gruyter, 1977), pp. 173–82. It is clear, however, that if the historical reasons for the inability of the northern rulers were known to the deuteronomistic writer, they played little or no role in the way in which he chose to structure his history.

III. Rehoboam to Jehoiachin: Lessons Provided and Lessons Ignored—Ideology and History

These two counter-symbols represented by David and Jeroboam characterize the tensions existing in the religious ideology of the deuteronomistic writer and in the social world that he was constructing. The dialectic between divine mercy and divine retribution could be mediated by obedience to the covenantal stipulations and the prophetic word. For the remainder of the history of Israel and Judah, the actions of the kings of each state would provide the basis for the deuteronomistic judgment on each. As had been ritually instituted by Samuel at the end of his career (1 Sam 12:20–25), the fate of the people would be reliant upon the proper covenantal actions of the king. While the debate whether or not this narrative was based upon written sources and was intended as "history" remains unresolved,[33] it seems most obvious that a simple recounting of the achievements or failures of the kings was not the focus of the writer of these materials. Rather, the deuteronomistic ideology of the centralization of all worship in the temple and the command for absolute purity in all matters of the cult pervades every aspect of the "history" of the monarchies. Those rulers who failed to act in accord with the deuteronomistic standards were condemned; those few who succeeded were praised. The formulae evaluating the rulers became a standard part of the presentation of the reigns of the kings of each monarchy.[34]

The presentation, however, was structured by more than simple formulaic evaluations. The deuteronomistic writer has arranged large blocks of material paratactically to present explicit synchronizations of

---

[33] Contrast the differing positions of Van Seters (*In Search of History*, pp. 1–7, 354–62) and Halpern (*The First Historians*, pp. 1–35) on the "historical" nature of the deuteronomistic narrative.

[34] For a study of these formulae, see Weippert, "Die deuteronomistischen Beurteilungen der Könige von Israel und Juda und das Problem der Redaktion der Königsbücher," pp. 301–39). For a critique of the differing treatments of the judgment formulae, see I. W. Provan, *Hezekiah and the Books of Kings: A Contribution to the Debate about the Composition of the Deuteronomistic History* (Berlin/New York: de Gruyter, 1988), pp. 33–55. These evaluatory comments are often used as evidence for differing redactional layers of composition in Kings. Recent studies which focus on these elements date the initial edition of Kings to the time of Jehoshaphat, Hezekiah, Josiah, or the exile. These ideological evaluations constitute part of a larger regnal formula that is applied throughout the remainder of the book. For a discussion of the genre represented by the regnal formula and ancient Near Eastern parallels, see Long, *1 Kings*, pp. 158–64.

the events in the reigns of the kings of Israel and Judah. The result is that the regnal periods constitute a story that is told "without a strictly linear flow of time."[35] What is instructive about this method of synchronizing the events of the various reigns is the way in which "good" and "evil" kings and their deeds are juxtaposed by the writer. Nearly every ruler of Israel received a negative judgment for continuing the sins of Jeroboam.[36] In contrast, the rulers of Judah are divided into two groups: those who did what was right in Yahweh's eyes and those who did what was evil.[37] The events recounting the history of the Israelite monarchy are synchronized with the reigns of those kings of Judah who receive the qualified approval of the deuteronomistic writer in five of the six divisions of the history.[38] The presentation of the loss of the ideal kingdom and the continuing history of the remaining monarchic states is structured around the conditional aspects of the covenantal demands regarding the purity of worship and the centrality of the cultus. Whatever historically accurate materials may be contained in the account are subjugated completely to the ideological positions that structure the work.

The fate of the northern kingdom of Israel had been sealed in the narrative account of the deeds of Jeroboam. He had failed to obey the stipulations of the covenant offered by Yahweh through Ahijah and, as a

---

[35] Long, *1 Kings*, p. 22. R. D. Nelson has described this organizing system as a "temporal 'folding over' pattern"; "The Anatomy of the Book of Kings," *JSOT* 40 (1988) 44.

[36] For references, see above, n. 30. Elah, the son of Baasha, is condemned for his own sins and those of his father (1 Kgs 16:13), who in turn had been condemned for following Jeroboam's ways (1 Kgs 15:34). For Shallum, there is no evaluation given by the historian at all (see 2 Kgs 15:13–15). Hoshea, the final Israelite king, while condemned for having done evil in Yahweh's eyes, is distinguished from those kings who ruled before him (17:2) and is not compared to Jeroboam, as were most of the other kings.

[37] The kings who are positively evaluated by the historian, i.e., who "did what was upright in Yahweh's eyes" (*ʿāśâ hayyāšār beʾênê yhwh*), were David (cf. 1 Kgs 15:3–5), Asa (15:11), Jehoshaphat (22:43), Jehoash (2 Kgs 12:3), Amaziah (14:3), Uzziah/Azariah (15:3), Jotham (15:34), Hezekiah (18:3), and Josiah (22:2; cf. 23:25). Those who received negative evaluations, i.e., who "did what was evil in Yahweh's eyes" (*ʿāśâ haraʿ beʾênê yhwh*) or who "did not do what was upright in Yahweh's eyes" (*lōʾ ʿāśâ hayyāšār beʾênê yhwh*), were Solomon (1 Kgs 11:6), Rehoboam (14:22), Abijam (cf. 15:3–4), Jehoram (2 Kgs 8:18), Ahaziah (8:27), Ahaz (16:2), Manasseh (21:2), Amon (21:20), Jehoahaz (23:32), Jehoiakim (23:37), Jehoiachin (24:9), and Zedekiah (24:19).

[38] Jotham, who also receives the qualified approval of the writer (2 Kgs 15:34–35), comes to the throne as co-regent during the reign of Azariah, his father. For the purposes of this structure, his reign may be interpreted as a continuation of his father's.

result, his dynasty would not endure. But even more important, his deeds had brought about the prophetic condemnation of Israel as a whole. The narratives concerning the remaining kings of Israel, then, are already predetermined, in a sense, if Yahweh can be relied upon to uphold the prophetic pronouncements. From this perspective, the accounts of the Israelite kings and their deeds serve as didactic episodes designed to instruct and guide Judah in its history and relationship with Yahweh. If the deeds of Jeroboam determined the final fate of the northern monarchic state, would similar failures by the southern Davidides produce the same disastrous results? This constitutes one of the major questions that the deuteronomistic writer attempts to resolve.

The Davidic line had received the same conditional form of divine guarantee to the throne that had been given to Jeroboam and, implicitly, to his successors. At the same time, David, who had been Yahweh's own choice as king, had been given prophetic assurance of the eternality of his throne, a guarantee that had also been reflected in the deliverance of the major portion of the kingdom to Jeroboam. This paradoxical nature of the divine will provides the ideological background for understanding the remaining history of the kingdoms. The positive evaluations of the selected kings of Judah provide the theme of dynastic stability and continuity against which is presented the continued apostasy of their Israelite counterparts. Hence, the history of Israel from Nadab through Ahab (1 Kgs 15:25–22:40) is presented "in the time of Asa" of Judah; the period from Ahaziah through Jehu, "in the time of Jehoshaphat" (1 Kgs 22:52–2 Kgs 10:36); from Jehoahaz through Jehoash, "in the time of Joash" of Judah (2 Kgs 13:1–25); Jeroboam II's reign, "in the time of Amaziah" (2 Kgs 14:23–29); and the period from Zechariah through Pekah, "in the time of Azariah/Jotham (2 Kgs 15:8–31).[39] The continued apostasy and dynastic failures of the northern rulers contrast directly with the proper actions of these selected southern monarchs who provide a sense of stability to the promises to David and the continuation of Judah. The final section of the presentation of the history of Israel, that which recounts its destruction and the divine explanation for that action, is recounted "in the time of Ahaz" (2 Kgs 17:1–41). This particular presentation could hardly be coincidental, since Ahaz himself "went in the way of the kings of Israel" (*wayyēlek bĕderek malkê yiśrāʾēl*, 2 Kgs 16:3). The destruction and exile of Israel provided the final object lesson that should

---

[39] See the schematic diagram of the interrelatedness of these narrative blocks presented above on pp. 25–27 and adapted from Long, *1 Kings*, p. 23.

be needed by Judah. Apparently, the southern state would be spared only if the rulers acted in accord with the divine commands or, less frequently, if Yahweh chose not to fulfill the promised punishment.[40]

But the evaluations of these kings are not completely positive, with two exceptions, Hezekiah and Josiah, neither of whom is accorded the same place in the overlapping structure of the presentation as those rulers noted above. In the case of each of these "positive" evaluations, a qualification is noted. Every king of Judah from Rehoboam until Hezekiah, and then from Manasseh to Josiah, allowed the "high places" to continue to exist in violation of the basic command for cultic centralization. Associated with these cultic installations[41] were a variety of paraphernalia and practices that were not allowable according to the deuteronomistic ideals of cultic purity.[42] As the kings of Israel were condemned for following in the sins of Jeroboam, by analogy, the kings of Judah were also condemned for continuing in the apostate ways of Solomon, for which the kingdom had been divided in the first place (1 Kgs 11:4–13). For the deuteronomistic writer, only pure Yahwistic practices as established in the deuteronomic blueprint of Israelite identity would be acceptable to Yahweh. All else would be interpreted as a violation of the covenant.[43]

---

[40] Apart from its occurrence in the oracle giving the northern kingdom to Jeroboam (1 Kgs 11:12, 13, 32, 34), the decision not to destroy Judah "for the sake of David my servant" is noted only three times (2 Kgs 8:19; 19:34; 20:6; cf. 1 Kgs 15:4).

[41] With the exception of the reforms of Hezekiah and Josiah, the "high places" (bāmôt) are presented as though they were a standard part of the religion of Judah throughout its history. G. W. Ahlström has argued that the bāmôt constituted the national shrines of the country surrounding Jerusalem and that these cultic centers constituted part of the royal administration of the religion of the realm; *Royal Administration and National Religion in Ancient Israel* (Studies in the History of the Ancient Near East 1; Leiden: E. J. Brill, 1982), p. 66.

[42] For the specialized deuteronomic and deuteronomistic terminology that is used with respect to the cultic reforms in the books of Kings, see Hoffmann, *Reform und Reformen*, pp. 341–63. As Hoffmann has noted, Deut 7:5 and 12:2–3 present the basic deuteronomic law for cultic reform to which all the deuteronomistic reports are related (pp. 341–42). Despite the assuredness with which scholars discuss the various practices and cultic objects referred to in the texts, most of these matters, such as the meaning of the references to bāmôt, maṣṣēbôt, or ʾăšērîm, remain quite unclear.

[43] Certain Mesopotamian materials, e.g., the Akitu Chronicle, the Weidner Chronicle, and the Synchronistic History, present conceptual parallels to the presentation and evaluations contained in the deuteronomistic judgments of the reigning monarchs. For a discussion of these texts, see A. K. Grayson, *Assyrian and Babylonian Chronicles* (Texts from Cuneiform Sources; Locust Valley, NY: J. J. Augustin, 1975), pp. 35–36, 43–45, 51–56. While these texts do not qualify as "history"

This emphasis upon centralization of worship and cultic purity culminates in the narrative in the accounts concerning Hezekiah and Josiah. Until the times of these two rulers, the kings of Judah had failed to remove the *bāmôt* from the land and had failed to eliminate forbidden cultic practices. Despite various cultic reforms that were ascribed to individual rulers, none stopped the practices associated with these non-sanctioned places of worship. Until the reigns and reforms of these two kings of Judah, the implications of engaging in such non-Yahwistic practices had been demonstrated throughout by the fate and fortunes of the kingdom of Israel. The alternating pattern of the presentation of the history from the division of the kingdoms until the destruction of Israel provided the deuteronomistic writer with the opportunity to develop a narrative that stressed the basic necessity of cultic purity if the deuteronomic law were to be fulfilled. For the people in exile, the religious practices surrounding them were all to be interpreted as "abominations" which they must avoid if they were to survive. The old nation of Israel had failed to do so and had been dissolved (1 Kings 12–2 Kings 17). This constitutes the first major section of the deuteronomistic history that stressed the necessities of obedience and prophetic guidance. The second major section of the narrative addresses the fate of Judah, which lost its symbols of power and polity, but not necessarily all hope for a future (2 Kings 18–25). Both parts are governed by the covenantal ideology established throughout the narratives instituting and developing ideal kingship, security for the land, and proper temple worship.

For the period following Solomon's dedication of the temple, the deuteronomistic writer uses the failure to remove the *bāmôt* as a condition to the approval given to all six kings of Judah who are said to have "done what was upright in the eyes of Yahweh" who rule before the destruction of Israel. Likewise, in the cases of the remaining kings of this era condemned by the historian, the references to the *bāmôt* seem to be crucial. Solomon's sin had been that he built these structures. Rather than removing them, Solomon's successor, Rehoboam, allowed the forbidden practices to proliferate: the people made *bāmôt*, *maṣṣēbôt*, and *'ăšērîm* "upon every high hill and under every luxuriant tree" (1 Kgs 14:23). In addition, during his reign certain cultic functionaries known as the *qādēš* were in the land (14:24).[44] From the deuteronomistic perspective, these

---

as a recognizable narrative genre, they do demonstrate that ideology exerts very powerful influences on historiography, both ancient and modern.

[44] Cf. 15:12; 22:47; 2 Kgs 23:7. Such functionaries are explicitly forbidden for Israel in Deut 23:18–19. While the *qādēš* and *qĕdēšâ* are most commonly interpreted as male

actions were "like all the abominations of the nations (kĕkol tôʿăbōt haggôyīm)[45] that Yahweh had driven out from before the Israelites" (14:24b).

This particular form of the judgment passed upon Rehoboam and the people of Judah for their actions is structurally important for the presentation of the remainder of the history and the deuteronomistic evaluations that provide interpretations of the actions throughout. The deeds of Rehoboam were judged to have been a complete reversal of the religious practices that had defined Israel as a people. Deut 18:9 provides the basic text that confirms the importance of this evaluation: "When you come to the land that Yahweh your god is giving to you, you shall not learn to do like the abominations of those nations" (kĕtôʿăbōt haggôyīm hāhēm). After detailing some of these "abominable" practices, the deuteronomic writer notes that they constituted the reason that Yahweh would drive them out (18:12b). Israel's obligation was to be blameless (tāmîm) before Yahweh (v. 13). The covenantal instructions were clear. Rehoboam's actions were in direct violation of the boundaries formed by deuteronomic prescriptions. Rather than undo the cultic improprieties of his father Solomon, he had returned the land to its pre-conquest state. The "identity" of Israel had been placed in jeopardy.

Significantly, the phrase "to do like the abominations of the nations" (ʿăśâ kĕtôʿăbōt haggôyīm) occurs only this once in Deuteronomy and in only three instances in the deuteronomistic history.[46] It is used three times to pass judgment on kings of Judah, each at critical points in the narrative and each creating conceptual parallels among the three rulers. Along with Rehoboam, Ahaz (2 Kgs 16:3) and Manasseh (2 Kgs 21:2) are judged for having done "like the abominations of the nations" (kĕtôʿăbōt haggôyīm). Since, in the final form of the deuteronomistic history it would be the deeds of Manasseh for which Judah would be condemned to destruction (2 Kgs 21:10–16), the direct comparison of Rehoboam and Manasseh implied by the use of this formula demonstrates the danger in which Judah's existence was placed because of these acts. Hence, at the

---

and female cultic prostitutes, there is some reason to question this identity. For this position, see R. Oden, *The Bible without Theology: The Theological Tradition and Alternatives to It* (San Francisco: Harper & Row, 1987), pp. 131–53.

45 Omitting the definite article of the MT on the construct tôʿăbōt (cf. BHS).

46 The phrase occurs only three times outside the deuteronomistic corpus. Two of these instances parallel the deuteronomistic text (2 Chr 28:3 // 2 Kgs 16:3; 2 Chr 33:2 // 2 Kgs 21:2), and the third occurrence (2 Chr 36:14) is clearly dependent on the deuteronomistic usage.

very beginning of the history of the divided state, Judah's identity and existence are thrust into the quandary of the divine paradox. The comparison with Ahaz that is also produced by this judgment demonstrates the danger implied by these acts even more explicitly. Since the final demise of Israel is narrated during the "time of Ahaz" (2 Kgs 17:1–41), and since Ahaz's deeds are compared explicitly to those of the kings of Israel (16:3), Judah might be considered to be under a similar threat. In the judgments concerning the kings of Judah, the deuteronomistic writer makes it clear that the religious apostasy of Rehoboam was as heinous as that of Jeroboam.

Since Abijam, son and successor of Rehoboam, continued in "all the sins of his father" (1 Kgs 15:3), Judah remained under the threat of the covenantal curses. But in this instance, the retributive aspect of the dilemma would not be actualized, but rather the promises to David would postpone the divine reprisal. "For the sake of David" (*lĕmaʿan dāwīd*) Yahweh refrained from destroying Judah (15:4; cf. 11:13, 32, 34, 36; 2 Kgs 8:19; 19:34; 20:6).[47] The threats that were explicit in the covenantal grant to Solomon (1 Kgs 9:6–9) could be suspended or postponed only by Yahweh and only at his decision. At the beginning of the history of Judah and Israel, there exists little to distinguish one from the other in the presentation of the historian. If Judah were to survive, it would be either by the gracious acts of Yahweh or by the righteous leadership of its kings. This second category of the kings of Judah serves to further the perceptions of the necessities of obedience to the covenantal demands. The next king, Asa, "did what was upright in the eyes of Yahweh as had David his father" (15:11). This judgment is passed on Asa because he reversed the deeds of "his ancestors" (15:12–13),[48] establishing himself as the first of several "cultic reformers" in Judah, each of whom would appear in the narrative at a critical time.

At the same time, the deuteronomistic writer is quick to point out that despite his "uprightness," Asa failed to remove the *bāmôt* (15:14)

---

[47] It is interesting to note that the author was completely aware of David's murder of Uriah (15:5), and recounts it within the context of David's "perfection" throughout his whole career. Though the deuteronomistic writer clearly condemned this action, it should be noted that it did not affect the historian's "memory" of David's covenantal perfection *vis-à-vis* the cult.

[48] On the nature of the reforms attributed to Asa, see Hoffmann, *Reform und Reformen*, pp. 87–93. As Hoffmann points out, the passage is thoroughly deuteronomistic in composition, a fact that brings the historical reliability of the report under scrutiny (pp. 89–92).

from the land. Such an evaluation is double-edged, for though Asa did what was upright and "his heart was complete with Yahweh all his days,"[49] his failure to eliminate the *bāmôt* maintains the cultic situation of Judah at the same point as it was at the end of the reign of Solomon. Still, for the deuteronomistic writer's presentation, this degree of covenantal loyalty was sufficient to reestablish the stability of Judah in contrast to the instability of Israel. During the "time of Asa" (15:25–22:40), the reigns of six kings of Israel representing at least four dynasties were recounted. This period of instability would culminate with the reign of Ahab, the "worst" king to rule over Israel to that time (1 Kgs 16:30–33; 21:25–26). Such a comparison is telling, since one of Ahab's predecessors had been Jeroboam. Against the background of the positive reforms of Asa and the stability thus established for Judah were recounted the negative reforms of Ahab and the ensuing condemnation of his line.[50]

In contrast to the situation related concerning Judah, with its traditions of the eternal promise to David and "upright" kings, the prophetic condemnation of Jeroboam's line and of Israel itself (cf. 1 Kgs 14:7–16; 15:25–30) created special situations for the deuteronomistic writer. If the prophetic words of Ahijah were to be fulfilled immediately, then the continuation of Israel and its kingship required explanation. Such is found in the accounts concerning Ahab and the Omride dynasty. Despite the evil done by these kings, especially by Ahab, Israel was not immediately destroyed. The reason for this is found in the pietistic response of Ahab to the condemnation delivered by the prophet Elijah (1 Kgs 21:20–29). The line of Ahab would be destroyed as had been Jeroboam's (21:22), but due to Ahab's repentant actions, not in his lifetime (21:27–29). This postponement of punishment of prophetically delivered condemnations is characteristic of the deuteronomistic ideology. Though the prophet's words might not be immediately confirmed, the "true" Mosaic successor would be exonerated (Deut 18:18–22). Ahijah's condemnation of Jeroboam (1 Kgs 14:14–16), not fulfilled until the time of his son Nadab (1 Kgs 15:27–30), and Jehu ben Hanani's condemnation of the dynasty of Baasha (16:1–4, 7), not fulfilled until the time of his son Elah (16:9–13), prepare the background for this delay of punishment pattern as it would

---

[49] On the clear covenantal implications of the phrase *lēb(ab) šālēm*, see M. Weinfeld, *Deuteronomy and the Deuteronomic School* (Oxford: Clarendon, 1972), pp. 77, 269.

[50] For more extended considerations of the literary structuring of these positive and negative reigns, see E. T. Mullen, Jr., "The Sins of Jeroboam: A Redactional Reassessment," *CBQ* 49 (1987) 212–32, and "The Royal Dynastic Grant to Jehu and the Structure of the Books of Kings," *JBL* 107 (1988) 193–206.

be applied to the house of Ahab, the destruction of which would not occur until the time of Jehu (2 Kgs 9:14–10:17).[51] The narrative projection of the pattern of prophetic pronouncement-delay-divine fulfillment into the historical past of the monarchies provided a traditional base for the deuteronomistic writer's claims to his own prophetic authority.

For Judah, the presentation of Ahab's reign and the evaluation he received became relevant on two counts: though Ahab was condemned as the worst ruler to take the throne of Israel for the variety of non-Yahwistic practices he introduced (1 Kgs 16:30–33), his response of humility and repentance delayed the enforcement of the divine punishment. Additionally, two kings of Judah, Jehoram and Ahaziah, ally themselves with the house of Ahab and are directly compared to him (2 Kgs 8:18, 27).[52] In structural terms, the comparison of these two kings of Judah with Ahab of Israel implies a similarity of fates. The negative evaluations received by these two offset the previous positive evaluation of Jehoshaphat (2 Kgs 22:43–44) and subject Judah to the same potential punishment that had been pronounced against Israel. For the construction of the deuteronomistic history, the repentance of Ahab and the divinely announced delay of the punishment of his household provide for the transition to the corresponding period in Judah.

Contrasting with Ahab was the "upright" ruler Jehoshaphat of Judah (1 Kgs 22: 43–44), during whose "time" the demise of the dynasty of Ahab was recounted. This contrast between "upright" king of Judah and "evil" king of Israel, however, disappears with the accounts of Jehoram and Ahaziah of Judah. Now, both Israel and Judah stand in violation of the covenantal obligations. Again, if divine justice were consistently retributive, each would have to be destroyed. But both delay of

---

[51] This same pattern is applicable to the history concerning Judah, for the punishment of Solomon, proclaimed by Ahijah, is postponed until the time of Rehoboam (1 Kgs 11:34–36). One might suggest further that Nathan's condemnation of the house of David also contains an element of the prophecy-delay-fulfillment ideology (2 Sam 12:10). It is an apparent basis for the presentation of Samuel's condemnations of Saul (1 Sam 13:13–14; 15:22–23) and the extended narrative delay prior to their fulfillment (cf. 1 Sam 31:1–13; 2 Sam 5:1–4).

[52] The fact that a Jehoram and an Ahaziah rule over Israel and Judah for approximately identical periods creates a number of interesting possibilities for historical reconstruction. For a discussion of the possible identity of these kings who are presented as separate individuals and the possibility of a political unity of the kingdoms in this period, see J. M. Miller and J. H. Hayes, *A History of Ancient Israel and Judah* (Philadelphia: Westminster, 1986), pp. 280–84. The role and status of Athaliah have been discussed above in chap. 2.

destruction and merciful refusal to instigate deserved punishments provide important aspects of the deuteronomistic ideology of divine activity. The seriousness of the comparison of Jehoram to Ahab is analogous to Abijam's failure to reverse the cultic actions of Rehoboam. The implementation of the covenantal curses is avoided only by virtue of Yahweh's faithfulness to the promise made to David: "But Yahweh was not willing to destroy Judah for the sake of David his servant" (wĕlōʾ-ʾābâ yhwh lĕhašḥît ʾet-yĕhûdâ lĕmaʿan dāwīd ʿabdô, 2 Kgs 8:19a). The king of Judah and, concurrently, Judah itself had earned the same punishment that had been pronounced upon Israel; but due to Yahweh's decision, it would not be invoked on Jehoram. The case was not so clear, however, with Jehoram's successor, Ahaziah, for during his reign the continuation of the line of David on the throne of Judah was clearly brought into question.

Ahaziah's military alliance with Jehoram, the final member of the Omride house to rule Israel, brought the two kings together in the valley of Jezreel (2 Kgs 8:28–29). There, the rulers of each state would die in the rebellion led by Jehu, a *coup* that would fulfill the prophecy against Ahab's house and would create a crisis in the Davidic ideology (9:14–10:17). Such a crisis would carry with it the prophetic sanction of Elisha, the figure who appointed one of the members of his prophetic group to anoint and commission Jehu. Jehu's subsequent murder of Ahaziah and 42 of his relations (9:27–28; 10:13–14) cleared the way for the Omride Athaliah to claim the throne of Judah and bring to an end the dynasty of David (11:1). The paradox created by the continued faithfulness of Yahweh to his promise to David could be alleviated with the destruction of the succession and then the destruction of the country. The promise that a Davidide "would never be cut off from the throne"[53] was about to be broken. Unless some type of reform were to take place, the new non-Davidic line of Judah could expect the same prophetic rejections and punishments as those directed against Israel.

The destruction of Judah was averted, however, by the reinstitution of the Davidic line. Jehoiada's ploy to save Jehoash until an appropriate time to oust the non-Davidic Athaliah from the throne (11:9–20)[54]

---

53   1 Kgs 2:4; 8:25; 9:5.

54   Though it is clear that Athaliah enjoyed the full powers of "kingship," her six-year reign is not so credited by the deuteronomistic historian, who refused to use the standard regnal formula to introduce her reign. Instead, the writer notes only that she was "reigning over the land" (mōleket ʿal-hāʾāreṣ, 11:3). In this manner, the break in the reign of the promised Davidides is relegated to the category of an interruption.

resulted not only in the ritually realized "continuation" of the line of David, but also in a series of extensive temple repairs and reforms that carried the approval of the deuteronomistic writer (12:3–4, 5–17).[55] These reforms of Jehoash present a parallel with those of Jehu in the North, thus once again creating a comparison between the two peoples. Jehu is credited with destroying the worship of Baal from Israel (2 Kgs 10:28), an act clearly approved of from the deuteronomistic perspective. Still, however, Jehu had not done all that was required, for he had failed to turn aside from the "sins of Jeroboam," identified explicitly with the "golden calves in Bethel and Dan."[56] Nonetheless, Jehu's actions were sufficient to gain him a limited dynastic promise that four of his sons would follow him on the throne of Israel (10:30). Such a promise is made to Jehu explicitly "because" he had done what Yahweh had required with respect to the house of Ahab and the worship of Baal. The reform efforts attributed to both Jehu of Israel and Jehoash of Judah reestablished a degree of security for their dynastic histories and allowed the deuteronomistic writer to compare the fates of each. Despite the positive aspects of the accounts of these two rulers, neither received the unqualified approval of the author. Jehoash still did not remove the *bāmôt* from Judah (12:4), just as Jehu had failed to eliminate the calves made by Jeroboam.[57]

The first section of the presentation of the histories of the kingdoms culminates with the events narrated during the "time of Ahaz." This period is differentiated from the previous periods recounted during the times of various kings of Judah because Ahaz is not only the final king

---

[55] On the serious textual problems associated with this passage, see M. Delcor, "Le trésor de la maison de Yahweh des origines à l'exile," *VT* 12 (1962) 360–66. An analysis of the form of the report and the suggestion that it reflects early post-exilic priestly concerns is presented by Hoffmann, *Reform und Reformen*, pp. 118–24.

[56] Compare the *šĕnê ʿăgālîm* of 2 Kgs 17:16, which appears as a gloss on the "molten image" (*massēkâ*). In the present context, the reference to the "golden calves" connects the failures of Jehu to the earlier deeds of Jeroboam (1 Kgs 12:28–30) and to the final explanation of the destruction of the kingdom (2 Kgs 17:16).

[57] An interesting parallel to Yahweh's continuation of the line of David is found in the account of the dynasty of Jehu. During the time of Jehoahaz, son of Jehu, the writer notes that Yahweh became angry with Israel and gave it into the power of Hazael and his son Benhadad. As a result of the oppression, Jehoahaz implored Yahweh, who responded by raising up a deliverer (*môšîaʿ*), who then led Israel out from under the power of Aram (13:1–9). Likewise, Yahweh decided not to "blot out the name of Israel" during the reign of Jeroboam II (14:27), showing once again that Yahweh would remain faithful to those who acted faithfully with him. The dynasty of Jehu was granted four successors, and so it endured.

during whose time the events affecting Israel are recounted, but is also the only such ruler who was condemned by the deuteronomistic writer for his deeds. It is an appropriate didactic construction, since Ahaz is presented as having completely reversed all the "upright" things done by the kings who had preceded him (16:1–20). Ahaz is the first king of Judah since Solomon (1 Kgs 3:3b; cf. 11:4–10) who is said explicitly to have sacrificed at the bāmôt (2 Kgs 16:4). Since this was the cultic offense that led to the division of the kingdom in the first place, its recurrence in the narrative carries critical implications. Additionally, Ahaz's deeds are likened to "the abominations of the nations" (2 Kgs 16:3b),[58] creating a direct comparison with Rehoboam in the past and Manasseh in the future (cf. 1 Kgs 14:24; 2 Kgs 21:2). So evil was Ahaz regarded because of his deeds that he was likened to the kings of Israel (16:3), a comparison made during the times of Jehoram and Ahaziah when the Davidic dynasty had almost been destroyed. Additionally, the introduction of non-Yahwistic practices in the temple as a result of the alliance with Assyria[59] brought the fate of Judah into a direct comparison with the fate of Israel. Each was equally apostate; each had failed to fulfill the covenantal demands that formed and defined them as people and states.

Immediately following this negative account of the status of Judah under Ahaz is recounted the destruction of the northern kingdom of Israel (17:1–41). This destruction and resettlement, explicitly interpreted by the deuteronomistic writer as the culmination of the punishment brought about by Jeroboam's actions (17:7–17), now stands to condemn Judah and to confirm the power of the prophetic pronouncement. The condemnation of Jeroboam and Israel had been placed in the narrative at the beginning of the accounts and was only now fulfilled. The words of the true prophet were and would be exonerated by the actions of the deity—at the appropriate time. Following this final discourse concerning the fate of Samaria, the structure of the presentation changes. The object lesson for Judah that the accounts of the continued apostasy of Israel had provided had been concluded. No longer was there an opposite kingdom with which the kings of Judah could be compared. With the reign of

---

[58] See above, pp. 270–72.

[59] For the deuteronomistic writer, Ahaz's activities constituted a cultic low that would be outdone only by Manasseh. On the relationship of Ahaz's deeds to those of other Israelite and Judean rulers, see Hoffmann, *Reform und Reformen*, pp. 139–43. On the significance and possible interpretations of Ahaz's innovations, see J. McKay, *Religion in Judah under the Assyrians* (SBT 26; Naperville, IL: Alec R. Allenson, 1973), pp. 5–12.

Ahaz and his completely negative cultic reforms, the fate of Judah could be different from that of Israel only as the result of one of two things: either by an expression of Yahwistic mercy and fervor for his promise to David, an occurrence that had been noted twice in the post-Solomonic history to this point (1 Kgs 15:4; 2 Kgs 8:19), or by the appearance of a king who would "do the upright in the eyes of Yahweh as all which David his father had done."

With the reign of Hezekiah, the dialectic contained in the divine paradox is dissolved, for both of these responses occur (2 Kgs 18:3; 19:34 [= Isa 37:35]; 20:6). Because Hezekiah removed the *bāmôt* and conducted other cultic reforms required by the deuteronomistic writer,[60] he is given a completely positive evaluation (18:3–4). Further, Hezekiah "trusted" Yahweh and clung to him, never turning aside from following him or from fulfilling the commands spoken by Yahweh to Moses (18:5–6). As Ahaz had placed Judah on the same destructive path as Israel, so Hezekiah had, if only temporarily, removed Judah from the punishments that would be expected. So good was this king that the author could proclaim that "after him there was none like him from among all of the kings of Judah" (18:5; cf. 23:25). Despite the "upright" nature of this ruler, he nonetheless faced the threat of destruction from the attack of the Assyrian king Sennacherib.[61] Yahweh delivered Hezekiah from this threat "for the sake of David" (19:34; 20:6).

The two sides of the paradox concerning Judah came together in the account of Hezekiah's reign. For the deuteronomistic writer, the proper actions of the king and the gracious deliverance of Yahweh converged to reestablish Judah as the people of Yahweh. The analogy created between Judah and Israel by the deeds of Ahaz was annulled by the righteous activity of Hezekiah. To provide a further commentary on Hezekiah's righteousness, the author points out that it was to the prophet Isaiah that Hezekiah turned for help when he was under siege by the Assyrians

---

[60] L. K. Handy suggests that the cultic actions attributed to Hezekiah are more accurately described as the actions of a king in response to an invading and conquering army than as a sustained effort at cultic reforms; "Hezekiah's Unlikely Reform," *ZAW* 100 (1988) 111–15.

[61] The materials concerning Hezekiah's reign presented in 2 Kgs 18:13–20:21 constitute a complex problem for the reconstruction of supposed underlying historical events. Whether Sennacherib conducted one or two campaigns against Judah and whether the present materials represent a compilation from different sources remain debated issues among scholars. For a thorough investigation of the relevant issues, see F. J. Gonçalves, *L'expédition de Sennachérib en Palestine dans la littérature hébraique ancienne* (Ebib 7; Paris: Gabalda, 1986).

(19:1–9a). For the deuteronomistic viewpoint throughout in the narrative, turning to Yahweh and his prophet constituted the essence of trusting in and clinging to Yahweh. In return, an oracle of deliverance was given (vv. 6–7). When the attack was renewed (vv. 8–13), Hezekiah again responded in the prescribed manner. He implored Yahweh for help and received divine assurance of deliverance from Isaiah (vv. 14–19, 20–34). To confirm the nature of the prophetic word, the historian records its fulfillment in the rescue of the city and the death of the aggressor.

This narrative of the first king since David to act in the proper Yahwistic mode is presented by way of a lengthy alternation of stories of oppression, faithful reliance on Yahweh, and deliverance. This is the very structure of the vision of the community that the historian has attempted to reconstruct from his deuteronomic outline. Yahweh's oppressed people could be delivered from their oppression by maintaining the identity outlined by the covenantal demands. Failure to remain "Israelites" would bring only further oppression and, ultimately, destruction. The latter is demonstrated in the final account of the story of Hezekiah. When he received the envoys of the Babylonian king and showed them the treasures of the realm (20:12–13), Isaiah appeared to condemn the king and announce the coming despoliation of the land (vv. 17–19). For the deuteronomistic vision of faithfulness, reliance on Yahweh had to be complete.[62] In his latter days, like Solomon, Hezekiah had failed to follow Yahweh; in each case, a prophet emerged to pronounce the delayed sentence on the ruler and his kingdom.

But the lessons of history were fitted neatly into the deuteronomistic ideology. The prophetic pronouncement of a coming exile prepared the way for the complete undoing of all the upright deeds of Hezekiah by his son and successor, Manasseh. Quite simply, Manasseh was the complete opposite of his father. He "did more evil than those nations Yahweh had destroyed from before the Israelites" (21:9), and his actions were comparable to "the abominations of the nations that Yahweh drove out from before the Israelites" (21:2). As with Ahaz and Rehoboam, the king of Judah had acted in such a way as to render the land comparable to its pre-conquest state. The boundaries that defined "Israel" by its dedication

---

[62] C. T. Begg notes that nowhere in the remaining chapters of Kings does there appear an appeal or intercession addressed to Yahweh; "2 Kings 20:12–19 as an Element of the Deuteronomistic History," *CBQ* 48 (1986) 37. The deuteronomistic evaluation of the uniqueness of Hezekiah (18:5) might be based on this factor, since no other ruler, not even Josiah, would demonstrate such continued reliance on Yahweh.

to Yahweh were dissolved by the cultic misdeeds committed by Manasseh (21:2–7). Judgment was announced by Yahweh "by means of his servants, the prophets" (*běyad-ʿăbādāyw hannĕbîʾîm*, 21:10). Judah and Jerusalem would be destroyed, as had been Israel and Samaria (vv. 11–15). Divine mercy would not intervene this time to save the kingdom.

Buried in the structure of this presentation, however, was the ideology of the efficacy of the prophetic word, one presentation of which remained to be confirmed before the completion of the history could be reached. The famous prophecy of the "man of God" from Judah against the altar of Bethel (1 Kgs 13:2) that had proclaimed the actions of a Davidic king by the name of Josiah had not yet been fulfilled. The divine punishment of Judah would be postponed until the prophetic word had been realized. Though Josiah would return the kingdom to the days of David, the time of the original ideal age, it could not last.[63] The demise of the kingdom had been proclaimed. Josiah, for all his righteousness, could present only one final vision of the way in which the king should lead the people. His extensive cultic reforms (2 Kgs 23:1–24)[64] stand in the same relation to the evil deeds of Manasseh as the righteousness of Hezekiah had stood with respect to the actions of Ahaz. But there was one irrefutable difference; in reaction to Ahaz's sinfulness, destruction had been threatened by implication, but in response to Manasseh's, it had been prophetically proclaimed. Even Josiah's Davidic "perfection" (22:2) could not offset the efficacy of the prophetic pronouncement against Judah and its royal house. This is confirmed by the oracle of Huldah (22:15–20), a prophetic response to the discovery of the "book of the *tôrâ*" during the temple repairs. The punishment proclaimed would be exacted (vv. 16–17). Josiah's righteousness, like that of Hezekiah, would spare him the experience of the disaster (vv. 18–20).

The greatness of Josiah was to be found in the fact that despite the absolute confirmation of the disaster that was to befall Judah, he continued his reform. Following the guidelines of "the book," by which the writer clearly seems to have intended Deuteronomy, Josiah engaged in a covenant renewal, a complete cleansing of the cultus of any non-Yahwistic practices, and defiled the *bāmôt* that dated back to the days of Solomon (23:13). More importantly, he fulfilled the prophecy against the

---

[63] On the reforms of Josiah and the manner in which they reconstituted the deuteronomic and deuteronomistic ideals of Israelite identity, see chap. 3, pp. 76–85.

[64] For an analysis of the reform reports in the account of Josiah's reign and the relationship of these accounts to other cultic reforms reported in the deuteronomistic history, see Hoffmann, *Reform und Reformen*, pp. 169–270.

altar at Bethel (23:15–20). The newly recreated covenantal "Israel" then celebrated the Passover in a manner unequaled since the time of the judges (23:22).[65] In ritual terms, "Israel" had been redefined in the days of Josiah by the deuteronomic boundaries provided in this "book of the *tôrâ;*" because of that same covenantal charter, this recreation could not last. Despite Josiah's efforts, Judah had been condemned by Yahweh's prophets. Yahweh would not fail to bring their proclamations to fruition (23:26–27).

With this reconfirmation of the fate of Judah, the history takes on a laconic tone.[66] Such a shift in tone need not suggest a later editing of the story. Instead, it might serve to reemphasize the concept of the final confirmation of the prophetic word that dominated the entire presentation of kingship in the narrative reconstruction of Judah's past. The period from the death of Josiah to the release of the last of the Davidic kings, Jehoiachin, from his Babylonian prison cell is presented in a highly compressed narrative form (23:31–25:30). This style of presentation is very much like that used to describe the final years of Israel. Unlike the account of Israel's fall, however, the destruction of Judah and Jerusalem does not end with an extended or even an emotional peroration, for from the "ashes" of Judah would emerge the new "Israel." A new history would begin, understood now in terms of the ideal past that had been forfeited by the people's failure to recognize and maintain their distinctive relationship with their god.

---

[65] The last narrated celebration of the Passover occurred in Josh 5:10–12.

[66] Cross, *Canaanite Myth and Hebrew Epic*, p. 288.

9

POSTSCRIPT: THE EXILE AND THE PARADOX OF THE FUTURE

The approach developed in the foregoing analysis of the narratives composing the deuteronomistic history has attempted to present a new interpretation of both that history and the historian who wrote it. Addressing the narratives in their basic final form and placing the composition of those materials within the context of the exilic situation open the way for approaching these materials as prophetic visions concerning the composition and recomposition of the ethnic/national group that was known as Israel and Judah but that now faced the danger of complete assimilation into the nations due to its defeat at the hands of foreign powers. In order to address the problems of religious, national, and self-identity that would have arisen within the context of the exile, the deuteronomistic historian produced a narrative account of the existence of Israel and Judah from the entry into the land until its exile in Babylon.

This history recounted by the deuteronomistic writer came to a closure, but not to an end, with the account of the exile. Though Jehoiachin was still under house arrest in Babylon, the line of David still existed and Yahweh's promise to establish the Davidic line had not been broken. Yet the promises to David and his descendants constituted only a part of the relationship of Yahweh with the people whom he had chosen for his own possession. In order to realize and maintain its position as Yahweh's chosen people, Israel willingly accepted the obligations of the covenantal demands. For the deuteronomistic writer, these demands found their most authoritative expression in the materials contained in the "law of Moses" expressed in what is now the book of Deuteronomy. It was within the demands for religious, cultural, and ethnic distinctiveness set forth in this book that the deuteronomistic writer found a manifesto that presented the boundaries by which Israel might be defined as a distinct people apart from all the other nations. At the same time, the proclamations of that book also provided an outline for the ways in which Israel might be reconstituted and reenvisioned in times of conquest. The distinctiveness of Israel would be defined by the ways in which the people fulfilled the commands of the covenant that formed the basis of the nation's ethnic identity, demands that required interpretation and implementation in the new situations in which the people discovered themselves.

Against the backdrop of the prophetic interpretation of the *tôrâ* as it was to be applied to the Israel of the exile and following, the deuteronomistic author undertook a recounting of the traditions concerning the past that were now refracted through the interpretive lens provided by that writer's understanding of the demands of Deuteronomy. What results, then, is a form of national and ethnic myth, cast in the form of a history, that contains the essential elements for group boundaries and identification: myths of origin, ancestry, migration, liberation, golden age, decline, and rebirth. The realization of such ethnic distinctiveness finds its ultimate expression in Israel's actions in the land promised to its ancestors. Retaining the land is made dependent upon the maintenance of the distinctive ethnic and religious identity required of the people.

Understood in these ways, the deuteronomistic history constitutes a two-way vision: it looks to the past to understand the present and to the future to restore the ideals that have been described as part of that past. The groups who would accept or reject this vision would ultimately decide if the prophetic authority of this "speaker" had been established and was to be supported by and incorporated into their symbolic universe. Since the symbols of that universe were in the process of significant transition, if not in complete disarray, a societal situation was created in which the need to reconfirm the identity of "Israel" was paramount for selected groups of the former state of Judah. The destruction of the monarchic state and the major supporting groups for the dynastic religion created an incontrovertible perception of dissonance for many of those involved. Into this "gap" between the divine commands and obligations that defined the proper "Israel" stepped the deuteronomistic author with his particular concept of the power of the prophet to intermediate the covenantal demands that would, if followed, recreate this people as the original group that they had been intended to be from the standpoint of their divinely chosen "origins."

By constructing the covenantal demands around the figure of Moses, the leader from Egyptian bondage and the intermediator after whom all "true" prophets would be patterned, the historian placed the prophetic power to present and interpret the divine will, both temporally and spatially, into the context of "Israel's" origins. The ideal charter presenting the boundaries by which "Israel" had defined itself and should continue to define itself occurred outside the land and was presented via the farewell speech of Moses himself. The deuteronomistic writer's attempt to show the failures of the past generations to fulfill these demands and the resulting loss of its major external identifying symbols created a twofold thrust for his ideological interpretation of "Israel's" past: the losses of the kingdom, temple, and land were all placed within the context of the "original" social manifesto of "Israelite" identity, and the ways to regain this ideal age were implied throughout. The extensive nature of the narrative past produced demonstrated the complexities of identifying oneself as "Israelite" and of accepting both the internal and external obligations that would bring.

For the deuteronomistic writer, such self-identification would mean the willing acceptance of the covenantal demands outlined in Deuteronomy and, ultimately, all those that came to be associated with the events occurring at Horeb/Sinai. To be "Israelite" would require one to be separated from all other groups, to be dedicated to Yahweh alone, and to avoid the dangers of association with those outside the group. The ethnic unity of "Israel" was one to be recreated from the traditions, history, and culture that had so nearly been lost in the flames that destroyed the old state of Israel and that had now nearly enveloped Judah. The reformation and recreation of this new "Israel" would depend on the ability of the various peoples concerned to incorporate and internalize this vision of the ideal as the only true way of understanding themselves. If this were to be done, i.e., if the prophetic voice of the deuteronomistic writer were followed, then the forgiving and merciful side of the divine paradox that provided one of the dialectics of the deuteronomistic history might be rekindled and, after an appropriate delay, the symbols of land, temple and king might be reinstituted in the new "Israel" that would coincide with the ideal created in the archaic past.

After all, the kingdom may have ended, but a Davidic king and his sons still lived and were recognized by the Babylonians as the legitimate rulers. The curses of the covenant had been visited on the people, for the land had been devastated and the people exiled, but they remained the chosen of Yahweh. The promises to the ancestors concerning the land had not been revoked. "Israel" had simply failed to take possession of it in the appropriate way and to institute the covenant as the only defining characteristic of the group. Where ambiguity over direction or obligation might exist, the prophetic voice of the deuteronomistic writer stood to clarify it. The authority of the voice had been demonstrated throughout the history itself, for the words of Samuel, Ahijah, the unnamed prophet from Judah, Huldah, and a host of others had not brought about their pronounced realities immediately. Such "traditional" authorities as these provided the exoneration to the prophetic tradition concerning the power to influence the symbolic universe inhabited by his hearers. The historical lessons of the past, selected by the ideological presuppositions of this prophet who perceived himself as the heir to Moses, provided a pattern and paradigm for the reformation of a new "Israel" and a reconstitution of the ideal age lost due to the failures of the people. The older symbols were still available for use; it was up to the leadership of the dispersed elements of Judah to inject them with new meanings. This deuteronomistic history represented one such reenvisioning of "Israel's" religious and ethnic distinctiveness.

SELECTED BIBLIOGRAPHY

Ackerman, J. S. "Knowing Good and Evil: A Literary Analysis of the Court History in 2 Samuel 9–20 and 1 Kings 1–2," *JBL* 109 (1990) 41–60.

——. "Who Can Stand before YHWH, This Holy God? A Reading of 1 Samuel 1–15," *Prooftexts* 11 (1991) 1–24.

Ackroyd, P. R. *Exile and Restoration: A Study of Hebrew Thought of the Sixth Century B. C.* OTL; Philadelphia: Westminster, 1968.

Aharoni, Y. "The Province-List of Judah," *VT* 9 (1959) 225–46.

Ahlström, G. W. *Royal Administration and National Religion in Ancient Israel.* Studies in the History of the Ancient Near East 1; Leiden: E. J. Brill, 1982.

——. *Who Were the Israelites?* Winona Lake, IN: Eisenbrauns, 1986.

Albrektson, B. *History and the Gods. An Essay on the Idea of Historical Events as Divine Manifestations in the Ancient Near East and in Israel.* Lund: C. W. K. Gleerup, 1967.

Albright, W. F. *Samuel and the Beginnings of the Prophetic Movement.* The Samuel H. Goldman Lectures; Cincinnati: Hebrew Union College, 1961.

Alonso-Schökel, L. "Erzählkunst im Buche der Richter," *Bib* 42 (1961) 143–72.

Alt, A. "Das Königtum in den Reichen Israel und Juda," *VT* 1 (1951) 2–22.

Amit, Y. "Judges 4: Its Contents and Form," *JSOT* 39 (1987) 89–111.

——. "Hidden Polemic in the Conquest of Dan: Judges xvii–xviii," *VT* 40 (1990) 4–20.

Anderson, A. A. *2 Samuel.* WBC; Waco, TX: Word, 1989.

Anderson, B. *Imagined Communities: Reflections on the Origin and Spread of Nationalism.* London: Verso, 1983.

Andreasen, N.-E. A. "The Role of the Queen Mother in Israelite Society," *CBQ* 45 (1983) 179–94.

Arens, W. *The Man-Eating Myth: Anthropology & Anthropophagy*. Oxford: Oxford University Press, 1979.

Auerbach, E. *Mimesis: The Representation of Reality in Western Literature*. Princeton: Princeton University Press, 1953.

Auld, A. G. "Judges 1 and History: A Reconsideration," *VT* 25 (1974) 261–85.

———. "Gideon: Hacking at the Heart of the Old Testament," *VT* 39 (1989) 257–67.

Baltzer, K. "Considerations Regarding the Office and Call of the Prophet," *HTR* 61 (1968) 567–81.

Barbour, I. "Paradigms in Science and Religion." Pp. 223–45 in *Paradigms and Revolutions: Appraisals and Applications of Thomas Kuhn's Philosophy of Science*. Ed. by Gary Gutting. Notre Dame: University of Notre Dame Press, 1980.

Barré, L. M. *The Rhetoric of Political Persuasion: The Narrative Artistry and Political Intentions of 2 Kings 9–11*. CBQMS 20; Washington, DC: Catholic Biblical Association of America, 1988.

Barrick, W. B. "What do we really know about 'high-places'?," *SEÅ* 45 (1980) 50–57.

Barth, F. "Introduction." Pp. 9–38 in *Ethnic Groups and Boundaries: The Social Organization of Culture Difference*. Ed. by F. Barth. Boston: Little, Brown, 1969.

Begg, C. T. "2 Kings 20:12–19 as an Element of the Deuteronomistic History," *CBQ* 48 (1986) 27–38.

Ben-Barak, Z. "The Status and Right of the *Gĕbîrâ*," *JBL* 110 (1990) 23–34.

Berger, P. *The Sacred Canopy: Elements of a Sociological Theory of Religion*. Garden City, NY: Anchor, 1969.

——— and T. Luckmann. *The Social Construction of Reality: A Treatise in the Sociology of Knowledge*. New York: Doubleday, 1966.

Beyerlin, W. "Gattung und Herkunft des Rahmens im Richterbuch." Pp. 1–29 in *Tradition und Situation: Festschrift A. Weiser*. Ed. by E. Würthwein. Göttingen: Vandenhoeck & Ruprecht, 1963.

Birch, B. C. "The Development of the Tradition on the Anointing of Saul in I Sam 9:1–10:16," *JBL* 90 (1971) 55–68.

———. *The Rise of the Israelite Monarchy: The Growth and Development of I Samuel 7–15*. SBLDS 27; Missoula, MT: Scholars Press, 1976.

Blenkinsopp, J. "Structure and Style in Judges 13–16," *JBL* 82 (1963) 65–76.

Boling, R. G. *Judges*. AB 6A; New York: Doubleday, 1975.

——— and G. E. Wright, *Joshua*. AB 6; Garden City, NY: Doubleday, 1982.

Boorer, S. "The Importance of a Diachronic Approach: The Case of Genesis-Kings," *CBQ* 51 (1989) 195–208.

Booth, W. C. *The Rhetoric of Fiction*. 2nd ed. Chicago: University of Chicago Press, 1983.

Brentjes, B. "Zur 'Beulen' Epidemie bei den Philistern in 1. Samuel 5–6," *Altertum* 15 (1969) 67–74.

Brettler, M. "The Book of Judges: Literature as Politics," *JBL* 108 (1989) 395–418.

Bright, J. *A History of Israel.* 3rd ed. Philadelphia: Westminster, 1981.

Brueggemann, W. *David's Truth in Israel's Imagination and Memory.* Philadelphia: Fortress, 1985.

Buccellati, G. *Cities and Nations of Ancient Syria: An Essay on Political Institutions with Special Reference to the Israelite Kingdoms.* Studi Semitici 21; Rome: Istituto di Studi del vicino Oriente, 1967.

Campbell, A. F. *The Ark Narrative.* SBLDS 16; Missoula, MT: Scholars Press, 1975.

———. *Of Prophets and Kings: A Late Ninth-Century Document (1 Samuel 1 – 2 Kings 10).* CBQMS 17; Washington, DC: The Catholic Biblical Association of America, 1986.

Carlson, R. A. *David, the Chosen King: A Traditio-Historical Approach to the Second Book of Samuel.* Stockholm: Almqvist & Wiksell, 1964.

Carmichael, C. M. *The Laws of Deuteronomy.* Ithaca: Cornell University Press, 1974.

Carneiro, R. L. "The Chiefdom: Precursor of the State." Pp. 37–79 in *The Transition to Statehood in the New World.* Ed. by G. D. Jones and R. R. Kautz. Cambridge: Cambridge University Press, 1981.

Chaney, M. "Ancient Palestinian Peasant Movements and the Formation of Premonarchic Israel." Pp. 39–90 in *Palestine in Transition: The Emergence of Ancient Israel.* Ed. by D. N. Freedman and D. F. Graf. SWBA 2; Sheffield: Almond, 1983.

Charsley, S. R. "The Formation of Ethnic Groups." Pp. 337–68 in *Urban Ethnicity.* Ed. by Abner Cohen. London: Tavistock, 1974.

Clements, R. E. "The Deuteronomistic Interpretation of the Founding of the Monarchy in I Sam. VIII," *VT* 24 (1974) 398–410.

Clifford, R. J. "The Tent of El and the Israelite Tent of Meeting," *CBQ* 33 (1971) 221–27.

Clines, D. J. A. *The Theme of the Pentateuch.* JSOTSup 10; Sheffield: JSOT, 1978.

Cody, A. *A History of Old Testament Priesthood.* AnBib 35; Rome: Pontifical Biblical Institute, 1969.

Cogan, M. and H. Tadmor. *II Kings.* AB 11; Garden City, NY: Doubleday, 1988.

Cohen, A. "Introduction: The Lesson of Ethnicity." Pp. ix–xxiv in *Urban Ethnicity.* Ed. by A. Cohen. New York: Tavistock, 1974.

Conrad, L. I. "The Biblical Tradition for the Plague of the Philistines," *JAOS* 104 (1984) 281–87.

Coogan, M. D. "A Structural and Literary Analysis of the Song of Deborah," *CBQ* 40 (1978) 143–66.

Cook, S. A. "The Theophanies of Gideon and Manoah," *JTS* 28 (1927) 368–83.

Coote, R. and K. Whitelam. *The Emergence of Early Israel in Historical Perspective.* SWBA 5. Sheffield: Almond, 1987.

Craigie, P. C. "A Reconsideration of Shamgar ben Anath (Judg 3.31 and 5.6)," *JBL* 91 (1972) 239–40.

Crenshaw, J. L. *Samson: A Secret Betrayed. A Vow Ignored.* Atlanta: John Knox, 1978.

Cross, F. M. *Canaanite Myth and Hebrew Epic.* Cambridge: Harvard University Press, 1973.

———— and G. E. Wright. "The Boundary and Province Lists of the Kingdom of Judah," *JBL* 75 (1956) 202–26.

Crüsemann, F. *Der Widerstand gegen das Königtum: Die antiköniglichen Texte des Alten Testaments und der Kampf um den frühen israelitischen Staat.* WMANT 49; Neukirchen-Vluyn: Neukirchener Verlag, 1978.

Curtis, J. B. "A Folk Etymology of nābîʾ," *VT* 29 (1979) 491–93.

Damrosch, D. *The Narrative Covenant: Transformation of Genre in the Growth of Biblical Literature.* San Francisco: Harper & Row, 1987.

Debus, J. *Die Sünde Jerobeams: Studien zur Darstellung Jerobeams und der Geschichte des Nordreichs in der deuteronomistischen Geschichtsschreibung.* FRLANT 93; Göttingen: Vandenhoeck & Ruprecht, 1967.

Delcor, M. "Le trésor de la maison de Yahweh des origines à l'exile," *VT* 12 (1962) 353–77.

Demsky, A. "Writing in Ancient Israel and Early Judaism: Part One: The Biblical Period." Pp. 2–20 in *Mikra.* CRINT, sec. 1; Assen/Maastrict/Philadelphia: Van Gorcum/Fortress, 1988.

DeVries, S. J. *1 Kings.* WBC; Waco, TX: Word, 1985.

Dietrich, W. *Prophetie und Geschichte. Eine redaktionsgeschichtliche Unversuchung zum deuteronomistischen Geschichtswerk.* FRLANT 108; Göttingen: Vandenhoeck & Ruprecht, 1972.

Donner, H. "Art und Herkunft des Amtes der Königmutter im Alten Testament." Pp. 105–45 in *Festschrift Johannes Friedrich.* Ed. by R. von Kienle, *et al.* Heidelberg: Karl Winter, 1959.

————. *Geschichte des V lkes Israel und seiner Nachbarn in Grundzügen.* GAT 4/2; Göttingen: Vandenhoeck & Ruprecht, 1986.

Driver, S. R. *Notes on the Hebrew Text and the Topography of the Books of Samuel.* 2nd ed. (a reprint of the 1912 Oxford edition). Winona Lake, IN: Alpha, 1984.

Eissfeldt, O. "Gilgal or Shechem?" Pp. 90–101 in *Proclamation and Presence.* Ed. by J. L. Durham and J. R. Porter. Richmond: John Knox, 1970.

Eppstein, V. "Was Saul among the Prophets?," *ZAW* 81 (1969) 287–303.

Estess, T. L. "The Inennarrable Contraption," *JAAR* 42 (1974) 415–34.

Exum, J. C. "Promise and Fulfillment: Narrative Art in Judges 13," *JBL* 99 (1980) 43–59.

————. "Aspects of Symmetry and Balance in the Samson Saga," *JSOT* 19 (1981) 3–29.

Flanagan, J. W. "Succession and Genealogy in the Davidic Dynasty." Pp. 35–55 in *The Quest for the Kingdom of God: Studies in Honor of George E. Mendenhall*. Ed. by H. G. Huffmon, F. A. Spina, and A. R. Green. Winona Lake, IN: Eisenbrauns, 1983.

Fokkelman, J. P. *Narrative Art and Poetry in the Books of Samuel, Volume II: The Crossing of Fates (I Sam. 13–31 & II Sam. 1)*. SSN 11; Assen, The Netherlands: Van Gorcum, 1986.

————. "Saul & David," *BibRev* 5 (1989) 20–32.

Frick, F. *The Formation of the State in Ancient Israel*. SWBA 4; Sheffield: JSOT, 1985.

Friedman, R. E. *The Exile and Biblical Narrative*. HSM 22; Chico, CA: Scholars Press, 1981.

————. "From Egypt to Egypt: Dtr¹ and Dtr²." Pp. 167–92 in *Traditions in Transformation: Turning Points in Biblical Faith*. Ed. by B. Halpern and J. D. Levenson. Winona Lake, IN: Eisenbrauns, 1981.

Gager, J. *Kingdom and Community: The Social World of Early Christianity*. Englewood Cliffs, NJ: Prentice-Hall, 1975.

Garsiel, M. *The First Book of Samuel: A Literary Study of Comparative Structures, Analogies and Parallels*. Ramat Gan, Israel: Revivim, 1985.

Geertz, C. *The Interpretation of Cultures: Selected Essays by Clifford Geertz*. New York: Basic, 1973.

————. *Local Knowledge: Further Essays in Interpretive Anthropology*. New York: Basic, 1983.

Gellner, E. *Nations and Nationalism*. Ithaca, NY: Cornell University Press, 1983.

Gerbrandt, G. E. *Kingship According to the Deuteronomistic History*. SBLDS 87; Atlanta: Scholars Press, 1986.

Gonçalves, F. J. *L'expédition de Sennachérib en Palestine dans la littérature hébraïque ancienne*. Ebib 7; Paris: Gabalda, 1986.

Goody, J. *The Logic of Writing and the Organization of Society*. Studies in Literacy, Family, Culture, and the State. Cambridge: Cambridge University Press, 1986.

Gottwald, N. K. *The Tribes of Yahweh: A Sociology of the Religion of Liberated Israel, 1250–1050 B.C.E.* Maryknoll, NY: Orbis, 1979.

————. "Religious Conversion and the Societal Origins of Ancient Israel," *Perspectives in Religious Studies* 15 (1988) 49–65.

Graham, W. *Beyond the Written Word: Oral Aspects of Scripture in the History of Religion*. Cambridge: Cambridge University Press, 1987.

Grayson, A. K. *Assyrian and Babylonian Chronicles*. Texts from Cuneiform Sources; Locust Valley, NY: J. J. Augustin, 1975.

Green, R. M. *Religion and Moral Reason: A New Method for Comparative Study*. New York: Oxford University Press, 1988.

Greenstein, E. L. "The Riddle of Samson," *Prooftexts* 1 (1981) 237–60.

———. "On the Genesis of Biblical Prose Narrative," *Prooftexts* 8 (1988) 347–54.

Grimm, D. "Der Name des Gottesboten in Richter 13," *Bib* 62 (1981) 92–98.

Gruber, M. "Hebrew *Qĕdēšah* and Her Canaanite and Akkadian Cognates," *UF* 8 (1986) 133–48.

Gunn, D. M. *The Fate of King Saul: An Interpretation of a Biblical Story*. JSOTSup 14; Sheffield: JSOT, 1980.

Haag, H. "Gideon-Jerubbaal-Abimelek," *ZAW* 79 (1967) 305–14.

Habel, N. C. "The Form and Significance of the Call Narrative," *ZAW* 77 (1965) 297–323.

Halpern, B. "Levitic Participation in the Reform Cult of Jeroboam I," *JBL* 95 (1976) 31–42.

———. *The Constitution of the Monarchy in Israel*. HSM 25; Chico, CA: Scholars Press, 1981.

———. *The First Historians: The Hebrew Bible and History*. San Francisco: Harper & Row, 1988.

Handy, L. K. "Hezekiah's Unlikely Reform," *ZAW* 100 (1988) 111–15.

Hanson, P. D. "The Song of Heshbon and David's *Nîr*," *HTR* 61 (1968) 297–320.

———. *The Dawn of Apocalyptic*. Philadelphia: Fortress, 1975.

———. *The People Called: The Growth of Community in the Bible*. San Francisco: Harper & Row, 1986.

———. "Israelite Religion in the Early Post-exilic Period." Pp. 485–508 in *Ancient Israelite Religion*. Ed. by P. D. Miller, Jr., P. D. Hanson, and S. D. McBride. Philadelphia: Fortress, 1987.

Haran, M. *Temples and Temple Service in Ancient Israel: An Inquiry into Biblical Cult Phenomena and the Historical Setting of the Priestly School*. Oxford: Clarendon, 1978; reprinted Winona Lake, IN: Eisenbrauns, 1985.

Harris, R. "Woman in the ANE." Pp. 960–63 in *The Interpreter's Dictionary of the Bible, Supp*. Ed. by K. Crim. Nashville: Abingdon, 1976.

Hauser, A. J. "The 'Minor Judges'—A Re-evaluation," *JBL* 94 (1975) 190–200.

———. "Judges 5: Parataxis in Hebrew Poetry," *JBL* 99 (1980) 23–41.

Hermann, S. *A History of Israel in Old Testament Times*. Philadelphia: Fortress, 1975.

Hertzberg, H.-W. *Die Bücher Josua, Richter, Ruth*. 2nd ed. ATD 9; Göttingen: Vandenhoeck & Ruprecht, 1959.

———. *I & II Samuel*. OTL; Philadelphia: Westminster, 1964.

Hobbs, T. R. *2 Kings*. WBC 13; Waco, TX: Word, 1985.

Hobsbawm, E. *Bandits*. Rev. ed. New York: Pantheon, 1969.

———. "Introduction: Inventing Traditions." Pp. 1–14 in *The Invention of Tradition*. Ed. by E. Hobsbawm and T. Ranger. Cambridge: Cambridge University Press, 1983.

Hoffmann, H.-D. *Reform und Reformen: Untersuchungen zu einen Grundthema der deuteronomistischen Geschichtsschreibung.* ATANT 66; Zürich: Theologischer Verlag, 1980.

Holladay, W. *Jeremiah 1.* Hermeneia. Philadelphia: Fortress, 1986.

Huffmon, H. B. "The Treaty Background of Hebrew *Yadaᶜ*," *BASOR* 184 (1966) 31–37.

Huizinga, J. "A Definition of the Concept of History." Pp. 1–10 in *Philosophy and History: Essays Presented to Ernst Cassirer.* Ed. by R. Klibansky and H. J. Paton. New York: 1963.

Isaacs, H. R. "Basic Group Identity: The Idols of the Tribe." Pp. 29–52 in *Ethnicity: Theory and Experience.* Ed. by N. Glazer and D. P. Moynihan. Cambridge: Harvard University Press, 1975.

Ishida, T. *The Royal Dynasties in Ancient Israel: A Study on the Formation and Development of Royal-Dynastic Ideology.* BZAW 142; New York: de Gruyter, 1977.

Jagersma, H. *A History of Israel in the Old Testament Period.* Philadelphia: Fortress, 1983.

Jay, N. "Sacrifice, Descent and the Patriarchs," *VT* 38 (1988) 52–70.

Jobling, D. *The Sense of Biblical Narrative: Structural Analyses in the Hebrew Bible, II.* JSOTSup 39; Sheffield: JSOT, 1986.

Jones, G. H. *1 and 2 Kings,* Vol. 2. NCB; Grand Rapids, MI: Eerdmans, 1984.

Jüngling, H.-W., S. J. *Richter 19—Ein Plädoyer für das Königtum.* AnBib 84; Rome: Pontifical Biblical Institute, 1981.

Kenik, H. A. *Design for Kingship: The Deuteronomistic Narrative Technique in 1 Kings 3:4–15.* SBLDS 69; Chico, CA: Scholars Press, 1983.

Klein, R. W. *Israel in Exile: A Theological Interpretation.* OBT; Philadelphia: Fortress, 1979.

———. *1 Samuel.* WBC 10; Waco, TX: Word, 1983.

Kuhn, T. *The Structure of Scientific Revolutions.* 2nd ed. Chicago: University of Chicago Press, 1970.

Lasine, S. "Guest and Host in Judges 19: Lot's Hospitality in an Inverted World," *JSOT* 29 (1984) 37–59.

Lemche, N. P. "David's Rise," *JSOT* 10 (1978) 2–25.

———. "'Hebrew' as a National Name for Israel," *Studia Theologica* 33 (1979) 1–23.

———. *Early Israel: Anthropological and Historical Studies on the Israelite Society before the Monarchy.* VTSup 37. Leiden: E. J. Brill, 1985.

Lemke, W. E. "The Way of Obedience: I Kings 13 and the Structure of the Deuteronomistic History." Pp. 301–26 in *Magnalia Dei: The Mighty Acts of God.* Ed. by F. M. Cross, W. E. Lemke, and P. D. Miller, Jr. Garden City, NY: Doubleday, 1976.

Levenson, J. D. "Who Inserted the Book of the Torah?," *HTR* 68 (1975) 203–33.

———. "1 Samuel 25 as Literature and as History," *CBQ* 40 (1978) 11–28.

———. "The Davidic Covenant and its Modern Interpreters," *CBQ* 41 (1979) 205–19.

————. "From Temple to Synagogue: 1 Kings 8." Pp. 143–66 in *Traditions in Transformation: Turning Points in Biblical Faith*. Ed. by B. Halpern and J. D. Levenson. Winona Lake, IN: Eisenbrauns, 1981.

Levin, C. *Der Struz der Königin Atalja. Ein Kapitel zur Geschichte Judas im 9. Jahrhundert v. Chr.* Stuttgarter Bibelstudien 105; Stuttgart: Katholisches Bibelwerk, 1982.

Lewis, B. *History—Remembered, Recovered, Invented*. Princeton: Princeton University Press, 1975.

Lincoln, B. *Discourse and the Construction of Society: Comparative Studies of Myth, Ritual, and Classification*. New York/Oxford: Oxford University Press, 1989.

Liverani, M. "L'histoire de Joas," *VT* 24 (1974) 438–53.

Lohfink, N. "Kerygmata des Deuteronomistischen Geschichtswerks." Pp. 87–100 in *Die Botschaft und die Boten. Festschrift Für H. W. Wolff zum 70. Geburtstag*. Ed. by J. Jeremias and L. Perlitt. Neukirchen-Vluyn: Neukirchener Verlag, 1981.

————. "The Cult Reform of Josiah of Judah: 2 Kings 22–23 as a Source for the History of Israelite Religion." Pp. 459–84 in *Ancient Israelite Religion: Essays in Honor of Frank Moore Cross*. Ed. by P. D. Miller, Jr., P. D. Hanson, and S. D. McBride. Philadelphia: Fortress, 1987.

Long, B. O. *The Problem of Etiological Narrative in the Old Testament*. BZAW 108; Berlin: de Gruyter, 1968.

————. "Prophetic Authority as Social Reality." Pp. 3–20 in *Canon and Authority*. Ed. by G. W. Coats and B. O. Long. Philadelphia: Fortress, 1977.

————. "Social Dimensions of Prophetic Conflict," *Semeia* 21 (1982) 31–53.

————. *1 Kings with an Introduction to Historical Literature*. FOTL 9; Grand Rapids, MI: Eerdmans, 1984.

————. "On Finding the Hidden Premises," *JSOT* 39 (1987) 10–14.

Malamat, A. "The Danite Migration and the Pan-Israelite Exodus-Conquest: A Biblical Narrative Pattern," *Bib* 51 (1970) 1–16.

Mantovani, P. A. "Circoncisi ed incirconcisi," *Henoch* 10 (1988) 51–67.

Marcus, D. *Jephthah and his Vow*. Lubbock, TX: Texas Tech Press, 1986.

————. "In Defense of Micah: Judges 17:2: He was Not a Thief," *Shofar* 6 (1987) 72–80.

Margalith, O. "The Meaning of ʿplym in 1 Samuel v–vi," *VT* 33 (1983) 339–41.

Mayes, A. D. H. *Israel in the Period of the Judges*. SBT 29; London: SCM, 1974.

————. "The Rise of the Israelite Monarchy," *ZAW* 90 (1978) 1–19.

————. *Deuteronomy*. NCB; Grand Rapids, MI: Eerdmans, 1979.

McBride, S. D., Jr. "Polity of the Covenant People: The Book of Deuteronomy," *Int* 41 (1987) 229–44.

McCarter, P. K. "The Apology of David," *JBL* 99 (1980) 489–504.

————. *I Samuel*. AB 8; Garden City, NY: Doubleday, 1980.

————. *II Samuel*. AB 9; Garden City, NY: Doubleday, 1984.

McCarthy, D. J. "II Samuel and the Structure of the Deuteronomic History," *JBL* 84 (1966) 131–38.

———. "The Inauguration of Monarchy in Israel: A Form-Critical Study of I Samuel 8–12," *Int* 27 (1973) 401–12.

———. *Treaty and Covenant: A Study in Form in the Ancient Oriental Documents and in the Old Testament*. AnBib 21A, rev. ed.; Rome: Biblical Institute Press, 1978.

McKay, J. *Religion in Judah under the Assyrians*. SBT 26; Naperville, IL: Alec R. Allenson, 1973.

McKenzie, S. L. *The Chronicler's Use of the Deuteronomistic History*. HSM 33; Atlanta: Scholars Press, 1984.

Mettinger, T. N. D. *Solomonic State Officials. A Study of the Civil Government of Officials of the Israelite Monarchy*. Lund: C. W. K. Gleerup, 1971.

———. *King and Messiah: The Civil and Sacral Legitimation of the Israelite Kings*. Lund: C. W. K. Gleerup, 1976.

———. *The Dethronement of Sabaoth: Studies in the Shem and Kabod Theologies*. ConBOT 18; Lund: C. W. K. Gleerup, 1982.

Milgrom, J. "Religious Conversion and the Revolt Model for the Formation of Israel," *JBL* 101 (1982) 169–76.

Miller, J. M. and J. H. Hayes. *A History of Ancient Israel and Judah*. Philadelphia: Westminster, 1986.

Miller, P. D., Jr. and J. J. M. Roberts. *The Hand of the Lord: A Reassessment of the "Ark Narrative" of 1 Samuel*. Baltimore: The Johns Hopkins University Press, 1977.

Miscall, P. *1 Samuel: A Literary Reading*. Bloomington/Indianapolis: Indiana University Press, 1986.

Moore, G. F. *Judges*. Edinburgh: T. & T. Clark, 1895.

Moran, W. L. "The Ancient Near Eastern Background of the Love of God in Deuteronomy," *CBQ* 25 (1963) 77–87.

Mullen, E. T., Jr. "The 'Minor Judges': Some Literary and Historical Considerations," *CBQ* 44 (1982) 185–201.

———. "Judges 1:1–36: The Deuteronomistic Reintroduction of the Book of Judges," *HTR* 77:1 (1984) 33–54.

———. "The Sins of Jeroboam: A Redactional Reassessment," *CBQ* 49 (1987) 212–32.

———. "The Royal Dynastic Grant to Jehu and the Structure of the Books of Kings," *JBL* 107 (1988) 193–206.

Murray, D. F. "Narrative Structure and Technique in the Deborah-Barak Story (Judges IV 4–22)." Pp. 155–89 in *Studies in the Historical Books of the Old Testament*. Ed. by J. A. Emerton. VTSup 30; Leiden: E. J. Brill, 1979.

Nelson, R. D. *The Double Redaction of the Deuteronomistic History*. JSOTSup 18; Sheffield: JSOT, 1981.

———. "The Anatomy of the Book of Kings," *JSOT* 40 (1988) 39–48.

Neusner, J. "'Israel': Judaism and Its Social Metaphors," *JAAR* 55 (1987) 331–61.

Newman, M. "The Prophetic Call of Samuel." Pp. 86–97 in *Israel's Prophetic Heritage*. Ed. by B. W. Anderson and W. Harrelson. New York: Harper & Row, 1962.

Nicholson, E. W. *Deuteronomy and Tradition: Literary and Historical Problems in the Book of Deuteronomy*. Philadelphia: Westminster, 1967.

Niditch, S. "The 'Sodomite' Theme in Judges 19–20: Family, Community, and Social Disintegration," *CBQ* 44 (1982) 365–78.

Noth, M. "Das Amt des 'Richters Israels.'" Pp. 404–17 in *Festschrift Alfred Bertholet*. Ed. by W. Baumgartner. Tübingen: Mohr and Siebeck, 1950.

——. *The History of Israel*. Rev. ed. New York: Harper & Row, 1960.

——. "The Background of Judges 17–18." Pp. 68–85 in *Israel's Prophetic Heritage: Essays in Honor of James Muilenburg*. Ed. by B. W. Anderson and W. Harrelson. New York: Harper & Row, 1962.

——. *Überlieferungsgeschichtliche Studien*. 3rd ed. Tübingen: Max Niemeyer, 1967.

——. *A History of Pentateuchal Traditions*. Englewood Cliffs, NJ: Prentice-Hall, 1972.

O'Doherty, E. "The Literary Problem of Judges, 1,1–3,6," *CBQ* 18 (1956) 1–7.

Oden, R. *The Bible Without Theology: The Theological Traditions and Alternatives to It*. San Francisco: Harper & Row, 1987.

Olyan, S. M. *Asherah and the Cult of Yahweh in Israel*. SBLMS 34; Atlanta: Scholars Press, 1988.

Overholt, T. *Prophecy in Cross-Cultural Perspective: A Sourcebook for Biblical Researchers*. SBLSBS 17; Atlanta, GA: Scholars Press, 1986.

——. "The End of Prophecy: No Players Without a Program," *JSOT* 42 (1988) 103–15.

——. *Channels of Prophecy: The Social Dynamics of Prophetic Activity*. Minneapolis: Augsburg/Fortress, 1989.

Parker, K. I. "Repetition as a Structuring Device in 1 Kings 1–11," *JSOT* 42 (1988) 19–27.

Perlitt, L. *Bundestheologie im Alten Testament*. WMANT 36; Neukirchen-Vluyn: Neukirchener Verlag, 1969.

Polzin, R. *Moses and the Deuteronomist: A Literary Study of the Deuteronomic History*. New York: Seabury, 1980.

——. "Reporting Speech in the Book of Deuteronomy: Toward a Compositional Analysis of the Deuteronomic History." Pp. 193–211 in *Traditions in Transformation: Turning Points in Biblical Faith*. Ed. by B. Halpern and J. D. Levenson. Winona Lake, IN: Eisenbrauns, 1981.

——. *Samuel and the Deuteronomist: A Literary Study of the Deuteronomic History, Part 2*. San Francisco: Harper & Row, 1989.

——. "1 Samuel: Biblical Studies and the Humanities," *RelSRev* 15 (1989) 297–306.

Porten, B. "The Structure and Theme of the Solomon Narrative (I Kings 3–11)," *HUCA* 38 (1967) 93–128.

Provan, I. *Hezekiah and the Books of Kings: A Contribution to the Debate about the Composition of the Deuteronomistic History*. BZAW 172; Berlin: de Gruyter, 1988.

Purvis, J. D. *The Samaritan Pentateuch and the Origin of the Samaritan Sect*. HSM 2; Cambridge: Harvard University Press, 1968.

Rainey, A. F. "Compulsory Labour Gangs in Ancient Israel," *IEJ* 20 (1970) 191–202.

Redford, D. B. *History and Chronology of the Eighteenth Dynasty of Egypt: Seven Studies*. Toronto: University of Toronto Press, 1967.

Reviv, H. "On the Days of Athaliah and Joash," *Beth Mikra* 47 (1970/71) 541–48 [Hebrew].

Richter, W. *Die Bearbeitungen des "Retterbuches" in der deuteronomischen Epoche*. BBB 21; Bonn: Peter Hanstein, 1964.

———. "Zu den 'Rictern Israels,'" *ZAW* 77 (1965) 40–72.

———. *Traditionsgeschichtliche Untersuchungen zum Richterbuch*. BBB 18; Bonn: Peter Hanstein, 1966.

———. *Die sogenannten vorprophetischen Berufsberichte*. FRLANT 101; Göttingen: Vandenhoeck & Ruprecht, 1970.

Rosenberg, J. *King and Kin: Political Allegory in the Hebrew Bible*. Bloomington/Indianapolis: Indiana University Press, 1986.

Rost, L. *Die Überlieferung von der Thronnachfolge Davids*. BZWANT III/6; Stuttgart: W. Kohlhammer Verlag, 1926 (*The Succession to the Throne of David*. Trans. by M. D. Rutter and D. M. Gunn [Historic Texts and Interpreters in Biblical Scholarship 1; Sheffield: Almond, 1982]).

Royce, A. P. *Ethnic Identity: Strategies of Diversity*. Bloomington/Indianapolis: Indiana University Press, 1982.

Rösel, H. N. "Jephtah und das Problem der Richter," *Bib* 61 (1980) 251–55.

Rudolph, W. "Die Einheitlichkeit der Erzählung vom Sturz der Atalja (2 Kön 11)." Pp. 473–78 in *Festschrift Alfred Bertholet*. Ed. by W. Baumgartner, et al. Tübingen: L. C. B. Mohr/Paul Siebeck, 1950.

Saggs, H. W. F. *The Encounter with the Divine in Mesopotamia and Israel*. London: Athlone, 1978.

Sanders, J. "Hermeneutics in True and False Prophecy." Pp. 21–41 in *Canon and Authority*. Ed. by G. W. Coats and B. O. Long. Philadelphia: Fortress, 1977.

Scholes, R. and R. Kellogg. *The Nature of Narrative*. New York: Oxford, 1966.

Schunck, K.-D. "Die Richter Israels und ihr Amt." Pp. 252–62 in *Volume du congrès international. Genève 1965*. VTSup 15; Leiden: E. J. Brill, 1966.

Seebass, H. "בָּחַר (bachar)." Pp. 73–87 in *Theological Dictionary of the Old Testament*. Vol. II, rev. ed. Ed. by G. J. Botterweck and H. Ringgren. Grand Rapids, MI: Eerdmans, 1977.

Smend, R. "Das Gesetz und die Völker: Ein Beitrag zur deuteronomistischen Redaktiongeschichte." Pp. 494–509 in *Probleme biblischer Theologie: Festschrift für Gerhard von Rad zum 70. Geburtstag*. Ed. by H. W. Wolff. Munich: Kaiser, 1971.

Smith, A. D. "War and Ethnicity: The Role of Warfare in the Formation, Self-Images and Cohesion of Ethnic Communities," *Ethnic and Racial Studies* 4 (1981) 375–97.

———. "National Identity and Myths of Ethnic Descent," *Research in Social Movements, Conflict and Change* 7 (1984) 95–130.

———. *The Ethnic Origins of Nations.* Oxford: Blackwell, 1986.

Smith, D. *The Religion of the Landless: The Social Context of the Babylonian Exile.* Bloomington, IN: Meyer Stone, 1989.

Smith, H. P. *The Books of Samuel.* ICC; Edinburgh: T. & T. Clark, 1969 (first printed 1899).

Smith, J. Z. *Imagining Religion: From Babylon to Jonestown.* Chicago: University of Chicago Press, 1982.

———. "'Religion' and 'Religious Studies': No Difference at All," *Soundings* 71 (1988) 231–44.

Smith, M. *Palestinian Parties and Politics that Shaped the Old Testament.* London: SCM, 1971.

———. "A Note on Burning Babies," *JAOS* 95 (1975) 477–79.

Smith, M. S. *The Early History of God: Yahweh and the Other Deities in Ancient Israel.* San Francisco: Harper & Row, 1990.

Soggin, J. A. *Joshua.* OTL; Philadelphia: Westminster, 1972.

———. "Das Amt der 'kleinen Richter' in Israel," *VT* 30 (1980) 245–48.

———. *Judges.* OTL; Philadelphia: Westminster, 1981.

———. "'Ehud und 'Eglon: Bemerkungen zu Richter III 11b–31," *VT* 39 (1989) 95–100.

Sollors, W. "Introduction: The Invention of Ethnicity." Pp. viii–xx in *The Invention of Ethnicity.* Ed. by W. Sollors. New York: Oxford, 1989.

Spicer, E. H. "Persistent Cultural Systems," *Science* 4011 (1971) 795–800.

Spina, F. A. "The Dan Story Historically Reconsidered," *JSOT* 4 (1977) 60–71.

Spiro, M. E. "Religion: Problems of Definition and Explanation." Pp. 85–126 in *Anthropological Approaches to the Study of Religion.* Ed. by Michael Banton. London: Tavistock, 1966.

Sturdy, J. "The Original Meaning of 'Is Saul Also among the Prophets?' (I Samuel X 11, 12; XIX 24)," *VT* 20 (1970) 206–13.

Talmon, S. "The Cult and Calendar Reform of Jeroboam I." Pp. 113–39 in *King, Cult and Calendar in Ancient Israel: Collected Essays.* Leiden/Jerusalem: E. J. Brill/Magnes, 1986.

Thompson, T. L. *The Historicity of the Patriarchal Narratives: The Quest for the Historical Abraham.* Berlin: de Gruyter, 1974.

Tigay, J. H. *You Shall Have No Other Gods: Israelite Religion in the Light of Hebrew Inscriptions.* HSS 31; Atlanta: Scholars Press, 1986.

Toorn, K. van der. "The Nature of the Biblical Teraphim in the Light of the Cuneiform Evidence," *CBQ* 52 (1990) 203–22.

Tov, E. "The Composition of 1 Samuel 16–18 in the Light of the Septuagint Version." Pp. 97–130 in *Empirical Models for Biblical Criticism*. Ed. by J. H. Tigay. Philadelphia: University of Pennsylvania Press, 1985.

Trible, P. *Texts of Terror: Literary-Feminist Readings of Biblical Narratives*. OBT; Philadelphia: Fortress, 1984.

Tucker, G. "Deuteronomy 18:15–22," *Int* 41 (1987) 292–97.

Turner, V. *Dramas, Fields, and Metaphors: Symbolic Action in Human Society*. Ithaca: Cornell University Press, 1974.

———. "Social Dramas and Stories about Them." Pp. 137–64 in *On Narrative*. Ed. by W. J. T. Mitchell. Chicago: University of Chicago Press, 1981.

Vaihinger, H. *The Philosophy of 'As if': A System of the Theoretical, Practical and Religious Fictions of Mankind*. Trans. by C. K. Ogden. New York: Barnes & Noble, 1935.

Van Seters, J. *Abraham in History and Tradition*. New Haven: Yale University Press, 1975.

———. "Tradition and Social Change in Ancient Israel," *Perspectives in Religious Studies* 7 (1980) 96–113.

———. *In Search of History: Historiography in the Ancient World and the Origins of Biblical History*. New Haven: Yale University Press, 1983.

de Vaux, R. *Ancient Israel: Its Life and Institutions*. New York: McGraw-Hill, 1965.

———. *The Early History of Israel*. Philadelphia: Westminster, 1978.

Veijola, T. *Die ewige Dynastie. David und die Entstehung seiner Dynastie nach der deuteronomistischen Darstellung*. Annales academiae scientiarum Fennicae B 193; Helsinki: Suomalainen Tiedeakatemia, 1975.

———. *Das Königtum in der Beurteilung der deuteronomistischen Historiographie: Eine redaktiongeschichtliche Untersuchung*. Annales academiae scientiarum Fennicae 198; Helsinki: Suomalainen Tiedeakatemia, 1977.

———. *Verheissung in der Krise: Studien zur Literatur und Theologie der Exilszeit anhand des 89. Psalms*. Annales academiae scientiarum Fennicae 110; Helsinki: Suomalainen Tiedeakatemia, 1982.

von Rad, G. *Studies in Deuteronomy*. SBT; London: SCM, 1953.

Wagner, R. *The Invention of Culture*. Rev. ed. Chicago: University of Chicago Press, 1981.

Wallace, A. F. C. "Revitalization Movements," *American Anthropologist* 58 (1956) 264–81.

Walters, S. D. "Hannah and Anna: The Greek and Hebrew Texts of 1 Samuel 1," *JBL* 107 (1988) 385–412.

Warner, S. M. "The Dating of the Period of the Judges," *VT* 28 (1978) 455–63.

Warton, J. A. "The Secret of Yahweh: Story and Affirmation in Judges 13–16," *Int* 27 (1973) 48–66.

Webb, B. G. *The Book of Judges: An Integrated Reading.* JSOTSup 46; Sheffield: JSOT, 1987.

Weinfeld, M. "The Period of the Conquest and of the Judges as Seen by Earlier and Later Sources," *VT* 17 (1967) 93–113.

———. "The Covenant of Grant in the Old Testament and in the Ancient Near East," *JAOS* 90 (1970) 184–203.

———. "The Worship of Molech and of the Queen of Heaven and its Background," *UF* 4 (1972) 133–54.

———. *Deuteronomy and the Deuteronomic School.* Oxford: Clarendon, 1972.

———. "The Origins of Apodictic Law: An Overlooked Source," *VT* 23 (1973) 63–75.

———. "The Emergence of the Deuteronomic Movement: The Historical Antecedents." Pp. 76–98 in *Das Deuteronomium: Entstehung, Gestalt und Botschaft.* Ed. by N. Lohfink. BETL 68; Lueven: University Press, 1985.

Weippert, H. "Die deuteronomistischen Beurteilungen der Könige von Israel und Juda und das Problem der Redaktion der Königsbücher," *Bib* 53 (1972) 301–39.

Westermann, C. *Basic Forms of Prophetic Speech.* Tr. by H. C. White. Philadelphia: Westminster, 1967.

White, H. "The Value of Narrativity in the Representation of Reality." Pp. 1–23 in *On Narrative.* Ed. by W. J. T. Mitchell. Chicago: University of Chicago Press, 1981.

Whitelam, K. W. "The Defence of David," *JSOT* 29 (1984) 61–87.

———. "Israel's Traditions of Origin: Reclaiming the Land," *JSOT* 44 (1989) 19–42.

Wilcoxen, J. A. "Narrative Structure and Cult Legend." Pp. 43–70 in *Transitions in Biblical Scholarship.* Ed. by J. C. Rylaarsdam. Chicago: University of Chicago Press, 1968.

Wilkinson, J. "The Philistine Epidemic of I Samuel 5 and 6," *ExpTim* 88 (1977) 137–41.

Wilson, R. *Prophecy and Society in Ancient Israel.* Philadelphia: Fortress, 1980.

Wright, G. E. "The Literary and Historical Problem of Joshua 10 and Judges 1," *JNES* 5 (1946) 105–14.

———. *The Old Testament Against Its Environment.* SBT 2; London: SCM, 1950.

———. *Biblical Archaeology.* Philadelphia: Westminster, 1957.

Würthwein, E. *The Text of the Old Testament.* Grand Rapids, MI: Eerdmans, 1979.

———. *Die Bücher der Könige, 1. Kön. 17 – 2 Kön. 25.* ATD 11/2; Göttingen: Vandenhoeck & Ruprecht, 1984.

———. *Die Bücher der Könige: 1. Könige 1–16.* ATD 11/1; Göttingen: Vandenhoeck & Ruprecht, 1985.

Biblical Passages Cited

Judges

1 Samuel

2 Kings

AUTHOR INDEX

General Index